THE STATE AND THE SUBALTERN

A propaganda poster published in the Republic of Turkey during the Atatürk era.

THE STATE AND THE SUBALTERN

Modernization, Society and the State in Turkey and Iran

Touraj Atabaki
Editor

I.B.Tauris *Publishers*
London • New York
in association with
The International Institute of
Social History, Amsterdam

Published in 2007 by I.B.Tauris & Co. Ltd
6 Salem Road, London W2 4BU
175 Fifth Avenue, New York, NY 10010
www.ibtauris.com

In the United States of America and Canada distributed by Palgrave Macmillan, a
division of St Martin's Press, 175 Fifth Avenue, New York, NY 10010

Library of Modern Middle East Studies 66

ISBN: 978 1 84511 339 1

A full CIP record for this book is available from the British Library
A full CIP record for this book is available from the Library of Congress

Library of Congress catalog card: available

Typeset in Adobe Garamond Pro by A. & D. Worthington, Newmarket, Suffolk
Printed and bound in India by Replika Press Pvt. Ltd

Contents

Contributors

Touraj Atabaki is Professor of History of the Middle East and Central Asia at Leiden University and Senior Research Fellow at the International Institute of Social History. He is the author of *Azerbaijan: Ethnicity and the Struggle for Powers in Iran* (London: I.B.Tauris, 1993), of *Beyond Essentialism: Who Writes Whose Past in the Middle East and Central Asia?* (Amsterdam: Aksant, 2003), editor of *Post-Soviet Central Asia* (London: I.B.Tauris, 1998), of *Men of Order: Authoritarian Modernisation in Turkey and Iran* (London: I.B.Tauris, 2004), of *Central Asia and the Caucasus: Transnationalism and Diaspora* (London and New York: Routledge, 2005), and *Iran and the First World War: Battleground of the Great Powers* (London: I.B.Tauris, 2006). His current work focuses on the historiography of everyday life and comparative subaltern history.

Umut Azak is an instructor in Islam and Politics in Turkey at Utrecht University. She is currently concluding her PhD thesis on Continuity and Change in the Discourse of Secularism in Turkey (1946–1966) at the University of Leiden.

Kaveh Bayat is an independent researcher working in Iran. He has published extensively in Persian on modern history, especially military history, and tribal and ethnic politics.

Stephanie Cronin is Iran Heritage Foundation Fellow in Iranian History, University of Northampton. She is the author of *The Army and the Creation of the Pahlavi State in Iran, 1910–1926* (London: I.B.Tauris, 1997), and editor of *The Making of Modern Iran: State and Society under Riza Shah, 1921–1941* (London and New York: RoutledgeCurzon, 2003) and *Reformers and Revolutionaries in Modern Iran: New Perspectives on the Iranian Left* (London and New York: RoutledgeCurzon, 2004). Her recent publications include *Tribal Politics in Iran: Rural Conflict and the New State 1921–1941* (London and New York: Routledge, 2006), and an edited collection, *Subalterns, Social Protest: History from Below in the Middle East and North Africa* (forthcoming).

Vangelis Kechriotis is Assistant Professor at the History Department, Boğaziçi University, where he teaches Balkan history and the history of non-Muslims in the Ottoman Empire. He holds a PhD from the University of Leiden, the title of his thesis being *The Greeks of Izmir: An Ottoman Non-Muslim Community between Autonomy and Patriotism*. He is a member of a research group on historiography and the theory of history, which since 1999 has published the review *Historein*. He is also fellow of a project for the publication of a four-volume *Discourses of Collective Identity in Central and Southeast Europe (1770–1945): Texts and Commentaries* by CEU Press, Budapest. He has also published articles on Izmir and the Greek Orthodox of the Ottoman Empire.

Hülya Küçük is Associate Professor of the History of Sufism at Selçuk University, Konya. She is the author of *Tasavvuf Tarihine Giriş* (Konya: Nükte, 2004, 2nd ed), *The Roles of the Bektashis in Turkey's National Struggle* (Leiden: Brill, 2002), *Kurtuluş Savaşında Bektaşiler* (Istanbul, Kitap, 2003), and *Sultan Veled Ve Maarif'i. Kitâbu'l-Hikemiyye adlı Maârif Tercüme ve Şerhi* (Konya: Konya Büyükşehir Belediyesi, 2005). Her current study focuses on the history of Sufism in classical times and today.

Afsaneh Najmabadi is Professor of History and of Studies of Women, Gender, and Sexuality at Harvard University. Her most recent book is *Women with Mustaches and Men without Beards: Gender and Sexual Anxieties of Iranian Modernity* (Berkeley: University of California Press, 2005), a study of cultural transformations in nineteenth-century Iran centred on reconfigurations of gender and sexuality. She is currently working on several projects, 'Sexing Gender, Transing Homos: Travail of Sexuality in Contemporary Iran', 'How an Aqa became an Agha: Women's Sociality and Sexuality in Qajar Iran', and 'Genealogies of Iranian Feminism'. She is an associate editor of a six-volume project, *Encyclopedia of Women and Islamic Cultures*, with volume 1 published in 2003 and volume 2 in 2005 (Leiden: Brill). Previous publications in English include *The Story of Daughters of Quchan: Gender and National Memory in Iranian History* (Syracuse and New York: Syracuse University Press, 1998), and *Women Autobiographies in Contemporary Iran* (editor and contributor) (Cambridge and London: Harvard University Press, 1991).

Nicole A.N.M. van Os studied Middle East Studies at Nijmegen University, the Netherlands. After receiving her MA degree she moved to Turkey, where she taught at Koç University, Istanbul. During her ten-year stay in

Turkey, she published several articles on women in the Ottoman Empire. She is the author of 'Müstehlik değil müstahsil (Producers, not Consumers): Ottoman Muslim Women and Millî İktisat', in Kemal Çiçek et al (eds), *The Great Ottoman–Turkish Civilization*, vol. 2 (Ankara: Yeni Türkiye, 2000), 'Ottoman Women's Organizations: Sources of the Past, Sources for the Future', *Islam and Christian–Muslim Relations*, XI, 3 (Winter 2000), and 'The Ottoman State as Bread Giver: The Muinsiz Aile Maaşı', in Erik-Jan Zürcher (ed), *Arming the State* (London: I.B.Tauris, 1999). She is especially interested in the interrelatedness of nationalist and feminist movements in the first decade of the twentieth century.

Donald Quataert is Professor of History at Binghamton University and a recent Fellow of the John Simon Guggenheim Memorial Foundation. He is the author of *The Ottoman Empire, 1700–1922* (Cambridge: Cambridge University Press, 2000), *Ottoman Manufacturing in the Age of the Industrial Revolution* (Cambridge: Cambridge University Press, 1993), *Workers, Peasants and Economic Change in the Ottoman Empire, 1730–1914* (Istanbul: Isis Press, 1993), *Manufacturing and Technology Transfer in the Ottoman Empire, 1800–1914* (Istanbul: Isis Press, 1992), and *Social Disintegration and Popular Resistance in the Ottoman Empire, 1881–1908: Reactions to European Economic Penetration* (New York: New York University Press, 1983).

Erik-Jan Zürcher holds the chair of Turkish Studies at the University of Leiden. He has published *The Unionist Factor* (Leiden: Brill, 1984), *Political Opposition in the Early Turkish Republic* (Leiden: Brill, 1991) and *Turkey. A Modern History* (London and New York: I.B.Tauris, 1993) and has co-edited *Socialism and Nationalism in the Ottoman Empire* (London and New York: I.B.Tauris, 1994), *Workers and Working Class in the Ottoman Empire* (London and New York: I.B.Tauris, 1995), *Arming the State: Military Conscription in the Middle East and Central Asia* (London and New York: I.B.Tauris, 1999), *Identity Politics in Central Asia and the Muslim World* (London and New York: I.B.Tauris, 2001), and *Men of Order, Authoritarian Modernization in Turkey and Iran* (London: I.B.Tauris, 2004). His main research interest is the political and social history of the late Ottoman Empire and the early Turkish Republic.

Acknowledgements

The idea for this volume arose out of a workshop I organized at the International Institute of Social History in 2003. The workshop was held in honour of Erik-Jan Zürcher, who during his ten years as head of the Department of Turkish at the International Institute of Social History contributed significantly to collecting archival materials as well as conducting research on modern Turkey.

In organizing this workshop I greatly enjoyed the support of Jaap Kloosterman, the director of the International Institute of Social History, and Marcel van der Linden, the head of the Research Department.

In the process of editing this volume, I benefited from the indispensable assistance of David and Alison Worthington, Hans Timmermans, Mieke Stroo and Zeynep Altok, who were kind enough to spend considerable time reading the manuscript and sharing their editorial comments with me.

I would like to offer my sincere thanks to all of them.

Note on Transliteration

Transliteration is always a thorny problem when one is dealing with several languages and alphabets at once. The system adopted in this work for Persian and Ottoman Turkish is a modified version of the system used by the *International Journal of Middle East Studies* (*IJMES*). For the sake of convenience diacritical marks have been omitted, with the exception of *'ayn* (') and *hamzah* (') for the Persian and in representing the vowels for Ottoman Turkish. In the case of Azerbaijani words, a modified Persian system has been followed, except again in representing the vowels. Current English spelling of names such as Azerbaijan, Kerman, Istanbul, Isfahan, Sheikh, Reza, Hafez and Hussein have been retained. With the exception of Dr Cronin's article, in which she opted for a different transliteration system, every effort has been made to observe the utmost consistency in style and transliteration in this volume.

Introduction

Touraj Atabaki

Compared to other trends in historiography, the social history of the Middle East is a terrain that still lacks many explorers. As was the case with European historiography, up to the twentieth century the historiography of the Middle East was dominated by political, dynastical and genealogical historiography as well as narratives of the life and times of individual elites. Nevertheless, by 'the remarkable and worldwide growth of sociology as an academic subject and fashion'[1] especially during the last 50 years, the social history of Middle Eastern societies was gradually acknowledged as a legitimate academic field by many historians. Albert Hourani's work on the history of the Arab peoples,[2] Halil Inalcik's volume on the social history of the Ottoman Empire[3] and Abdulhussein Zarinkoub's accounts of the Iranians' early reaction to the Arab invasion of the seventh century[4] are among the most renowned examples of Middle Eastern social historiography. It was indeed with the recognition of social history that the grassroots history, or, as Eric Hobsbawm referred to it, history from below or the 'history of common people',[5] found its way into the Middle Eastern historiography. Although history from below is a new trend in Middle Eastern historiography, one can mention some studies in this area: Ervand Abrahamian's study of the crowd in Iranian politics,[6] which follows George Rudé's distinguished study of the crowds' role in the French Revolution, and Huri Islamoğlu-Inan's account of state and peasant relations in Ottoman Turkey.[7]

In studying the practice of modernization in the Middle East in general and in Turkey and Iran in particular one also faces very serious deficiencies in historical accounts and analysis on accommodation and resistance to the changes that the Turkish and Iranian societies have been confronted with during the last 200 years. Although the study of modernization in Turkey and Iran has been the subject of numerous academic studies, these studies examine the practice of modernization exclusively from above, i.e. the measures adopted by political regimes in changing societies, introducing new rules and regulations, and founding new social and political institutions. However, what is still absent from these studies is how the society reacted to these reforms and changes originating from above.

Modernization was a global project which almost concurrently, although with different pace in different regions, was launched into our world. In the political sphere modernization was juxtaposed with the birth of civil society and the emergence of individualism and individual autonomy; the latter presented itself more than anywhere else in the individual's political and civic rights.

The age of modernity in northwest Europe began when the basic unit of modern society was the individual rather than, as with agrarian or peasant society, the group or community. Communal solidarity and ethnic particularism and cultural awareness have not only vanished through a high degree of social mobilization and technological and economic integration, but have been modernized, articulated and intermingled with individualism and individual autonomy, both being an indispensable part of modern man's perception of civility. Consequently the individualism that was embodied in the liberty and autonomy of the individual provided a new definition embracing the new association between the individual and the polity. According to this new association, the individual in a modern society, in principle at least, was not anymore the subject of a particular king or priest, sultan, shah or sheikh, endowed with divine or prescriptive authority, but rather acted according to rational and impersonal precepts formulated in laws. The investiture of new juridical and political rights, including the right of representation, was indeed the conclusion of this new association, and the emerging commercial and industrial urban middle class was inextricably linked to this individualism.

However, if in northwest Europe the process of modernization was associated with the gradual development and expansion of critical reason and individual autonomy, and with the emergence of a civil society, in Ottoman Turkey and Iran the reverse was true. Following the successive military defeats both countries suffered in the eighteenth and nineteenth centuries, the calls for change and reform, for a modernized politics and society, gradually became the prevailing political discourse. The failure of some early attempts during the first half of the nineteenth century in both countries to implement change and reform from below enabled the intelligentsia to pursue modernization exclusively from above. Bureaucrats and military officers were sturdily convinced that, in the presence of colonial powers, any endeavour to seek change and reform from below was nothing but a cause of political chaos, jeopardizing their country's sovereignty.

The efforts of nineteenth-century and early twentieth-century reformers had not protected these countries from the challenges they faced, either from the separatism of minorities or from occupation by European powers. The setback that the Iranian constitutional movement (1905–9) suffered in the years before the outbreak of the First World War, the political disintegration and partial occupation of Persia during the war, the traumatic loss of the European provinces of the Ottoman Empire in the Balkan War and its subsequent defeat in the First World War, the threat of imminent disintegration after the war: all of these left the middle classes and the intelligentsia no other option than to look for a *man of order*, who, as an agent of the nation, was to modernize society, sometimes even against the will of the people, and install a centralized, powerful (though not necessarily despotic) government capable of solving the country's growing problems of underdevelopment, while at the same time safeguarding the nation's unity and sovereignty. The practice of authoritarian modernization in post-First World War Turkey and Iran was embedded in the perceived failure of earlier attempts to introduce modernization both from below as well as from above.

The accommodation and resistance to modernization, the relation between the common people and state in Turkey and Iran, is the subject of the essays included in this volume. In the spring of 1999 the International Institute of Social History in Amsterdam organized a workshop on 'Authoritarian Modernization in Turkey and Iran', where participants examined the modernization process in Turkey and Iran from 'above', i.e. from the perspective of the state and its elites. Some of the articles presented in this workshop were later published in the volume *Men of Order: Authoritarian Modernization in Turkey and Iran* (London: I.B.Tauris, 2004). The follow-up of this workshop was a second one which aimed at the study of modernization in Turkey and Iran from 'below'. By pursuing this project, it was intended to have a comparative, contrasting and inclusive historical study of modernization in modern Turkey and Iran. The history of labourers and subaltern groups, with specific reference to historiography and methodology, gender, ethnicity, industrial and non-industrial urban labour, rural labour, unemployed and immigrant labourers, were among the themes studied in this workshop.

My use of the word 'subaltern' is based on the description given by Antonio Gramsci. In his *The Modern Prince* and *The Prison Notebooks*, Gramsci defines the subaltern as those classes subordinated by hegemony and excluded from any meaningful role in a regime of power.

The contributions to this volume were written, with some exceptions, as a result of a workshop on 'The Triumphs and Travails of Authoritarian Modernization in Turkey and Iran: Twentieth-Century History from Below', which was organized at the International Institute of Social History (IISH) in autumn 2003. This volume is dedicated to Erik-Jan Zürcher who, during his ten years as head of the Department of Turkish at the International Institute of Social History, contributed significantly to collecting archival materials as well as conducting research on modern Turkey at the IISH.

1

Time, Labour-Discipline and Modernization in Turkey and Iran: Some Comparative Remarks[1]

Touraj Atabaki

The features of modernity and the requirements for modernization itself are commonly associated with a new apprehension of time, of measuring time and the ability to synchronize and match times exactly. Secularization of time as an arbitrary abstract system of measurement associated time to an impersonal, universal and interchangeable unit. The exact measurement of time became a precondition of modern science and technology and hence a prerequisite of both private and public life in a modern society. Thus the clock and the timetable are both instruments by which modernity is experienced.

The advent of the public mechanical clock in Europe began in the early fourteenth century, and by the early eighteenth century church clocks and public clocks had appeared in all major cities and large market towns. In Persia and the Ottoman Empire, although the earliest public mechanical clocks were erected in Tabriz (sixteenth century), in Isfahan (seventeenth century) and in Istanbul (mid-nineteenth century), it was not until the late nineteenth/early twentieth century that this feature of public time was gradually acknowledged by the urban populace.

The earliest wave of industrialization, which began in the nineteenth century, introduced a new perception of time, of teamwork, of organization and cooperation, in harmony if not in unison. Work-discipline was chiefly based on new working-day regulations encompassing a fixed timetable and a predetermined interval, replacing the pre-modern interval related to the moments of dawn and sunset. Moreover the introduction of both telegraphic communication and modern public transport, particularly the railway, covering a great distance in a fixed time period, with predetermined departure and arrival times, was a chief factor in bringing on the meticulous precision in the measurement of time. However, it was only in the twentieth century and through the adaptation of worldwide international uniform times, as well as early labour legislation, that severely enforced new nationwide work-disciplines, that a modern perception of time was finally experienced in Turkey and Iran.

It is the aim of this chapter to study the measures adopted to bring time into the public domain and enforce work-discipline, so as to assess the response of the public to this process as well as the internalization of time by the population in both countries. How far was it imposed and how far was it assumed?

The clock goes public

Mechanical clocks with an escapement came into use in Europe some time around 1285. These timepieces had a verge and foliot, which were used for the mechanism that sounded a bell. The name *clock*, which originally meant *bell*, came into use when there were very large mechanical time indicators installed in bell towers in the late Middle Ages.[2] Prior to the invention of the mechanical clock a churchman was in charge of tolling the bell, summoning people for Holy Mass. But with the installation of public mechanical clocks in churches, the function of the tolling man gradually vanished.

The initial reaction in Persia and the Ottoman Empire to the introduction of public clocks was mixed. Muslims in both countries, even in religious circles, welcomed the employment of the mechanical timekeeping instrument, but denounced the striking clock because its bell, which was reminiscent of the striking bells in churches, undermined the function of the local *muezzins*. The Persian-Arabic *naqus* or the Turkish *çan* was an icon of Christianity, an instrument calling the Christian to prayer, which if utilized hourly could undermine the practice of *muezzin*. The following verse of Khaqani, a Persian poet of the twelfth century, displays the association that *naqus* had with Christianity, as opposed to the practice of everyday Islam:

> Subhah dar kaf miguzashtam bamdad
> Bang-i naqus-i mugan birun fitad

> Rosary in hand I was passing in the morning
> When the bell of the church was tolled

When in 1554 Ogier Ghiselin de Busbecq travelled to Istanbul in his capacity as ambassador of the Holy Roman Empire to the Sublime Porte, he displayed his disappointment on many occasions. For example, he asserted that the 'Turks have no idea of chronology and dates and make a wonderful mixture and confusion of all epochs of history'.[3] Moreover, he claimed that if public clocks were introduced, the authority of their *muezzins* and their ancient rites would be thereby impaired.[4] A similar appraisal, this time of the Persians, can be found in the remarks of the English diarist John Evelyn, who in 1683, in referring to his dialogue with traveller Jean Chardin, stated that the Persians 'had neither clocks nor watches'.[5]

Certainly one can view with scepticism such essentialist comments by Busbecq and Evelyn on the exploitation of the timekeeper – *horologium* – in Persia and the Ottoman Empire. The genesis of the mechanical clock in the Western Europe of the early fourteenth century was certainly influenced by the idea of the water clock, which was known in pre-Safavid Persia and pre-Ottoman Asia Minor. Except for the escapement, which made the mechanical clock possible, all of its other features, such as automata, weight-drive, gear trains and segmental gears, were present in *clepsydra*, or water clocks. Moreover, as far as the mechanical clock is concerned, there are references indicating that as early as the fifteenth century some Persians and Ottomans were acquainted with it. Muhammad Hafez Isfahani in *Sih risalah dar san'at*, from the early sixteenth century, refers to what may have been the first clock brought from Europe to Herat. According to Hafez Isfahani, 'since the time keeper was a very valuable instrument in giving an accurate time for daily prayers', in Herat the Timuri king decided to 'discover' it and then locally produce it. However, after a long search to find an expert, they eventually found Hafez Isfahani, who was at that time in Tabriz, to fulfil the task, which he did successfully.[6] It is interesting to note that in Hafez Isfahani's narrative, Tabriz is mentioned as a city enjoying experts familiar with the mechanism of the clock. Such remarks concur with other references on Tabriz's scientific status in the sixteenth century.

In the sixteenth century – contemporaneous with Busbecq's visit to Istanbul – Mustafa Çelebi and later Taqi al-Din b. Muhammad b. Ahmad (1520–85), an Egyptian astronomer who erected the Istanbul observatory, wrote a treatise on clocks operated by weights and springs.[7] In a work of 1565, Taqi al-Din 'described the construction of a weight-driven clock with verge and foliot escapement, a striking train of gears, an alarm and a representation of the moon's phases. He also described the manufacture of a spring-driven clock with a fuse escapement. He mentions several mechanisms invented by him, including, for example, a new system for the striking train of a clock. He is known to have constructed an observatory clock and mentions elsewhere in his writings the use of the pocket watch in Turkey.'[8]

However, since the sixteenth century there were non-striking clocks and watches being widely used by Ottoman and Persian Muslims, and they were found particularly useful in mosques to fix the time of the five daily prayers. In Iran, even in different holy shrines such as that of Imam Reza in Mashhad, the non-striking public clock was installed as early as the seventeenth century or in the shrine of Shahchiragh of Shiraz in the nineteenth century.[9] However, the public striking clock still was being rejected.

The first reference to the existence of a public mechanical clock in Persia comes from the early sixteenth century. Michele Membré in his travelogue describes that in the northern Iranian city of Tabriz he had seen a public clock built by a Persian housed in a pavilion in the city's bazaar:

> It was set inside a square enclosed pavilion of painted planks four ells high and two wide. ... On the summit of the said pavilion there was a bell with a clapper that struck the hours which stood in the middle of the pavilion on the top, and in front of the said pavilion there were two men with horses and lances, as big as a hen, next to two buffoons as big as a large mouse, the size of those in a house, so that, when it came to strike the hour, however many hours the bell had struck, then so many times those horsemen with the lance thrust them forward, and those buffoons banged their foreheads together, and that all at once; it also showed the moon during the eclipse.[10]

There are also references to other public clocks in Iranian cities such as Isfahan and Mashhad. In Isfahan in the time of Shah Abbas (1588–1629), 'the Augustinian fathers presented the shah with a large clock, which was installed at the entrance of the royal bazaar. A church bell that had been captured during the conquest of Hurmuz in 1622 was mounted on its top but never sounded.'[11] During the reign of Shah Abbas II (1642–66) a 'special clock pavilion was built in the royal square (*maydan*) of Isfahan, on the occasion of his coronation'.[12] In 1703 the Dutch painter Cornelis de Bruijn, who visited Isfahan, refers to both of these clocks as 'striking clocks above the gate of the bazaar'.[13]

In the Ottoman Empire, as early as the sixteenth century, the erection of clock towers in the churches and market places was common in the regions where the Christian communities lived. For example, in Izmir in the seventeenth century there was a striking clock tower in the Aya Fotini church. However, the practice of establishing public clocks in towers or other structures in the regions where a titular Muslim community lived remained alien until the nineteenth century. The gradual building of non-striking clock towers began in the early nineteenth century, and it was in 1901, on the occasion of the silver jubilee of Sultan Abdulhamid's reign, that the Ottoman government passed a decree ordering the construction of a non-striking clock tower in every big city of the empire.[14]

On his return from his first trip to Europe in 1873 Nasir al-Din Shah, the Qajar king, decided to build a European-style palace in Tehran known as Shams al-ʿImarah. Moreover, he ordered the installation of a public clock on top of one of the towers of the building, a four-sided striking clock, striking every hour. This resulted in a public outcry. The rumour soon spread throughout the capital that the ringing of the bell was harmful to the sick and potentially could lead to premature childbirth in pregnant women. The public remonstration eventually forced the king to order the wrapping of the bell with a piece of felt in order to reduce its sound.

> Shams al-ʿImarah's clock was four sided. This enabled the people to spot it from all corners. There was also a large bell attached to this clock, which rang on the hours. Old people believed that the song of the bell could be heard from far away, and it caused the sick to be shocked and to faint. There was also a belief that the pregnant women by hearing its song would lose their babies. The widespread grumble by people finally forced the King to order that the bell be wrapped by a piece of felt. [15]

Despite these early examples of public clocks in Persia, and also some references by foreign traders such as Fraser (1826) to clocks and watches being listed among possible exports for the Persian market,[16] until the nineteenth century the clocks and watches were used almost exclusively as gifts and were in government or private possession and rarely were the object of commercial transactions in Persia. This state of affairs gradually altered owing to the import of low-priced timekeepers from Europe, where production had already started in the eighteenth century.

In studying the adoption of clocks and watches, the issue of repairing them is another territory worthy of mention. Maintaining the mechanical clock was always a headache for the authorities. Taking into service foreign clock repairers was a steady demand of the Persian and the Ottoman kings in their correspondence and negotiations with the European powers since the fifteenth century. As early as the sixteenth century in both the Ottoman and Persian Empires there was a group of foreign clockmakers who enjoyed a certain status at court. By the eighteenth century the number of clock and watchmakers in the capital increased. In Istanbul and Tehran a district was gradually formed mainly accommodating watchmakers.

If in the early days most of these watchmakers were subjects of European countries, by the late nineteenth century native watchmakers were finding their way into this new guild. Moreover a culture of repair with its own terminology emerged in this new guild, which explicitly exhibited the popular reception and rejection of the process of modernity going through these societies.

Becoming punctual

Prior to the invention and construction of the mechanical clock, it was only in astronomical calculations that the rule of equal hours, the day consisting of 24 hours of equal length throughout the year, was known. In everyday life, both in Europe as well as in the Orient, people reckoned in temporal hours, where the periods of daylight or darkness were divided into 12 equal parts to give hours that varied in length from day to day. The length of the days varied according to season: during the summer the day hours were longer than the night hours, and during the winter the opposite was true. Water clocks also worked on the principle of 'unequal' hours. It was, however, by the invention and common exploitation of the mechanical clock, both in the West and in the Orient, that temporal hours died out in everyday life and equal hours took their place. The exploitation of the mechanical clock in big cities gradually became one of the various points of reference characterizing industrial and urban life.

For Ottomans and Persians, however, the adoption of equal hours turned out differently. Both reckoned the temporal hours of the day as being divided into 24 equal parts, but a new day started at sunset, so one counted twice 12 hours from dusk to dusk. That led to setting the clocks and watches everyday at sunset. The Persians called it *ghurub kuk*, or evening setting, and the time based on it was known to the Europeans as the hour *alla turca*, as distinct from the European *alla franca*.[17]

What brought on the rapid adoption of the *alla franca* timing in the Middle East, particularly in Turkey and Iran, was the pace of industrialization affecting every area of public life during the second half of the nineteenth century. Urban and industrial life are highly structured, and industrialization requires cooperation, teamwork and organization in harmony if not in unison, with different actors playing different parts in a common purpose. The ability to synchronize, to match times exactly, and for this purpose to measure times exactly, becomes an essential feature of modernity and therefore a requirement of modernization.

> The precise measurement of passing time is of course a prerequisite of modern science and technology – both scientific, so obvious as usually to be taken for granted, of both private and public life in a modern society. The timetable of a sequence of events taking place at predetermined intervals defined and demarcated with meticulous exactitude – is basic. In many ways the least dramatic and most powerful instrument of change in the whole process of modernization, it seems to have begun with the railroad – the earliest form of organized public transport covering ever greater distances at fixed time, and available to all who buy a ticket. ... The railroad brought the timetable to the Middle East

and was followed by all the other modalities of modern transport and hence of modern life.[18]

Numerous other forms of public transport, covering ever greater distances at ever greater speeds, followed the railway, and the timetable, indicating times of departure and arrival, became a feature of everyday life.

> Without a timetable of one sort or another, neither society nor the economy could function, and the state would rapidly decline through confusion to chaos. Even such essential feature of modern life as parades and demonstrations, political parties and business corporations, school curricula and armed forces at all levels, from vast armies to simple infantry platoons, would be impossible.[19]

But urban life surely could not set the tone of the national culture. In a society composed essentially of an upper class of literati and a large mass of peasants who counted their time in 'days and months, not in minutes or hours, the clock had little chance to play the role of a useful practical contrivance'.[20]

In the absence of watches and clocks, what made workers conscious of time-discipline in the workplace was a horn or klaxon, usually assembled in the top of towers. Twice a day, early morning and early evening, the horn indicated the shift of the workforce, the working day being divided into two 12-hour shifts.

In the north of Iran, in the region south of the Caspian Sea, the horn was called *sisto* (from the Russian word *svistok*, meaning the horn or klaxon apparatus). One of these *sistos* was assembled in a silk preparation factory in the Amin al-Zarb district of the city of Rasht. In Khuzestan, in the oil industry, the horn was called *faydus*, hooting twice a day at seven o'clock in the morning and five o'clock in the afternoon. On Thursdays, owing to the shorter working hours, it was done at noon only.

Calendar reform was eventually adopted during the time of Reza Shah and Mustafa Kemal. In Turkey on 1 January 1926 the Gregorian calendar was officially adopted and, furthermore, the 24-hour clock was confirmed as the only legally valid method of measuring time.[21] The Iranian parliament in 1927 adopted a resolution confirming the solar calendar as the official calendar of the country and the 24-hour clock as the official clock.

The new calendar and the timetable had an enormous effect on the shaping of the public sphere. Nevertheless, if the reception of the 24-hour clock in the public sphere was rather swift, in the private sphere, dawn, noon, sunset and prayers for a long time remained the point of reference for the majority of commoners. 'An hour after morning prayers, two hours after lunch, three hours before dusk' were common references in daily conversation.[22] Furthermore, when the summer-time regulation was introduced later, the reaction of people who regarded it as anti-Islamic became marked.[23]

In 1977, with social and economic unrest increasingly rising, the Iranian government adopted a policy of daylight-saving time in order to tackle the power shortages chronically paralysing the densely populated centres, especially the capital city Tehran. The clock was set forward an hour in spring and set back again in autumn. This was indeed the second highly controversial decision taken by the Iranian government concerning time. In 1976 the shah changed the starting date of the Iranian calendar from the Islamic *Hijri*, corresponding to the migration of the Prophet Muhammad from Mecca to Medina in 622AD, to that of the calendar originating in the Achaemenian era. Consequently the current Iranian year was changed from 1355 Anno Hegira (solar) (in the year of solar *Hijra* – AH) to the year 2535 Anno Cyri (in the year of Cyrus – AC).[24] However, the new calendar did not last long and two years later, in the summer of 1978, it was changed back again to the old solar *Hijri* system.

The public criticism of the new time amendments, both changing the calendar as well as adopting daylight-saving time, was vociferous. The clerics declared the introduction of the new calendar as another symptom of the shah's treacherous policy on Islam and called on the people to continue with the old one. On the implementation of the daylight-saving time, however, the reaction was more vigorous:

> Thousands of complaints were registered against the plan. The Department of Energy was swamped by daily protest letters and phone calls. Iran's daily newspapers printed hundred of letters and editorials decrying the idea as absurd and futile. Comedians capitalized on the arbitrary nature of the official time as they sought to mobilize public ridicule of the government. Many people rejected the plan outright and adhered to the old time. Others kept both times. When you asked someone for the time of the day, the immediate response was 'which time do you mean, the old time or the new time?'[25]

In both cases, rejecting the government's innovations soon became an icon of protest against the shah's regime. However, the nature of the protests was different in these cases. Since the adoption of the new *shahanshahi* or imperial calendar was somehow related to legitimizing the institution of the monarchy, the protest largely remained within the boundaries of the private sphere. Nevertheless, in the case of the adoption of the new daylight-saving time, as an economic policy, the protest was more overt. One should also consider the period when the innovations were applied. While in 1975 the Iranian government still had a complete grip on society, in 1978 its absolute authority had gradually begun to crack. Based on an opinion poll in 1978, four weeks after daylight-saving time going into effect in Tehran, Movahedi came to the following conclusion:

> The analysis of data collected from 767 respondents revealed widespread opposi-
> tion to the time measurement. Anti-government sentiments did show a correla-
> tion with the unfavourable attitude towards daylight-saving time. However, the
> most interesting response pattern was the correlation attitude towards daylight-
> saving time with any response or item, which appeared to tap secular-sacred,
> modernity-traditionality, or sensate-ideational mentality.[26]

Ironically enough, while the Iranian clerics considered the exercise of
daylight-saving time as an interference in people's daily religious observ-
ances, following the revolution of 1979 one of the first measures adopted
by the new revolutionary government was to return to daylight-saving time.
Three months after the revolution, on 26 May 1979, 'a barrage of radio
and television commentaries called the opposition to the shah's time change
heroic and revolutionary, and exhorted the people to show comparable zeal
this time in support of time measure'.[27] Finally Ayatullah Khomeini issued
a public decree, exhorting people to 'prove their revolutionary zeal and
consciousness by following the daylight saving time ordinance'.[28]

Labour-discipline

It was Marx's allegation in *Das Kapital* that the length of the working day
is a direct indicator of capitalist exploitation.[29] However, it is noteworthy
to examine if such a Eurocentric assumption marks also a watershed in the
introduction of modernity in West Asia, namely Turkey and Iran.

Up until the nineteenth century in the Ottoman Empire and Persia,
the workforce was rarely represented outside the guilds[30] and the guilds
were often concentrated in the local bazaars. The working day of Persian
bazaars was from dawn, or two hours after dawn, until dusk in summer or
half an hour before dusk in winter. According to the accounts of travellers,
the main gates of city bazaars and caravanserais were customarily closed an
hour following sunset, and that was the indicator of the end of the working day.[31] Although Friday was considered the day of communal worship
in Islam, the day when people came together, and designated as the market
day on which also some amusements were provided, nevertheless, unlike
the Jewish Sabbath or the Christian Sunday, it was never considered as a
free day. Moreover some Islamic theologians 'disapproved of the practice of
some Muslims who refrained from doing work on Friday in imitation of the
Jewish and Christian weekly holidays'.[32]

In the Ottoman Empire no day of the week was set aside as a day off for
wage earners, rural or urban, even for those who lived far off from family.
Even on Friday, as a day of Muslim communal worship, the Muslim workers

returned to work after the noon prayer. For the Christian workers a similar scheme had been set up, except for Sunday morning Mass.

The first reference to the introduction of some kind of day-off discipline in the Ottoman Empire goes back to the early nineteenth century, during the period of the Egyptian pashas' rule in Çukurova. During his seven-year rule, Ibrahim Pasha introduced measures to modernize the region and improve the people's living conditions. Among such measures was the introduction and extension of a labour-free Thursday afternoon and Friday. The implementation of the new measure in 1834 allowed agricultural wage earners to terminate their weekly working day on Thursday afternoon, before dusk, in order to avoid facing any possible harassment on their way to visit their families. The labourers' reaction to the new decree was appreciative and enthusiastic. Even after a century the people of Çukurova still remember the act of Ibrahim Pasha in their prayers through the following blessing:

Akşama bereket, sabaha kuvvet, Ibrahim paşa'ya rahmet, büyüklerimize nusret.[33]

Abundance to the evening, strength to the morning, the mercy of God be upon Ibrahim Pasha and efficient aid to our elders.

More than 20 years after the introduction of Ibrahim Pasha's regulation, new guidelines for the working day were introduced when the telegraph, steamship and railways found their way into the Ottoman and Persian Empires.

The first telegraph line in Turkey was laid during the Crimean War and the first message was sent in September 1855. In Persia the first telegraph line joined Tehran to Sultaniyah, one of the Qajar king's holiday resorts, in 1858. The introduction of the telegraph line was followed by the construction of the railway system. The first railway in Ottoman Turkey linked Izmir with Aydin through the Menderes Valley. It was some 120 kilometres long and was opened to traffic in 1866. Others, including the Istanbul–Edirne line, which with some 320 kilometres became the first stage of the Orient Express line, followed the Izmir–Aydin railway. By the end of the nineteenth century a burst of rail construction increased the railways of the Ottoman Empire from several hundred to several thousand kilometres of track including the Hejaz Railroad linking Damascus with Medina, which began in 1900.[34] In Persia, the first track linking Tehran to Rey was opened to the public in 1887. Nevertheless, the railway system never observed punctuality.[35]

Working in the telegraph offices had its rules and regulations. Often the 24 opening hours of the telegraph offices led to the recognition of fixed working hours. As for telegraphic communication, the introduction of the railway, covering a great distance in a fixed time period, with predetermined departure and arrival times available to all, not only was a chief factor in bringing on the meticulous precision in the measurement of time, but also a new labour-discipline.

However, while the Ottoman and Persian rulers were fascinated by the idea of bringing modernization to their countries by introducing new technical innovations, especially in the field of communications, enabling them to sustain their authority over their realm, it was the ruled rather than the rulers who endeavoured to harmonize different dimensions of the new capitalist pace. One can indeed trace the endeavour and pressure from below for a better adjustment to modernity in Ottoman Turkey and Persia as early as the late nineteenth century.

In the nineteenth-century Ottoman Empire, a long working day, sometimes more than 16 hours, was commonplace.[36] The working condition of the miners in the Zonguldak coalfield during 1848–65 has been portrayed in the following terms:

> Zonguldak villagers worked in the mines like slaves in colonial countries. Arbitrary working hours set in two shifts namely 'sunrise shift' and 'sunset shift'. The ponies' stables were more hygienic than the workers' barracks. There were no first aid facilities or doctor even around big coal pits. If a miner got injured or became ill, the company would throw him out. When a miner was seriously injured, the coal company would put him on a pony and send him to his village. That was a common practice.[37]

It is noteworthy that the European companies active in the coal industry of the Ottoman Empire implemented a different work-day policy back in their homeland. In mid-nineteenth century the average working week of the miners in the British coalfields was 60 hours, compared to the 100–120 hours of the miners in the Ottoman coalfields.[38] The Anatolian and Baghdad Railroad Companies, who were also active in some European countries, adopted different pay policies in different countries. In the late nineteenth century, while in European countries the company's pay was based on the monthly work, in the Ottoman Empire it adopted the policy of paying workers for task-work or by the hour.[39] In 1908 the union of workers and employees of the Anatolian and Baghdad Railroad Companies published a pamphlet recording a long list of demands, including a shorter working day and double pay for night work.[40] Following the denial of their claim, published in their *beyaname* (declaration), the railway workers launched a strike and marched through the streets of Istanbul.[41] However, the strike ended in failure and the working hours remained as long as 12 per day, with task-pay a common practice.[42] Except for ratifying some general labour codes, the Young Turks' profound engagement with territorial issues left their government a lesser amount of time to deal with workers' living conditions, and by the outbreak of the First World War the issue went utterly into the shadows.

In Kemalist Turkey some sectors of the Turkish economy, owing to the shortage of labour, employed prisoners and military personnel, chiefly the conscripts of the armed forces.[43] Although in 1921 the mineworkers of Zonguldak adopted an eight-hour working day, the laws were impressive only on paper and had little impact on workers' everyday life. The ten- to twelve-hour working day was common in Kemalist Turkey. In 1930 the Hygienic Act (*Hıfzıssıhha Kanunu*) was introduced. While forbidding the working of 12–16-year-olds in the evening after eight o'clock, it nevertheless left the working hours issue unanswered.

The *Hıfzıssıhha Kanunu* was followed by another decree published in 1932, in which the paid weekly day off and public holidays were acknowledged and the weekly day off changed from Friday to Sunday. However, it was by the Labour Act (*İş Kanunu*) of 1936 that the limit of working hours per day was eventually addressed. According to the Act, the working day was fixed on a standard 48 hours a week, with possible overtime of three hours a day. Moreover, the Act proscribed the total overtime working days exceeding more than 90 a year. This was certainly a step forward in regulating the working day throughout the country. Nevertheless the Labour Act retreated from the Hygienic Act when it lifted the compulsory recognition of the paid day off and public holidays.[44]

In Iran, the first legislative attempt at regulating the working day was in 1913 in Kerman. When the deputy governor of Kerman laid down the new conditions to be maintained in the carpet factories, the carpet weavers welcomed his initiative. However, it caused discontent among the agents of the employers, most of them European companies, who took sanctuary at the British consulate to protest against the 'social regulation'.[45] The state of affairs became even more blistering when the British consulate interfered in favour of the European companies. The weavers called for a strike, which lasted for some days but finally ended in failure following a negotiation between the deputy and the British consulate.[46]

Following the failure of the Kermani carpet weavers to adopt a new working day regulation came Reza Khan's coup of 1921, when the question of working conditions was once more raised, first in the capital Tehran:

> The new government led by Sayyad Zia had indeed prepared various measures, which were to be executed by the Welfare Department of the Municipality of Tehran (*Idarah-i Umur-i Khayriyyah-i Baladiyyah-i Tehran*), which were made

public in April 1921. Apart from measures in the field of public health and consumer protection, action would be taken to combat unemployment. To that end a Labour Council (*Shuray-i Mashghalah-i Kargaran*) was established, which was charged with finding jobs for unemployed workers, both skilled and unskilled. It had, moreover, to assist them when destitute, and to defend their rights, especially where their working hours and weekly rest period were concerned.[47]

In the same year the government issued another working regulation with regard to the carpet industry of Kerman. Among the new measures adopted in the new regulation was one to limit the working day to eight hours. However, the strong objection of the employers to the eight-hour working day did not make the government retreat from its early mandate, and two years later, in 1923, another decree declared that:

- The working day shall not exceed eight hours.
- On Fridays and public holidays work shall be suspended and workers will continue to receive their normal wages.[48]

The question of working regulations for pregnant women in the carpet industry was also raised in a decree published by the government in 1924, entitling 'a woman who had to give birth to five weeks' vacation on half pay'. Furthermore the new directive once more referred to a working day of eight hours and a week of 48 hours, rest period excluded, which was set during midday at one and a half hours. Overtime – based on agreement between the employer and employee – was set at a maximum of two hours per day and 12 hours per week, with a proportional increase of 50 per cent in pay.[49]

During the 1930s the Iranian parliament ratified a number of decrees designed to improve the conditions of workers and government employees, such as the Factory Act of 1936, which was for a while rejected by the Anglo-Persian Oil Company (APOC), the 1937 act on the employment of prisoners in industrial and agricultural sectors, and the 1939 act on the working conditions of medical personnel in government service. In most of these decrees the question of fixing working hours was addressed. However, the question remained as to what extent the labour-discipline imposed by external pressure was practised and, moreover, the internalization of this discipline.

In 1929 the workers at the Abadan refinery launched a strike for better working conditions and pay. Among the demands of some 9,000 striking workers, out of the 15,000 total oilfield workforce, was the call for a shortening of the working day from ten hours to seven hours in the summer and eight hours in the winter.[50] The strike was crushed by the police, and the call for the shortening of the working day was left unanswered.

Following the unsuccessful strike at the Abadan refinery, in May 1931 the workers of the Vatan textile factory in Isfahan launched a strike to improve their working and living conditions. 'The strike was almost total, and even eight-year-old children participated. A few workers of the weaving department who wanted to continue to work were induced to strike as well.'[51] Marching towards the city centre, the workers formulated their demands, including:

- Changing from task-work to monthly salary in order to change the early ill treatment of the workers.
- An eight-hour working day with sufficient pay, which should not be less than five qeran.
- Leisure time for half a day with pay in order to be able to enjoy a leisure day properly and fortify themselves, so that they could perform the task in the factory the next week properly,
- The maximum working day not to exceed ten hours, i.e. only to include a maximum of two hours' overtime.

Following a police attack on the marchers and the arrest of a number of ringleaders, the workers returned to the factory the next day but stopped work after eight hours as planned. More police harassment could not convince the workers to give up their demands. Finally, following some intense negotiations between the representatives of the government, the director of the factory and the representatives of the workers, the government reached an agreement with the workers and accepted most of their demands, including the working-day regulation, in the following terms:

- The working day was to be reduced from 12 to nine hours.
- The lunchtime was to be changed from half an hour to one hour.

Throughout the 1930s the Isfahan textile workers' achievement in fixing the working-day regulations remained as a point of reference for not only the Iranian workers' desire to fix their working day but also for the government in introducing the new legislation observing employer–employee association.

In 1936 the Iranian Ministry of Mining and Industry introduced new legislation observing the working conditions in the country's industrial units. While in the new legislation the health and safety regulations of the workplace were addressed, the question of working time was somehow over-looked.[52] It was indeed in the post-Second World War period that the newly founded Ministry of Labour adopted the nationwide maximum eight-hour day and the 48-hour week.[53]

The requirement of adopting the structured secular time went even beyond the ideological framework of the Islamic government in Iran. Following the revolution of 1979, the noon prayer at the solar noon became part of the officially sanctioned religious ritual in Iran:

> All industrial, business, and office workers had to stop at the solar noon to conduct prayers. This practice led to such chaos and confusion in the daily affairs of government agencies, banks, schools, factories, etcetera, that a new ordinance issued by Ayatullah Khomeini abolished it. Workers and public employees are now required to postpone their noon prayers until after working hours are officially over.[54]

Conclusion

Contrary to the general assumption among some European Orientalists, neither Persians nor Turks had an aversion to accommodating timekeepers in their public life. Their resentment was solely against the striking clock, which for them was nothing less than an icon of Christianity. As far as the adoption and assumption of punctuality based on the 24-hour modern time was concerned, there was indeed a disparity between the practice of time with regard to work-discipline and the realm beyond the workplace. The existence of such a gap, which was not peculiar to these two countries, was related to the quest for modernization during the nineteenth and twentieth centuries in Turkey and Iran. For many Iranian and Ottoman elites seeking changes and reforms in their countries, the clock and the timetable, the calendar and the programme were certainly the icons of modernity, and they believed that by adopting them a society could be modernized.

The inspiration for rapid and authoritarian modernization, while demanding swift understanding and colossal sacrifice on behalf of the working population and the subaltern class, denied the agencies of such groups a role in reshaping the countries' social and political life. In other words, the elitist characteristics of the authoritarian modernization in both countries left no room for autonomy on behalf of the non-elites, especially the subaltern. In studying the adoption of modernity in Turkey and Iran and the way the people reacted to the authoritarian trends imposing change and reform by the *men of order*, one should certainly consider the social and political changes which both countries experienced in their pre- *men of order* era. If one compares and contrasts the Iranian constitutional movement of 1905–

11 with the Young Turks' revolt of 1908, the elitist characteristics of the political events in Turkey become even more vivid. Following the 1908–10 strikes, which were not tolerated by the *Ittihad va Taraqqi* government, it took more than 35 years up until 1946 for the working class to once more appear on the country's political scene, establishing their role in the country's daily political life. The reason for such a long period of isolation can certainly be attributed to the low profile the political parties enjoyed in late Ottoman and early republican Turkey. On the other hand, in Iran, with the reformist political parties, especially the leftist parties, playing significant roles in the constitutional and post-constitutional period, the period of absence of working people in the country's political life did not exceed more than ten years. By 1941 when the old king was forced to abdicate and public participation in the country's political life somehow became possible, the Iranian subaltern did not hesitate in participating once again in the public life of the nation, even with a degree of autonomy.

2

Workers and the State during the Late Ottoman Empire[1]

Donald Quataert

Most historians of the nineteenth-century Ottoman Empire fondly write about the state and its works. They have examined in some detail how the Ottoman state transformed itself and debate about whether the changes were mere Western imitations or indigenously powered. While this is all to the good, most historians continue to avoid labour history – the story of workers, their organizations and their contribution to the ebb and flow of events in the Ottoman world. To help fill this void, this chapter focuses on workers and their role as a bulwark against the ambitions of the Ottoman state. It seeks to determine the extent to which Ottoman workers curbed, challenged, curtailed and moulded the power of the state.

This is not a romantic enterprise, one seeking to assign workers a powerful status that they did not possess. From the outset I concede that the Ottoman regime was a powerful, indeed the dominant partner in the worker–state relationship during most of the nineteenth century. But the relationship was not a one-way exchange in which the state dictated and workers obeyed or simply rebelled. Workers have their own story and their own goals. It seems incumbent on all Ottoman historians to seek to apprehend that story and those goals if we are to appreciate the dynamics of late Ottoman society. And so the stress here is on Ottoman labour and workers, their organizations and their power in an era of the steadily more powerful and encroaching state.

The historiography of Ottoman labour

In Ottoman studies, history from below remains unusual, even though economic history writing has been a major trend for several decades and we have fine studies on commerce, agriculture and, to a lesser extent, manufacturing and mining. There has, however, been little attention given to the individuals and groups working in those sectors. Merchants have received some attention but peasants, artisans, miners and other workers have not. Ottoman history is a stage on which there are few actors from the popular classes. They almost always are in supporting roles or waiting in the wings. On stage, the cast remains replete with characters drawn from the state elites. And, abandoning the stage metaphor, Ottoman history is one that is largely devoid of conflict in social relations.

The causes of this state of affairs are several. The first two are more general issues that Ottoman history from below shares with other historical fields. The other factors seem more particular to Ottoman historical studies. Let us begin with the self-evident notion that history from below concerns persons and groups who leave few written records about themselves and their lives. The sources for such history usually are state and corporate archives and, in general, the records of the literate classes, materials that typically are hostile or indifferent to peasants, workers and miners. These class barriers, by definition, make the task of writing history from below more difficult than, for example, that of a literate member of the elite, such as, in the Ottoman case, the intellectual Mustafa Ali or the politician Midhat Pasha. The successes of the *Annales* school and that of *Alltagsgeschichte*, however, demonstrate that the obstacles to good history from below can be overcome.

A second factor concerns the archival materials for Ottoman history that are drawn from European sources, both private and public. The diplomatic and commercial correspondents of the various European powers possessed many cultural differences with the Ottoman objects of their concern and they usually viewed the Ottoman Empire as a backdrop against which their particular interests were played out. These foreign observers, who had their own concerns and culture, held Ottoman subjects at a remove, at a distance. Thus Ottoman historians examining workers, miners and peasants and using materials generated by foreigners of a different class and culture find the research task doubly difficult.

A third factor is the nature of the abundant documentation available in the Ottoman archives. The study of these numerous documents written by government officials remains very exciting but poses difficulties that have not been addressed sufficiently. To begin with, the prevalence of such documents helps to perpetuate a static perspective on the past. Ottoman bureaucratic and military officials wrote about what concerned them and their state and they were not seeking to capture the totality of this lost world, as historians collectively seek to do. The state documenters usually discussed workers as producers of wealth and as taxpayers, as objects and not as agents with everyday lives. In recent years, happily, Ottomanists have begun to recognize this as a difficulty that requires correction. Also, the sheer quantity of the documents often has mired scholars in the archives, causing them to ignore other kinds of relevant materials. Thus family business records as well as state documents located outside the central state archives have largely been unexplored.

Having said that, labour history quite recently has emerged as a legitimate, if very minor, field of specialization in both Ottoman and Middle Eastern studies. A number of works have appeared that offer the beginnings of a foundation for future research. These include early books by Beinin and Lockman (1987), Lockman (1994), Quataert and Zürcher (1995), and Goldberg (1996).[2] More recently Beinin has offered us a helpful survey of peasants and workers (2001), while Chalcraft presents a path-breaking analysis of Egyptian workers.[3] Overall most of the few historians who worry about labour (including the present author) over-emphasize certain groups of workers and workers' experiences at the expense of others. For example, they feature organized workers, those in guilds and/or unions, stressing urban, mobilized, active, protesting or striking workers, often those with a socialist consciousness. Such a focus derives partly from the ready visibility of such workers, because organized or activist labour produces more documents than unorganized or quiescent workers. Both in this present essay and generally in Ottoman labour history, urban workers who were organized or activist have received almost all of the scant attention given to those labouring in the lower reaches of society. And yet, vast numbers of unorganized (and often politically quiescent) workers laboured both in the rural areas and in the towns and cities as well. There were very many thousands of men and women worker-cultivators in the Ottoman countryside who grew crops and raised animals for subsistence and for sale and also manufactured for local, foreign and distant markets. Because they laboured in widely scattered locations, they often remained invisible and therefore, despite their economic and numeric importance, neglected.[4] Similarly, as shown below, labour in many urban areas was only loosely organized, if at all. For example, the increasing use of Singer sewing machines for commercial production in the latter part of the century usually occurred in small workshops and homes, sites of unorganized labour.[5]

Protesting workers, for their part, are emphasized partly because they attracted the attention of contemporaries, who left records. In addition, this emphasis organically emerges out of the modernization paradigm. Modernizationists examine those who are moving upward on the evolutionary scale, in this case towards self-consciously working-class workers who represent themselves through vigorous action. It is for this reason that we see the flurry of scholarly activity around the strikers of 1908 (see below).

Politically active workers are fascinating people. But we must also remember that workers can be agents without having organizations, without explicitly expressing working-class consciousness and without striking. They can have an agenda and successfully pursue goals via other, less public means of representing their interests.[6]

Introduction to Ottoman labour and the state

The history of Ottoman labour and state relations in the nineteenth century is framed by two epochal events. These are, firstly, the annihilation of the Janissaries in 1826 and, secondly, the great wave of labour strikes that immediately followed the Young Turk Revolution of 1908. In one of its first acts of self-assertion of the modern age, the centralizing Ottoman state destroyed the Janissary Corps and thus violently eliminated its armed source of worker opposition. At the other end of the period, we find another violent confrontation between state and labour in the Ottoman world. In 1908, after 80 additional years of centralization, the state sent troops and enacted new laws to crush striking workers. The strike-related events show that despite all the achievements of nineteenth-century state building, workers still posed a grave threat to the Istanbul regime.

The workers involved in the two sets of events seem to have been quite different. Although there is some uncertainty about this, it appears that unskilled workers may have played the most important single role in the 1826 events. Most visible, perhaps, were the porters whom the state quickly punished for their participation. In the 1908 strikes, most mobilized workers, that is, those who went on strike, were of the skilled variety. Railway workers, for example, played a visible and important role in the strikes.[7] Both sets of events – the Janissaries' destruction and the 1908 strikes – occurred in Ottoman urban centres and among organized workers.

In the realm of organized urban labour, guild-like *esnaf* organizations predominated for most of Ottoman history. Among the *esnaf* workers, the porters and port workers remained the most visibly well organized and powerful during the nineteenth century. Overall it seems likely that service-sector *esnaf* persisted most successfully among all organized workers. By 1908 craft *esnaf* guilds in a number of Ottoman towns and cities had fallen on hard times and had disappeared. This occurred when (1) the products they made were replaced with European goods, and/or (2) wages and prices fell in response to foreign competition and non-*esnaf* replaced *esnaf* Ottoman labour in making goods that successfully competed in the Ottoman marketplace. We actually know little about the behaviour, actions, objectives and goals of organized *esnaf* workers during the final Ottoman century. They certainly were not what prevailing wisdom, that which follows the lead of the scholar Gabriel Baer, suggests. He influentially but nonetheless incorrectly argued that *esnaf* guilds were to be understood as bodies primarily existing to serve as administrative links to the state. Thus, he and others have implied, labour had no agenda separate from that of the regime. Such a view is to portray the *esnaf* members as objects, not agents, in their own history. They certainly did have their own goals.[8] But we continue to know very little about these nineteenth-century organizations. They may not have been chartered organizations like their European guild counterparts. Perhaps they were only informal organizations around which urban workers with a particular skill clustered. But Baer is partly correct, for they were officially sanctioned by the state. Our ignorance is largely, I believe, because scholarly proponents of the modernization paradigm considered *esnaf* as non- or antimodern relics of a past that inevitably would disappear. (Recall that such scholars were ignoring religion for the same reason.) Hence, modernization historians ignored the guilds, a subject that I will raise again in the conclusion of this essay. Whether or not *esnaf* vanished so inevitably is an open question. Many hundreds of them survived, in what health and form is not clear, into the twentieth century. Also, consider the contemporary spatial form of the retail stores and manufacturing workshops in many Middle Eastern cities. The continued clustering of similar activities certainly owes something to the *esnaf* heritage and suggests that they are alive in function, if not name, today. Guilds and *esnaf* in their early modern European and Middle Eastern forms and functions surely did vanish in the emerging new world of capitalism. But they remained a visible force throughout the period of interest here and have left an important legacy.

By 1908 the forms of organized labour were becoming very different from what they had been in 1825, just before the Janissaries' massacre. As the various *esnaf* thrived, hung on or disappeared, new kinds of labour organizations were appearing, often European in form and, sometimes, partly, in membership. Just prior to 1900, mutual aid societies, syndicates and unions began to appear in a number of the largest Ottoman cities, and mainly in places like Salonica, Istanbul and Izmir the new labour organizations became important. A real explosion in the number of these new organizations occurred during the 1908 strike wave, when workers often formed unions as they went on strike to express their grievances. These unions were frequently ephemeral in nature, enduring only as long as the strike that was their midwife. And in many cases state repression destroyed or drove them underground.[9]

Some of these unions and syndicates had emerged as early as 1889, evolving out of the mutual aid societies that some workers had formed. In that year, the state passed legislation forbidding the formation of workers' associations anywhere in the empire. The law was not directed against guilds, with which the state had long-established relations, but rather against Western-style unions and syndicates. Promulgation of the legislation perhaps demonstrates government unease with the new and unfamiliar forms of labour organization that were emerging during the late nineteenth-century era of direct foreign investment. But it is probably unfair to assume that it indicates actual government fear of worker power. Prevented from legally forming unions, the workers turned to mutual aid societies, whose form the state was willing to tolerate. Thus mutual aid societies emerged, for example, among the coal miners at Ereğli on the Black Sea coast, workers for the Istanbul Ferryboat Company (Şirket-i Hayriye), as well as workers at the state-run Feshane and Hereke textile factories. Similarly, workers and employees of the vast Anatolian Railway Company established a mutual aid society in 1895.[10] These new societies had several common features: they tended to promote the interests of the more skilled workers, all were located in enterprises that possessed comparatively large groups of workers massed in one or several locations, and all the firms in question employed foreign workers who were in the majority in certain job categories and companies. Also, except for the government establishments, all the corporations were owned by foreign capital.

The Janissaries as workers and their relations with the state

The eighteenth century may have been a golden era from the perspective of workers' power relative to the state.[11] This power is directly linked to the Janissaries, familiar actors in Ottoman history. In the writings of traditional Ottoman historians, the Janissary Corps has been represented as an institution of the Ottoman classical age that had become debased, corrupted and perverted. By the early nineteenth century, they were represented as having become crude, rude, vulgar and bloodthirsty, massing into an irrational, avaricious mob that routinely abused and raped women. For such an element, no crime was too great, not even religious hypocrisy. When they were destroyed in 1826, it was said that their housing quarters had been 'cleansed' and that 'scorpions' had been eliminated.[12]

For those who took charge of the Ottoman state and the writing of its history in the nineteenth century, the Janissaries have served well as a key symbol of Ottoman decline, of what had gone wrong with the empire. The Janissaries' defeat in political battles meant that later observers read

only the winners' accounts and thus overlooked the identity, interests and
economic-political functions of the losers. This neglect notwithstanding, it
is clear that the Janissaries were based in specific social groups and represented particular economic and political interests during the eighteenth
and nineteenth centuries. Some historians have argued that the Janissaries
controlled virtually all the professions and trades in cities as far apart as
Aleppo and Edirne.[13] And yet, a closer look does not suggest a broad occupational base encompassing all or even most artisan categories. For example,
with one exception, no textile manufacturers seem to have been included
among Janissary-related workgroups. This is noteworthy since, after food
processing, textiles were the largest single urban industry. If it is true that
Janissaries came to control virtually all trades and professions, this must
have occurred very late in their history, probably not before 1800. My
surmise is that they began to enhance their economic and political influence only after 1740; it then accelerated very rapidly near the turn of the
nineteenth century.[14] The Janissaries (at least in Istanbul and Aleppo) seem
to have represented the predominantly Muslim lower working-class strata,
with a large proportion of them working as porters, boatmen, day labourers and fruit-peddlers. They monopolized access to worksites, organized the
labour force and represented the workers in negotiations with owners and
merchants.[15] Were Janissaries, as some would argue, instruments by which
unskilled and semi-skilled workers terrorized the rest of the urban working class? Perhaps not. The evidence is not conclusive, but they might well
have been participants in a mutually advantageous alliance that protected
Ottoman urban workers of many different kinds against the encroachments
of the state.[16] As some contemporaries asserted, the Janissaries were the
instruments of popular sovereignty, guarding the urban population against
the power of the throne, the central bureaucracy and officialdom in general.
They had become 'a national militia attached to the immediate interests of
the people'.[17] When the final Janissary revolt began in June 1826, the rebels
clearly focused on the state itself and sought to assure merchants that their
properties were safe. In the view of some observers, the destruction of the
Janissaries meant that the 'sole rampart against absolute power had been
overthrown, that their [the people's] liberty had been destroyed'.[18] With the
destruction of the Corps, it seems plausible to argue, workers in Istanbul
and other Ottoman cities with Janissary garrisons lost their armed protec-
tors. Thereafter the *esnaf* and other workers had to rely on other, less direct
mechanisms when they addressed the state in search of redress (see below).

The porters and port workers of Istanbul

There is an important postscript to these 1826 events concerning the use of state power to replace a group of workers of one ethnicity with those of another.[19] In 1826 Sultan Mahmud II commanded the Armenian Patriarch of Constantinople to provide 10,000 men as replacements for the exiled and killed porters, who had been of Turkish and Kurdish ethnicity. At this time, Armenians already constituted an important, perhaps even dominant, source for the recruitment of Istanbul porters.[20] By fiat, they now assumed control over sectors of the profession that Muslims, with their Janissary alliance, had dominated. The subsequent political role of these Armenian porters is uncertain. In the days of the Janissaries, the Kurdish and Turkish porters, in their poverty and their intimate knowledge of the Istanbul streets, often had fought against the government to protect the interests of the Corps and its artisan members. The newly appointed Armenian porters of 1826, however, owed their jobs to the state. If they were used by it against opponents of the reform legislation, they may have been part of the fundamental realignment of Ottoman politics inaugurated by the destruction of the Janissaries. Alternatively the state, having neutralized the once troublesome porters, may have sought to allow only economic tasks to the Armenian porters. Without more information, this subject cannot be explored further.

The growing economic influence of the European powers and of the Ottoman Christians during the nineteenth century, however, worked to undermine the position of the Armenian porters in Istanbul and not only those who owed their jobs to the events of 1826. In August 1896 a group of Armenian revolutionaries seized the Ottoman Bank at Galata in Istanbul, entering it disguised as porters, hauling sacks ordinarily filled with money but this time carrying explosives. In response, Muslim crowds, organized and armed by the Ottoman government, attacked the Armenians who, significantly, were from 'the lower classes in Stambul, the *hamals* or porters'.[21] In all, 5,000–8,000 Armenians perished in the riots, including many hundreds of porters. The surviving Armenian porters were exiled from the capital and sent back to their homes while Turks and Kurds, who came from the same eastern Anatolian provinces, took their jobs.[22]

Thereafter Kurds dominated the ranks of the Istanbul porters, and their close alliance with Sultan Abdulhamid II is well known in Ottoman history. But these Kurdish porters were hardly mere tools of the state. Rather, they vigorously and successfully pursued goals of their own, frequently to the detriment of the Ottoman government and its economic well being. As I have already written about this elsewhere, let me summarize one of their more notable successes. In the later nineteenth century, many of them, as well as port workers of different ethnicities, found their jobs threatened by the formation of the French-capitalized Istanbul Quay Company. The company sought to construct a set of modern port facilities that immediately threatened to make redundant many porters and port workers. But these workers fought, literally, and for years kept their jobs. Finally the company won out, firing many and breaking their guilds' monopolies. There the matter might have rested but for the Austro-Hungarian annexation, just after the July 1908 Young Turk Revolution, of the Ottoman provinces of Bosnia and Herzegovina. Unable to mount a military response, the Young Turks declared an empire-wide boycott of Austro-Hungarian goods and turned to the porters and port workers (including those in Istanbul) for its enforcement. In the ensuing months, these workers did their part to maintain the boycott and, after its successful conclusion, received their reward. Numbers of the previously fired porters were re-hired and *esnaf* guild privileges reinstated.[23]

The strikes of 1908

The Young Turk Revolution of July 1908 is famed for the re-establishment of the Ottoman constitution of 1876 and for the end of the absolutism of Sultan Abdulhamid II. In the history of worker–state relations, the revolution is significant because of the labour unrest that followed. In the immediate aftermath of the July Revolution there was tremendous uncertainty. The sultan restored the 1876 constitution that he himself had once set aside, but it was very unclear what it meant, where power actually resided and what might be allowed. Workers began probing to find the meaning of the revolution and the restoration that had just occurred. A series of tests started and with increasing assertiveness they demanded wage increases to offset the sharp price hikes of the past several years.[24] In this climate of uncertainty, workers were likely emboldened by the apparent pro-worker posture of some Young Turks, positions dating back to pre-revolutionary days. In their effort to overthrow the sultan, elements among the Young Turks secretly had sought out aggrieved workers (and peasants) and helped to organize strikes and other labour actions. In the context of governmental confusion, apparent Young Turk support and steadily increasing experience in labour mobilization, workers pressed their grievances forward with increasing assuredness. Some workers focused solely on wage demands, but others moved on to a host of other work-related issues. Within less than a month of the Constitutional Revolution, scores of unions and syndicates appeared. Then strikes began erupting and, in the following month, a wave of strikes washed over the empire, peaking in mid-September 1908.[25] These strikes were sometimes quite violent and literally terrified the regime. For example, strikers closed down, for brief intervals, the greatest coal mines in the Middle East while others shut down whole sections of the Ottoman railway system, severing links between the capital, the major cities and the provinces. It seemed as if nearly every urban worker was striking. Significantly the newly formed unions account for the vast majority of all strikes recorded in the 1908 strike wave.

The state responded by dispatching mediators, gunboats and soldiers. In dealing with the workers, the state always, or almost always, granted all or part of the wage demands. But it never, to the best of my knowledge, recognized or legitimized the many demands for a workers' say in management. And worse, in early October 1908, it adopted stringent anti-strike legislation that required arbitration and effectively outlawed strikes. These actions had their effect. In the ten years following the passing of the law, there were an estimated 46 strikes, fewer than half the number that had erupted in the few months after the July 1908 revolution. Both strikes and unions remained illegal for many subsequent decades, well into the history of the succeeding Turkish Republic.[26]

Conclusion

If we look at the period between the sets of events in 1826 and 1908, how successfully did Ottoman labour confront and curb the power of the state? Obviously, without access to an armed group for support, labour *militarily* was less confrontational in 1908 than it had been on the eve of the 1826 events. In this way, the state was in a stronger position in 1908 than in the early nineteenth century. Its 1908 bureaucracy and military were vastly larger and superior, by many orders of magnitude, to their 1826 incarnations.

It is not certain how often and successfully labour directly confronted the state in the decades after 1826 and before the 1908 eruption of strikes. The available materials show scattered incidents where, throughout the period, workers directly and successfully confronted the state. Altogether, there are several dozens of these direct, recorded conflicts over the period 1826–1908 that are presently available (and many more incidents likely await discovery). The petitions of workers, both *esnaf* guild and union, tell us much about their relative strength in a given situation and circumstance. In these petitions they were variously obsequious, deferential and self-confident depending on the circumstances and effectiveness of the strategy being employed. The issues at stake were the preservation of their own privileges, their encroachment on the monopolies of others and taxation levels. In all these cases of petitions, workers directly were addressing the state in an effort to influence its behaviour.

But there are many other forms of behaviour that workers employed in order to shape, curb or circumvent state policy and power. For example, workers ignored state demands to adhere to fixed price schedules or to restrict output. They avoided paying taxes. They reached outside of guild structures when necessary to remain competitive, employing non-guild labour as a means of lowering prices or increasing output. Such pursuits of labour self-interest, in sum, were commonplace in late Ottoman history but not yet adequately documented.

The power of some *esnaf* guilds, notably the porters and port workers, indicates major successes for organized labour. A large number of guilds did persist until the end of the Ottoman Empire, certainly in Istanbul and perhaps elsewhere as well. There is, for example, a government listing of 287 guilds in Istanbul, dated 1887. The overwhelming majority were craft and provisioning *esnafs*: a sample recorded the names of 72 guilds and of these a full 78 per cent were manufacturing guilds, making one thing or another, from thread to quilts to silver wire. The survival of such guilds demonstrates that, at some level, they had been able to protect their own interests.

The recorded persistence of these *esnaf* guilds into the twentieth century raises another issue, which concerns the strike wave of 1908. To begin with, it is certain that guild labour was still an important part of the workforce in many Ottoman cities in 1908. And, surely, guild labour was being hurt by the relative wage declines of the pre-1908 era. When, however, we turn to the enumeration of striking workers in 1908, the *esnaf*-organized artisan workers – with only a couple of *sui generis* exceptions such as the bakers – are not visible. Perhaps there were strikes among small-scale artisans but so diffuse and scattered as to remain unrecorded, but, given the documentary record available at this particular time, such an absence seems unlikely. The development of Ottoman capitalism suggests that these guilds must have been in serious difficulties. Why, then, were there so few strikes among manufacturing guilds?

The fact that many *esnaf* workers owned the means of production obviously played a role. Against whom, after all, would they strike? Themselves? For journeymen and apprentices, the explanation must be more complex. Perhaps the bonds of affection and loyalty linking them to the masters, who may have played the role of *paterfamilias*, prevented these workers from taking such hostile actions. But such was not the case in Damascus, where militant journeymen in the textile guilds frequently struck or agitated against the oppressive actions of their masters.[27]

The answer may lie chiefly in the weakened condition of the journeymen and apprentices, in their fragile vulnerability. Manufacturing *esnafs* generally were on the defensive as a result of the cheapening price of most goods during the nineteenth century and the official elimination of guild monopolies. The journeymen and apprentices may have felt that their jobs were too vulnerable and thus were reluctant to risk overt action. As I suggested above, there were other forms of negotiation besides strikes that could have been used to increase wages. Or they may not have agitated at all, joining with the masters in supporting a state that they considered a bulwark of last resort against foreign competitors. From positions of weakness, negotiation may have been the preferable course. Labour need not be in conflict in order to exert influence or change the direction of state initiatives. The *esnafs* historically had offered mutual benefits to labour and state and during the nineteenth century, and after 1826 they obtained frequent (if unreliable) official support for monopolies and price regulations, i.e. protection from untrammelled market forces. That is, *esnafs* were obtaining tangible benefits from their relationship with the state. And finally, preservation of *esnafs* suggests that these forms of labour were exerting sensible pressures on the state, which found their continuation useful.

Thus manufacturing but not transport *esnaf* guilds largely were absent while unionized and syndicated workers formed the vast majority of the recorded strikers in 1908. And when we speak of the striking or mobilized unions and syndicates of 1908, we need to remember that such bodies constituted only one part of a larger labour force that either was unorganized or existed in guild-like *esnaf* organizations.

In the Ottoman labour–state equation, mutual aid societies, unions and syndicates were a new and unfamiliar variable. Unlike *esnaf* guilds, these unions and societies originally did not result from some internal set of dynamics at work inside the Ottoman world but rather were imported from outside, often travelling with the workers down the railway lines from the Balkans. Labour unions at first were outside of the standard channels of labour–state negotiation that had developed and evolved over the Ottoman centuries. There was no normal method of negotiation between the state and these newly arrived bodies on the Ottoman scene and the evolution of such relations occurred during an era of crisis in the evolution of the Ottoman state, as the Young Turk contenders were challenging the Hamidian regime. Caught in an intra-elite struggle for domination, the Hamidian holdovers and the Young Turks were thus less ready and able to flexibly respond to unrest from below.

The tactics that unions employed to present their grievances were often novel. On the one hand, the language of the petitions and statements that they sent for newspaper publication or that they printed in pamphlet form was often that of the *esnaf* guilds. The new unions were polite and careful, acknowledging the authority of the state and asserting their own patriotism. But in many other ways they differed radically from the guilds' approach. When they asked for participation in company management, unions went far beyond what any guilds might have demanded. Their words often were deferential, within the norms of customary behaviour and politeness, but their actions were not. The unions' strike format, adopted in a widespread fashion only through the emboldening atmosphere following restoration of the constitution, was an unacceptable form of negotiation in the eyes of the nineteenth-century Ottoman state. This stoppage of work stood outside the accepted framework for negotiating workers' claims, in part because it was so public.

In addition to the public aspect of their action, unions were novel in yet another way, in their ethnic and religious hierarchies. Overall Muslims formed the majority of the Ottoman non-agricultural workforce, but perhaps not of the factory-based industrial and rail-based transportation sectors. We know that the Ottoman workforce in the modern sector – here mean-ing the European-capitalized corporations – was ethnically and religiously stratified, with the Muslims on the bottom and, in ascending order, the Ottoman Christians and the Europeans at the top. European and Ottoman Christians disproportionately predominated in most, if not all, of the new unions. Furthermore it is clear that either foreign subjects or recently natu-ralized foreigners, all Christians (and perhaps a few Jews), led these new labour organizations. This hierarchy was different from the religiously heter-ogeneous *esnaf* guilds where Muslims and Christians participated without one group or the other in a clear position of dominance. The net effect of such union hierarchies perhaps was to weaken labour in its struggle with capital and also with the state that ended up allying with capital.

If we look beyond the end of the Ottoman Empire to the Turkish Republic of the 1920s, we see that labour in these same endeavours, for example rail-ways, was overwhelmingly Muslim, mostly Turkish. What had happened? The answer is not simply that Ottoman Greeks and Armenians had vanished from the republican Turkish scene because of population exchanges and massacres between 1915 and 1923. The shift away from non-Muslims already was under way before these epochal events. Between July 1908 and the First World War, there had been a number of boycotts against Austro-Hungarian, Bulgarian and Greek goods. As a result, Christian-ness became less palatable, more risky.

So labour lost many of its leaders who were Christian, and in the early Turkish Republic the labour force in the modern sector was often headless. How this affected its ability to confront the state remains an open question.

Disgruntled Guests: Iranian Subalterns on the Margins of the Tsarist Empire[1]

Touraj Atabaki

*Every year throughout spring in the mountains on the frontier you could see thou-
sands of poor and ill-fated Iranians barefoot and in tattered clothes, in groups of
forty to fifty, illegally crossing the borders of the Empire in search of work. Any
attempt to hinder this labor passage would have a devastating effect on our
booming economy.*
(Extract from a report compiled by the governor of Elizabethpol in 1887)

Suffering from two consecutive military defeats at the hands of the expanding Tsarist Empire in 1813 and 1828, Iranian society went through gradual
but significant political as well as socio-economic transformations. One of
the ultimate consequences of these was a series of major social dislocations
in Iranian society. Urbanization and migration to neighbouring countries
in pursuit of work or political shelter were the vivid manifestations of such
social dislocations. The migration of Iranian subalterns and political activists
began in the mid-nineteenth century.[2] Imperial Russia, India, the Ottoman
Empire, and North and West Africa were the most favoured destinations
for the Iranian migrants. Of these destinations, the margins of the Tsarist
Empire, the Caucasus and Central Asia were the favourite constituencies
for the people of central and northern Iran. The flourishing economy of the
nineteenth century and the relatively liberal political setting of the Caucasus
and Central Asia attracted many Iranian migrants. The economic and
political migration of Iranians to this region gradually became the major
migration trend in nineteenth-century Iran, and by the time of the Russian
Revolution in 1917 hundreds of thousands of Iranians had settled throughout the southern districts of the Tsarist Empire. In the Caucasus region
these Iranian migrants, most of whom came from Iranian Azerbaijan and
lived in the Caucasus among their co-ethnic and co-linguistic group, were
known as *hamshahri* (fellow countryman), and they maintained a separate

sense of identity that marked them out from the local population to the north of Iran's frontier.

Although the life and times of the Iranian migrants at the margins of the Tsarist Empire during the nineteenth century has been the subject of a number of academic studies, the need for a new inquiry still seems well founded. One reason is that since the demise of the Soviet Union the archives of the Soviet as well as of the Tsarist period have become more accessible. Furthermore in the past ten years the availability of archival documents, especially those relating to the Qajar and early Pahlavi periods in Iran, has added significantly to our understanding of the nineteenth- and early twentieth-century history of the region.

Another reason for a new inquiry stems from the quality of previous studies. The historiography of the Russo-Iranian connections suffers to a large extent from essentialist deficiencies. One example is the question of Iranian migration to the Tsarist Empire. By reducing the forces causing the migration to an economic motive, the dominant historiography denies the existence of other social and political incentives to migration. By closely studying the history of Iranian migration, one might also conclude that throughout the long period of the nineteenth and early twentieth centuries there were times when, notwithstanding constant non-linear economic factors, other factors became more decisive in driving people to the north. The study of the causes of migration is not the only field where such reductionism is so vividly marked. In studies of the life of the Iranian migrant community in Imperial Russia the essentialist approach denies, by highlighting notions such as class and class solidarity, the existence of other sets of solidarities massing people together and driving them to fill the vacuum between their origins and their actuality.

By examining the scale of the migration and the living conditions of the Iranian subaltern residing on the margins of the Tsarist Empire, this article will present an overview of political developments within this community in the Caucasus in conjunction with political changes in Iran and the Caucasus.

Forces causing the migration

Iranian society's reaction to the military defeats of the early nineteenth century was a precipitous endeavour to introduce a series of changes and reforms throughout the country. Although it was initially the political elites, both inside as well as outside the political establishment, that were calling for changes and reforms, it soon became a public plea joined by the country's merchants, craftsmen and urban wage earners. The messianic

Babi movement of the 1840s was the grand manifestation of this popular demand. Within a few years, the Babi movement had mobilized an amalgam of different but discontented urban social classes, as well as some rural groups.[3] As will be shown later, although the brutal suppression of the Babi movement put an end – at least for the next 40 years – to any endeavours to implement reform from below, the ruling political elites nevertheless continued with their reformist agenda from above. Gradually it changed the political features of the country – guiding it towards the Constitutional Revolution of 1905–9.

The political concessions, commercial capitulations and economic penetration that were the direct consequences of the military defeats led the Iranian economy to become more dependent on the international market and its fluctuations. The decline of the domestic and external value of the Iranian currency, the increase in the level of the country's foreign trade, the commercialization of agriculture and the decline in non-export agricultural products and traditional crafts, the rise in the production of cash crops, and the gradual increase in the country's population from 5 or 6 million in 1800 to about 10 million in 1914[4] resulted in class dislocation and population displacement.[5] Such changes brought a new pattern of consumption and subsequently changed social norms, social stratification and the traditional power structure. This pattern of change was intensified further in 1869 by the excavation of the Suez Canal, which provided easier access to the Indian Ocean for European ships. At the same time, the importance of the Tabriz–Trebizond route diminished. The closure of this route, which for centuries had been the most important one joining Europe to the Indian subcontinent, was an extra burden on the Iranian economy, which was already going though a drastic decline, creating mass unemployment.

During the nineteenth century Iran suffered from outbreaks of famine more frequently than during any previous century. The main cause of the famine was the loss of the country's 'grain store'. For centuries the agricultural lands north of the Araxes river, especially the Nakhjivan region, were providers of grain for northern and central Iran. The annexation of the region by Imperial Russia not only deprived Iran of its grain store, but the manpower working on the land was also lost. However, there were also other reasons for famine. That of 1859–60, for example, was caused by the export of grain to Russia, which was followed by social disturbances and an increase of between 70 and 400 per cent in the price of all essential supplies.[6] Famine once more swept through Iran in 1871–72 and 1895–96. Both were caused by local magnates hoarding grain.

In Iranian Azerbaijan and the provinces of Isfahan and Khorasan, the cyclical bread shortages of the 1870s through to the 1890s, which again were mainly caused by local governors hoarding grain, caused a massive influx of refugees from some provincial cities. As a result of the widespread official practice of closing all the city gates during an economic crisis to prevent the influx of refugees, the only option left for displaced people was to cross the border illegally into neighbouring countries. According to a report by the French consul in Tabriz in 1895,

> the shortage of grain, which for some years has caused serious political unrest in the province, was mainly the result of the corrupt conduct of the local governor. By gradually purchasing the entire province's farming land and hoarding the grain for selling at higher prices, the governor created a disastrous economic crisis in the province.[7]

The people's failure in their petition to the central government to secure intervention in their favour paved the way for mass migration and urban as well as rural riots. After months of confrontation, these riots only eased once grain entered the market again.[8]

With the decline of the traditional economy and the limited potential of the new economy to provide work for thousands in their traditional locality, leaving rural areas for the cities in pursuit of jobs gradually became a new trend. However, with cities having only limited potential to provide jobs and shelter to the newcomers, and often having closed their gates to immigrants anyway, the regions beyond the borders became the most prominent alternative calling the Iranian subaltern.

The practice of arbitrary rule at each and every level of public life had always been a force behind migration throughout Iranian history. Nevertheless, if in the presence of a strong and effective government the exercise of arbitrary rule at the provincial level by local governors and tribal chiefs was somehow checked by the central government, in the nineteenth century – with the country's economy in decline and the weakening of central control over the provinces – the practice of arbitrary rule was incontestably extended throughout the country. The enduring incursions and looting of villages in northwest Iran by Kurdish tribes during the nineteenth century forced tens of thousands of peasants, especially the Christians (mainly Armenians and Assyrians), to leave Iran for Imperial Russia. According to Nafisi, during the first half of the nineteenth century more than 60,000 Christians left Iran.[9] In addition to the threat from local tribes, one should also consider Russia's far-reaching Christian repatriation policy in the region, which encouraged the Iranian Christian community to move to the southern constituencies of Tsarist Russia.[10] In Iran the Christian community was subjected to a range of discriminatory policies, including having to pay a different poll tax. But in introducing 'Caucasus development planning' the Russian authorities exempted the new migrants from paying taxes during the first two years of their arrival in Imperial Russia.[11]

The discriminatory economic policy towards the Christian community was not the only factor causing religious minorities to migrate. Another and more serious factor was religious persecution, and especially the uninterrupted harassment of the Babis. The mass persecution of Babis in the second half of the nineteenth century, especially after the failed attempt on the life of the Qajar king, Nasir al-Din Shah, in 1852,[12] added to the influx of migrants to the north. The persecution and the gruesome slaughter to which the Babis were condemned was a signal to the populace, whether sympathetic to the Babis or not, of the consequences of challenging the existing order – a spectacle to remind as well as to avenge.[13] According to one chronicle,

> At Milan, a village near Tabriz (in northern Iran), a large number of the inhabitants had been converted to the religion of the Bab. Following the attempt on the life of the Shah, a group of government servants and soldiers came from Tabriz and fell upon the helpless Babis of the village and sacked their houses. A number suffered martyrdom immediately while a further group was taken to Tabriz.[14]

During the following years, Ashgabat and Baku, on the southern frontiers of Imperial Russia, provided shelter for thousands of Babis fleeing from subjugation in their home country. While Baku, with its dominant Shi'ite Muslim population and with a strong link to the Iranian clerical Shi'ite hierarchy, was considered a less favourable destination, Ashgabat, with its dominant Christian population, proved to be a safe haven, where the Babis were able to construct their own places of worship.

Finally, in studying the economic and political forces behind Iranian migration to the north, one should also consider the economic and political changes that swept through Russia during the nineteenth and early twentieth centuries. Russia's strong state-oriented policy of industrialization, and the development of massive mining projects and expansion of domestic industries, led to an apparent labour shortage in Russia. By adopting a policy of importing the labour force it required, Russia aimed not only to supply the manpower it needed for its labour-intensive industries but also for the expanding agricultural lands and industries, including its tea plantations. This policy certainly appealed to many of its neighbouring countries, including Iran.

In the political sphere, one of the major consequences of the annexation of the Caucasus to the Tsarist Empire was the consolidation of ethnic solidarity among the Georgians, the Azeris and the Armenians. The public desire for independence gradually became one of the main engagements of the new educated middle class within each of these ethnic communities. By the end of the nineteenth century Georgian, Azeri, and Armenian nationalism held sway over the southern Caucasus. Moreover, the political changes in Russia also affected everyday life in the Caucasus. In the second half of the nineteenth century the Caucasus became one of the most important backyards of Russian revolutionary and reformist organizations. For many politically minded Iranians, the Baku and Tbilisi of the late nineteenth century were cultural magnets where they could become acquainted with new ideas and practise their aspirations. Living in such a political environment refashioned their political consciousness and made their contribution to political change in their homeland more vivid.

The political changes and upheavals in Russia and Iran had an effect on the number of migrant subalterns. For some years the Russo-Japanese War of the early twentieth century, which was followed by the Russian Revolution of 1905 and the Iranian Constitutional Revolution of 1905–9, hindered the progress of migration to the north (see Figure 1, p 41). Moreover, although the Iranian government benefited directly from the income the migrant subaltern returned to the country, there were nevertheless occasions when the number of migrants reached such high levels that the government endeavoured to hinder migration, mainly by diplomatic negotiations and by ratifying protocols with Russia demanding that the latter refuse to accept new migrants. However, migration was too strong a force to be stopped by diplomatic treaties.

Formation of the Iranian subaltern community in the Caucasus

The Iranian migration to the Caucasus dates back to the early nineteenth century. Prior to this period, the southern Caucasus khanates, although they enjoyed extended autonomy, nevertheless still considered themselves part of the Persian Empire. With the endorsement of the Gulistan and Turkmenchay treaties of 1813 and 1828, the people of the region were separated from each other along the political borders dividing Iran from Russia. The annexation of the southern Caucasian region forced the subjects of 13 khanates to accept the citizenship of Tsarist Russia. They were mainly Georgians, Armenians and Azeris. The most significant of these groups were the Azeris, or, as the Russians called them, the local Tatar, who lived along the Araxes river. While the status of the northern Azeris was changed – they accepted citizenship of the Tsarist Empire – the people south of the Araxes remained within the realm of the Persian government and retained their Iranian citizenship.

The annexation of the southern Caucasus to the Tsarist Empire had far-reaching consequences. For centuries, people in this region used to travel freely up to the Black Sea. Now, with the imposition of a new border between the two countries, people on both sides of the Araxes had to cross a border that had been drawn without their consultation. Regardless of the many attempts by both countries to formalize the travellers' movement across this new border, the problems relating to the border and border crossing remained a major concern for both countries. In the early years of annexation, Russia endeavoured to counter the mass migration and illegal cross border trafficking by introducing new laws and regulations. Iranians wanting to cross the border were required to obtain visas from Russian consulates within the border provinces. On arrival in Russia, they were also asked to register with the local authorities and obtain residence permits.

With the Iranian economy in gradual decline during the nineteenth century, the flourishing economy of Russia had been attracting many Iranian subalterns. They moved, in search of work, by different routes, legally or illegally, to the southern region of the Tsarist Empire, especially the Caucasus. The influx of these seasonal and non-seasonal labourers reached such high proportions that it eventually became a cause of great unease to the Iranian government. The Iranian government's apprehension was demonstrated noticeably in the treaty of 1844 signed between the two countries. Among other issues, what was significant in this agreement was the influx of Iranian subjects into Russia and the guarantee of Russian citizenship offered them by the Tsarist authorities. Under this agreement, those Iranians intending to adopt Russian nationality had to obtain the Iranian government's written permission.

On the other hand, although the Russians were eager to formalize the existence of their new border with Iran, as far as migration was concerned they adopted their own agenda and continued their policy of importing labour when required. According to an article in the journal of the Ministry of Internal Affairs of the Tsarist Empire, published in 1845, 'there was a huge arrival of Iranian and Ottoman masons and carpenters in the southern Caucasus and they somehow monopolized the local labour market'.[15] According to another source, in 1858 a total of 4,852 passports were issued to those crossing the Russian–Iranian frontier in search of work in Tbilisi, Elizabethpol, Shusha, Shamakhi, Yerevan and the other southern Caucasian cities.[16] The number of passports issued corresponds to the number of migrants who crossed the border legally. The long natural border between the two countries provided many possible routes enabling illegal migrant workers to avoid the eyes of the eager border guards. Although there are no statistics available, the number of illegal migrants would definitely have exceeded the number of legal migrant labourers.[17]

The free exploitation of the oil deposits in the Apsheron peninsula on the Caspian coast in 1872 caused the mass migration of Iranian labourers to the Caucasus and Central Asia. The rapidly growing oil production of the Caucasus soon elevated the region to supplier of 95 per cent of all Russia's consumer oil and holder of the second largest oil deposits in the world, after the United States. Along with the British, French and German companies operating in the region, it was Russia that anticipated benefiting from underground resources in a territory that, on the eve of its occupation and annexation, was considered of solely geopolitical and military importance.

The strong Russian state-oriented industrialization policy of the late nineteenth century paved the way for a massive expansion of domestic industries, the development of huge mining projects and a dazzling extension of railway networks into the southern regions of the Tsarist Empire.[18] The construction of roads and railways such as the Trans-Caspian network, connecting the Caucasus with Central Asia, increased labour migration and resulted in an even greater population dislocation, as well as the expansion of the ancient cities and the building of new industrial zones. Baku is one such example: as a result of the 'oil rush', its population rose from 13,000 in 1859 to 112,000 in 1879 and to 300,000 in 1917. The workforce in the oilfields rose from 1,800 in 1872 to 30,000 in 1907.[19]

In such an increased tempo of economic activity, labour shortages soon became evident. It was not only labour-intensive industries that faced serious shortages; the expanding agricultural lands and industries were also affected. Consequently, along with local people, hundreds of thousands of Russians, Armenians and Dagestanis migrated to mining areas and the oilfields, as well as to other industrial regions. Nevertheless, many branches of production in Russia still faced severe labour shortages, and the import of foreign labour turned out to be the first priority for the Russian authorities in the region.[20] It was believed that nineteenth-century Iran – with its declining economy and outstretched border with Russia – could supply the cheap labour needed for the fast-growing Russian economy.

Although a large proportion of the Iranian migrant subalterns went to the southern Caucasus, the number of migrants seeking work in the various parts of Central Asia was also significant. In addition to using the perilous route that passed the Turkmen desert, there is evidence to show that migrant workers reached Central Asia by way of Transcaucasia. For example, in 1886 Nikolskii, in an account of his travels, reported that 'In Baku our ship took on three hundred Iranian workers, on their way to work on the Trans-Caspian railway.'[21] Consequently, within ten years the number of Iranians in Central Asia rose from 23,191 in 1897 to 55,000 in 1907, and they became the main immigrant community in the region.[22]

The Iranian migrants resided in various places in the Russian Empire: Baku, Yerevan, Tbilisi, Elizabethpol, Batum, Astrakhan, Ashgabat, Marv, Samarkand, the northern port cities on the Volga, and also in the less important industrial centres, such as Alaverdi and Nukha. In 1885, in a memorandum addressed to the Russian Ministry of Foreign Affairs, the Russian government commissioner in charge of immigration to the Caucasus raised the issue of guaranteeing Russian citizenship to thousands of Iranian labourers who had migrated to Russia prior to 1870. The Ministry of Foreign Affairs responded positively, but in a communiqué dated 17 March 1886 it was mindful of the 1844 Russian–Iranian agreement on cross-border issues – which prevented either country from guaranteeing citizenship to subjects of the other country – and underlined the 'need for further vigilance in dealing with the scheme and to accomplish it in absolute tranquillity'.[23] Meanwhile, as regards the possibility that Russia's citizenship practices might eventually be revealed, the communiqué urged the Russian representatives in Iran to claim that, in the event of a possible protest from the Iranian government, the Iranian authorities must themselves 'be held responsible for their incompetence in controlling their own northern frontiers'.[24]

As expected, the Iranian government gradually became concerned by the mass migration of the Iranian subaltern to Russia, and on more than one occasion it approached the Tsarist government's representative in Tehran to ensure mutual cooperation in order to extradite thousands of Iranian émigrés living on Russian soil. In 1886, in a letter to the governor of Baku, the Russian government commissioner in charge of immigration to the Caucasus urged the governor, '[while] considering the Empire's economic interest, [to] apply appropriate measures in order to diminish the tension between the two governments'.[25] Accordingly the governor of Baku decided to deport some of those migrant Iranian subalterns who had settled in Russia after 1870 and who were employed in the marginal sector of the province's economy. Hundreds of migrant workers were expelled in groups of 50 to 100, while the authorities refused to allow them to take their personal possessions with them.[26]

While by such diplomatic gestures the Tsarist government endeavoured to demonstrate its commitment to bilateral agreements with Iran, it never

closed its border to the influx of cheap labour from its neighbour. Local
landowners, oil companies and industrialists were hostile to the government
adopting any measures hindering the immigration of Iranian labourers.
According to the governor of Yerevan, 'any measure to limit the migration
of the Iranian labourers could result in disastrous shortages of manpower in
the region'.[27] As a result, the Russian government issued a new law in 1887
allowing the Iranians to reside in the Russian border provinces for a maximum of six months without the need for appropriate permission or visas. A
year later, this was extended to other provinces and included all of Russia.
According to an official report, in 1889 there were thousands of Iranian
labourers in the Caucasus who had neither an official work permit nor an
entry visa.[28]

Towards the beginning of the twentieth century, the rapid influx of Iranian
subalterns crossing Russia's frontiers was constantly increasing. Russian
consulates in Persia, especially in the northern provinces of Azerbaijan,
Gilan and Khorasan, issued work permits and visas to thousands of Iranians
wanting to leave their country in pursuit of work. Documents from the
Russian consulates in the northern frontier cities of Tabriz, Mashhad, Rasht
and Astarabad indicate that between 1876 and 1890 an average of 13,000
Iranians per year acquired work permits and visas to enter Russia legally. By
1896 this figure had reached 56,371. The number of work permits issued by
the Russian consulate in Tabriz rose from 15,615 in 1891 to 32,866 in 1900
– an increase of 110 per cent in nine years.[29] In the province of Khorasan, the
influx of people seeking 'work in the Transcaspian region in 1909 increased
so fast that the number of villages with offices for granting external passports rose from ten to twenty-five'.[30] In 1904 the number of visas issued to
Iranian migrant labourers reached a total of 71,407,[31] and seven years later,
in 1911, of a total of 192,767 labourers entering Russia legally 160,211 were
Iranians.[32]

Figure 1. Legal Migration of Persians to Russia, 1900–1913

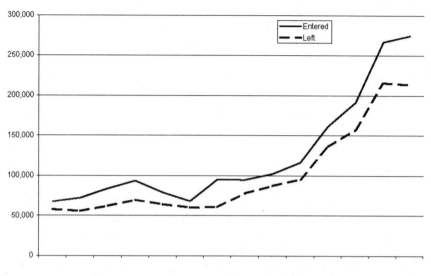

Source: Marvin L. Entner, *Russo-Persian Commercial Relations, 1828–1914* (Gainesville, FL, 1965), p 60.

However, one should realize that these figures do not cover those migrant workers who crossed the frontier illegally. If one recognizes that in nineteenth-century Iran crossing the frontier was common practice among those residing in the border regions, then the actual number of Iranian migrants must definitely have exceeded the recorded figures. Moreover, crossing the border illegally allowed poor migrant workers to avoid paying a range of fees imposed discriminately on them. These fees included the costs of 'visas', 'passing the gate', a 'donation to charitable organizations', and of helping various projects such as the 'Russian railroad projects'.[33] The same fate awaited them on their return to Iran. The Iranian border guards and customs officers refused to let the returnees pass until they had parted with much of their savings.[34] Ardabil and its vicinity was the main region sending illegal migrant labourers to Russia. According to Illinskii, the number of illegal migrants from this region was more than 20,000 a year.[35] Tigranov puts the figure at 30,000 to 40,000 per year.[36] In April 1897 the newspaper *Kaspii* reported that 'lately every ship coming from Persia to Baku carries some 150 to 200 Persian subjects, illegally entering the Caucasus to seek work'.[37] Strigunov argues that by the turn of the century the number of illegal workers in Baku province had reached 18,000.[38]

Seasonal workers comprised the mainstream of the labourers cross-ing the frontier. Returning home after harvest to avoid the cold winter of the Caucasus, they worked some seven to eight months of the year on the cash-crop plantations. For example, in 1900, while 67,304 Iranian workers crossed the Russian frontier legally, 57,489 returned to Iran. In 1906 these figures reached 95,132 and 60,524 respectively, and 274,555 crossed into Russia while 213,373 returned in 1913.[39] Nevertheless the process of migra-tion to Russia was so entrenched that Iranian emigrants constituted a large labour force in the region. On the eve of the Russian Revolution of 1905 the Baku oilfields employed some 10,000 Iranian workers,[40] and in the copper mines and industrial plants of Alaverdi in the north of Yerevan there were 2,500 Iranian workers, who accounted for 70 per cent of the total workforce there. In the other industries in the Caucasus and Central Asia, Iranian workers constituted 30 per cent of all labourers and they were the largest of the foreign groups residing there. In the city of Tbilisi, the number of Iranian labourers reached 5,000 by 1910.[41]

The steadily growing number of migrant workers in the southern part of Imperial Russia was halted by the political upheavals following the Russian Revolution of 1905. For example, in January 1906 the total number of workers employed by 75 oil companies operating in the southern Caucasus dropped by 6,000.[42] Nevertheless the trend soon changed again, owing first to the Constitutional Revolution in Iran and also to political stability in the Tsarist Empire. In 1907 the Caucasus and Central Asia witnessed a massive influx of Iranian migrant subalterns. Thousands of poor peasants from Persia's northern provinces of Azerbaijan and Khorasan crossed the frontier seeking a job.[43] According to Wladikavkaskaia railway documents, during the three days of 12, 13 and 14 September 1907, 1,500 labourers arrived in Baku.[44] In the same year the number of workers in Baku's oil and other industries returned to its earlier level of 50,000.[45]

Gender, ethnicity and age of the Iranian subaltern

Although the available data on Iranian migrant workers do not provide an inclusive picture of the gender composition of Persian migrant workers, nevertheless by comparing two sets of data derived from the first national census of the Russian Empire carried out on 28 January 1897, we can derive a sketchy picture of gender divisions among Iranian migrants in the late nineteenth-century Caucasus and Central Asia. Table 1 shows the number of women at work in the city of Baku and its fringes. At 8.6 per cent, the textile industry was the largest employer of women; as a whole, women accounted for no more than 2.5 per cent of total workers in 1897.

Table 1. Women in Work, Baku and Suburbs (1897)

Branches of Baku industries	Total number of workers	Women workers	Percentage of women
Mining	4557	12	0.3
Chemical	1029	8	0.8
Metal	2892	15	0.5
Wood	539	10	1.9
Textile	755	65	8.6
Dairy food	203	-	-
Minerals processing	123	6	4.9
Food	958	49	5.1
Printing	147	4	2.7
Construction	3161	-	-
Railways	1136	22	1.9

Source: I.V. Strigunov, *Iz Istorii Formirovaniya Bakinskovo Proletariat* (Baku: 1960), p 138.

Concerning the total number of Iranians living in the Russian Empire, the first national census of 1897 divided the community into two categories. The first group consisted of those who spoke Persian but did not hold Iranian nationality. They had been residing in the region for centuries and formed a solid community, especially in the big cities. The second group, known as the Iranian subjects, consisted mostly of newly arrived migrant workers. However, while the national census considered the gender dimension of both groups and noted that women constituted some 20–25 per cent of the total number of Iranian migrants living in the Caucasus and Central Asia, it did not explain what percentage of these Iranian women worked in industry.

Although Table 2 demonstrates the gender composition of Iranian migrants, we do not – as noted earlier – know what percentage of these women went to work outside the home. The only available information on Iranian women workers is for a later period and covers just Baku's oil industry. In an article published in 1926, Irandoust (his real name was V.P. Ostrov) argued that of the 22,840 Iranians working in the Baku oil industry at the beginning of the twentieth century 8.3 per cent were women. By 1920 they accounted for 7.7 per cent of a total of 24,958 Iranian workers.[46]

Table 2. Gender Composition and Geographic Distribution of Persian-Speaking and Persian Subjects in the Caucasus and Central Asia (1897)

Regions and cities	Males and females	Males	Females	Percentage of females
Caucasus	71,432	54,687	16,745	23.5
Baku	29,941	22,012	7,929	26.4
Tbilisi	10,133	7,749	2,384	23.5
Yerevan	8,458	5,239	3,219	38.0
Elizabethpol	13,014	8,391	4,623	35.5
Dagestan	3,571	2,582	989	27.0
Central Asia	23,191	18,455	4,736	20.4
Tran-Caspian	16,914	14,059	2,855	16.8
Samarkand	2,915	2,390	525	18.0
Sir Darya	1,661	1,031	630	37.9
Farqaneh	1,876	1,565	689	36.7

Source: A.Z. Arabadzyani and N.A. Kuznetsovoy (eds), *Iran, Sabornik Statey* (Moscow, 1973), pp 195–214, and Hassan Hakimian, 'Wage Labour and Migration: Persian Workers in Southern Russia, 1880–1914', *IJMES* 17 (1985), p 445.

There were obvious cultural barriers making it improbable that Iranian women of the nineteenth century could leave their locality in pursuit of work across the border. The furthest they could travel in search of work was to provincial centres or the country's capital, where they were mainly engaged in the domestic sector or the carpet-weaving industry. The seasonal migrants were mainly composed of male subalterns. However, considering the working traditions in the region, one could assume that working in the domestic sector and carpet-weaving industry was widespread among the female members of Iran's non-seasonal working families.

We have useful data on the ethnic composition of the workforce in the Baku oilfield. Unfortunately, there are no comparable data available that provide as clear a picture of the ethnic composition of migrant workers in labour-intensive industries in other regions of the Caucasus. In the case of the Baku oilfield, Iranian workers constituted the majority of unskilled foreign workers in the region. According to Thompson, who visited the region in the early twentieth century, 'the daily work on the properties, such as cleaning the setting tubs, chutes, etc, was done exclusively by Persians'.[47] The labour market in the Baku oilfield was initially segmented by race, with oil companies hiring mainly Russians and Armenians for jobs requiring skill and literacy, and Muslim workers, Iranians, local Tatars and Dagestanis for lower-paid unskilled jobs. However, as the result of a policy of favouring the empire's local Muslims the unskilled job sector was gradually allocated exclusively to migrant workers, the main group among them being the Iranians. By sustaining traditional barriers between migrant and non-migrant groups on the shop floor, these hiring practices not only averted labour conflict but also pushed the migrant worker to the margins of society.

Furthermore, this labour discrimination went beyond segregation in employment policy. As we shall see, employers perpetually discriminated in terms of wages too. For identical work, different wages were paid based mainly on the worker's nationality. Even for skilled jobs, Iranian migrant workers earned less than Russians, Armenians, and even less than local Muslim workers.[48] It is noteworthy that contrary to what one might expect the prevailing shortages of unskilled workers and the incessant demand for migrant labour did not alter employment conditions in favour of the latter group. Nor did they exclude ethnic discrimination in the form of professional segregation.

Table 3. Ethnic Composition of the Workforce in the Baku Oilfield (1893 and 1900)

| Ethnic origin | 1893 | | 1900 | |
	Percentage of non-skilled workers	Percentage of skilled workers	Percentage of non-skilled workers	Percentage of skilled workers
Local Tatars (Azeris)	21.5	3.0	19.0	12.3
Russians	13.7	54.3	10.9	42.9
Armenians	26.4	27	24.3	30.8
Dagestanis	19.1	1.0	17.0	2.8
Iranians	14.0	-	24.7	4.7
Others	5.3	14.7	4.1	11.2

Source: I.V. Strigunov, *Iz Istorii Formirovaniya Bakinskovo Proletariata* (Baku: 1960), pp 143–5.

Concerning the data presented in Tables 1 to 3, one should realize, as Hakimian has pointed out, that since the national census was conducted in January,

it is clearly seasonably biased as it excludes all those people who returned home in the cold months of Winter. Moreover, it does not include all working branches, especially those traditionally engaging women workers, such as domestic work. Besides the high incidence of illiteracy coupled with the illegal-alien status of many Persians could make a strong case for possible underestimation of the final results.[49]

Child labour is another issue that deserves attention. According to the 1897 Russian national census, the age composition of Baku's workforce was as set out in Table 4. In a study on the living conditions of Iranian subalterns on the margins of Tsarist Russia, Bahram Agayev, a member of the Iranian migrant community in the Caucasus, presents a devastating account of the children taken by a mediator (*pochtalion*) who had been touring Iranian villages in the Northern provinces in order to recruit children for the Caucasus industries:

> *Pochtalyon* recruited children by promising to pay their parents 40 rubles per year. In each tour, after recruiting about 100 children, the *pochtalyon* made them walk to Baku. The journey took 7 to 8 days. During the journey, the *pochtalyon* provided no food and the children had to collect their food from the villages on the road. On arrival, they were assembled in 'common houses' and were carefully checked and chosen by visiting tradesmen who eventually paid an average of 100 rubles per child to *pochtalyon*.[50]

Table 4. Percentage of Age Distribution of the Workforce in Baku District (1897)

Industries	12 years & younger	13–14	15–16	17–19	20–39	40–59	60 years & older	Unknown
Mining	0.2	1.0	4.0	12.0	73.0	8.6	1.1	0.1
Chemicals	0.6	1.1	3.1	8.4	72.6	12.8	1.4	-
Metals	2.6	4.0	7.3	13.0	62.0	12.8	1.4	0.1
Wood	2.2	5.4	10.8	11.1	53.1	15.9	1.5	-
Textiles	5.3	2.8	7.0	8.2	52.3	19.0	5.3	0.1
Dairy food	4.9	1.0	9.4	17.7	53.2	10.9	2.9	-
Minerals processing	0.8	0.8	2.4	4.9	68.3	17.9	4.1	0.8
Food	3.6	2.2	4.8	10.3	57.4	17.1	4.4	0.2
Printing	3.4	8.8	7.5	21.1	54.4	4.1	-	0.7
Construction	1.2	1.6	3.7	8.3	53.2	26.8	5.1	0.1
Railways	0.1	0.5	0.5	3.1	77.5	17.7	0.6	-

Source: I.V. Strigunov, *Iz Istorii Formirovaniya Bakinskovo Proletariata* (Baku: 1960), p 134.

In 1901 44.7 per cent of workers engaged in tobacco production were aged 15 or 16. The figure for the printing industry for the same year was 32.2 per cent; this compares with 7.5 per cent for 1897, which implies a rapid increase of 429 per cent.[51] Moreover the average wage of the children was a half or as little as one-third that of adult workers.[52]

The working and living conditions of the Iranian subaltern

Iranian migrant workers consisted for the most part of common labourers taking simple manual jobs in the Caucasus and Central Asia. They can be divided into four categories: agricultural labourers receiving wages, agricultural labourers paid in kind with crops (*ranjbar*), porters or dockworkers, and industrial labourers (*muzdur*). According to a report compiled by the governor of Elizabethpol, 'certain categories of hard and dirty jobs were exclusively carried out by the foreign labourers'. These included 'cleaning the water channels affected by malaria, [working on] rice plantations, cotton-picking and sulphating grapes'.[53]

Furthermore Belova indicates that in Elizabethpol it was almost exclusively the Iranians who worked on the land. Every year, thousands of Iranians migrated to this province to take up occupations normally refused by local workers because of the inferior pay and conditions.[54] Here a comparison with the segregation policy imposed on black labourers in the American South is illuminating. In his study of the labour market in the American South during the segregation era Michael Honey points out that:

> [In the 1930s] occupational segregation remained as evident in the factories as in the crafts. Wherever they worked, the racial barriers imposed on them by white society insured that the better paying positions went to white males. While white males worked as mechanists, superintendents, inspectors, mechanics, repairmen, and in product finishing, black men swept floors, lifted and hauled materials, or did semi-skilled fabricating and production work.[55]

In a report on migrant workers published in 1900 in the *Saratovski vestnik* newspaper, the author asserted that throughout Russia Iranian workers consistently took on the heavy work. He referred, for example, to the port of Astrakhan, where the dockworkers were exclusively Iranian.[56]

The living conditions of these dockworkers were extremely poor. In an article published in *Taraqqi* in 1911, Muhammad Amin Rasulzadah portrayed their deprived state:

> The Iranian workers in the Caucasus were working the hardest and meanwhile they were the poorest workers in the Caucasus. They worked 15 to 18 hours a day – sometimes even at night. The daily average wage of the dockworker *hamshahri* was 50 to 60 kopeks. Their earnings were some 20 per cent less than the average earnings of the other simple wage laborers. They ate badly and often 10 to 15 of them shared one room, paying 50 kopeks per month for it. These rooms, which looked like stables, lacked very basic and essential hygiene.[57]

An official survey of the living conditions and earnings of foreign labourers in the Caucasus compiled by Russian officials estimated that, on average,

Iranian labourers in the region earned some 25 per cent less than local workers.[58] Furthermore, according to the same survey, a large number of seasonal workers were unable to cover the cost of accommodation and had no other option but to sleep in the open air, under bridges or along walls.[59] Having to survive on a staple diet of bread, cheese and onions, the majority of these workers suffered from malaria and diarrhoea.[60] According to another eyewitness account, the Iranian labourers survived 'on the simplest and meanest of diets, their food being almost exclusively confined to bread and, in the proper season, raw cucumber, watermelons, grapes, etc, when sufficient may be purchased for a kopek or two to last a day'.[61] The living conditions of non-seasonal workers were no better either. After working a 12- to 18-hour day, mineworkers gathered in wooden barracks known as *artel*, which accommodated an average of 100 workers and had no sanitary facilities.[62]

The various reports compiled by the Iranian consulates in Baku, Ganjeh and Tbilisi also portray the outrageous conditions of these workers. For the dockworkers, the decayed and rotten state of the docks usually caused hundreds of them to drown.[63] Working conditions in the oil sector were no better. According to one of these reports:

> In Baku's district of Sabunchi and Balakhani the private holders of the oil wells employ exclusively Iranian well diggers. In this region, in order to reach oil, the depth of the wells varies between 35 and 45 meters. Usually, after 30 meters of digging, the ill-fated Iranian workers cannot stand the gas inside and are poisoned and pass away. No information on working condition is available, and with no knowledge of what awaits them at the bottom of the well the Iranian diggers accept the pay of 20 to 40 mantas a day and meet their unfortunate fate. It is almost every day that news of the death of 4 or 5 of these diggers appears in the local press.[64]

According to a different source, the job security of the Iranian workers was extremely limited:

> Very few had permanent jobs, and even the oil workers in Baku were no exception to this. Under a 1903 law, employers no longer had any responsibilities for accidents involving foreign workers. Moreover, the economic and political insecurity of foreign workers was further dramatized when, following the 1905 labour unrest throughout Baku, the Russian authorities forced the extradition of thousands of them.[65]

The first recorded news of protest among Iranian workers was of the three-day strikes in 1903 in the tobacco factory of Mirzabekianc. The strike was launched exclusively by Iranians, who composed one-quarter of the 800 workers at the factory. There are no records of other workers taking

part. During the strike, leaflets in Persian were distributed, listing workers' demands.[66] It is not known where these leaflets were published. In his
masterpiece *Tarikh-i mashrutah-i Iran* (History of the Iranian Constitution),
Kasravi refers to a customs employee in Julfa called Bakhsh'ali, who passed
revolutionary literature across the border with the Caucasus.[67] Two years
later, in 1905, 700 Iranian workers in the copper mines of Alaverdi in the
north of Yerevan instigated a strike. Iranian miners accounted for 2,500 of
the 3,000 to 4,000 miners there.[68]

Among the 28 points of their demands were shorter working hours (a
seven-hour day), a 20 per cent increase in wages and better working conditions. As a result of the mediation of the Iranian consulate, the workers dropped their call for a wage increase, while insisting on their other
demands.[69] After almost five months, the governor-general of the Caucasus
crushed the strike by dispatching military forces to the region. Twenty-
nine miners were killed, and all the Iranian miners were arrested and later
deported to Iran.[70] Following the Alaverdi strike, the Tsarist police became
more concerned about the activities of Iranian migrant workers and, according to some secret reports, on more than one occasion Iranian labour
militants charged with initiating unrest were arrested and expelled from
Russia.[71]

Crafting a political consciousness

Since the early days of their mass migration to Russia, the Iranians had
endeavoured to establish a set of connections to bring them together. The
first attempt involved setting up Persian schools. In Baku they founded
Ittihad in the city centre, and Tamadon in the Sabunchi district. The activities of these schools went beyond conventional education for migrant children. They were soon turned into a cultural club where the migrant Iranians
could assemble and discuss social issues. The Ittihad School, for example,
had an active association called the *Sanduq-i Ta'avon-i Madrasah-i Ittihad-i
Iraniyan-i Baku* (Cooperation Fund of the Iranian Ittihad School in Baku),
which held weekly meetings.[72]

The political upheavals that followed Russia's defeat in the Russo-Japanese
War of 1904–5 and the Iranian Constitutional Revolution of 1905–9 also
altered the political environment for the Iranian migrant subaltern. The
southern Caucasus, which had links with the Russian social-democratic
network, hosted a leading community of Iranian political activists and
offered exceptional shelter to Iranian political groups for their headquarters.
Alongside the local branches of all-Russian political parties and organizations, the Iranians too established their own parties and societies. The most

important of the political organizations were *Firqah-i Ijtima'iyun Amiyun-i Iran* (Social Democratic Party of Iran), founded with the help of the social democratic group of Caucasian Muslims (*Himmat*) in 1904;[73] *Firqah-i Ijtima'iyun-Inqilabiyun* (Social Revolutionaries Party);[74] *Hizb-i Demokrat-i Iran* (Iranian Democrat Party); *Hizb-i 'Adalat* ('Adalat Party), which later adopted the name 'Communist Party of Iran'; *Jam'iyat-i Ma'arif-i Iran* (Iran's Knowledge Society), a front for the 'Adalat Party; and *Hizb-i Istiqlal-i Iran* (Iran Independent Party), a pro-Iranian government party.[75]

Following its formation, the 'Adalat Party launched a widespread campaign among the Iranian subalterns. The dominant egalitarianism inspired by the Russian Revolution of 1917 affected many Iranians. It was during this period that 'Adalat Party activists occupied the Iranian consulate in Baku. They made a series of demands, including the abolition of a special annual tax each individual migrant worker had to pay to the consulate. They also called for a permanent delegate at the Iranian consulate to be responsible for migrants' affairs.[76] The Iranian consulate eventually conceded to the protestors' demands, and migrant workers chose Asadollah Qaffarzadah, a veteran social democrat, as vice-consul in Baku.[77]

Concerning the non-Iranian political parties, the approach of the Iranian migrant workers was twofold. While they remained reluctant to join local leftist organizations, they took a blunt stand against the nationalism gradually gaining ground in the region. Creating a Greater Azerbaijan – bringing together the Azeris on both sides of the Araxes – was the main aim of the Caucasian Azeri nationalists. Since the majority of Azeri-speaking people lived in a large region within northern Iran, the nationalists' ultimate hope was to persuade the Azeris of Iran to support their proposed project for unity. To achieve their ultimate goal, they regarded the Iranian migrant Azeris as one of the main target groups for their political propaganda and recruitment. According to Sa'id Maraghah'i – the Iranian consul in Baku – there were some 70,000 Iranians living in Baku during the First World War,[78] and among them the Azeris from Iran's Azerbaijan province constituted the titular ethnic group.

With the fall of the Tsarist regime in October 1917, the Caucasian nationalists dispatched an emissary to Tabriz, urging local politicians to secede from Iran and join with Baku to form a great federation. However, the Iranian Azeris rejected their proposal.[79] Following their failure to convince the Iranian Azeris to join an independent federation, in January 1918 the nationalists published an editorial in *Açiq Söz* (Candid Speech), the main periodical of the local Azeri nationalists, which directly tackled the question of Iranian Azerbaijan. In a rather haughty style, the editorial defined the

historical boundaries of Azerbaijan as stretching to the Caucasian mountains in the north and to the central Iranian city of Kermanshah in the
south, with Tbilisi forming the western frontier and the Caspian Sea the
eastern frontier. The Russian expansionists and Iranian ruling classes were
blamed for having adopted policies that resulted in the dismemberment
of the nation of Azerbaijan. Furthermore, according to the author, it was
the 'natural right of the southern Caucasian Muslims to call their territory
Azerbaijan' and to hope that 'one day their brothers in the south could join
them'.[80]

Interestingly enough, the first reaction to *Açiq Söz*'s stance came from
Iranian Azeri migrants in the Caucasus. In their perception the view
expounded in the editorial was nothing less than a nationalist plot, which
menaced Iran's sovereignty and territorial integrity. Though speaking the
same language as the people of their adopted country, the Iranian Azeris
nevertheless remained a self-contained community with a distinctive identity as migrant subalterns. In terms of social ties they were closer to other
non-Azeri Iranians than to local Azeris. Their political ties were mainly
with Iranian leftist organizations and, above all, with the Iranian Democrat
Party. The Caucasian branch of the Democrat Party was founded in 1914
and its members were recruited from migrant subaltern groups living in
Baku and the border district. During the First World War, the local branch
of the Democrat Party became the most high-profile and active organization among Iranian migrant workers.

With the escalation of nationalist activities in the Caucasus, the Democrat
Party gradually adopted a defensive stand against the propaganda initiated
by local Azeri nationalists. Disturbed by the nationalist stance of *Açiq Söz*,
the Iranian Democrats initiated a political campaign in the region and on
10 February 1918 launched a bilingual newspaper, *Azarbayjan, Juz'-i la-
yanfak-i Iran* (Azerbaijan, an Inseparable Part of Iran).[81]

In addition to promoting political change and reform in Iran, the newspaper declared its task to be one of 'displaying Iran's glorious past and its
historical continuity',[82] as well as of 'hindering any attempt to diminish the
national consciousness of Iranians'.[83] Similarly it contended that Azerbaijan
shared a history with the rest of Iran, and strove to foster self-confidence
and a sense of belonging to territorial Iran. While glorifying the name of
Azerbaijan and its 'key position in Iranian history', the newspaper frequently
referred to 'the many centuries during which Azerbaijan governed all of Iran'.
Pointing to the geographical front-line position of the province, the newspaper 'declared it to be the duty of Azeris' to confront the hostile outsiders
and to safeguard Iran's 'national pride' and 'territorial integrity'.

With a persuasive political agenda, *Azarbayjan, Juz'-i la-yanfak-i Iran* pursued what it had proclaimed in its first issue to be its duty, and continued to publish even after the early takeover of Baku by the Bolsheviks. However, it was forced to close down in May 1918 when the Musavatists – the local nationalists – regained power and formed a national government. Subsequently, all Iranian societies were dissolved.[84]

Conclusion

In narrating the history of the Iranian subaltern community in the Caucasus, I have endeavoured to depict a migrant community formed within the boundaries of prevailing pre-capitalist relationships. The absence of individualism and equality before the law, which manifested itself in second-class citizenship for these Iranians, was one characteristic of such relationships, which drove them towards an alternative identity as a means of protection. The majority of this community were Iranian Azeris who, while in Iran, were considered an ethnic minority; in their host country they lived largely among their co-ethnic-linguistic group, the Azeris of the Caucasus. The persistence of inequality before the law created a bond between these migrant workers and also a sense of defensive territorial-Iranian commonality rather than ethno-linguistic or class solidarity with the native workers in their adopted country.[85] Furthermore, by upholding their territorial-Iranian identity the Iranian subaltern community crafted a significant and unbroken link with a seminal past that could fill the vacuum between their origins and their actuality.[86] As Nipperdey has remarked, for this migrant community, territorial-Iranian solidarity provided the driving force in shaping their cultural identity and promoting their political actions.[87] Crafting such an inclusive culture created a community defined by political loyalty and attachment to a territorial identity that took precedence over their other forms of loyalty, in particular their ethnic, linguistic and class loyalties.

4

The Modernization of the Empire and the Community 'Privileges': Greek Orthodox Responses to the Young Turk Policies

Vangelis Kechriotis

The concept of 'equality before the law' for all the subjects of the sultan, which was introduced by the new constitutional regime in 1908, was part of a political project aimed at bringing all Ottoman subjects under a common political umbrella by implementing equal civic rights whatever their reli-gion or ethnic origin might be. This policy had been initiated already in the *Tanzimat* period (1839–76). However, although it had permitted the limited participation of non-Muslim communities in the regional adminis-tration, through the official endorsement of their elites in the local councils, it rather enhanced autonomy than promoted a common 'Ottoman' identity. The re-emergence of this project, after the Young Turk movement, would provide, it was initially believed, the Greek Orthodox communities, espe-cially in the urban centres, with a unique opportunity to translate their social and economic prosperity into political authority. Soon, however, it became clear that the 'Ottomanist' project was not compatible with such an ambition.

The main challenge against the non-Muslim communities was the elimi-nation of their autonomy on educational and religious matters that had been institutionalized by the *Tanzimat*, but pre-existed in various forms well before that. These 'privileges' (*imtiyazlar*, προνόμια) formed the main point of contention between the Ottoman government and the Greek Orthodox communities throughout this period and until the end of the empire. As a matter of fact, the strife had already been instigated in the 1880s and 1890s with two crises, which had shaken the relations between the Patriarchate and the Ottoman authorities. The Young Turk movement thus fuelled an already existing conflict. However, as will become apparent, the qualitative change in the new regime was its determination to impose state regulations. The crises of the 1880s and 1890s, as well as the ultimate round of the clash in the period 1908–10, is known in Greek historiography as the 'Privileges Question' (*Προνομιακό Ζήτημα*).

The structuring of Ottoman society on the basis of ethno-religious communities allowed certain non-Muslim elite groups, which might have had diverse cultural affiliations, to collectively identify with the Ottoman state. However, although the members of the elite groups that flourished in the course of the *Tanzimat* participated in the administration and shared the power of their Muslim colleagues, the community institutions (religious courts, schools, charitable foundations) would always provide a vehicle of social and political participation for the broader strata of the population as well.[1] Thus the efforts of the Ottoman administration to modernize the empire, by curtailing the power of the elite groups to administer their communities, were perceived by the bulk of the population as a violation of their autonomy. The reactions can partly be attributed to the failure of the Ottoman state to impose and disseminate its own self-image,[2] but also to the process of secularization, which transformed these communities from religious to national ones.[3] In this sense, reactions to state-oriented modernization were not only limited to the elite groups. Resentment could also be traced in the acts of protest and demonstration that brought together large crowds, particularly in the urban centres.

In this chapter, my aim is, firstly, to provide a comprehensive historical account of the conflict up to 1908, which will then enable us to focus on the crucial period of 1908–10. Accordingly, within this context, I wish both to discuss the political discourses articulated among the elite groups either in the parliament or in individual accounts and relate them to larger popular mobilization, in an attempt to conceptualize both as a form of reaction 'from below'. Under these circumstances, the reactions were both of an ethnic-cultural as well as a social character. In any case, however, they had immense political repercussions.

The reforms and the building up of the tension

The reform of the structure of community administration initiated by the *Tanzimat* consolidated the organization of the Ottoman society in *millets*, as not only religious but also political entities. Each community would develop its own internal hierarchy, which would permit a significant part of the community to have a say in decision making. At the same time, it would facilitate the incorporation of the community administration to the secular state administration. In the centre, this integration would be achieved through the subjugation of religious offices to the legal jurisdiction of the state and the substitution of previous incomes with salaries. Moreover, Greek Orthodox members of the Ottoman administration were now involved in the administration of the Patriarchate, functioning as mediators between the two institutions. A similar integration would also take place on a local level with the participation of the elders (*ihtiyarlar*, γέροντες) in the provincial administration on several levels, the most important being the county councils (*Meclis-i Idare-yi Vilayet*, Νομαρχιακό Συμβούλιο). The most crucial development of this period, however, was that, whereas the administration of the Patriarchate was undergoing a process of secularization or rather laicization,[4] with the establishment of a new council, the Mixed National Council (*Karma Milli Meclis*, Μικτό Εθνικό Συμβούλιο), dominated by lay members, which, from then on, would curtail the authority of the Holy Synod, the Patriarch himself was recognized as the leader of his nation (*milletbaşı*, εθνάρχης).[5] This inconsistency indicated the hybrid nature of the reforms. In other words, the Ottoman state undertook a project of secularizing the structure of society, but retained the only available form of organization of the population, that is the organization in religious communities.[6]

One of the most crucial issues around which the controversy revolved was the right of the Greek Orthodox to educational autonomy. Therefore an overview of the major developments in this field, since the *Tanzimat*, will help us place the later conflicts into context. The *Hatt-ı Şerif* of 1839 did not specifically refer to educational or other institutional issues. It was the *Islahat Fermanı* of 1856 which postulated for the first time that non-Muslims would be accepted in state schools, but they were also given the right to organize and administer their own schools. It allowed 'within certain limits, the educational activity of the communities and the confessions'. However, it also made clear that 'though preserving the religious privileges of the non-Muslim communities, the other privileges will be examined and modified'.[7] Thus schools were considered part of the activity that the ethno-religious communities were allowed to undertake. It becomes obvious, however, that the same text paves the way for the curtailing of the aforementioned privileges, a process that relied on the differences between religious and non-religious affairs.[8] On the other hand, we should also mention that the *Islahat Fermanı* postulated for the first time the full incorporation of the Patriarchate and the religious prelates into the Ottoman administration through paid salaries in order to prevent irregular payments and donations. The implementation of this decision, despite the reaction it would trigger, was a decisive step on the part of the Ottoman state in legally curtailing the autonomy of the ecclesiastical authorities. In other words, while 'religious' or 'spiritual' affairs, including education, remained under the jurisdiction of the Patriarchate, the Patriarchate officials were integrated into the Ottoman bureaucracy.[9]

In the 'Regulation for the General Education' (*Maarif-i Umumiye Nizamnamesi*) of 1869, this contention is apparent. The education of the non-Muslims was considered their own affair, as opposed to the education of the Muslim community. However, in the non-Muslim schools, while religious teaching would be organized by the respective religious authorities, teaching of other courses would be supervised by the state. According to Ozil, this can be considered as an attempt by the state to partially secularize education. Accordingly schools were divided into private and public. Private schools were those established by the communities or by individuals who also had authority over their financial administration. Teaching materials and teachers themselves were to be approved by the Ministry of Education. Thus, already in the *Tanzimat* period, the Ottoman state sought to establish a control over community education. The reason this attempt did not bear fruit is related to the broader inconsistency of the reforms that we have already tackled. Education is a good example where one can see how the state allocates the duty for pursuing the secularizing reform agenda to the religious community authorities. Thus, under these circumstances, the outcome was not a standardized secular education but many parallel ones.[10]

The first controversy with respect to the privileges of the Patriarchate appeared in the early 1880s. The atmosphere was considerably different from that of the *Tanzimat* period. The recognition of an autonomous Bulgarian Exarchate on the part of the Ottoman government in 1870 had escalated the tension with the Patriarchate. Moreover, after the suspension of the 1876 constitution and the imposition of autocratic rule by Sultan Abdulhamid, a process of political centralization had been initiated. In the summer of 1883, the Patriarch Ioachim III,[11] in a memorandum to the Ottoman government, protested against the violation of the 'privileges'. He referred to orders issued to the provincial authorities, according to which the civil affairs of the Orthodox clergy should be presented at the local *kadı* courts, and, in criminal cases, the clergymen should be judged by the newly established civil courts in each region. Moreover, the Ministry of Justice did not recognize the definite character of the decisions taken by religious courts in cases of heredity rights. On the contrary, it considered that if someone thought himself mistreated in the religious courts, he had the right to appeal to the civil ones. In his memorandum, Ioachim III also protested against restrictions imposed in the construction and repair of churches and schools.[12] The memorandum was sent in July 1883, followed by a new one in September, in which the Patriarch demanded the issuing of a *ferman* which would confirm his authority. In case this was not provided, Ioachim

III would resign. The Ministry of Education replied that the status of 'privileges' had not been violated, while what the Patriarch now asked for was a novelty.[13] However, there could not exist two parallel legal systems, and in cases where there was a conflict between the civil system and the religious one based on the privileges, the state had the right to intervene. This escalated the tension. Ioachim III declared that he abstained from his duties and thus the Christmas service that year was not held in any of the churches in Istanbul.

The ministerial *tezkere* and also the minutes of a relevant discussion in the cabinet were notified to the Holy Synod and the National Mixed Council, which, however, could not make any final decision. Charis Exertzoglou, who studied these crises, rightly points out that this reluctance to clearly support the Patriarch revealed a conciliatory attitude on the part of the aforementioned administrative bodies.[14] At the same time, the government demonstrated an equally conciliatory attitude, when, in March 1884, it issued the *ferman* demanded by the Patriarch. In May the government, with a new *tezkere*, announced its full compliance with the 'ancient regime', thus terminating the crisis, at least temporarily. The event was celebrated with ceremonies in honour of the sultan and the publication in the official newspaper of the Patriarchate, *Ekklisiastiki Alithia*, of several incidents demonstrating the application in practice of the official instructions. Ioachim III, however, had already resigned. He would withdraw to Mount Athos until his re-election in 1901.

The second crisis broke out in 1890, when, again, news reached the Patriarchate regarding the violation of the 'privileges'. It was clear that the articles of the 1884 *ferman* concerning family affairs had been disregarded. There were also rumours about the intentions of the Ottoman government to impose the teaching of Turkish in the Greek Orthodox schools. In fact, already in 1862–63, teaching of Turkish had become compulsory for secondary schools (*Ruşdiye*) and in 1876 Turkish had been proclaimed as the official language of the state. However, it seems that these decisions had not been properly implemented.[15] In 1889 a newly established committee elaborated on certain modifications on the *Nizamname* with the purpose of facilitating its implementation. Moreover, in 1890, with a relevant *tezkere*, the Sublime Porte declared its intention to intervene in the appointment of teachers and boards of trustees (*mütevelli*) in the Greek Orthodox schools. It also wished to have a say in the curriculum.[16] Both the Patriarchate and the communities considered that these issues were under their jurisdiction and that the government could not act unilaterally. The Patriarch Dionysios resigned, massive demonstrations were held in the major urban centres and the Orthodox Church was declared 'under siege'. The Patriarchate demanded that the 'privileges' remain intact, especially the ones concerning family affairs. Whatever conflict might emerge, it should be resolved by the ecclesiastical authorities. It also demanded retention of the right to put clergymen under arrest in case of a civil offence and to intervene with the authorities in criminal cases. As for education, the Patriarchate demanded the right to retain control of the Greek Orthodox schools.[17] Eventually the Ottoman government preferred to compromise, issuing an *irade* that once again reasserted the 'privileges'.

In this first stage of the conflict, two things became apparent. On the one hand, the Ottoman government considered its policies as a continuation of the modernizing efforts of the *Tanzimat* period. On the other hand, despite the authoritarian political atmosphere and the determination to implement the proclaimed reform agenda, the government preferred resorting to a negotiation with the institutions that were disturbed by these reforms. What is more, since institutions such as the Patriarchate formed part of the internal structure of Ottoman society, the Ottoman government could not sever their authority without jeopardizing social cohesion. Thus the Ottoman administration found itself in a dilemma, which, until the Young Turk movement, it did not manage to resolve.

On the part of the Patriarchate, the reference to the ancient status of the 'privileges' had a twofold effect. On the one hand, it was a reminder that the Orthodox hierarchy formed an integral part of the Ottoman state, an arrangement which, moreover, had been in accordance with Islamic law. On the other hand, however, it demonstrated the will of the Orthodox centre to fulfil its role as an ecumenical force. Throughout the period of the conflict, both sides defended their positions with remarkable persistence. The Ottoman government tended to downplay the political importance of the conflict, insisting on recognizing the Patriarchate as a religious authority, whereas the Patriarchate stressed the political aspect of the conflict. Most telling was the conflict with the Bulgarian Exarchate, which was perceived by the Ottoman state as a conflict between two churches, which should have equal rights in protecting their congregations. Thus for the Patriarchate, it was a matter of vital importance to claim and protect its unchallenged rights in administering the Orthodox populations against the challenges both from the Ottoman government but also from the Bulgarian Exarchate or the Hellenic state. The Patriarchate did not perceive itself as one more authority. It was the only authority.[18]

The Young Turk movement and the Greek Orthodox elites

The conflict that broke out in the second constitutional period is of a different quality. It has been argued that, even if the politicization of the masses proved to be a difficult endeavour, the Young Turks, contrary to the first adherents of Turkish nationalism, managed to introduce notions pertinent to a kind of 'political nationalism'.[19] The aim was the homogenization of Ottoman society based on political, secular principles, and the establishment of a state that would rely on this homogenization. However, Sia Anagnostopoulou claims, the only element that allowed for the political articulation of Turkish nationalism and the construction and proliferation of a national identity among the Muslims was again religion. Thus the reintroduction of the distinction between Muslims and non-Muslims in the political discourse of the Young Turks undermines the very concept of equality, whereas the secularization of the organizational structures of the society was being achieved again through religion. The new regime constituted a system of representation not of the whole of society as a political entity, but of the ethno-religious communities separately. Moreover the maintenance of the *milli* (ethno-religious) mechanisms, through which the political existence of the non-Muslims was constituted, led to the politicization of the *milli* institutional frame, and thus to its 'nationalization'.[20]

In this approach lie two different assumptions. The first is that the ethno-religious community had not yet been politicized, and thus 'nationalized', in the previous period. Let us here take advantage of the otherwise schematic distinction between 'political' and 'cultural' nationalism, to suggest that 'culturally' the *millet* had been already 'nationalized'.[21] To this effect, an important role should be attributed both to the Patriarchate and to the secular middle-class elites that had emerged in the previous period. This 'cultural' nationalization provided the necessary substratum for the 'political' nationalization of this period. Secondly, rather than seeking to trace the reasons behind this nationalization to the influence of the propaganda the Hellenic state exerted on Greek Orthodox populations, it would be more accurate to suggest that this development had been an intrinsic effect of the very policies of the new regime. The important difference between the 'politicization' of this period compared to the 'cultural nationalization' of the previous one, was, as Anagnostopoulou herself suggests, that the mandate was not anymore conveyed by the Ottoman authorities to the religious leaders, but by every community to its elected representatives. These were members of the middle-class groups and were compelled to 'secularize' these entities according to the principles of the new regime. This process, however, would ultimately also 'politicize' them.[22]

As a matter of fact, the religious leaders did not seem to share the enthusiasm expressed by their flock for the restoration of the constitution. This reaction alienated them from their people. In the case of the Armenians, in particular, it led to an open conflict when an enraged group reached the Patriarchate and ousted the Patriarch Malahia Ormanian. The demonstration of the Greek Orthodox against Ioachim III, who had returned to the patriarchal throne, had been scheduled for three days later, on 19 July. However, after the tension created by the Armenian incident, nobody dared to bear such a responsibility.[23] A great deal of the Greek Orthodox elite, out of their confidence that the constitution and the new regime would promote the secularization of the *millet* and would result in the weakening of the Patriarch's authority rather than out of sympathy for the Young Turks, saw in this development the opportunity they sought for and turned into supporters of the Young Turks and opponents to the Patriarch. Thus it would be these elites that, from then on, would take over the political representation of the Greek Orthodox population.[24]

Indeed, within the new regime, with the abolition of the *millet* system, the recognition of the Patriarch as leader of the *millet* (*milletbaşı*, εθνάρχης) by the Ottoman authority lost ground. Since the Patriarch was no longer an integral part of the Ottoman administration, his role as the national ruler of the Greek Orthodox vanished.[25] In political terms, this development would take some time to be accomplished. For instance, as far as education was concerned, according to the new legislation, community schools were preserved, while the state safeguarded their financial control and inspected their programmes and syllabuses, thus removing this authority from the hands of the Patriarchate. The separate educational system was preserved, but the authority of the Patriarch was removed. In other words, whereas before education was considered 'Ottoman', whatever its content might have been, as long as it was subjected to the jurisdiction of the Patriarch, who was acting as the representative of the government, now it would be considered 'Ottoman' only if it was subjected directly to Ottoman authority. However, as Anagnostopoulou points out, in this new era 'the previous 'privilege' of education would constitute the legitimization for the claim of the 'political' right to a separate education'.[26] The argument of the government was that if, in this new era, it accepted the 'political right' of the Greek Orthodox community to have a separate education, a right legitimized by the previous 'privilege', Greek education would be recognized as 'Ottoman' and the whole effort of the state to remove the Ottoman legitimacy of the *millet* system would be undermined. Thus eventually the debate focused on the term 'Ottoman', but also on the question whether an 'Ottoman nation' existed or not. The debate, especially on the 'privileges', would determine the fate not only of the non-Muslim communities but also of the state itself, as the interrelation became more and more clear. In other words, the annihilation of the 'Ottoman' character of the communities (where the term means non-Turkish) would entail the annihilation of the 'Ottoman' state itself.[27]

The representation of the Greek Orthodox population would be now taken over by the civil leadership in Istanbul, namely the parliamentary deputies and the Society of Constantinople, a secret organization that supported their activity. We will refer to them later on. But it is important to stress here that this leadership developed a discourse pertinent to the 'administering of the political rights of the Greek Orthodox' within the frame of the parliamentary system, while at the same time it reproduced principles common to the whole Hellenic nation. Thus we can agree with Anagnostopoulou who claims that despite their declared loyalty to the Ottoman state and the principles of 'Helleno-Ottomanism',[28] their political discourse failed their intentions.[29] Even if this loyalty could be taken for granted, it is also true that both the Ottoman state and these Greek Orthodox elite groups with related aspirations belonged to the past, whereas the new regime was transforming the state into something different. Thus the Greek Orthodox elite groups might remain loyal to 'Helleno-Ottomanism', but the social and cultural preconditions of this ideology had since long ceased to exist.[30] However, it was necessary for the Greek Orthodox elites to legitimize the administration of the political rights of their community within the Ottoman political context. This I aim to demonstrate through certain examples.

The Society of Constantinople, the Patriarch and the violation of 'privileges'

A crucial role in decision making during this period was attributed both by the Hellenic state and the Patriarchate to the secret Society of Constantinople (Οργάνωσις Κωνσταντινουπόλεως) which was established by Lieutenant Athanassios Souliotis-Nicolaidis, together with the diplomat and prominent intellectual Ion Dragoumis.[31] After the successful outcome of the Young Turk movement, despite the initial mistrust, Greek attitudes towards the Unionists had become friendlier. This did not last long, though, as the policy of the Unionists shifted to more authoritarian measures over time. Thus both the Hellenic state and the Society supported the opposition liberal party. However, as Caterina Boura has described,[32] this was not a unanimous decision. Sixteen among the Greek Orthodox parliamentary deputies complied with this policy and formed the Greek Political Association (Ελληνικός Πολιτικός Σύνδεσμος), an alter ego of the Society, also directed by Souliotis-Nicolaidis. Certain among the remaining eight deputies, most prominent being the Izmir deputy, Pavlos Carolidis, were more positively disposed towards the Young Turks, supporting them on certain issues.[33]

In the political programme set up by Ion Dragoumis and Souliotis-Nicolaidis, immediately after the proclamation of the constitution, the concern for the 'privileges' is high on the agenda:

> It should not be considered that since the Turks do not touch the issue of 'privileges', we should not touch it ourselves. If the Turks have not in mind to attack the 'privileges', we are not in danger; on the contrary, we remove the actual suspicion and enmity, which is harmful, particularly for us. If, however, as we are afraid, they challenge them [the 'privileges'] in a way that would not instigate an uprising or when the Ottoman state becomes strong, the danger of the annihilation of the Hellenic ethnicity (ελληνική εθνότητα) is increased.[34]

The most important of these 'privileges' was certainly education. However, in the political discourse of the Society and the parliamentary deputies, a separate education was not considered a political right of non-Muslim Ottoman citizens but a political right of the 'nation', a claim that was legitimized by the very existence of the 'privileges'. What is more, the 'privileges' as a political right within the new environment safeguarded the political and national unity of a population that was geographically but also culturally dispersed and which ran the danger within the new regime of losing its distinctive character. It has been suggested that in this approach it becomes apparent that a part of the Ottoman population, while recognizing the legitimacy of the existence of an Ottoman state, denied the existence of an Ottoman nation as a political entity.[35] However, as was obvious from the discourse of the deputies, the issue at stake was not the existence of the Ottoman nation as a political one, but as a cultural one.[36]

The Patriarch Ioachim III was probably the only one who, from the very beginning, had reacted with scepticism to the Young Turk movement. In response to the two *tezkeres* (memoranda) regarding the issue of the autonomy of educational institutions, which were sent to the Patriarchate on 22 December 1325/1909, Ioachim III pointed out that:

> the Patriarchate, since ages had had the right, for religious, linguistic, national and educational purposes, to take care of the creation of schools, their maintenance, the appointment of the appropriate individuals as teachers and the safeguarding of the religious and moral education of the Greek nation. Thus, it considers it fair that the same law will be valid in the future too, since it is not going to have any effect contrary to the decisions and the high edicts regarding the education and the schools of the State.[37]

Later on a committee consisting of members from the two bodies of the

Patriarchate, the Holy Synod and the National Mixed Council, prepared a memorandum in which it was stated that despite the fact the other religions were also tolerated, the polity had essentially remained Muslim. Therefore it was impossible for a Muslim state to undertake the education of Christian children. This not only concerned strictly religious education but also customs and manners, namely attitudes in social and family life. The differences between the Muslim and the Christian world were so enormous that any interference would be catastrophic.[38]

In Turkish historiography it has been frequently suggested that the Patriarch was claiming political and not religious 'privileges', something that was definitely rejected by the Ottoman government. For instance, in a recent work, drawing vastly on archival material, Bülent Atalay describes how, when the Patriarchate claimed that it would not abandon its 'privileges', it was notified by the Minister of the Interior (Nazır-ı Dahiliye), Talat Pasha, that the Patriarch was recognized only as a religious and not as a political leader.[39] In other instances, the government, probably following the tradition of negotiation with what was still an Ottoman institution, explained that it was not against the 'privileges' of the Patriarchate; however, certain modifications were necessary under the constitutional regime.[40] This attitude, according to Atalay, was due to the painful experiences that the administration had had at the hands of the Patriarchate in the past.[41] Moreover the Patriarchate even then did not refrain from expressing itself negatively with regard to the 'Ottoman Union' (İttihad-ı Osmani).[42] Consequently, according to this simplistic approach, the Patriarchate and the government were at odds with each other. On the one hand, the government was trying to keep the Greek Orthodox population away from the propaganda of the Patriarchate, while, on the other hand, the Patriarchate was trying to prevent the Greek Orthodox from any contact with the Ottoman authorities.[43]

What is disregarded in this approach is the challenging of patriarchal authority from inside its own domain, which compelled it to negotiate with all sides. This is better illustrated in the debates on another issue, which created frustration among the Greek Orthodox, namely the mobilization of the Christian Ottoman subjects in 1910, after the decision of the parliament that they would also be recruited into the army. There were complaints that the mobilization had been very hasty and no precautions had been taken. Therefore the Patriarch addressed the Ministry of Justice and Religions and suggested the conditions under which the Christians should join the army.[44] What is interesting in this case is that following the publication of the patriarchal letters, a note was published as a response to the fact that, 'the pious congregation of the Capital and the provinces, due to the mobilization of the Christians, under emotional tension and frustration for the unforeseen practice and the consequences of the law, put the blame for the precarious situation on the Patriarchate, suggesting that it did not take the necessary measures on the mobilization issue'.[45]

At the conclusion of this brief note, it is stated that the patriarchal authorities and the deputies were ready to support the Christians in any legal endeavour. As a matter of fact, it was already clear that the Patriarch was losing control and was facing harsh criticism from the laity. Decision making in the Patriarchate was slipping into different hands. This became more obvious when, very soon, the Greek Orthodox deputies decided to work jointly with the Bulgarians in order to fight against Young Turk authoritarianism. The debate on a rapprochement between Greeks and Bulgarians must have started already in 1909. In *Ekklisiastiki Alithia* we read that indeed such discussion over the removal of the schism with the Exarchate had found its way through newspapers of the empire and abroad. However, it was argued, after all the crimes that the supporters of the Bulgarian Exarchate had committed against the Greek Orthodox, 'no respectful, unbiased, thoughtful Christian would have the courage to suggest the above-mentioned understanding, reconciliation and unification'.[46] It is well known that Ioachim III did not at all appreciate joint action with the Bulgarians. He was very suspicious of their attitude, and even on the eve of the Balkan War he asked for a written reassurance that if and when the Bulgarian army would enter Istanbul, it would never dare approach Aghia Sofia. Consequently we can assume that it was after pressure by the Political Association that he conceded to this joint action.

Soon afterwards the parliament was closed down and new elections were called for the spring of 1912. The CUP offered the Greek Orthodox deputies the possibility of cooperating and thus safeguarding their seats. The Political Association asked for guarantees regarding the 'privileges' of the Greek Orthodox community. Its demands, however, were not satisfied. As a result the Political Association joined forces with the Liberal Party headed by Prince Sabahaddin. To its despair, this coalition was badly beaten in the elections that became known as *sopalı seçim* (elections with a beating stick), because of the excessive violence used by the Committee members. However, the decision making over the electoral coalitions and the debate over the motives and sincerity of Young Turk activity also instigated a conflict between the representatives of the Political Association, who were supported by the Hellenic state, on the one hand, and the local Metropolitans and community authorities both in Istanbul and in other areas with large Greek

Orthodox populations, on the other. The Patriarch himself had realized that his authority had totally vanished and even when the representatives of the Ottoman government visited him to present their offer, to their amazement they received the answer that the Patriarchate was a religious and not a political institution and that the Patriarch had no jurisdiction to negotiate with them. After years of conflict over the character of the Patriarchate and all its efforts to impose its political authority, the very moment that the Ottoman state recognized this authority, the Patriarchate was fatally resigning from any such claim.[47]

Parliamentary deputies and the perceptions of 'Ottoman unity'

The study of parliamentary debates reveals that the deputies-members of the Society demonstrated remarkable audacity when protesting in parliament against what they considered as the violation of 'national privileges'. One of the highly controversial issues concerned reforms in education. The attitude of the Ottoman government on this issue, as we have already seen, was bound to the need to protect the Ottoman legitimacy of education. The Sublime Porte considered the teaching of Turkish as the *sine qua non* of the cultural unification of the diverse communities of the empire. Thus, in order to counterbalance the influence of the Patriarchate, the state funded the construction of schools in areas where non-Muslims lived but no public schools were available. Thus, when the 'Schools Question' came up in a meeting at the Patriarchate on 11 June 1909, Ioachim III declared that the government was violating the 'privileges' of the community, and wondered why the changes implemented in the Greek Orthodox schools were not also introduced in the foreign schools.[48]

In the ensuing discussion in parliament, Istanbul deputy Pantelis Cosmidis took it upon himself to ask for the reformulation of Article 16, which concerned the monitoring of educational institutions. According to the new formulation 'the instruction related to the religious creeds of the diverse communities should not be disturbed' (*ve milel-i muhtelifenin umur-ı itikadiyelerine müteallik olan usul-i talimiyeye halel getirilmemek*). Cosmidis suggested that the formulation should read, 'the age-old recognized instruction of the diverse communities should not be disturbed' (*ve milel-i muhtelifenin kadimen mer'i usul-i talimyerlerine halel getirilmemek*).[49] He explained that, as was the case in the Muslim schools, so also in the Greek Orthodox ones, apart from the religious courses, there were courses on geography and literature. A child in these schools would also study Plato and Aristotle. He then pointed out that, 'I am sure that the Ottoman unity we have accomplished is not a fused ethnic unity [*ittihad-i hercümerci kavmi*][50] but a political one [*ittihad-i siyasi*]. Each of the Ottoman nations preserves its own religion, its own ethnicity, but at the same time accomplishes the political unity which is the common interest of the motherland [*vatanın menafi-i umumiyesi*].' [51] As a matter of fact, the religious authorities at the time declared similar views regarding their expectations from the constitution: 'when we talk about constitution, we wish to mention the coexistence and political unification [σύνταξη και πολιτικήν συνένωσιν], not of one and the same nation, but rather of many nations which differ in language and religion, whose ideas on equality, justice and freedom basically are the same. Under this tripartite and undividable flag, each one retains his one paternal language and his own God.' [52]

However, the instructions of the Ministry of Education pointed out that the law would be applied so that 'the education of all Ottoman citizens will be of the same form and order' (*tebea-i Osmaniyenin terbiyesi bir siyak ve intizam üzere olmak*). This would entail that, apart from religious courses, the other courses would be taught in Turkish. However, Cosmidis claimed, the constitution, which postulated that 'within the prescribed boundaries, everything is free' (*Kanun-i esasinin tayin ettiği hudut dairesinde serbestir*), did not permit such a violation. Thus only the amendment he suggested would guarantee these rights. To a comment by Nafi Pasha that in that case all ethnicities would want to preserve their own programme and that the majority should decide, Cosmidis replied that these issues should not be decided by the majority and that, definitely, each ethnicity should preserve its own education.[53] In order to make his point clearer, he brought an example from his own everyday experience. He referred to the Great School of the Nation (*Rum Mekteb-i Kebir*, Μεγάλη του Γένους Σχολή), which stands on the top of the Fener (Phanar) Hill, which used to be his neighbourhood.[54] His concern, and consequently the concern of the community, was, concluded Cosmidis, whether a school like this would survive or not.[55]

During the same discussion, Georgios Choneos,[56] Salonica deputy, referred to the 'ancient character of the community education' (*minelkadim mer'i olan usulü talimiyeleri*). What is impressive in his argument is the attempt to reconcile Greek language and education with those of the Ottomans:

> The Greek Orthodox ethnicity [*rum kavmi*] which possesses an exceptional literature [*edebiyat-ı fevkaladeye*] of 3000 years ... is never going to abandon it [*hic bir vakit vaz geçmiyecektir*]. However, the Ottoman language [*lisan-ı Osmaniyi*] will also be taught since it is possible to combine both of them [*ikisinin de yekdiğerine telifi mümkündür*]. On the contrary, if one of the two prevails at the expense of the other, it will destroy the 'Ottoman unity' [*İttihad-ı Osmaniyi ihlal olacağız*].[57]

It becomes clear that the discussion on education always shifted into a debate about the essence of the 'Ottoman nation'. In this case, both Cosmidis and Choneos start their interventions by reminding their colleagues that the 'Ottoman nation' is composed of many 'ethnicities' (*Millet-i Osmaniye akvamı muhtelifden mürekkebtir*, or *Osmanlıları herkes bilir ki birçok akvamdan mürekkebtir*).[58] Here we have the first interesting distinction between the terms *millet* and *akvam*. We can assume that the Greek deputies felt compelled to make this distinction in order to underline that the new 'Ottoman nation' was related to the way society will be organized in the new regime, whereas the 'ethnic groups' were independent of any arrangement. In this sense, the first is a political configuration, whereas the others are cultural entities. Cosmidis sets out by describing that, parallel to the state schools, there is a system of education, beginning with the primary schools, which are built next to the church of the neighbourhood (*bir mahallede kilisenin yanında bir İbtidai mektebi*) up to the high schools (*Idadi derecesinde*). In these schools, apart from religious classes, *akaid dersler*, there are courses on Greek literature, Christianity (*Yunan edebiyatı, Hıristiyanlık*) etc, and all these are offered in Greek. It is important that these schools survive, since the knowledge provided there does not concern only 'religious matters' (*umuru itikadiye*) but also 'ethnic matters' (*umuru kavmiye*); it constitutes an 'ethnic knowledge' (*malumat-ı kavmiye*).[59]

Choneos, in his turn, makes an interesting comparison between the period of absolutism (*Devr-i Istibdat*) and the regime of freedom (*Hürriyet-i Idare*), and he considers it impossible that the distinctive character of education (*terbiye hususunda mazhar oldukları*), respected in the previous period, was going to be abolished now. On the contrary, his concern being the unity and the love of the motherland (*Ittihad ... muhabbet-i vataniye*), he believes that separate education should be maintained, since this will enhance Ottoman unity and love (*Ittihad ve muhabbet-i Osmaniyeyi teyit etmek*) and serve the interests of the nation greatly (*menfaat-ı millete büyük bir hizmet etmiş olacağı*).[60]

Another important controversy concerned the distribution of churches and schools in Macedonia. According to Atalay, the Patriarchate was trying to manipulate the debate by instructing the Greek Orthodox deputies to postpone any discussion in parliament.[61] The Greek Orthodox deputies who handled the issue, especially Cosmidis and Carolidis, claimed that only the Patriarchate had the authority to settle the dispute.[62] Another argument put forth by Cosmidis was that there was not any actual difference between the Greeks and the Bulgarians, since they all belonged to the same confession. Everybody had contributed to the building of these churches and thus there was no way that these could be distributed among them.[63]

During the relevant discussion in the Senate (*Meclis-i Ayan*) on 27 June 1910, Alexandros Mavrogenis claimed that the issue was a very simple issue of land ownership (*emlak meselesi*). The Orthodox who had dissociated themselves from the Patriarchate did not have any right of ownership over any of the buildings which had been constructed in the name of the Patriarchate. All this property belonged to the spiritual centre (*ruhani merkez*). In response to this, however, Besarya Efendi pointed out that the owner of all churches was, in fact, the government and not the Patriarchate, because it was only with the government's permission that anything could be accomplished.[64]

Eventually the famous *Rumeli'de kain münazaun-fih kilise ve mektepler hakkında kanun* or *Kiliseler Kanunu* was voted and published on 3 July 1910. Against the law, many protests were organized. According to Atalay, the Sublime Porte had anticipated these demonstrations and thus had given permission for them beforehand.[65] One of the largest was organized in Izmir by the Metropolitan Chrysostomos. During the demonstration, Izmir deputy Pavlos Carolidis addressed the crowd. In his speech he suggested that despite the allegedly legal character of the decision, it is an 'unfair' one, and the 'Hellenic race' (ελληνική φυλή) had every right to protest. He also added that they should all work for the enhancement of the role of the Patriarchate, 'our national centre'. The newspaper *Amalthia* commented on the event as follows:

> In the declaration voted by the community, among other things, it is stressed that imperial *fermans* of eternal value are violated and are deemed invalid by a parliamentary majority, eternal privileges and mutual conventions between the Orthodox Christian Church within the Empire and the Ottoman Polity, conventions, which if they have safeguarded on the one hand the freedom and independence of the Church, on the other hand, they have also safeguarded the existence and the independence of the whole state of the Ottomans. ... Because this law is contrary to the 'historical law', which since centuries ago was conceded to the Christian Church by all the Islamic Polities, since the time of the first great caliphs, until the time of the glorious Ottoman Sultans, a 'law' which so vehemently became part of the public law of the Ottoman state. ... In any event, the rights of the nations are beyond any vote from any parliament.

There are two points in this passage which deserve special attention. The first regards the 'mutual conventions' between the Church and the Ottoman state. The author, probably Sokratis Solomonidis, the editor of *Amalthia*, points to the danger that such a law would entail for the existence of the Ottoman state itself. Probably the stress here is on the survival of the 'state'. However, as we have already pointed out, the abolition of the privileges challenged not only the 'Ottoman character' of the non-Turkish communities of the empire, but also, more importantly, the 'Ottoman character' of the 'Ottoman state' itself. Thus, if the state survived, it ran the danger of not being 'Ottoman' any more. And this is what eventually happened. The second point regards the political arguments utilized in order to support this thesis. Whereas the constitutional regime was up to that time glorified as the only guarantee against any violation of the rule of law, it is now depicted as a formality, and the right of the majority to decide the fate of the country is rejected. Instead 'Islamic law' is mobilized in order to legitimize the 'national claims'. This is the expression of the ideological leanings of a large part of the Greek Orthodox elites, which wished to reconcile civic loyalty to the new constitutional regime with the 'historical rights' of these elites who fought until the end to produce and disseminate an alternative ideology of the Eastern Empire or the new Ottoman Empire, even if it was not ready to abandon the references to the past.[66]

Out of these several demonstrations that took place all over the empire, telegraphs were sent to the capital, signed by the 'Orthodox community' or the 'Greek people', and not by the Metropolitans. This could point to a political activity of a broader participation. However, it has also been presented as a deliberate action in order to conceal the fact that the real instigators behind these demonstrations were the Metropolitans themselves.[67] It has become clear, we believe, that despite the common interests that the Patriarchate shared with the deputies, the Metropolitans and the local communities, it was less and less capable of imposing its own will. An interesting incident, again from Izmir, demonstrates this tension in the instructions regarding the protests. When Ioachim III had ordered for the closing down of all churches as a measure against the violation of the 'privileges', the Metropolitan of Izmir, Vassilios, did not abide by the order because this would hurt his income.

Conclusion

In this essay, my purpose has been to describe the conflict, which revolved around the 'privileges' of the Greek Orthodox community in the Ottoman Empire, as these were challenged by the modernization efforts of the Ottoman government during the first years of the second constitutional period. The programme of reforms aimed at eliminating the distinctions among ethno-religious communities (*millet*) was fiercely opposed by the Greek Orthodox communities, which related their very existence to the preservation of their 'privileges'. However, as we have seen, the demand for a unified system of education or justice, which would transform a compartmentalized society into a homogeneous one, was not new. The crucial feature of this period, though, can be traced to two factors. Firstly, the governments of this period did not wish to negotiate any more, at least in the manner that the traditional institutions of the Ottoman society were used to. On the contrary, they were determined to impose their agenda. On the other hand, because of the abolition of the *millet* system and thus the weakening of the institution of the Patriarchate as the only authority of the Greek Orthodox, we witness the emergence of secular elite groups which challenged this patriarchal authority and were using the 'politicization' of the *millet* in order to take over its representation, mainly through parliament. Moreover, the participation of larger segments of the population in political activities paved the way for a more radical opposition, which did not rely so much on 'religious' but rather on 'national' grounds. Thus the challenges of the new political environment led to a reshuffling of loyalties within the community itself. While one would expect that this ultimate struggle for the defence of the community would be handled by the 'historical' leader who personified these 'privileges', a gradual shift of authority had taken place. Ioachim III was obviously considered a remnant of the past not only by the Young Turks but also by certain elite groups in the community. In this sense, contrary to what is frequently suggested, the Greek Orthodox secular elites, as was the case with the Hellenic state already in the 1880s, shook the legitimization of the Patriarch more than the Young Turk movement could ever manage to do.

However, waging a war for the defence of the 'privileges' and, at the same time, undermining the Patriarch does not fit in with the 'Ottoman' state of mind. This is exactly where the incompatibility of the political discourses can be traced to. The Greek Orthodox elites, even if they remained faithful to the 'Ottoman nation' and to 'Ottoman unity', obviously attributed to these terms a content that corresponded to earlier historical circumstances. Whether they realized this or not, they still claimed a role relevant to their own understanding of the modernization process. At a time of liberal ideas and promises of emancipation, the Greek Ottoman elites and the Hellenic activists were convinced that this was the appropriate time to enhance autonomy and, in the long run, to achieve a significant role in the ruling of the empire, a role which was justified by their economic and social profile. To their disappointment, they soon felt that the Young Turks not only did not seriously intend to share authority with them but were also challenging their already existing autonomy. The last battleground upon which this fight was going to be fought was the 'privileges'.

Reform from Above, Resistance from Below: The New Order and its Opponents in Iran, 1927–29

Stephanie Cronin

The early Pahlavi period in Iran has conventionally been seen through the prism of its state-building effort. Attention has been focused almost exclusively on the high politics of the Tehran elite and a positive or negative balance sheet drawn up according to assessments of this elite's success in transforming Iran into a modern, politically independent nation-state.[1] This preoccupation with the Tehran regime and its version of modernity has typically been accompanied, as the other side of the same coin, by an almost complete silence regarding other interests and perspectives. Little attempt has been made to elucidate either the historical narrative or the perception of their own experience of, for example, non-elite groups such as the Tehran crowd, of non-metropolitan groups including the guilds and the bazaars of the provincial cities, or of any social category in the countryside. The authoritarian modernization imposed by the Riza Shah regime was aimed at transforming precisely these elements, but it was neither received passively nor opposed blindly by them. The arrival of the new order rather evoked complex and multi-faceted responses from different layers and sectors of Iranian society. Whereas the restoration of relative order and stability in the first half of the decade had been widely welcomed, as the regime embarked on a more radical phase of modernization, especially during the years 1927–29, substantial social groups, especially subaltern groups, resorted to strategies of avoidance, opposition and sometimes resistance. In describing these responses and strategies, the account which follows hopes to make some attempt at representing the 'history from below' of these years.[2]

The new order in Iran

In 1927, following the stabilization of his new dynasty, Riza Shah launched a programme of radical secularizing, centralizing measures and, in the years that followed, enforced the new policies aggressively, often through the use of the army.[3] His regime's programme was essentially that formulated by the intelligentsia of the constitutional period, and was popular with the nationalist elite. However, when imposed on the population at large it provoked widespread hostility and occasionally active defiance. 1927–28 saw the introduction and determined enforcement of the key measures which came to symbolize the era. In 1927 the first sustained attempts were made at the implementation of the census registration and conscription, the judicial system was reorganized along secular lines, the first major effort was made at mass tribal relocation, in Luristan, while a generalized policy of nomadic settlement began to be formulated, and work began on the Trans-Iranian Railway. In 1928 a civil code was introduced, capitulations were abolished and the Majlis passed the Uniform Dress Law and effective legislation for the registration of title deeds to landed property and real estate. The same year the opium monopoly, one in a series of *etatiste* economic measures, was introduced, to be followed the next year by the tobacco monopoly. This major reform drive coincided with the ascendancy of the shah's principal lieutenants, Ali Akbar Davar, Firuz Mirza, and particularly Abd al-Husayn Taymurtash.

These measures were central elements of the nationalist drive to create a strong state capable of governing a modern and homogeneous society. Yet wherever they were imposed they were experienced by the general population as highly oppressive. The fiscal and military reforms weighed especially heavily, the draining of money and manpower from the provinces resulting in few reciprocal social, infrastructural or educational benefits. Opposition to the new state's agenda accordingly erupted at intervals over the years 1927–29 throughout the provinces, in various towns and cities, and among different rural groups. It was led, in general, by middle-ranking clerics and the guilds in the urban centres and by junior tribal khans and aghas in the countryside.

The first half of the 1920s had been essentially a period of power struggle within the elite, the political changes of these years possessing little social content. However, once the outstanding constitutional and political issues had been resolved in favour of the establishment of a military–monarchical dictatorship, the regime was able to embark on a programme of far-reaching and profound modernization. The driving force behind this programme was the triumvirate of Taymurtash, Davar and Firuz, and between 1927 and 1929 the new state was at its most dynamic and confident. In many of its individual reform measures, as well as in its overall direction, the new regime was giving effect to long-standing demands of Iranian constitutionalism, and it accumulated much nationalist support on that account, the activism of the new state contrasting sharply with the passivity and helplessness of its Qajar predecessor. However, the increasingly dictatorial character of the regime had a profound effect on the manner in which it implemented its reform agenda. Preferring rapid and radical change imposed by force over a slower pace of change encumbered by any democratic process, the regime's key personnel, heavily influenced by the martial temper of Riza Shah himself, developed a commandist approach, seeking to impose their will across vast geographical areas and intricate social contexts by diktat, backed up by the threat of military intervention. These methods produced in civilian officials and especially in army officers a tendency to underestimate and sometimes even deliberately minimize the complexities and difficulties of their task, and often provoked and aggravated opposition as much or more than the reforms themselves.

The legislation of the second half of the 1920s affected directly and profoundly the lives and daily experience of wide layers of the population. Informed by the nationalist elite's overall objective of incubating a society Europeanized in appearance and modern in social and cultural mores, the innovations of these years were often devastating in their impact on non-metropolitan, non-elite groups, and tended actually to worsen the lot of the poor and to increase the gulf between the elite and the rest of the population. Conscription, for example, a long-standing demand of the constitutionalist intelligentsia, was enforced initially and primarily on the poor, the better-off easily able to purchase exemption.[4] The dress laws were welcomed by the educated modern elements in the cities, who were in any case in the process of adopting Western fashions, but were anathema to provincial clerical and tribal elements, who felt their role and identity undermined, and to the poor everywhere, who found the new sartorial requirements beyond their means and who lacked any cultural understanding of the new styles of clothing. The new secular law courts, which the Western states found so appealing, were in reality more expensive, less accessible and less familiar to the mass of the population than the old judicial system administered by the ulama in the cities and by the khans for the tribal populations. The legislation providing for the registration of land and property benefited landlords and khans, who were able to register in their names land to which their title was dubious;[5] the introduction of state monopolies on crops such as opium hit hard the peasant cultivators and also the large numbers of small shopkeepers and peddlars who depended on trading in opium sap;[6] and tribal disarmament and settlement, although unopposed by the great khans who were already being absorbed into the urban elite, threatened the foundation of the nomadic and semi-nomadic way of life.

Popular opposition and then resistance to the imposition of these dramatic changes first erupted in an urban context although Tehran, where the state's new mechanisms of control (the police and the army) were most effective, saw only brief episodes of protest. The cities and towns of the provinces, however, were the sites of major confrontations between local populations and the representatives of the modernizing state, chiefly the military and the political elite.

The succession of challenges offered to the new regime and its radical reform agenda began in the provincial urban centres of the south. In the latter part of 1927 the towns of southern Iran, especially Isfahan and Shiraz, were gripped by a mass movement of opposition to conscription. The following year Tabriz manifested profound and violent hostility to both conscription and the clothing reforms. Finally in 1929, with government authority barely intact in the provincial towns, a succession of tribal and peasant revolts broke out. One by one, the rural areas of western, southern, south-central and southeastern Iran erupted into rebellion. The most prolonged and serious of these rebellions were those in Fars and Isfahan, among the Qashqa'i, the Khamsah and the Bakhtiyari, the south almost slipping out of government control altogether. But, although for the duration of the uprisings only a shadow of Tehran's authority remained, even in the cities of Isfahan and Shiraz, and although the tribes were able to wrest temporary concessions from the government, they, like the urban opposition which had preceded them, failed to arrest the long-term centralizing drive of the regime.

Urban opposition: Shiraz and Isfahan

The first major example of mass popular resistance to the new order was centred on the cities of Isfahan and Shiraz and was provoked by the efforts of the interior and war ministries to impose conscription. It began at the beginning of October 1927, continuing until the end of December, and was led by the ulama of Isfahan and Shiraz, fully supported by the bazaars and especially the guilds of both towns.

In the early 1920s the notables of the southern towns, especially the merchants, had welcomed the establishment of order and security, the army's control of the roads allowing trade and commercial activity to flourish. By 1927, however, these traditional urban middle classes had begun to harbour doubts about the new regime in Tehran. They were concerned at the increasingly *etatiste* direction of state economic policy, and at wider processes of centralization which augured the marginalization of the provincial towns and their own loss of local power and influence. They resented the ever higher levels of taxation which were demanded from them, and the draining of resources from their own towns to satisfy the apparently insatiable demands of the military budget and the Trans-Iranian Railway. They had been unenthusiastic about the change of dynasty and found the omnipresent provincial military authorities oppressive and brutal. They particularly disliked the interference of the interior ministry and the army in the Majlis elections[7] and were also deeply affected by the burgeoning discontent of their traditional allies, the ulama. The guilds had been specifically antagonized by the abolition in 1926 of the guild tax whereby the state removed from the guild elders the power of determining how much each member paid in taxes. This measure had apparently been purposely designed to sap the control of the craft and trade masters over their apprentices, artisans, journeymen and labourers, and struck a severe blow at guild organization.[8]

Many members of the ulama had, like the merchants, welcomed Riza Khan's coming to power, seeing in him a source of salvation for Iran and for Islam. Between Riza Khan's becoming prime minister in 1923 and his accession to the throne in 1925, they had, in general, been willing to cooperate with the new regime, an inclination which was only briefly interrupted by the republican movement of early 1924. But by 1927 the ulama were aware that the balance of power between themselves and the regime was about to alter decisively to their detriment. Although on the defensive, they were bracing themselves for a struggle. They were angry at the reorganization and secularization of Iran's judicial system which was pushed through during 1927 and which threatened their role, status and income, which altogether deprived large numbers of minor clerics of their livelihoods. They disliked the cabinet's decision in early August to make the 'Pahlavi hat', similar to the French kepi, the official headgear for Iranian men, perceiving it to symbolize rapid and profound cultural secularization.[9] They had been made anxious and fearful by the rise of Abd al-Husayn Taymurtash, the shah's new minister of court and a strong advocate of modernization, whom they believed had particularly influenced the shah against them. They had been especially provoked in August 1927 by the formation, by Taymurtash and other leading secularizers, of the New Iran party, from membership of which anyone not wearing the Pahlavi hat was expressly debarred, a provision aimed at themselves. They also shared the cynicism and anger widely felt by the general population at the authorities' manipulation of the elections to the Sixth Majlis.

During the passage of the conscription bill through the Majlis, between 1923 and 1925, clerical deputies had put up little opposition, religious disquiet having been neutralized by a concession granting exemption to all religious students.[10] Nonetheless underlying clerical dislike of the secularizing impact of military service was increasingly apparent, and there was particular concern over the fact that the new law gave to the state the power to decide who, among the broad ranks of those engaged in religious study and activity, was entitled to exemption. By 1927 conscription for the ulama had become an issue of central importance and one enmeshed in a web of hostility to the central government and the shah.

Conscription was also, however, an issue of central importance to the regime. Universal military service had been an integral element of Iranian programmes of defensive modernization since the early nineteenth century and, for the nationalist ideologues of the early twentieth century the construction of a strong national army, based on conscription, was an essential element of state-building and nation-formation. For Riza Shah, the new army was at the heart of Iran's regeneration and he was determined to expand radically the human resources on which the military might draw. Not only would conscription enable the shah to realize his objective of an army numbering 100,000 men under arms, but it would, according to its supporters, bring with it a number of other benefits. The act specifically stated that conscription would give the Iranian army a national character and would give all families in the country an interest in defending their nation and their independence. It would also result in an increase of patriotic sentiments among the Iranian people, mutual good feeling between various classes and the creation of feelings of equality, and would embody the virtues of the avoidance of discrimination and the equality of all before the law.[11]

These benefits, however, were largely lost on the populations visited by the recruiting commissions. During 1926 the enforcement of conscription progressed extremely slowly, but by early 1927 the government felt sufficiently strong to begin to apply the law more energetically throughout the country. Recruiting offices were established and call-up notices posted in all the provincial capitals. However, strong opposition immediately appeared. Disturbances broke out in provincial towns following the arrival of recruiting officers, the bazaars were closed and the recruiting commissions attacked.[12] Nonetheless the government pressed on, although the general dislike of the prospect of military service was everywhere aggravated by the gross corruption of the recruiting officers.

During the summer of 1927, although resentment at conscription was intense, it resulted only in sporadic and spontaneous defiance. However, the attempt to impose conscription on the towns of southern Iran in the autumn of 1927 produced concerted resistance. Even the rural areas of southern Iran were unaccustomed to providing soldiers, the agriculturally based *bunichah* system of recruiting, inherited from the previous century, normally not having been enforced in the south. The sudden and unprecedented imposition of conscription on the towns of the south was intolerable to the urban populations, and opposition immediately appeared, led by the ulama with strong support from the bazaar, especially the labour guilds.

During the spring and summer of 1927 the increasing friction between the regime and the ulama had given rise to a number of protests in the southern towns, notably over census registration and the Pahlavi hat, but nevertheless in the autumn the military authorities prepared to begin recruiting conscripts. The day designated for the first call-up in Shiraz was 8 October. On that day the bazaars in Shiraz closed down and remained closed in protest and trade came to a standstill.[13] Similar action was taken in Isfahan and to a lesser extent in Kirmanshah, Qazvin and Tehran. The bazaars in Isfahan and Shiraz, where opposition was most determined, were to remain closed for three months. The occupational guilds in Shiraz and elsewhere organized general strikes, and carpenters, masons, brickmakers and others stopped work. Even in Tehran the bazaars closed and there were attempts by crowds to demonstrate in front of the Majlis, although these were prevented by the police.

In Isfahan, the aged mujtahid Ayatullah Haj Agha Nurullah Isfahani, in response to a request from the people of the city, agreed to go to the shrine city of Qum to take *bast* and from there lead a campaign against conscription.[14] Isfahani and several of his colleagues, including another senior Isfahan cleric, Ayatullah Mirza Husayn Fishariki, accordingly took up residence in Qum where they were joined by clerical representatives from Tehran and many provincial towns, including Shiraz, Hamadan, Mashhad and Tabriz, and from Najaf in Iraq. However, the ulama who joined Isfahani in Qum were, with one or two exceptions, very minor figures, and this weakened his position. But the major setback to the movement was its failure to enlist the support of the clerical establishment in Qum. The Isfahanis and Shirazis had hoped that the most important cleric resident in Qum, Ayatullah Shaykh Abd al-Karim Ha'iri, might be persuaded to take an active part in the campaign.[15] However Ha'iri, who had a personal history of political non-involvement, openly declared his neutrality.

The anti-conscription movement in the south was becoming a complex phenomenon, in fact a coalition involving a multiplicity of grievances and demands. The ulama, firmly established as the leadership of the movement, were motivated not just by dislike of conscription itself but by opposition to the general direction of the regime's reforms and by the steady diminishing of their own power. The opposition of the population in general to conscription was spontaneous, genuine and profound, and aggravated by the corruption of the recruiting commissions, while the more politically aware had wider grievances against the government, the most important being their resentment at the interference of the shah, the military and the government in the elections. Indeed the view was almost universally held that the Majlis then in session had been elected unconstitutionally.

In their defence the shah and his officials, both in the capital and the provinces, relied heavily on the argument that conscription had been introduced by the Majlis and only the Majlis could enact changes, the shah, as a constitutional monarch, having no choice but to give effect to the law.[16] This line of argument, however, only exasperated the protesters. In Shiraz, when the governor-general arranged for a delegation from the opposition to meet the Shiraz Majlis deputies, specifically on the grounds that it was the Majlis deputies who were responsible for the conscription law, the delegation bluntly denounced both the legitimacy of the Majlis and the regime's perversion of constitutional procedure. The Shirazis told their deputies to their face that their election had been imposed by force and that, since other laws passed by the Majlis were flouted and ignored by the government, as far as the protesters were concerned the conscription law could suffer the same fate.[17]

The ulama in *bast* in Qum seized on the issue of constitutionalism and legality, making it central to their opposition to conscription. They demanded that the constitution be respected and that the shah be a constitutional monarch, leaving government to a fully responsible cabinet; that the elections be free and the deputies not be appointed by the shah or the army; and, most crucial of all, they wanted implemented the constitutional provision for a supreme committee of five mujtahids able to scrutinize all bills introduced into the Majlis to ensure that nothing was done which contravened the *Shari'a*. In pursuance of this last point they argued that all laws passed by the Majlis in the absence of this committee were in fact unconstitutional and illegal. These opinions were a potent weapon. The ulama were apparently aiming especially at the legislation of the Fifth and Sixth Majlis, and specifically at the act which deposed the Qajars, thus threatening the legitimacy of the shah's newly established dynasty.[18]

At first the shah, on the advice of his entourage, had treated the southern movement with contempt. This attitude, however, became increasingly untenable as the imposition of martial law and the arrival of troop reinforcements in Isfahan and Shiraz made no impact on the strikes. Although the

shah had been greatly angered by the protests, nonetheless his acute understanding of political reality and his ready appreciation of political danger
indicated the necessity of a tactical retreat, coupled with the appearance of
compromise. In this way the government hoped to avoid aggravating the
crisis while it decided upon a strategy.

On 24 October the shah summoned groups of ulama, merchants and
deputies and made to them a lengthy speech, the theme of which was his
personal devotion to Islam. The government issued orders to the police and
the military to deal leniently with anti-conscription demonstrators in Tehran,
and the shah also gave orders for leniency in the carrying out of conscription. On 12 November conscription ceased entirely in Tehran. Early in
November the shah sent his minister of court, Taymurtash, to Qum to meet
the ulama who had taken refuge there from Isfahan, although they declined
to see him.[19] Hints were dropped about leniency and exemption, and the
intention to rely on the peasantry, the government clearly attempting to
defuse the opposition of specifically the better-off urban elements, particularly the guilds, without abandoning the central tenets of the conscription
policy.

After the failure of Taymurtash's mission to Qum the shah realized that
the situation was becoming dangerous. Despite press censorship, news of
the strike was being carried throughout the country and its duration began
to convey an impression of powerlessness on the part of the central government and of the decline of the control, civil and military, of the Pahlavi
regime. At first the shah continued to insist that amendment of the conscription law rested with the Majlis, while the president of the Majlis, replying
to the ulama of Shiraz, and the prime minister, replying to leaders of the
merchants, repeated platitudes about leniency in taking conscripts. By early
December the shah's impatience for a settlement was becoming overwhelming. On 10 December he again sent Taymurtash to Qum, accompanied by
the prime minister and two compliant Tehran clerics. This time the mission
met with a different response.

The ulama in Qum themselves were by now also keen to reach a face-
saving compromise as support for the protests in Shiraz and Isfahan had
begun to crumble. For some time the big merchants had surreptitiously been
doing a certain amount of business, but those of smaller substance were
experiencing genuine distress while the severe hardship of the apprentices,
petty shopkeepers and guildsmen was only alleviated by an arrangement
giving them half-pay.[20] The ulama themselves were spending a considerable amount of money on sustaining the strike, Ayatullah Isfahani himself
personally financing the movement in Isfahan. By December the people

of Isfahan and Shiraz had become extremely battle-weary and the onset of winter had further undermined both their resolve and that of the *bastis* in Qum. By early December the bazaars in Isfahan had already begun to reopen.

Taymurtash's second visit to Qum produced the basis for a settlement. The shah and Ayatullahs Isfahani and Fisharaki exchanged complimentary telegrams, which were published in the press.[21] A few days later two of the ulama from Qum came to Tehran, returning with the government's signature to the acceptance of five conditions.[22] The conditions were:

1. A revision of the conscription law to be made by the next Majlis.
2. Five high-ranking mujtahids to form a committee to supervise the Majlis, as provided by the constitutional law.
3. Ecclesiastical supervisors for the provincial press to see that nothing anti-Islamic is printed.
4. A strict veto on practices which are forbidden by Islam, such as drinking of wine, gambling, etc.
5. Reintroduction of the numerous small religious courts for dealing with personal status, the administration of oaths, etc, which had been newly centralized in the Central Court of Justice by the ministry of justice.

The government apparently also gave some verbal promises concerning other matters, including an undertaking that there would be no government interference in the next elections.

Although this agreement had been negotiated between Taymurtash and Isfahani, it produced a great deal of consternation and confusion among the *bastis* in Qum who found it unsatisfactory and unlikely to be implemented. But on 26 December Isfahani, a man of nearly 90 who had been unwell for some time, died.[23] This deprived the anti-conscription movement of its leader and also weakened the influence of the remaining ulama over the population in general. There was widespread demoralization at the death of Isfahani and next day the strikes in Shiraz ended. The crisis was over and the general perception was of a government victory, little prestige having accrued to the ulama, the general population believing that the agreement with the government to be hardly worth the paper on which it was written.

Urban opposition: Tabriz

For the next six months the work of the recruiting commissions proceeded haltingly and with difficulty, and they concentrated their efforts on the settled peasantry in the villages who were incapable of the organized, collective and sustained opposition shown by the better-off elements led by the guilds in the towns. But around the middle of 1928 the shah apparently decided the time had come to enforce conscription with renewed determination and an energetic campaign was launched in both the national and local press in support of conscription as a patriotic duty. Nonetheless the recruiting commissions continued everywhere to encounter opposition, sometimes spontaneous, sometimes more organized.

The renewed recruiting drive coincided with an intensifying effort on the part of the civil and military authorities to oblige the male population to abandon their traditional headgear and adopt the Pahlavi hat. This effort had begun with the cabinet's decision in early August 1927 to make the Pahlavi hat the official headgear for Iranian men, and during 1928 the shah himself had become the chief and most vocal protagonist of the move to banish turbans and 'abas. At each weekly reception in his palace he urged his subjects to modernize their dress and as the year wore on he began having those wearing turbans actually turned away from his receptions. On 25 December 1928 a bill drafted by Taymurtash, calling for the compulsory adoption of the Pahlavi hat and the short coat by all male Persians, was introduced into the Majlis. The bill outlined a few strictly limited exceptions, and fixed a scale of punishments, including fines and imprisonment, for those failing to comply. The bill was discussed in the Majlis sittings of 25 and 27 December and after some minor amendments passed by a very large majority. The law was to come into effect at Nawruz (21 March) 1929.

However, the police had not waited for the Majlis decision but instead, during the latter part of 1928, had begun exerting strenuous pressure on the male populations of many Iranian cities to begin wearing the Pahlavi hat immediately. Except among the small numbers of the Westernized elite, the Pahlavi hat was extremely unpopular and the actions of the police produced further resentment and indignation. Those wearing turbans, for many of whom the new clothes were not just unbecoming but actually tainted with heresy, were publicly insulted and their headgear forcibly removed by the police. The general unease was compounded by the prevalence of apparently credible rumours that Nawruz 1929 was also intended to witness the compulsory abolition of the veil.[24]

In 1928 it was Tabriz, the provincial capital of Azarbayjan, which was to be the site of the major protest against the two major reforms, and the second and last significant episode of urban resistance to the new order in this period. Here too, as with the previous year's protests in southern Iran, dislike of conscription and clothing reform enmeshed with wider resentment at the impact of the imposition of reform to produce an explosive and general challenge to the tightening control of the Tehran regime.

By early 1928 nothing had yet been done to enforce conscription or even census registration in Tabriz. When, in the latter part of the year, the renewed determination of the authorities to impose conscription and, simultaneously, the wearing of the Pahlavi hat, reached the city, considerable unrest immediately manifested itself. The bazaars were closed and protest meetings were held in mosques, these actions culminating in a demonstration on 17 October by a crowd of about 10,000 who apparently intended to take *bast* in the Soviet consulate-general. This demonstration, however, was broken up by the police and the army with some violence.[25] During the past year the regime had stabilized and grown in confidence and assertiveness. It was now able to dispense with the negotiation and concession to which it had been obliged to resort in Shiraz and Isfahan, and immediately responded to opposition in Tabriz with military force in a brutal but largely successful bid to suppress the movement.

Although popular opposition in Tabriz was intense, both the ulama and the bazaar had been much more cautious in their attitude to the government than had been their counterparts in the south the previous year. One of the four mujtahids of Tabriz, Ayatullah Haj Mirza Abul Hasan Agha Angaji, for example, had resorted to quietism regarding disobeying the government. When deputations of the people of the city urged him to make some pronouncement regarding conscription, he was circumspect, replying that when faced with the dilemma of having to choose between submitting to the registration or abandoning their pilgrimages to Mecca, Karbala or Mashhad, people should give up their pilgrimages. The Pahlavi hat, however, was a more serious issue for him and his response had more activist consequences.[26] The cabmen of the city, who had discarded the new hat which they had been wearing for a few days, were called to the police stations and asked to sign a document promising to wear only Pahlavi hats. Having signed they then went to Angaji, who told them that a promise extorted was not binding, with the result that they reverted to their old headgear.[27]

The large demonstration of 17 October was actually led by low-ranking mullas, while the mujtahids, 'old and cautious men,'[28] and the rich merchants had initially been reluctant to take part in the movement, only popular pressure finally forcing them to take a stand. Nonetheless arrests, which had begun even before the demonstration took place and continued for some time afterwards, included a number of ulama and rich merchants who were later deported. Those banished included Ayatullah Angaji and another mujtahid, Ayatullah Mirza Sadiq Agha. The merchants, besides having refused to attend a ceremony in honour of conscription to which they had been invited at the governor-general's palace, were accused of having given money to the shopkeepers who had closed their shops and of having provided tea and carpets for the various meetings. In fact some of these merchants had only acted under intense popular pressure. One of the arrested, Haj Muhammad Agha Hariri, the leading merchant in the bazaar, had actually been forced by the people of the Shuturban (Davachi) quarter of the town where he lived, a quarter known for its religious sensitivities, to attend the protest meetings in the mosques.

The mainstay of the protest in Tabriz were the lesser-ranking mullas and the small shopkeepers who had put up the strongest resistance in the bazaar. These elements now faced serious consequences. They were accused of inciting the people to resist the authorities and of treason, and some were threatened with hanging, others immediately flogged. Through the end of 1928 and into 1929, as the military authorities pressed on ruthlessly with the reforms, many small shopkeepers were the first to be recruited into the army.[29] These men were often the only breadwinners of their families who were left on the verge of starvation. The hat policy was pursued with equal determination. Police and soldiers were seen every day in the streets, tearing off and trampling on the turbans of clerics, who went away with their bare heads covered by their 'abas. This policy was followed systematically, different quarters of the town being chosen on different days. The military authorities even embarked on the actual destruction of the physical core of the mercantile and clerical classes, under the guise of 'town planning'. They began to pull down large numbers of houses and many of the bazaars and to construct new avenues, one of which was to cut right through the Shuturban (Davachi) quarter, where recent opposition had been fiercest. Those so made homeless were then evicted from the mosques, where they had initially found shelter, and directed by the military authorities to the ajizkhanah, an institution where destitute vagrants might find shelter and bread.[30]

Rural opposition

In the rural areas the nomadic and semi-nomadic tribal populations, alarmed by Tehran's radical version of modernity, had been watching closely developments in the towns. With the military authorities still engaged on the brutal enforcement of their control in Tabriz, and the opposition to conscription and the imposition of the Pahlavi hat still fresh, the first tribal rising against the new order broke out in Azarbayjan. The Kurdish tribes generally resented the closer control which the local Persian authorities were attempting to establish, and feared the disarmament and conscription as well as the uniform dress, especially the despised Pahlavi hat, which they perceived would inevitably follow. In January 1929, when Mulla Khalil, a local religious leader, issued a proclamation calling on the tribes to resist these innovations by force of arms, his appeal met with an immediate response among the Kurdish tribes in the areas Sauj Bulak-Urumiyyah and Tabriz, and the revolt even began to take on a pan-Kurdish and nationalist complexion.[31] Alternate fighting and negotiation continued until June when the Kurdish forces, finding themselves unable to obtain assistance from broader tribal groups, weakened by a shortage of ammunition, and fearing for the safety of their families and homes, retreated into the mountains, their leaders taking refuge in Iraq.

But it was in the south that the tribal uprisings assumed their most dangerous dimensions. The epicentre of the southern tribal uprisings was located in the province of Fars.[32] In the spring of 1929 first the Qashqa'i tribal confederation and then the Khamsah rose against the central government. Some of the smaller tribal groups, especially the Kuhgiluyyah, as well as independent brigand chiefs and their bands joined in the movement, and the whole of Fars quickly became engulfed in conflict. At the beginning of June the movement spread northwards, to the province of Isfahan, where some sections of the Bakhtiyaris, principally Chahar Langs with a sprinkling of Haft Langs, also broke out into rebellion.[33]

Although each of the tribal groups had its own specific concerns, the insurgents shared certain major underlying grievances. The tribal populations throughout the south were angry at the attempts made by the government to disarm them, they were embittered over the ever increasing taxes they were forced to pay by the officials of the Finance Department, they hated the new dress law, feared the growing reach of the conscription commissions, and the imposition of the census registration which was their preliminary, resented the interference and corruption of the local military authorities, suffered from the establishment of new government monopolies on commodities such as opium and tobacco and were apprehensive at the activities of the Department for the Registration of Title Deeds and at rumours of forced sedentarization. The example of the Qashqa'i, who had suffered particularly at the hands of rapacious military governors in the three years since their former *ilkhani*, Isma'il Khan Sawlat al-Dawlah, had been deposed, was especially unsettling.

The extirpation of tribal power and autonomy was of absolute centrality to the state-building effort of the early Pahlavi period, and from the very moment of seizing power in Tehran the new regime had embarked on a sustained effort to establish its military and administrative hegemony over the tribal confederations. Like their contemporaries elsewhere in the Middle East, the newly empowered Iranian nationalists insisted that sovereignty and independence were only possible on the basis of the complete disarmament of the civilian population and the concentration of physical power in the hands of the state. For this trend the establishment of a single national authority in Iran, which commanded the universal and direct allegiance of the population and which alone conducted relations with foreign powers, was essential to the country's political survival. For them, furthermore, the nomads were the antithesis of modernity, with the regime and its supporters, and indeed the urban population at large, viewing the tribes as both primitive in themselves and as symbolizing Iran's backwardness. In its views of the tribal problem, as in relation to other central issues of state-building and modernization, the new regime was giving expression to attitudes first articulated by the reforming intellectuals of the nineteenth century and now commonly held among the nationalist elite.[34]

The years of Riza Khan's rise to supreme power, 1921–25, essentially a period of intra-elite power struggles, were also the years in which he undertook the subjugation of the political leaderships of the great tribal confederations. By 1925 he had coopted, neutralized or removed all the great tribal leaders and regional magnates. Yet, although the new state had occasionally embarked on a military solution to tribal recalcitrance, many of the most important tribal leaders had willingly, and sometimes enthusiastically, offered their support to the new regime. This was particularly true of the tribal magnates of southern Iran, including Isma'il Khan Sawlat al-Dawlah of the Qashqa'i, Ibrahim Khan Qavam al-Mulk of the Khamsah, the great khans of the Bakhtiyari, and Ibrahim Shawkat al-Mulk, amir of Qayinat and Sistan, only Shaykh Khaz'al of Muhammarah failing to come to an accommodation with the shah.[35]

Although the southern tribal leaderships had, broadly speaking and with only a few exceptions, cooperated with the new regime in Tehran, yet with their history of imperial patronage, political autonomy, reputation for the pursuance of their own interests and fractious unreliability, they could never provide a solid foundation for the construction of the new order in the south. Riza Khan in particular was especially vulnerable to perennial suspicions of their disloyalty or treachery. For the regime, the ultimate removal of the tribal aristocracies from their *ilkhaniships* and the establishment of direct central government over the tribes was a logical step in the progress towards the establishment of its own complete and unmediated control over the entire country. In 1925, after the submission of the shaykh of Muhammarah, and with the other southern leaders, Sawlat, Qavam and the great khans of the Bakhtiyari, acquiescent and safely resident in Tehran, the Qashqa'i became the first major southern tribal grouping to experience direct military control. Riza Khan removed the *ilkhaniship* from the family of Sawlat al-Dawlah, appointing instead an army officer as military governor.

By the late 1920s the tribal aristocracies were walking a tightrope, fearful of the regime's tightening grip, yet dependent on it to defend their claims as khans and landlords against the growing hostility of their own followers.[36] When the tribal populations finally rose against the government in the spring of 1929, the attitude of their old elites varied. The senior khans of the Bakhtiyari, for example, threw their weight firmly behind the regime, providing support first for a military response and, when that failed, a negotiated political solution. The family of Sawlat al-Dawlah adoped a more ambiguous attitude, Sawlat's younger son fighting with the tribal rebels, while Sawlat himself and his elder son offered their good offices to Riza Shah as mediators and as loyal subjects capable of restoring order. The insurgent tribes, for their part, found leaders and spokesmen elsewhere, among middle-ranking tribal leaderships, the Qashqa'i *kalantars* and dissident junior khans of the Bakhtiyari. Indeed the risings were, in some cases, actually directed against the khans, insofar as the khans had identified themselves with, and acted as agents of, the new state. Despite the uncertainty of their initial reaction, the old tribal elites were essential to the regime in its efforts to re-establish its authority over the confederations.

Political and finally military weakness and the rapid spread of the risings forced a reluctant shah to the expedient of negotiation and compromise, and obliged him to resort for its implementation to those very khans whom he now most distrusted.

Peasant rebellion and banditry

The tribal uprisings in Fars and Isfahan were largely predicated on the involvement of the armed and mobile nomadic populations, who were resisting what they perceived to be a fundamental assault on their pastoral way of life. The uprisings also, however, provided the context for the emergence of two related but quite distinct phenomena, peasant rebellion and banditry.[37] In their armed risings, the nomads were able to rely on a groundswell of peasant resentment while the social, political and economic chaos produced by the regime's authoritarian version of modernity in the rural areas, among pastoralists and cultivators alike, led to a retreat by fringes of these societies into permanent brigandry.

As well as conscription and Pahlavi hats, the nomads feared the forced settlement that the regime had begun to advocate openly. In fact, however, a process of sedentarization was already in train among the nomadic populations. Many former nomads in southern Iran had already voluntarily adopted a semi-settled or settled life, engaging in agriculture. But these sedentarized cultivators, too, were hard hit by Tehran's reforms, and were drawn into the opposition to the new order in the south. The overthrow of Tehran's authority in eastern Fars was clearly accomplished with the active support of the peasantry, albeit in alliance with their nomadic kin. In southern Fars, too, the imposition of the new order had produced unrest among the settled tribal populations. One example is provided by Mahdi Surkhi, who headed what became a substantial group of bandits. Mahdi Surkhi was a small landowner and khan of the Surkhi, a small tribe, allied but not actually belonging to the Qashqa'i, semi-sedentarized and heavily engaged in opium cultivation. With the generalized reappearance of banditry in the mid-1920s as a strategy of rural resistance, Mahdi was driven into becoming an outlaw by the oppression of the local authorities, and from 1926 onwards collected around him numbers of the disaffected, both Surkhis and from many of the smaller Qashqa'i clans.[38] The imposition of the opium monopoly in 1928 turned Mahdi from an outlaw into the leader of a peasant movement, as widespread resistance to the monopoly broke out among the settled cultivators across Fars, and he and his tribe actively involved themselves in the Qashqa'i rebellion.[39] Again the Bakhtiyari rebellion clearly shows a community of interest between the peasant cultivators and the nomadic tribes with their fringe of bandits. For example, in July the leader, named Khaybar, of one of the largest brigand bands, together with 200 Bakhtiyari, captured the village of Taghun, 11 miles west of Qumishah on the Isfahan–Shiraz road. He then, like the Baharlu in Darab, broke open the government opium store, took out the government share of 10 per cent, and returned the remainder to the peasants, taking receipts.[40] Although the tribal insurgencies of the summer of 1929 were to fade quickly, a generalized phenomenon of small-scale banditry was to persist across southern Iran throughout the next decade.

Perhaps the most important reason for the ultimate political failure of the rural resistance was its inability to connect with disaffected elements in the provincial cities who shared many of its grievances. A tribal capture of a major provincial city would have had the capacity to transform the national political balance of forces. Yet there was no significant community of action between the uprisings in the countryside and broader urban forces, even those, the lower-ranking clerical and bazaar elements, who had recently been most active in resisting Tehran's agenda. The Baharlu had proved themselves able to take control of the small towns of southeastern Fars for a period of time and many provincial towns elsewhere saw sporadic outbreaks of violence against the physical and human representations of the new order, for example the recruiting commissions and the local civil authorities, with rioting and attacks on the police and the *amniyyah*. But in general the people of cities such as Shiraz, Isfahan and Tabriz experienced only fear at the prospect of tribal descents on their cities, and panic was the usual reaction to the approach of tribal forces. Nonetheless, although there was fear at the prospect of the actual arrival of armed tribal fighters in the cities, there was at the same time considerable sympathy for their plight and their suffering at the hands of the army and the Finance Department. The urban populations, especially the poorer classes, were also happy to take advantage of the authorities' manifest weakness in the summer of 1929 to make bonfires of the hated Pahlavi hat, which they discarded with impunity and en masse.

The defeat of the 1929 uprisings and its consequences

The successive tribal uprisings of 1929 had a serious impact on Riza Shah and his regime. Although he was able to respond pragmatically on a practical level, throughout the summer he remained in a highly nervous state. The example of Afghanistan was not encouraging. There King Amanullah, whose radical modernizing reforms mirrored those of Riza Shah, had alienated both the ulama and conservative tribal groups, and he had been overthrown earlier in the year by a tribal rebellion. In Iran the shah now believed himself to be facing the gravest crisis since he had come to the throne and considered the very survival of his dynasty to be threatened.[41] He not only feared that southern Iran would slip out of government control altogether, but he was also convinced that the uprisings were the work of the British, who wished to reassert their power in Iran.

The British had certainly in the past had close links with both Qavam al-Mulk and the Bakhtiyari khans, although never with Sawlat and the Qashqa'i, but these relationships had, by mutual consent, evaporated in the early 1920s.[42] Nonetheless the shah held firmly to the belief that the British had instigated the tribal discontent, and official circles, especially the army, shared this view.[43] The shah's belief in British malevolence was aggravated by the outbreak of a strike by labourers in the southern oilfields in May 1929. Although Taymurtash dismissed the alleged communist threat, of which the Anglo-Persian Oil Company made much, the shah was outraged by the arrival of British naval vessels just outside Persian territorial waters in the aftermath of the strike.

As well as reawakening Riza Shah's old fears about British imperial ambitions, the upheavals of 1929 also aggravated his fears for the security of his dynasty and caused him to begin to doubt those who had been his most ardent supporters. His perennial fear of assassination was also much in evidence. In June Prince Firuz Farmanfarma, the minister of finance and, with Taymurtash and Davar, one of the triumvirate who had controlled the whole machinery of government for the shah since his accession to the throne, was arrested and imprisoned. On the same day the former governor-general of Fars, the Qajar prince, Akbar Mirza Sarim al-Dawlah, and General Fazlullah Khan Zahidi, the commander of the *amniyyah*, who had been in Shiraz during the tribal disturbances, were arrested and jailed in Tehran. A little later General Mahmud Khan Ayrum, the former commander of the southern army, was arrested and imprisoned and the former divisional chief of staff in the south, General Prince Muhammad Husayn Farmanfarma, a brother of Firuz, also fell under suspicion and was arrested. No reasons were given for the arrests, but hints were dropped in the newspapers *Ittila'at* and *Shafaq-i Surkh* that they were in connection with a plot to support the Qashqa'i revolt.[44] In fact, Firuz, Sarim al-Dawlah and General Muhammad Husayn Farmanfarma were all Qajar princes, and the shah appeared to suspect that the tribal rebellions were a precursor of an attempt to overthrow his dynasty and restore the Qajars, perhaps with British help.[45]

Prince Firuz was the first of Riza Shah's high officials to suffer the fate of disgrace, arrest and imprisonment. With his fall began a process which was to end in the death, imprisonment or exile of most of the shah's loyal officials, including Taymurtash, the minister of court, and Sardar As'ad, the minister of war. As well as casting a shadow over his loyal officials, the tribal rebellions of 1929 also sealed the fate of the tribal leaders themselves. In 1930 Sardar As'ad and Sawlat al-Dawlah did their best to demonstrate to Riza Shah their own loyalty and the continued reliability and usefulness of their tribal followers, furnishing substantial irregular contingents for the army's operations against the Buyir Ahmadi. But in the same year, Tehran renewed its efforts at tribal disarmament and pacification and in 1932 began to make serious efforts to implement the policy of sedentarization. At the same time Riza Shah aggressively pursued his objective of severing the southern tribes from their hereditary leaders and matters quickly came to a head. In August 1932 Sawlat al-Dawlah and his eldest son, Nasir Khan, were imprisoned, and in August 1933 Sawlat was murdered in prison. In November Sardar As'ad, still minister of war, a large number of Bakhtiyari khans, and Qavam al-Mulk were arrested and accused of plotting against the shah's life.[46] In April 1934 Sardar As'ad was murdered in prison and, in November, eight people implicated in the so-called Bakhtiyari plot were executed.[47] Among those executed were Ali Mardan Khan Chahar Lang, the Haft Lang Bakhtiyari khans, Sardar Iqbal and Sardar Fatih, and Sardar Fatih's brother-in-law, Sartip Khan Buyir Ahmadi, all leaders of the 1929 revolt who had previously been pardoned by the shah. Twenty other Bakhtiyaris were sentenced to long prison terms, including four khans to life.[48] With this, the southern tribal leaders were permanently removed as a factor in national political life.

For the tribal populations in general, 1929 was also a turning point. The summer of that year saw the last significant collective rural opposition of the Riza Shah period, its failure to delay, divert or moderate the regime's determination to impose its agenda ushering in a decade of extreme hardship throughout the countryside. Disarmed, heavily taxed, the pressure to settle only ameliorated by the corruption of the local authorities, with their khans executed or imprisoned, the tribal populations were profoundly demoralized. With the regime's assault on the nomadic way of life, and its attempted destruction of the pastoral economy, and with military control of their pastures and migration routes ever tighter, the tribes were no longer capable of asserting the political and military autonomy of the past. The peasantry too experienced worsening conditions during these years. Harshly taxed in order to provide revenue for the regime's prestige projects, the railway and the army, undermined by the spread of the cash economy, and largely unable, through lack of money or education, to make use of the new institutions such as the law courts or the Department of Land Registration, the peasants' main point of contact with the modern state was through the conscription commissions. Caught between forms of economic exploitation and political subordination which were, on the one hand 'traditional,' represented by subsistence agriculture and pastoralism and the rule of the khans and rural magnates, and on the other hand, 'modern,' represented by private property and the authoritarian state, the rural poor experienced a series of crushing defeats in the 1920s.

Nonetheless throughout the 1930s rural resistance continued to manifest itself, but now only through the widespread persistence of banditry, whereby pauperized rural, especially nomadic elements, sometimes allied to other marginal figures such as army deserters, continued to evade and defy the new state. Such banditry was neither a survival from the pre-modern era nor an anachronism, but was rather itself created by, and constituted a response to, conditions of rapid and authoritarian modernization and rural social disintegration.

The rural resistance to the new order which erupted across southern Iran during the spring and summer of 1929 ultimately failed to defend the nomadic and peasant populations from the modernist vision of the urban nationalist elite. The various manifestations of rural discontent of those months at no stage coalesced into a unified or sustained movement. The confederations were themselves internally divided, in no case did a tribal confederation as a whole rise against the government, and there was intense hatred between the confederations, particularly between the Qashqa'i and the Khamsah. Furthermore, the demands of the rebels were invariably defensive, calling for the removal or rescinding of new laws and institutions, and developed no wider political perspective or coherent strategy through which a challenge to the central government might be mounted. The tribal risings also petered out for more mundane, although compelling, reasons, including a severe shortage of ammunition and the needs of the pastoral economy, particularly migration, although not before they had starkly revealed the limits of the regime's coercive power.

The tribal uprisings did not persuade the senior khans to abandon their alliance with the new state. On the contrary, Sardar As'ad Bakhtiyari threw his full weight behind a military response and other senior khans were instrumental in re-establishing Tehran's authority. Even Sawlat al-Dawlah's ambivalence ended once he was restored to his former position in Shiraz, whereupon he was happy to act once more as a conduit for the transmission of Tehran's will to his resentful tribesmen. The consequent rise of the *kalantars* as more authentic spokesmen for the nomadic populations led to increased fragmentation and further reduced the tribes' capacity for unified action.

Only 20 years previously the Bakhtiyari khans had intervened decisively in national politics through their role in deposing the shah and restoring the constitution. Although the myth of 1909 was still vividly alive among the khans, a comparison of the situation in 1929 with the earlier rising reveals a very different context. In 1929 the junior Bakhtiyari khans could furnish no figure of the stature of Ali Quli Khan Sardar As'ad, the father of the present Sardar As'ad, capable of providing intellectual leadership and of uniting the confederation for the march on Tehran. Not only did the tribal risings lack leaders of sufficient calibre and vision, but they lacked urban and intellectual allies in general. In 1909 the Bakhtiyari had acted in concert with the radicals and constitutionalists in Isfahan, Tehran and elsewhere. By 1929 Riza Shah, having begun to implement many of the demands of the nationalist intelligentsia, still largely retained the support of this group which was, in any case, temperamentally disinclined to ally itself with tribal elements, unless in the most exceptional circumstances. By this time too, there was little or no chance of the tribal rebels mounting a successful assault on the capital. In Tehran, again in contrast to the earlier period, the control of the new state, embodied in the army and police, was complete.

Neither the tribal resistance of 1929 nor the ulama-led urban opposition which had preceded it proved able to arrest or divert Tehran's centralizing drive. The 'religious-radical alliance',[49] the cooperation between secular reformers and clerical dissidents, which had achieved such success in the past, and was to be so effective in the future, was, in the Iran of the late 1920s, inoperative. In his implementation of many of the demands of the nationalist intelligentsia, Riza Shah had sundered this alliance. Its two components were now at loggerheads, one lending enthusiastic support, the other firmly opposed, to the ascendancy of the shah and the character of his state-building project.

Just as the tribal insurgents had failed to acquire urban allies, and especially support in the capital, so the ulama lacked any strategy of linking their resentments to the growing unease among secular elements at the increasingly autocratic rule of the shah. Not only did the ulama lack secular support but they were themselves internally divided along elite/subaltern lines. Just as it was the tribal rank and file's horror at Pahlavi hats, conscription and forced settlement which provided the dynamic for the risings, while the leadership remained ambivalent, aloof or even hostile, so the clerical agitation in the provincial towns was largely driven by the fears of lower-ranking mullas, preachers and religious students. It was they who were primarily vulnerable to the new dress and conscription laws, routinely denied exemption by the state boards, and who lost their livelihoods by the secularization of the judicial system. Although leading provincial mujtahids such as Ayatullah Isfahani assumed, for a variety of local reasons, a leading role in the opposition movement, the most important senior religious figures, especially Ayatullah Shaykh Abd al-Karim Ha'iri, remained unwilling or unable to put themselves at the head of a challenge to the new state.

The resistance manifested between 1927 and 1929 to the new order by different social groups, urban and rural, elite and subaltern, was episodic and serial rather than sustained, expressing sectional, regional and local interests as and when these were challenged, and neither possessing nor generating any leadership capable of transcending these interests. It had, furthermore, largely exhausted itself by 1930. Yet, although this resistance had been overcome, it nonetheless had a serious impact on the regime. The traumatic events of 1929 aggravated Riza Shah's perennial inclination towards paranoia. Profoundly shaken by apparent assaults on his rule from many directions, he began to lose confidence in his supporters. The arrest of Firuz Mirza in mid-1929 began the inauguration of what was to become a reign of terror, decimating the Iranian elite and leaving the shah isolated and his regime directionless and demoralized.

6

The Ottoman Legacy of the Kemalist Republic

Erik-Jan Zürcher

The Kemalist experiment of the 1920s and 1930s was both a classic example of nation-building and a daring modernization project. The state that emerged in the shape of the Republic of Turkey in 1923 had to be built on the basis of an ethnically mixed population that was both impoverished and numerically decimated. To turn this mass of people into a nation, to make citizens out of subjects and to install a sense of patriotism in the population was one of the two main aims of the Kemalists. The other was to make society 'modern' (*muasir*) and 'civilized' (*medeni*). Both of these terms, which at times seem to have been used almost as synonyms, referred to contemporary European civilization, which the Kemalists, like the radical 'Westernizers' among the Young Turks before them, considered the only viable civilization in the world. These goals could only be reached by enlightening people's minds, which in turn meant forcing organized religion to relinquish its hold on people's minds, unless religion could be used as a state-controlled channel to spread the message of enlightenment.

The policies that resulted from this ideological programme, such as the abolition of the mystical fraternities (*tarikat*) and the introduction of the Swiss civil code to replace the religious law (*Shari'a*) constituted such a far-reaching form of interference in the daily and personal lives of the citizens that they aroused both resentment and resistance. This is ably demonstrated in the contributions of Umut Azak, Nicole van Os and Hülya Küçük in this volume. If we want to understand the Kemalists and their policies, however, we must take a step back and look at their shared past, in other words at the final years of the Ottoman Empire. That period shaped the future leaders of the republic as well as the country they tried to reshape. Both the material circumstances and the ideological toolkit were products of the constitutional period after 1908 and the decade of war between 1912 and 1922.

The new borders

One look at the map suffices to make clear that in geographical terms the new republic was very different from the empire of even 1912. The Arab provinces, which had formed part of the empire for 400 years, had been lost, as had the southern Balkan ('Rumelian') provinces, which had been Ottoman since the fifteenth, sometimes even the fourteenth, century and from which hailed the largest part of the Ottoman bureaucratic and military elite. Losing such important areas clearly was a traumatic affair. At the same time, it is important to understand the nature of the new borders. They were not 'natural' borders in any sense, but determined essentially by the political and military realities of 1918. The 'national borders' were laid down in the 'national pact' (*Misak-i Milli*) adopted by the last Ottoman parliament in February 1920. In essence these were none other than the armistice lines of October 1918 (although confusingly two versions of the text seem to have been in existence from the very start, one calling for independence of the Ottoman–Muslim majority within the armistice lines and the other within and without the armistice lines).[1] In other words, the territory of the republic was essentially that which was still defended by Ottoman arms in 1918, a fact which was recognized in so many words by Mustafa Kemal Pasha, the leader of the national resistance movement.[2] It is important to note that in 1918–19 not even nationalist officers like Mustafa Kemal objected to the terms of the Armistice of Moudros as such – they objected to the infringement by the Allies, primarily the British, of the terms that had been laid down.[3] These infringements in part consisted of the occupation of territory which had still been in Ottoman hands at noon on 31 October, when the armistice formally came into effect. The most important of these were the areas around Mosul in the east and that around Iskenderun on the Mediterranean. Who held what in the inland areas of the Syrian Desert was completely unclear. This would later create problems during the peace negotiations in Lausanne in 1922–23. The Turkish delegation came to Lausanne with a brief to insist on a new southern border which would run from a point south of Iskenderun on the Mediterranean coast, along the Euphrates and then on to the Iranian border, thus including the province of Mosul in the new Turkey. As we know, it was unsuccessful in its demands. The border with the French protectorate of Syria was determined at Lausanne as it had been in the Franco-Turkish agreement of 1920 and ran just south of the track of the Baghdad railway. Arbitration by the League of Nations awarded the province of Mosul to Iraq in 1926, but Turkey managed to regain the district of Iskenderun (or 'Hatay') in 1939. For the Arab provinces under British occupation on the day of the armistice, the 'National

Pact' demanded a plebiscite, but not automatic inclusion in the postwar Ottoman state. While disillusionment with the attitude of the Arabs during the First World War probably played a role, the leadership in Ankara was also realistic enough to see that re-conquest of the Arab lands was beyond their means. There were attempts to cooperate with Arab nationalists in 1919–21, but inclusion of the former Arab provinces (Damascus, Baghdad, Basra, Hejaz) was never seriously contemplated.

On the Caucasian border, the National Pact demanded a plebiscite for the three provinces of Kars, Ardahan and Batumi. These had been lost to Russia in 1878, regained after the collapse of the Russian army in 1918 and lost again to the British and their Armenian and Georgian allies in 1919. The Turkish nationalist General Kazim Karabekir conquered Kars and Ardahan in a short war against the Republic of Armenia in 1920–21, thus making the plebiscite superfluous in these two provinces. This left only the fate of Batumi to be decided. The threat of a clash with the Red Army and the need for Soviet military and financial support led to a compromise with Russia, which left Batumi and its hinterland in the hands of Soviet-controlled Georgia.

In the west, the National Pact foresaw a plebiscite in Western Thrace (*Garbi Trakya*) with its Muslim majority. When the Turkish delegation went to Lausanne, it also brought with it the claim that a number of Aegean islands adjoining the Anatolian mainland should be ceded by Greece. Like the demands for inclusion of Iskenderun and Mosul, these claims were rejected. In the end, the Turks acquiesced, although the fact that the Lausanne treaty left sizeable Turkish and Muslim communities outside the new national borders caused acrimonious debates in the Turkish National Assembly.[4]

Thus in essence the borders of 1918 which were recognized in the peace treaty of Lausanne in 1923 were no different in principle from those established in 1878 or in 1913 – they were what the Ottomans had managed to hold on to and not the result of any principled choice for a 'Turkish' homeland. In this sense the borders of Turkey were very different from the lines drawn in Eastern Europe after 1918, which at least pretended to do justice to the right to self-determination of nations. The Republic of Turkey was created within Ottoman borders and as a result the society within those borders was still a multi-ethnic, multi-lingual one, with a large majority of Turks and significant minorities of Kurds, Arabs and many smaller groups. It was far less multi-ethnic than it had been, however.

Demographic change

The composition of the population of the new state was very different even from that of the same geographical area in late Ottoman times. This was the result of large-scale migration and warfare in the decade prior to the proclamation of the republic in 1923. The demographic effects of the ten years of warfare between 1912 and 1922 cannot be overstated. Mortality among the Anatolian population had been incredibly high. The Ottoman army had recruited most of its soldiers from the peasant population of Anatolia, and a very large proportion of the 800,000 fatalities (half of them due to disease rather than wounds) of the campaigns in the Caucasus, Gallipoli, Palestine, Mesopotamia, Galicia and Romania turn up in the population statistics of Anatolia. Furthermore, from the spring of 1915 onwards, eastern Anatolia had become a war theatre itself. This had led to great suffering among the Muslim population, which in part had followed the retreating Ottoman armies. The movement of troops stimulated the spread of epidemics, notably typhus in winter and cholera in summer.[5] The decade of war also marked the end of the old Christian communities in Anatolia, primarily those of the Greek Orthodox and the Armenians. The Armenian community was ravaged by the large-scale persecutions organized by the Young Turks in 1915–16. Massacres, death marches and neglect combined to kill some 600,000–700,000 Armenians, which probably constituted at least 40 per cent of the community as a whole.

The First World War had been followed by an independence war during which campaigns had been fought in the east and the west, in addition to guerrilla action in the south and the west and civil war between supporters of the Istanbul government and the nationalists in the interior. On the western front the fleeing Greek forces had committed large-scale atrocities against the Muslim population and some of the advancing Turkish troops had acted with comparable brutality against the Greek Orthodox.

All in all, as a result of war, epidemics and starvation, some 2.5 million Anatolian Muslims had lost their lives, as well as up to 800,000 Armenians and possibly 300,000 Greeks. The population of Anatolia declined by 20 per cent through mortality – a percentage 20 times higher than that of France, which was the hardest hit Western European country in the First World War. The effects of war and disease were spread unevenly, however: in some eastern provinces fully half of the population had perished and another quarter were refugees. There were 12 provinces, most of them in the west, where more than 30 per cent of adult women were widows.[6] Turkey after the war was an empty country. Travellers who visited the country in the 1920s and 1930s without exception remark on the desertedness of the countryside.[7]

Apart from mortality, the Anatolian population also showed the effects of large-scale migration. All through the nineteenth and early twentieth centuries Muslims had fled, or been forced to flee, from territories which were lost by the empire to Christian states: Russia, Romania, Bulgaria, Serbia and Greece. Eventually these people had been resettled in Anatolia (often on former Armenian properties) and there they and their children now made up about a third of the postwar population. The loss of the predominantly Christian areas and the immigration of Muslims had meant that in 1913, for the first time in its entire history, the Ottoman Empire had a Turkish majority.

During and after the war almost all the surviving Armenians left the country for Russia, France or the United States. In the aftermath of the Balkan War up to 200,000 Greeks (out of 450,000 living on the Aegean coast) had been forced to leave western Anatolia. Three-quarters of them returned in the wake of the Greek occupation in 1919.[8] When the Greek army in Anatolia collapsed in 1922, almost the whole of the Greek community in the west fled to Greece. This situation was then made official with the agreement on the exchange of populations (the *mübadele*), which was added to the peace treaty of Lausanne. Under this agreement the last remaining Greek Orthodox communities of Anatolia, mainly those of the Black Sea coast (the 'Pontic' Greeks) and the Karamanlis (Turkish-speaking Orthodox from Central Anatolia), were exchanged for the Muslim community in Greece. In total about a million Greeks left Anatolia in 1922–24 and about 400,000 Muslims from Greece came in. The migratory movements of the First World War and after meant a net population loss of 10 per cent, which should be added to the 20 per cent loss due to mortality.

The changes in population meant that culturally Anatolia in 1923 was a completely different place from what it had been in 1913. The larger Christian communities were practically gone and the population of about 13 million was now 98 per cent Muslim, as against 80 per cent before the war. Linguistically only two large groups were left, Turks and Kurds, with half a dozen smaller but still important language groups. The country was also more rural than it had been. Only 18 per cent of the people now lived in towns of 10,000 inhabitants or over, as against 25 per cent before the war.[9] This reflected the fact that the Christian communities had been more heavily urbanized. They had also completely dominated the modern sector of the economy: the cotton mills of the Çukurova, the silk of Bursa, the exports of figs and raisins in the west, shipping, banking, the railways, hotels and restaurants. All had been almost exclusively in the hands of Christians before the war. In 1923 Turkey was not only a country almost without managers and engineers, but it was a country almost without trained waiters, welders or electricians. It would take at least a generation to rebuild the skills that had disappeared.

A new state?

The republic created out of the ruins of Ottoman Anatolia in October 1923 was, of course, legally and formally a new state. It was only one of the many new states that were created out of the Ottoman Empire and which carried part of the Ottoman heritage with them. Comparisons with the experiences of other successor states in the Balkans and the Arab world (such as pioneered by Carl Brown in his *Imperial Legacy. The Ottoman Imprint on the Balkans and the Middle East*) are helpful in understanding the way the Ottoman heritage continued to play a role in the new states. At the same time, it is evident that in some ways Turkey was a very different heir to the empire from, say, Syria or Albania. It was created by the dominant ethnic and cultural elements of the empire and it inherited not just one of the limbs, but the head and heart of the empire, its cultural and administrative centre. It took over a disproportionate part of the military and civil bureaucracy and of the people with political experience.

One could argue that this position made defining the identity of the new state more, not less, difficult than in any of the other successor states, which could distance themselves from the Ottoman past by redefining it as a foreign occupation and seek inspiration from a mythical 'national' golden age before the Ottoman conquest. In this respect, the Turkish experience can perhaps be usefully compared to that of Austria. Where pre-war inhabitants of the German-speaking parts of the Habsburg Empire had thought of themselves as subjects of a Catholic and dynastic empire and at the same time as Germans, the elite of the new republic of Austria almost had to invent a 'small Austrian' identity from scratch. So the Turks, too, who had thought of themselves as Muslim subjects of an Islamic empire, now had to start thinking of themselves as Turks. In the following sections we shall look at the legal, political and institutional aspects of this transition.

The legal framework

On the face of it, the question when the change from empire to republic took place seems easy enough to answer. After all, the Republic of Turkey (*Türkiye Cumhuriyeti*) was proclaimed on 29 October 1923. But the Ottoman sultanate had been abolished almost a year earlier, on 1 November 1922. The delegation that went to Lausanne that month represented 'the government of the Great National Assembly'. Very well, but what state was that the government of? One could argue that it was, in fact, the Ottoman Empire, because the imperial constitution of 1876, as modified in 1908–9, remained in force until the promulgation of the new republican constitution of April 1924. Nor had the dynasty altogether disappeared. After the deposition of the last sultan in November 1922, his cousin, Abdülmecit Efendi, had been proclaimed caliph. The concept of a purely religious caliphate was alien to both Islamic and Ottoman tradition, however, and there can be little doubt that in the eyes of the population Abdülmecit was as much a monarch as Vahdettin had been. Many in the leadership also felt an emotional bond of loyalty to the dynasty, which they and their forefathers had served.[10] This was in fact the main reason why the republican leadership decided to abolish the caliphate in March 1924.

On the other hand, as early as January 1921, the National Assembly in Ankara had proclaimed the 'Law on Fundamental Organization' (*Teşkilat-i Esasiye Kanunu*). This law has generally been regarded by Turkish historians as the first republican constitution. It is seen as the ultimate source of political legitimacy, as is shown by the fact that both the future leaders of the Democratic Party in their famous *dörtlü takrir* ('memorandum of the four'), which issued in multi-party politics in 1946 and the generals who staged a coup against the Democrats in May 1960 in their first official statement referred to it. Strictly speaking, this view is incorrect. The Ottoman constitution was not abrogated in 1921 and the Law on Fundamental Organization was primarily an instrument to enable the nationalist de facto government in Anatolia to function while Istanbul was occupied. It was in force side by side with the Ottoman constitution.[11] At the same time, it cannot be denied that the law, with its emphasis on unrestricted popular sovereignty, vested in the nation and exercised solely by the National Assembly on the nation's behalf, was an expression of republicanism in the radical tradition of the French Revolution and sits awkwardly with a system of constitutional monarchy.[12]

In the period between the abolition of the sultanate and the proclamation of the republic, Mustafa Kemal Pasha in his public statements said that the nationalists had founded 'a new state', although at this time he still maintained that it resembled neither a monarchy nor a republic and was, in fact, *sui generis*. The term 'Türkiye', which had been used occasionally as a synonym for 'Ottoman Empire' by him and others, now became the sole term describing the country.[13]

The conclusion, therefore, has to be that in the legal sense the transition from empire to republic was a gradual one, which took place between February 1921 and April 1924.

The leadership

The political leadership, both of the resistance movement between 1918 and 1922 and of the republic from 1923 onwards, consisted of a well-defined group of people who shared a number of characteristics. They were, almost without exception, people who had made their careers in the service of the state, predominantly military officers. They were also men of a certain age (between 38 and 45 years old in 1923), of Muslim descent (but not necessarily Turkish), born, more often than not, in the old *Rumeli* (Balkans) provinces or Istanbul. In fact 84 per cent of the leaders of the republic between 1923 and 1945 hailed from there, with 62 per cent coming from Europe.[14] They do not seem to have hailed from a particular social group in terms of wealth: the fathers include pashas and large landowners, but also small-time civil servants. They seem to have had an almost exclusively urban background, but their most distinctive characteristic was that they were products of the modern educational establishments of the empire, created by the *Tanzimat* reformers of the nineteenth century.

Apart from their social characteristics, they also shared a number of experiences. They had played a role in the politics of the second constitutional period (1908–18) and, even before that, in the preparations for the constitutional revolution. Almost without exception they were former members of the Committee of Union and Progress (*İttihad ve Terakki Cemiyeti*). They were bound together by a common past which included a number of the greatest upheavals in modern Ottoman history: the constitutional revolution of 1908; the suppression of the counter-revolution of April 1909 by the 'Action Army' (*Hareket Ordusu*); working as volunteers to organize the Beduin resistance in Tripolitania against the Italian invaders in 1911; the Balkan War disaster of 1913; the First World War and the resistance movement after the war. For the typical leading Kemalist politician of the 1920s these were all part of his personal curriculum vitae.

I have attempted to show in my own work[15] that the continuity extends beyond the fact that Young Turk and Kemalist leaders hailed from a common pool. My thesis is that it was in fact the leadership of the Committee of Union and Progress that planned and prepared the national resistance struggle after 1918 and that Mustafa Kemal Pasha and his circle of adherents only gradually gained control of the movement. Since then, both extended research on the Unionist underground in Istanbul[16] and on the earliest regional resistance organizations, which held 28 congresses between 1918 and 1920,[17] have yielded more information on the central role of the Unionist organizations and individuals.

The great military victory of August–September 1922 made Mustafa Kemal ('Gazi' since 1921) the undisputed political leader. In the years after the proclamation of the republic, more particularly between the promulgation of the 'Law on the Maintenance of Order' (*Takrir-i Sükun Kanunu*) in March

1925 and the political trials of June–August 1926, the remaining members of the top echelon of the former Committee of Union and Progress as well as those commanders of the national resistance movement who had played a leading role in the start of that movement (in some cases even before Mustafa Kemal Pasha arrived in Anatolia) were eliminated physically or politically.[18] From then on, Mustafa Kemal Pasha ruled unchallenged. Gradually younger men were brought into the political centre, but throughout the years of the Kemalist single-party state and to a certain extent even beyond it, into the 1950s, the key positions remained in the hands of people who had made their political and military careers during the Young Turk era.

The state apparatus

In the execution of its policies, the political leadership could count on the support of the large bureaucratic and military apparatus which had been built up under the empire from the 1840s onwards. This is not to say that the republic took over the servants of the empire unquestioningly. There had been purges in the recent past: many civil servants who had compromised themselves by corruption or spying on behalf of the Hamidian regime had been thrown out by the Young Turks after the constitutional revolution of 1908 (and sometimes chased out by the public). Many of the officers who had risen from the ranks under the old regime had been purged by Enver Pasha in 1913–14 and replaced by officers who had graduated from the modern military colleges. The Kemalists also resorted to purges. On 25 September 1923 Law 347 was passed, which made possible the dismissal of army officers who had not joined the national resistance movement. Three years later, on 26 May 1926, a similar law was passed (Law 854) for civil servants, but the scope of the purges seems to have been fairly limited, and as early as 24 May 1928 Law 1289 created a review panel for officers and civil servants who felt they had been wrongfully dismissed.[19]

In essence, therefore, the army of the republic was the army of the late empire. It was the army, and certainly also the gendarmerie, which allowed the republican regime to extend its control into every corner of the land and into every village, to a degree the empire had never achieved.[20] In fact one could argue that it was this establishment of effective control, more than any of the famous Kemalist reforms (clothing, alphabet or calendar), which heralded the arrival of the modern state in Anatolia. The bureaucracy by and large was the imperial bureaucracy. In the early years of the National Struggle, the nationalists weeded out members of the provincial bureaucracy who were considered unreliable because of their links to the Istanbul government. The persons concerned were mostly provincial and district governors (*valis* and *kaymakams*) who had been political appointees. On the lower levels the provincial administration remained intact and this enabled the nationalists to conscript soldiers and raise taxes in the areas under their control. Another branch of the bureaucracy, the Ottoman telegraph service, proved itself loyal to the nationalists and rendered sterling service to them. At the peace conference of Lausanne in 1923, the Turks first resisted Allied demands for a general amnesty after the conclusion of peace; then they gave in but reserved the right to ban 150 undesirable Ottoman Muslims from the country. The number of 150 was completely arbitrary and the names were only filled in (with some difficulty) more than a year after the conclusion of peace.[21] There were a number of army officers and bureaucrats among those banned, but obviously it concerned only a very small number of people.

In the field of finance, the republic inherited two separate bureaucratic structures from the empire. The one was the regular Ministry of Finance, which had been thoroughly modernized under the Young Turk finance minister, Cavid Bey, and the other the administration of the Ottoman Public Debt, which since 1881 had taken control of the collection of taxes, duties and excises in areas such as the sale of tobacco and tobacco products and salt and fisheries on behalf of the European creditors of the empire. Although the new Turkey shouldered part of the Ottoman debt at the peace of Lausanne in 1923, the autonomous operation of the Public Debt Administration was terminated and the existing monopolies were taken over by the Turkish state. In 1932 they were united under the Directorate of Monopolies. The monopolies provided vital income for the new state in the 1920s and 1930s.

Of all the branches of the state bureaucracy, the one to undergo the greatest change under the republic was undoubtedly the religious one. The passing of the law on the unification of education in 1924 and the introduction of a European-style family law in 1926 meant that the secular state now took direct control of these important fields and the role of the religious establishment contracted accordingly. The abolition of the caliphate and the simultaneous replacement of the office of the Sheikh al-Islam, the highest religious authority, by a directorate under the prime minister, certainly meant that the top of the religious establishment lost much of its room for manoeuvre. On the other hand, the reforms of 1916, when the Sheikh al-Islam had been removed from the cabinet and had lost his jurisdiction over the *Shari'a* courts, the foundations (*evkaf*) and the religious colleges (*madrasas*) had already severely circumscribed its function. The fact that Mustafa Kemal Pasha could push through his reforms almost without opposition from within the senior clergy is testimony to the degree to which the Ottoman religious establishment had already been bureaucratized and brought under state control in the late Ottoman Empire.

Not only were the important branches of the state inherited by the republic, but the means of reproducing these branches also remained virtually unchanged. The great schools of the empire, modelled on the French *grandes écoles*, which had bred the officers and civil servants of the *Tanzimat*, Hamidian and Young Turk eras, continued to do so under the republic. When the military academy was closed by the occupying powers in Istanbul, it was provisionally relocated to Ankara during the National Struggle. In 1923 the school moved back to Istanbul, but in 1936 it was moved to Ankara once more, where it has since remained. Its function and way of working remained essentially unchanged. The same is true for the Civil Service Academy (*Mülkiye*), which continued in Istanbul and was reconstituted as the Political Science Faculty in Ankara in 1935. It continued to provide the state with its governors, diplomats and administrators. In time both institutions also became centres of Kemalist indoctrination, where nationalism, republicanism and secularism were articles of faith for staff and students alike – a situation that continues to this day.

The Unionists had tried to reform the *madrasas*, by including science in their curriculum, but the Kemalists thought they were beyond redemption and closed them down in 1924. From now on the education of religious specialists was in the hands of the Faculty of Theology of the University in Istanbul and the two dozen *imam-hatip okulları* (schools for prayer leaders and preachers), but the former was closed down in 1935 and the latter over the years 1930–31. But the decline in the level of religious learning only became apparent when the older Ottoman-educated generation started to fade – something which can be roughly dated from the mid-1940s onwards.

The party

A new instrument at the disposal of the republican regime was the People's Party (*Halk Fırkası, Halk Partisi*), which from 1925 onwards and with the exception of a three-month period in 1930 was the only legal political party in Turkey.

Of course, the country had had quite wide experience of political parties since 1908, and between 1913 and 1918 it had already lived under a one-party regime, but there were major differences. In the second constitutional period, power ultimately rested with the secret, extra-parliamentary committee which dominated both the parliamentary party and the cabinet. In the republic, the party was created by Mustafa Kemal in the National Assembly and it functioned to a large extent as an annex to the state. Between 1925 and 1929, the emergency legislation in force meant that the parliamentary party abdicated all of its powers to the cabinet, so, ironically, the parliamentary party exercised no power at all during the time when most of the radical reforms were adopted. In these years reform laws were usually adopted unanimously or with very large majorities, but the number of votes cast was often less than half of the total.[22] From 1930 onwards, the People's Party, especially through its educational arm, the People's Houses, became an instrument for indoctrination and mobilization, but it always remained under tight state control. This culminated in the formal unification of state and party in 1936. The CUP had also reached out to the public through its 'clubs' and through the branches of the 'Turkish Hearth' (*Türk Ocağı*) movement, but these had never been under the kind of central state control that the People's Houses were under during the republic.[23]

Ideology

If it is true that there was a high degree of continuity in the political leadership and in the state apparatus, the picture is more complicated where the aims and underlying ideology of the regime are concerned.[24]

Before the outbreak of the Balkan War in 1912, the heated ideological debates among the Young Turks, all of whom were fundamentally concerned with ways to save the Ottoman state, had centred around two main questions. The first concerned the degree of Westernization needed to achieve the strengthening of state and society and in particular the way in which the use of Western science and technology could be reconciled with continued adherence to Turkish culture and Islamic civilization. As Mardin and Hanioğlu have shown, the vast majority of Ottoman intellectuals (who were at the same time in the service of the state) came to believe from the mid-nineteenth century onwards that Westernization was the only way to achieve material progress and political strength. There was a great deal of popular resentment against the Westernizing ways of the elite, but no strong anti-Western intellectual current to give it direction.[25] The debates among the elite were about the degree of Westernization needed and about the desirability of reconciling borrowing from Europe with the maintenance of an Islamic value system. Equally widespread was a belief in modern science and biological materialism. Relatively few Young Turks were committed positivists in the strict sense (Ahmet Reza being the best-known example), but nearly all were influenced by positivism in a broad sense. Its combination of belief in progress through science and intellectual elitism appealed to the Young Turks, many of whom were influenced by Le Bon's deeply distrustful ideas on mass psychology.[26] Without exception, however, Young Turk thinkers defended the idea that 'real' Islam (which they contrasted with the obscurantism of the clerics of their day) was receptive to, and quite compatible with, science. Even if they were not religious men themselves, they regarded religion as important 'national cement'.[27]

The second question, which often occupied the same Young Turk authors, was that of the communal basis of any future Ottoman state, whether it should be based on a single nationality, on a voluntary union of nation-alities or perhaps on religion. By the early twentieth century sincere belief in a 'Union of (ethnic) Elements' (İttihadı Anasır) was probably limited to some Greek, Arab and Albanian intellectuals and the 'Liberal' group led by Prens Sabahattin. The vast majority, certainly of the Unionists, already before the 1908 revolution subscribed to a kind of Ottoman Muslim nation-alism in which the dominant position of the Turks was taken for granted. There was a growing awareness of Turkishness, but for most Young Turks this was one facet of a complex identity in which being an Ottoman and a Muslim played equally important parts. From the start the organizers of the 1908 revolution opened up their ranks to non-Turkish Muslims, but not (or at least not automatically) to non-Muslims.[28] Contrary to what is often supposed, pan-Turkism was popular only among a very small circle of intellectuals in which Russian émigrés played a dominant role. Islamist or pan-Islamist sentiments were used politically by the Unionists, but played almost no part in their ideological makeup.

The Young Turk thinkers, their intellectual debates and the journals, which formed the mouthpieces of the different currents, have been described in detail.[29] However, with the outbreak of the Balkan War, theoretical ques-tions paled into insignificance. There was a national emergency and the most important issue now seemed to be the mobilization of all national resources. What was national was no longer in doubt by the end of 1912: the empire had been attacked by a coalition of Christian Balkan states, the sympathies of the Ottoman Christian communities were doubtful at best and the big powers of Europe did not lift a finger to help the empire in its distress. When the Young Turks organized the war effort through count-less political, social, economic and cultural organizations which all carried the title milli ('national') it was no longer in doubt what was meant by this term. It meant by and for the Ottoman Muslims. This tendency contin-ued throughout the years of the First World War (which was also officially declared a Jihad and which was partly fought out as a brutal ethnic/religious conflict in Anatolia) and beyond. The proclamations of the national resist-ance movement in Anatolia after 1918 make it abundantly clear that the movement fought for continued independence and unity of the Ottoman Muslims. The religious character of the movement was often remarked upon at the time. Religious ceremonies accompanied every major event and it was the only period in recent Turkish history when the country experienced prohibition of alcohol.[30]

After the war had been won in 1922, this ideological orientation changed quite suddenly. With the passing of the national emergency, the need for mass mobilization had also passed. The debates conducted before 1912 now resumed their importance and here the republican regime made some very deliberate choices. In the debate on the degree of Westernization, Mustafa Kemal and his circle identified themselves with the position of the most extreme 'Westernists' (*garbcılar*) of the Young Turk era, who held that European civilization was indivisible and should be adopted in toto.[31] There was no attempt to harmonize European civilization (*medeniyet*) with Turkish culture (*hars*), although these terms, which had been coined by Ziya Gökalp to differentiate between the acquired *Gesellschaft* and the organic *Gemeinschaft*,[32] remained in use. In fact the Kemalists envisaged a cultural revolution in which not only the 'high' Islamic civilization would be exchanged for that of Europe, but also the 'low' or popular culture would be transformed. Like the Young Turk ideological writers, Mustafa Kemal insisted that Islam was a 'rational' religion and adaptable to the contemporary world, but there was no attempt to turn a 'purged' Islam into a major constituent of the republican ideology. The *Jadidist* ideas of Akçura and Ağaoğlu were rejected as much as Gökalp's proposals for a Turkified Islam and Said Nursi's ideas on Islamic moral rearmament. Instead, secularism (*laiklik*, derived from the French laique) became one of the main planks of the Kemalist ideology. Scientism and biological materialism (as well as social Darwinism) were characteristic of Kemalist thinking even more than they had been of that of the Unionists – witness Mustafa Kemal's famous dictum, 'the only real spiritual guide in life is positive science' (*müspet ilim*), and the passage in his 1933 anniversary speech, where he says that 'the torch, which the Turkish nation holds in its hand while marching on the road towards progress and civilization, is positive science'.

On the issue of national identity, a radical choice was also made. Ottomanism obviously no longer was an option, but the Muslim nationalism of the years 1912–22 was now also abandoned, as it sat awkwardly with the ideal of wholesale adoption of European civilization. Instead an immense effort at nation-building within the borders of the new republic was made, based on the idea of a 'Turkish' nation. Although Turkish nationalism was territorial and based on a shared Turkish language, culture and ideals (with nationality being open to anyone willing to adopt these), a romantic idealization of the Turkish national character, with racist elements, became more and more important in the 1930s (in line with developments in Europe). In practice the adoption of Turkish nationalism led to the forced assimilation of the 30 per cent or so of the population which did not have Turkish as its mother tongue.

One aspect of ideology where there was marked continuity between the Unionists and the Kemalists was in their firm rejection of the role of classes and class struggle. Both Unionist and Kemalist policies aimed at the creation of a national bourgeoisie and rejected any kind of change in property relationships. The CUP had reacted to the wave of strikes after the constitutional revolution of 1908 with repressive legislation and its 'National Economy' programme after 1913 had been geared towards the creation of a class of Muslim traders and industrialists under state protection.[33] Corporatism gained a measure of popularity among the political elite both between 1913 and 1918 and in the early years of the republic. The creation of societies of traders and artisans by the CUP, after it had disbanded the old guilds, was an expression of the importance attached to professional organizations. This interest continued into the republic, but proposals such as those put forward by the nationalist ideologist Gökalp to base the political system on corporatist structures, were rejected.[34] Instead the republic adopted a rather vaguely defined notion of 'populism' (*halkçılık*) or national solidarity, which was partly derived from the Russian Narodniki and partly from the romantic nationalist *Halka doğru* (Towards the People) movement, founded in Izmir in 1916.[35] In practice, the republican regime supported the capitalists and left both peasants and workers at the mercy of the ruling coalition of officers, bureaucrats and large landowners and the 'national' bourgeoisie, which gradually grew up under its protection. Socialism, trade unions and strike action were all banned under the Kemalist republic and land redistribution was first made into a government policy in 1945.

The Kemalist mentality

More important perhaps, but less tangible and well defined, than the strictly ideological legacy of the late Ottoman Empire was the mentality or set of attitudes that the Kemalist republicans derived from their predecessors: a state-centred view, a strong educational streak, elitism and distrust of the masses, activism and a certain impatience, a belief in progress. They emphatically embraced change and, in stark contrast to traditional Ottoman values, which had always seen age and experience as prerequisites for authority, they put their trust in youth, which they saw as a very positive characteristic.[36] The

Young Turks had been young in a literal sense (most of them being in their late 20s at the time of the constitutional revolution) and they had felt that, being young and well educated, they understood the world much better than older generations. This feeling was also prevalent among the founders of the republic, by now middle-aged Young Turks, as well. Mustafa Kemal Atatürk emphasized his bond with the youth of Turkey (a theme taken up in countless school books of the republic until the present day) and made rousing appeals to the Turkish youth to act as guardians of the republic, most notably at the end of his six-day speech (*Nutuk*) before the Party Congress in 1927. Traces of this 'Young Turk mentality' are still much in evidence in Turkey at the start of the twenty-first century.

7

With or Without Workers in Reza Shah's Iran: Abadan, May 1929

Kaveh Bayat

In May 1929, in the early stages of a long and arduous confrontation between the Iranian government and the Anglo-Persian Oil Company (APOC) that for almost half a decade overshadowed, and for a brief period (1948–53) dominated, the contemporary history of Iran, a very significant strike occurred in the Abadan refinery, the heart of APOC's empire in Khuzestan.

The Abadan strike, the first major industrial action of its kind to occur in Iran, put the Iranian government in an awkward position. Considering the ongoing attempts by the government to curb the supremacy of the Anglo-Persian Oil Company in Khuzestan, in which defending the rights of the downtrodden Iranian labourers assumed an important political and moral significance, and at the same time an inherent apprehension by the Reza Shah's regime of any independent activity that could have been interpreted as an attempt to undermine its omnipresence, the course to be taken by the Iranian government was far from clear.

At the end, for a number of reasons such as the authoritarian nature of the Iranian regime and the British ability to brand the whole incident as a dangerous Bolshevik plot, the Iranian government decided to suppress the workers by use of force, but, as later developments proved, it was not only the Iranian workers in the oil industry who were suppressed as a consequence of these developments, but the nascent Iranian nationalism lost much of its momentum and impetus too.

Being excluded from the campaign against the APOC also meant being relegated to a relatively obscure and secluded domain of Iranian history. In most of the major Iranian studies on the history of the oil industry, not even a single footnote has been devoted to this subject.[1] The aforementioned prevailing view, coupled with the original attempts of the British sources to characterize the Abadan disturbances as a 'Bolshevik plot', fitted very well with some of the later studies' inclination to categorize it as an out-and-out 'workers' struggle',[2] and has done much to relegate this matter to its present minor and insignificant position.

The D'Arcy oil concession

In 1901 the Iranian government granted an oil concession to William D'Arcy – an Australian entrepreneur – to 'search for, obtain, develop, render suitable for trade, carry away and sell natural gas, petroleum...' throughout Iran for 60 years, except in the northern provinces that were considered to be in the Russian zone of influence. In April 1909, after seven years of exhaustive work to prove that there was oil in commercial quantities in Khuzestan, the Anglo-Persian Oil Company was incorporated to take over and develop the D'Arcy concession. After establishing administrative centres in Khoramshahr – the provincial centre – and Masjed Soleyman, where the oilfield was located, APOC constructed a range of long pipelines to carry the extracted oil from the plains of Khuzestan to the jetties on the Persian Gulf and also to the refinery that was being constructed in Abadan.[3]

By the end of the 1920s, as the production of oil had increased from 80,000 tons in 1913 to almost 6 million tons in 1929, the number of Iranian workers employed by the company had also increased from 5,708 in 1913 to 16,382 in 1928.[4] Although this rapid development of the oil industry in Khuzestan had its own benefits, such as providing a new source of income for the Iranians, it also had a number of drawbacks: the omnipresence of the APOC in the southwestern parts of Iran constrained Iranian sovereignty there, and a host of other issues, such as the appalling condition of the Iranian workers, were significant.

Abadan was an overcrowded township with a population estimated at 60,000. It consisted mainly of a large number of squalid and unsanitary dwellings, with no proper public services such as clean drinking water.[5] What made matters worse, besides this potentially explosive situation, was the lack of any established procedure to deal with any possible complaints and grievances of the workers. In the early 1920s the Indian and Arab workers and employees of the company – who could be considered to be more privileged than the Iranian workers – did manage to stage some sort of industrial action to demonstrate their grievances against the company, but the Iranian workers were not yet ready to take an active part in these actions or to organize their own.[6]

Disturbances in Abadan

On 2 May 1929 the APOC management, having been informed of the activities of a secret organization among the Iranian workers, decided to report the matter to the governor-general of Khuzestan – Brigadier Farajullah Khan Aghavli – and request his cooperation in an urgent and immediate action against any possible disturbances.

In a meeting between the governor-general, the governor of Abadan and E.H. Elkington, the general manager of the Abadan refinery, it was decided to arrange for a major crackdown on the workers' organization, and, in a series of operations led by Colonel Rukn al-Din Khan Mokhtary, the chief of police, 45 people were arrested. Of those, 20 were employed by the company and the rest were former employees.[7]

At the same time, T.L. Jacks, the resident director of the company, met Teymurtash, the all-powerful Iranian minister of court, in Tehran. After trying to convince him of the 'Bolshevik' nature of the whole affair for not only undermining the APOC operations but also setting the southern parts of Iran ablaze, he managed to win Teymurtash's approval for a tougher course of action by the local authorities in Khuzestan.[8] When, therefore, on 6 May a remnant of the workers' organization, in protest against the arrests of their comrades, attempted to prevent labourers from returning to work in the Abadan refinery and some riots ensued, a detachment of soldiers were on hand to be dispatched to Abadan to disperse the crowd.[9]

According to a report by the Iranian head of the Khoramshahr's Post and Telegraph Office, on that day, at about 9.30:

> When groups of Company's workers were going to work, a cry and hue of a great disturbance was heard and suddenly in a rush and haste [the workers] started to return. According to our information some people who wanted to protest against their meagre wages were arrested at the instigation of the Company a few days earlier. Today these workers wanted to take action against the Company and caused some damage. The moment the disturbance occurred, the police that had been informed about this matter, sent some forces by car, accompanied by Rukn al-Din Khan and the Governor [of Abadan, Asayesh] and they managed to prevent the workers from getting inside the oil installations and forced them back in front of the post office and the office of the Imperial Bank. When the Company tried to take a group of Rangooly in, the workers blocked their way. ... About three to four thousand people were standing in front of the post office, and suddenly a group of between three to four hundred persons broke out of them and rushed towards the installations of the Company.[10]

Although once again the police managed to disperse them, and for the time being the situation was under control, the disturbances were far from over.

In the meantime, even though more than 200 'suspect' workers were deported to the adjacent province of Lurestan, there were rumours in Abadan and Khoramshahr about the possibility of another attempt to utilize the Muharram ceremonies that coincided with 9–19 May of that year, to prevent the workers from going to work in the following days. But eventually the authorities managed by posting extra troops – including an armoured car – in Abadan to handle the Muharram processions and no serious complications occurred.[11]

By early June the disturbance in Abadan, which, for a period of time and especially because of its unexpected nature, had frightened the management of the APOC and the British embassy in Tehran so much that it asked for the presence of a British warship in the vicinity of Abadan in case of an emergency, had faded away.[12]

Communist activities

Communist activists did play a significant role in the developments that prompted the Anglo-Iranian authorities to suppress the nascent workers' organization of Abadan in May 1928.

After the Fifth Congress of the Comintern in June 1924 and Moscow's decision to 'Bolshevize' the international communist movement – a policy that was re-endorsed by the Sixth Congress of the Comintern in June 1928 – various communist groups were ordered to take a much more radical course of action in their respective countries.[13] Henceforth the Communist Party of Iran that had lost much of its initial dynamism after the Iranian–Soviet political rapprochement in the early 1920s took upon itself to launch a new course of action. In the second congress of the Iranian Communist Party (December 1927) it was decided to launch a new campaign to reorganize the Iranian working class,[14] and a number of trained agents such as Yusif Iftikhari, Rahim Hamdad and Ali Umid were dispatched to the Khuzestan oilfields.[15]

The appalling condition of the Iranian workers in the oil industry, the obvious discrimination between Iranian and foreign workers, the awful living conditions of the native workers, the low rate of wages, coupled with the initial stages of an official campaign to force the APOC to revise the 1901 D'Arcy oil concession in a way to check the power of the company and increase Iran's share of oil revenue, provided a favourable field of action for these agents.

The communist agitators who were sent to Khuzestan in the autumn of 1927 joined forces with some other communist activists and sympathizers who had been residing there. By taking full advantage of the current anti-British activities of the nationalists, including their attempts to organize the Iranian workers against the company, they contributed to the formation of the semblance of a trade union.[16]

After an early concentration of efforts on the APOC's Training Shop, which provided an accessible recruitment ground for the organizations, and having established a secret organization based on a series of loosely connected three-men cells, they started to expand the organization. According to Yusif Iftikhari:

> Because the oil workers and the majority of the Khuzestanies were against the Company and hated it, the founding and the expansion of the organization was not difficult. But when it came to running it, many problems arose; there were not enough educated and able workers available, so we had to devote much of our time and efforts to political and organizational matters.[17]

But despite these difficulties they managed to form an organization that in less than a year had prepared the ground for an open action against the company.[18]

The communist activists played a very important role in the education and organization of the Iranian workers in the oil industry at that time, but this was only one factor that contributed to the outburst of the turmoil. Even though some of these activities were secret in nature and were definitely carried out in accordance with communist instructions, their main field of operation was an open one and in complete compliance with a vigorous and well-established campaign by the Iranian nationalists to put an end to the omnipresence of the Anglo-Persian Oil Company in Khuzestan. This campaign enjoyed a much broader base of support.

Nationalistic agitation

After a brief military operation in 1924–25 that put an end to a long period of relative autonomy of Sheikh Khaza'al, the British local protégé in Khuzestan, the re-assertion of the central government authority there became one of the main targets of the nascent Iranian nationalism and it did not take long for this campaign to focus on the inappropriate activities of the Anglo-Persian Oil Company and especially the plight of the Iranians who were employed by it. As E.H. Elkington, the director of APOC in Abadan, in his 'Appreciation of the political situation in Khuzestan with special reference to the present unrest' pointed out, it was specially after Reza Shah's visit to Khuzestan in November 1928, with the aim of making it 'clear to the whole of Khuzestan that the hand of Government was strong in the land and that Khuzestan was as much a part of the Persian Empire as any other province', that the current campaign to downgrade the privileged position of the company took a much more dynamic course.[19]

It was during this trip that, despite the APOC's expectations and preparations, Reza Shah refused to visit the company's installations in Khuzestan. For *Shafaq-i surkh* which reported this incident, the popular dislike of the APOC was the main reason that induced Reza Shah not to visit:

> The Company doesn't deal fairly with people and only has its own interests in mind. The Company's officials do not see themselves as mere representatives of a commercial enterprise, they prefer to meddle in all affairs and they even have a political office ... that acts as the embassy of a powerful nation in a weak country. ... Generally speaking the attitude of the Company before the establishment of the Pahlavi dynasty was akin to the East India Company's stance in the India of two centuries earlier. It is for this reason and for hundreds of other minor issues that the people here don't like the Company. Consequently the public opinion was not in favour of seeing their King as a guest of the Company.[20]

According to Elkington, after Reza Shah's return, 'from the attitude of these government officials ... it was clear that instructions had been issued that although every assistance and protection was to be given to the Company, there was to be no question what so ever as to who was master of the house'.[21]

Apart from the widespread press campaign against the APOC in the late summer of 1928, the prime minister's comments in a speech delivered to parliament on 20 November 1928 that, 'the Imperial government doesn't believe in granting concessions in the bygone manners and conditions and would not permit the type of investments that may entail [foreign] influence' and especially his word of caution to 'holders of old concessions' that if they expect 'assistance from government they would have to realize that such an assistance depends on the holder of the concession's willingness to revise and amend' the terms of the concession,[22] could not have been interpreted as anything but the first shots in a serious war against the APOC.

The question of Iranian labour

The question of labour had always been a major concern of Iranians in their relations with the APOC. In D'Arcy's 1901 concession it was agreed to employ Iranians exclusively, except for managerial and technical staff, but the Iranians were always complaining about the large numbers of Indian and Iraqi workers employed by the company.[23] In one of the latest instances of this conflict, after some rumours in March 1928 about the APOC's intention to fire 10,000 Iranians and to replace them with Indian and Iraqi labourers, more than 2,000 Iranian workers gathered in front of the company's labour office in Abadan and threw stones at it.[24]

For a period of time, even though the Iranian authorities were more concerned about the 'quantitative' aspect of this question, that is the number of Iranians employed in the industry, and to ascertain that the company was observing the terms of the concession gradually – and specially after the change in the government's attitude towards the APOC – the 'qualitative' aspect of it, that is the working and living condition of the Iranian workers, became an important issue too.

In the press campaign that was initiated against the APOC in the late summer of 1928, apart from some left-leaning papers such as *Tufan*, which had always attacked British interest in Iran,[25] a number of mainstream and semi-official papers such as Tehran's *Ittela'at, Sitarah-i Iran* and *Shafaq-i surkh* took up the question of the terrible conditions of the Iranian workers in the oil industry. In addition, some other Persian newspapers such as *Habl al-matin* and *Chihrahnama*, published in Calcutta and Cairo respectively, had a much more forthright attitude towards the British in general and the APOC in particular.

'How the South Oil Company Deals With its Workers', an article by Mahmud Khuzistani that was published by *Shafaq-i surkh* on September 1928, is a telling sample of the type of material being published in the Iranian press at that time. According to Khuzistani the Iranian employees of the oil company,

> who normally owe around 50 to 150 Tuman to the shopkeepers of Abadan, have a nominal salary of 9 Tuman per month, but after the deduction of the holidays and fines that usually get imposed on them because of the negligence of the foremen, 7 and a half Tuman is the actual monthly pay they receive at the end. They have to live in dark hovels made of packing materials, and the utmost imaginable poverty and destitution is their lot. For those who have a family to support, it is much worse.[26]

The question of discrimination between Iranian and foreign labour was another source of dissatisfaction. Mahmud Khuzistani could find no reason for employing Indian labour 'with higher wages – including their transport costs –, better accommodation and living conditions', other than barring the ascendancy of the Iranian workers, 'lest they wanted to demand their rights, not to be dependent on them in different sections of the works'.[27]

And finally in examining the reasons why the company had been so successful in 'acting against our national interest', he criticized the Iranian officials, who are indifferent to public affairs and consider the Iranian workers as an ignorant lot who are not able to act in its own defence even if, for instance, a few workers do attempt to take action in defence of their rights. The Company can easily prevent any collective action and suppress them through 'patriotic officials'. Nowhere in the world can one find such a state of affairs; the employers and the workers are free to get organized and defend their rights, and the government takes it upon itself not to let capitalists oppress the workers. ... The Company and its dealings in Khuzestan are no more than a common labour and capital issue: the colonial aspirations of the young English employees of the Company who are mainly ex-South Persian Rifles or Indian Political Service veterans have been superimposed on the capitalist aims of the foreign shareholders and are strangling the wretched Iranian worker. ... If the government doesn't take serious defensive measures shortly, this moral state of colonialism that has been established at the head of the Persian Gulf, and the germs of this social leprosy, will contaminate not only Khuzestan or the southern parts of the country, but the whole of Iran.[28]

Popular opposition

A combination of local merchants and officials who were set against the overbearing attitude of the company and its constant meddling in local affairs formed the backbone of this campaign in Khuzestan. One such was Mirza Hussein Khan Muvaqqar, the parliamentary representative for Khoramshahr, who was a local entrepreneur who owned many shops and estates in Abadan and, because of his Bushehri lineage, was influential among the Bushehri and Tangestani communities of Khuzestan.[29] On the official side, considering his reports on the activities of the APOC, Muhammad Hasan Badi', the Iranian consul in Basreh, was another member of this local anti-British group,[30] as was Marzban, the chief inspector of customs in Khuzestan, who was even accused by the British of hiding a case of arms in his house.[31]

As a matter of fact the workingmen's clubs, which served as an important vehicle of workers' organization and education at this juncture, were established in the aftermath of Reza Shah's visit to Khuzestan and were sponsored by some leading personalities in the region such as Mirza Hussein Khan Muvaqqar. In the face of the company's objections, Muvaqqar's attempts to open a branch in Abadan failed and the clubs that had already opened in Ahwaz and Khoramshahr were closed down, but as Elkington wrote, 'Muvaqqar was driven to more subterranean methods for achieving his purpose. The Clubs were continued but from now on as a secret society, well provided with money and formed along definite communist lines.'[32]

The agitation that led to the May confrontation had a twofold character: the hardship of the Iranian workers who had to suffer under the drastic rule of the APOC, their meagre wages, poor living conditions (i.e. purely 'class' issues) constituted one aspect of this campaign, the other being the current struggle of the Iranians against British supremacy and the symbol of that supremacy, the APOC.

A proclamation distributed during this period is a telling indication of the dual nature of the struggle. In this appeal, which was addressed to 'Our Crowned Father, Government and Court Officials', the plight of the Iranian workers – 'the glorious and noble sons of Darius' – who had to suffer under the tutelage of the British and particularly their Indian clerks and middle-men, was depicted; the workers who had 'sacrificed everything in the path of the Anglo-Persian Oil Company, [now] have no better work to do than carry heavy pipes and material on [their] shoulders in the 125 degree heat of Khuzestan'. And in conclusion, asked Brigadier Farajullah Khan, who 'is the real protector and defender of the Persian nation's rights, to do us the favour of assisting the body of the workmen of Khuzestan and thus take the high hand of the APOC's tyranny off a handful of poor, unfortunate, oppressed toilers?'[33]

In the aftermath of the disturbances, even though the APOC officials, by circulating various reports and rumours on the alleged activities of Soviet agents and hinting at a probable connection between the presence of the Soviet merchant ship *Frunze* in Khoramshahr and the recent disturbances, did their utmost to depict the whole incident as an outright Bolshevik plot,[34] the reality was that they were more concerned about the Iranian aspect of the disturbances than the so-called 'Soviet' angle. Therefore the removal of those Iranian officials whom they considered as the actual sponsors of this campaign became a priority – people such as Muvaqqar and his relatives, and Marzban, the chief inspector of customs.[35]

With or without workers?

For the Iranian establishment the issue was much more complicated and the priorities not so clear. For example, Teymurtash at his first meeting with T.L. Jacks, the representative of the APOC, in Tehran on 5 May did not question his appreciation of the gravity of the situation in Abadan and did not hesitate to order the local authorities to cooperate in the suppression of the workers. In his second meeting with him, he showed a marked hesitation to comply with the wishes of the company, particularly the removal and punishment of those Iranian officials that the company suspected.

E.H. Elkington, in a report to Medlicott, attributed this 'unfortunate' change of mind to the misinformation and ill advice of 'certain elements who are hostile to our interests, amongst whom we strongly suspect Mirza Hussein Movvaquer [sic]. The result is most disturbing, and unless the

Minister of Court can be persuaded to re-adjust his views, a most dangerous reaction can be anticipated at our centres of operation.'[36]

Although once again the APOC's appreciation of the situation in
Khuzestan was exaggerated and no 'dangerous reactions' threatened those
centres of operations, what they considered as a change of mind and vacilla-
tion among the Iranian officials was quite correct.

In August 1929, when the APOC published its annual report, *Shafaq-i
surkh*, in an article under the title 'The Situation of the Iranian Workers and
the Annual Report of the Oil Company', pointed out that 'the policy of the
Anglo-Iranian [Company] in the south of Iran is based on the humiliation
and intimidation of the Iranian employees and workers. The administrators of the company, in dealing with the grievances of the Iranian workers
instead of trying to satisfy their demands, have always attempted to suppress
their feelings and keep them ignorant.'[37]

Then *Shafaq-i surkh*, in defence of the just demands of the Iranian workers, criticized Brigadier Farajullah Khan, the governor-general of Khuzestan,
who 'though being an honest official and a man of integrity, is not aware of
foreign intrigues' and without any justification was tricked into the suppression of an ordinary one-day strike.[38]

In refuting APOC's version of the incident, particularly their reports
on the 'Bolshevik' nature of the disturbances and the alleged intention of
the workers to set fire to the refinery, *Shafaq* also pointed out that 'our
officials, in the interest of the country and the exigencies of the prevailing
policy, for the time being are expedited to accept the irrational demands of
the Company in using force against the Iranian workers and to agree with
the arrest, imprisonment and banishment of a group of employees, but we
very much doubt they really believe that the Iranian employees and workers
were involved in a conspiracy and were influenced by collectivist ideas'. In
conclusion it asked the government 'to dispatch an able and patriotic official
to investigate the Khuzestan affair, so it could be proven that there has not
been any conspiracy to stage a riot or set fire to the refinery, and to find out
if any complaints had been aired that had to do with plain workers' grievances about meagre wages'.[39]

The Iranian establishment was well aware of the moral and political value
of having the Iranian workers on its side in the current campaign against the
Anglo-Iranian Oil Company but at the same time it was not quite sure how
to deal with it.

Muhammad Hasan Badi', the consul of Iran at Basreh, who had always
been critical of the APOC's activities in Khuzestan and particularly its treatment of the Iranian workers, in a detailed report on the Abadan disturbances

that he sent to Tehran after a tour of inspection there, gives an interesting picture of this dilemma. Even though he considered the Iranian workers quite justified in their claims against the company and even quoted one of the local authorities as saying that the whole incident had been 'highly exaggerated' by the British, and that 'the Company, in order to frame the Iranian workers and sack them, had brought in these accusations', nevertheless pointed out that 'the Governor of Abadan was right to act promptly ... because in a place like Abadan that is situated on the border it is not proper to let the workers [act in such a manner] as to give the British a pretext'.[40]

Being apprehensive about the potential dangers of an independent labour movement and at the same time being well aware of its worth in the current confrontation, Badi' recommended that a 'Permanent Commission' be set up, comprised of different Iranian officials such as the governors of Abadan and Khoramshahr, the head of Khuzestan's post office, the mayor of Abadan and a representative from the Ministry of Public Works as its chairman to deal with labour affairs. The workers had to address their complaints to this commission, and the commission in turn, 'by looking at the terms of the concession and the laws and regulations that were being abided by other oil companies, had to [satisfy their demands]. If the company was harassing the workers, to stop it and if the workers were in the wrong, to punish them.'[41]

For *Habl al-matin*, which considered the occurrence of industrial action such as that at Abadan an ordinary and common way of expressing labour dissatisfaction that was going to become normal practice in Iran, adopting a labour law was of the utmost urgency: 'the enactment of a law for this growing community in order to clarify the tasks of the proprietors and the obligations of the workers has to be the first priority of the State and parliament.'[42]

As far as we know, there was no 'competent and patriotic official' dispatched to investigate the Khuzestan affair to prove the innocence of the Iranian workers, nor was the adoption of a labour law contemplated. A 'Permanent Commission', such as Muhammad Hasan Badi' had in mind, was not formed and even if such a body had been established it is very doubtful whether it could have acted as a replacement for a genuine labour movement.

The fact is that after the May crackdown in Khuzestan and the suppression of the workers, the Iranian drive to force the Anglo-Iranian Oil Company to revise the 1901 D'Arcy oil concession lost much of its initial impetus. The campaign continued but in the meantime one of its main points of strength was discarded. From now on, most of the papers that had been particularly critical of the miserable situation of the Iranian workers tended to concentrate on less controversial aspects of the APOC's activities in Khuzestan.[43]

In November 1932, after the failure of a series of arduous negotiations with the APOC, the Iranians decided to announce the annulment of the D'Arcy concession. But it did not take the British long to persuade the Iranian government that they had no option but to give in. In a relatively short period of time Tehran had to negotiate a new concession that was not up to popular expectation. In contemplating the reasons why the government caved in so easily to the pressure of the British, the lack of any genuine local movement to rely on could be considered as an important factor.

In the early 1940s it seemed that for a short period of time the occurrence of a similar development in Iran was going to corner the government in the same awkward position: the outbreak of a series of sporadic industrial actions by the Iranian workers in the oil industry to seek better living conditions and higher wages, the prevailing attitude of the state in regard to 'labour unrest', and at the same time the emergence of a new movement against the British Oil Company, all pointed to the probable occurrence of the same dilemma. But the situation was totally different from the late 1920s. This time the workers were not excluded from the campaign. The collapse of Reza Shah's autocratic rule in the summer of 1941 and the gradual emergence of a democratic polity that in a short span of time gave rise to a popular and broadly based movement for the nationalization of the oil industry provided a harmonious outlet for what had hitherto tended to take a colliding and self-negating course.

8

Sufi Reactions Against the Reforms After Turkey's National Struggle: How a Nightingale Turned into a Crow [1]

Hülya Küçük

Over the past four decades Western experts on the Middle East and Islam have spilled much ink in accounting for the political role of those Islamic 'revivalist', 'resistance' and 'opposition' movements of the eighteenth and nineteenth centuries that seemed to derive their vitality from 'reformed' Sufi ideologies and institutions. According to many Western scholars, these ideologies and institutions arose in response to the new political and economic realities of the modern epoch, characterized, first and foremost, by Europe's growing ascendancy and the perceived decline of the Muslim world.[2] But what happened in the twentieth century and especially in Turkey in the 1900s is not fully treated. Only works describing some instances of opposition, like the Sheikh Sa'id revolt in 1925 and the Menemen Incident in 1930, are available.[3] In this study the whole story of what occurred in Turkey from 1925 onwards will be treated. Furthermore this study answers the question, 'How did Sufis react to the reforms presented after the National Struggle, in particular to the secularization of religious affairs?'

As is widely known, during the early years of Turkish reform,[4] Islam remained the state religion. In 1928, however, the article of the constitution declaring Islam as the state's religion was deleted.[5] While secularists did not oppose Islam as a faith, they condemned its dogmatism and alleged inherent opposition to technical and social progress. They assumed that religious movements were opposed to the republican regime. The prime examples of opposition were seen to be the Sheikh Sa'id revolt and the Menemen Incident. Secularization of social life took form partly as a struggle over symbols,[6] and partly as suppression of competing networks and focuses of loyalty, the Sufi orders being the most important of these. The Sufi orders had served vital religious, social and political functions throughout Ottoman history. According to Mardin, Islam's administrative vision can easily comply with the republican regime, as it holds everyone equal in the sight of God.[7] The only difference was that Mustafa Kemal wanted a community consisting of 'free' individuals seeing themselves as the source of legitimacy. Islam, on the other hand, binds people by religious rules or societies.[8] This difference in view made acceptance of Sufi orders in the new regime impossible. Hence, in spite of their support for the nationalists and their struggle, the Sufi orders had to be abolished.

On 30 August 1925 Mustafa Kemal made his renowned speech in Kastamonu. In it he launched the great attack on the *fez*, the gown, the *shalvar* and the other traditional garments of Turkish Muslims. Furthermore he spoke of the Dervish convents, retreats and brotherhoods, of their so-called saints and holy men, and of the tombs to which the ignorant and superstitious went to seek help and guidance.[9]

As Gologlu says: 'The structure and nature of [Turkish] man and community were not suitable for any kind of repressions. Therefore, in the Turkish Grand National Assembly (TBMM) the opposition never remained silent.'[10] Besides the general fact that change is not easily accepted in any level of society,[11] it was particularly difficult for Sufis of that time to accept it. One reason for this difficulty was that radical changes in these years brought the Sufis' credibility in society and their colourful life to an end: 'someone' turned into 'anyone'. Naturally they were saddened by this outcome. What would they be expected to do, or what could they actually do in response?[12] We will try to answer these questions by examining the reactions of famous Sufis who lived during and after that time. Our search for an answer is complicated by the fact that studies on Sufi activities after 1925, the year Sufi orders were closed down, are generally fragmentary and lack detail. Additionally it can be sometimes dangerous for scholars to write about the era,[13] and Sufis themselves were uncomfortable discussing or recording their memories of that time.[14] Consequently, how Sufis reacted to the events of the era is not easy to depict.

Generally speaking, although no public surveys were taken then or later,[15] we can state that Sufi reaction against the reforms carried out after the National Struggle was not homogeneous. There were rather progressive Sufis as well as those who were very reactionary. Some in the former category were acquainted with Western circles. They were close followers of the press of the second constitutional era and were acquainted with the intellectuals of the *Tanzimat* (Reforms) period. For them, the reforms were not unexpected; they considered the matters differently than others and accepted reforms easily.[16] There were even people who thought that it was only prophets or mystics who could make this kind of reform possible. But people like

İsmail Hakkı Baltacıoğlu (1886–1978)[17] disagreed with that idea, as they thought that seeds of reforms would be spread by thought and science.[18] In fact there was not much in the way of active reaction to the reforms from the community.[19] Ulama and Meshayikh, for instance, took the state's side a short time after any kind of reform. This was also true for the reforms after 1924, simply because the concept of 'state' was important in Turkish culture.[20] Some Sufis became silent in accordance with the Sufi rule that 'everything, good or bad, is from God. His grace, as well as his punishment is nice'.[21] Here it is important to emphasize that this did not mean that they neglected teaching Sufism to interested people around them.[22] Whether this new approach to teaching helped to build the type of community they desired is a matter of dispute among the Turkish Islamists. Some claim that the consequence of these 'secret teachings' was 'a nightingale turned into a crow' (that is, their secret work and effort did not produce the desired result, like a nightingale – in a country dominated by the crow – teaching her baby clandestinely how to sing as a nightingale; on the big day that the baby was thought to be ready, she sings like a crow).[23] Another group saw the reforms as part of 'state policy whose goals were unknowable but surely for the good of the community'. 'A group of them were already so fearful of the *Takrir-i Sükun Kanunu* (Maintenance of Order Law)[24] and Independence courts that they did not say a word concerning the reforms.'[25]

Another thing should be emphasized: although Mustafa Kara, an expert on Sufism today, says that the Malami Dervishes (who opposed the external manifestations or performance of Sufi practices openly in society, for example, using *tekke*s, Dervish costumes, etc) lived more comfortably than other Sufis in the republican era,[26] it was not always the case. For instance 'Abd al-'Aziz Mecdi Tolun (1865–1941), a Malami Dervish, refused any official job as a silent protest, a subject that will be treated further in this chapter. Here it should be kept in mind that the most recent Malamis (Muhammad Nuru'l-Arabi's (d.1305/1878) followers) had *tekke*s, although these were used only as a place for discussions on religious matters. Only on Fridays were there *dhikr* ceremonies, and these were conducted merely to follow the Sufi orders.[27] Another thing is that Malamism is not a Sufi order but a kind of Sufi disposition that can be found in each Sufi order.[28] There are also special Malami *silsila*s,[29] but latest Malami representatives did not give any *ijaza* to anyone.[30] In the 1920s there were Malamis who lived in Rumelia, Istanbul and around Izmir, especially in Tire, which was their centre.[31] Gölpınarlı gives a list of recent (that is 1920s) Malamis.[32] I tried to study those who lived after 1925 but could not acquire any specific information about their attitude towards the reforms, except 'Abd al-'Aziz Mecdi Tolun, who was not mentioned in Gölpınarlı's work.

In any case, we can definitely say that those who could easily integrate into or support the new reforms were in the majority. Because Sufism is based on an intimate and personal contact with God, and because the secularism presented in that period stressed the necessity of practising Islam privately, there seemed to be no conflict. Thus Sufis, who were not interested or involved in political activities, had no problems with the abolition of the caliphate and the Ministry of the *Shar'iyya wa Awkaf,* or banning the Sufi orders etc. Many were even ready to be used as a medium of legitimizing these reforms. However, their costumes, culture, tradition and cosmology would not be helpful to the modernization process. Therefore they were not selected as a legitimizing medium.[33] A couple of open/armed opposition incidents of which some Sufis were alleged to be the leaders have not been and cannot be studied objectively, as it is not possible to study first hand unpublished archival material. The official historiography is of the opinion that the people involved in these incidents belonged to Sufi circles. At the same time, Sufi circles deny any involvement in them. Therefore, with no concrete documentation, the problem remains unsolved. Here, we will first present some examples of the reactions of the period and then give an evaluation of them in the conclusion.

Opposition

(1) Those who supported the National Struggle but changed their attitudes soon after the reforms because they could not comply with them

Sheikh Şerafeddin Dağıstani (d.1936),[34] famous Naqshi sheikh. Despite his support during the National Struggle, he was sent to the Independence Tribunal because of his hostility towards the new government, as he changed his attitude soon after the caliphate was banned.[35] There is no clue as to the outcome of the trial in the sources. After the banning of the Sufi orders in Turkey in 1925, he went to Jordan.[36] After a while he returned to Turkey and was imprisoned in Eskişehir, together with famous Bediüzzaman Sa'id Nursi.[37] He died shortly after he was released.[38]

Salih Niyazi Baba, head of the Bektashi Babagan branch at that time,[39] when he heard about the decision to close down the *tekke*s, merely said, 'This means that we are not eligible for this task,' and left the *dargah.* However, he believed that although the buildings of *dargahs* could be closed, the real living place of Sufism, i.e. the hearts of individuals, could not be. He occupied himself as the manager of a hotel (the Anadolu Otel) at Ulus in Ankara. He tried to use the hotel as a *dargah,* but was not permitted to do so.

Nevertheless, according to Şevki Koca Baba's quote from his father (Turgut Koca), Salih Niyazi Baba managed to continue his activities clandestinely as *Dedebaba* until 1927. On 17 January 1930 he, together with some other *Mujarrad babas*, left Ankara for Tirana, Albania, and was welcomed warmly by the Bektashi community there. Bektash Baba and a group of *Mujarrad Babas* also went to Albania after Salih Niyazi Baba had left Turkey.

Salih Niyazi Baba tried to transfer the centre of Bektashism to Albania, but could not obtain permission from the Albanian king, (Ahmed) Zog, who believed that the real centre of Bektashism was in Turkey. Nevertheless the Bektashis looked upon the *tekke* in Tirana as their main *tekke*. Salih Niyazi Baba was elected to the post of *Dedebaba* of the Bektashi community in 1930, and held it until he was killed in 1941 (or 1942) by the Italian forces occupying Albania during their efforts to crush the liberation movement.[40]

Selman Cemali Baba[41] is understood to have left Istanbul for Albania earlier than Salih Niyazi and Bektash Baba, that is, after the hat reform. He took refuge in Albania, as he did not want to wear a hat. He served as *Baba* at the Elbasan *tekke* and possibly died there.

Mehmed Akif Ersoy. Although he was a neo-Salafi (who oppose some Sufi rituals and seek to change some Sufi innovations),[42] he had a mystical personality, as indicated by his stay at Taceddin *dargah* during the National Struggle[43] and by the mystic poems he wrote after 1925.[44] Also, in one of the letters he wrote during his first visit to Egypt (dated 8 March 1925), he said: 'My disposition towards Sufism is increasing as much as it can. Man should do his best to achieve his goal, but if he does not reach the goal, should not cry out. I feel that I am going through this point out of my will.'[45] As can clearly be seen, he was disappointed and saddened, with no more energy to continue as an activist. Nevertheless, as a good Sufi, he did not cry out. As his hopes to see the Turkish people lead unity among Muslim countries vanished after the new Turkish state was established with secularism as its main principle, he went again to Egypt, or rather went into seclusion (1926–36).[46] This great poet, writer of the *İstiklal Marşı* (Independence Anthem), did not write many poems in Egypt. Among those he did write while there, are *Gece*, *Secde* and *Hicran* which contain the concept of *Wahdat al-Wujud* (Unity of Being).[47] Before he went to Egypt, he was entrusted by the TBMM with performing the Turkish translation of the Holy Koran. He did the job in Egypt, but when he left the country, he gave the manuscript to one of his closest friends and said: 'If I can come back, I take it back. If not, you do not give it to anyone, and if they ask, you say "it does not exist".' (In another version of the story, he instructs him to 'burn it'.[48]) The motive behind this reaction may be the rumour at that time that the newly founded Turkish government, as part of reforms in the religious affairs, was planning to set up a Turkish Koran to be used in prayers instead of the Arabic text. The translation would be used for that purpose. Newspapers of the time were full of debates on the issue.[49]

Bediüzzaman Sa'id Nursi (d.1960). During the National Struggle he believed that the nationalists were really trying to save the sultan/caliph and, as a unionist, he supported them. For instance, he supported the anti-*fatwa* of the nationalists. At Mustafa Kemal's invitation he visited the TBMM towards the end of 1922, delivered a speech and prayed for their further success.[50] His statement to the MPs gives the impression that he would continue to support them if they would adhere to Islamic rules. This was not, however, the message Ankara expected; it wanted unconditional submission and support. Thus his approval came to nothing and he then became a fierce opponent of reform.

(2) The silent opposition

There were Sufis who did not accept any sort of official job as a sign of their silent opposition, although they did not become involved in any uprisings.

Süleymancıs (those affiliated with Naqshi Süleyman Seyfullah Efendi (1863–1946)) are an instance of what Gölpınarlı describes when he says that they did not accept even teaching positions for the secular regime, as in that case they would be obliged to teach some secular doctrines.[51]

'Abd al-'Aziz Mecdi Tolun (1865–1941),[52] a Kadiri-Malami (as a disciple of one of the last Malamis, Ahmed Amiş Efendi (d.1338/1919), who did not want to use the word 'Malami', and even forbade his disciples to use it[53]) is another distinctive instance. During the abolition of the Sufi orders, he worked in Ankara as an official at the *Shar'iyya wa Awkaf*. To avoid any possibility of being offered a position at the Directorate of Religious Affairs, he went to Istanbul. Never leaving the confines of his home, he occupied himself with praying, reading and writing religious books. To anyone asking 'why he does not accept any official job,' he replied, 'I do not want. If I am wanted, I can think about it.'[54] His attitude helped to increase his popularity and induced many people to visit him. Receiving approximately ten visitors a day, on holidays and holy nights, this number would increase (he kept a list of visitors).[55] As he had some adversaries from the ulama group and from some politicians (he was a unionist),[56] he was sometimes accused of defending Sufi orders. Although the authorities did not pay attention to these accusations,[57] he was very careful not to give the impression that he was a Sufi. He burnt the letters he received and kept a list of visitors as evidence in case the authorities asked who had been to see him and why.[58] He was also very careful not to speak on Sufi matters in public. He was very selective in his contacts and afraid of being reported to the authorities.

(3) Those who openly opposed the reforms/regime

A few who were not happy with the reforms opposed (or allegedly opposed) them openly: Sheikh Sa'id, Mustafa Çavuş and Veli Dede, some Sufis in the Free Republican Party, Sa'id Nursi (d.1960), Sheikh Es'ad Erbili (1867–1931) and 'Abd al-Hakim Arvasi (1865-1943), and Tijanis.

Sheikh Sa'id's revolt was an indication of the extent and type of unhappiness that the reforms caused. According to several sources, with the abolition of the caliphate, the most important symbol of Turkish–Kurdish brotherhood disappeared. It became possible to condemn the Ankara government as irreligious, an accusation that seemed to be confirmed by other measures it took.[59] The major motive behind the rebellion was the creation of an independent Kurdish state (where Islamic principles, violated in modern Turkey, were to be respected).[60] This independent state, which was granted by Articles 62, 63 and 65 of the Sèvres Treaty, signed on 10 August 1920, went against the *Misak-i Milli*, the goal of the National Struggle.[61] The case of the Kurds was not mentioned in the subsequent Treaty of Lausanne (signed on 24 July 1923), a great disappointment to Kurdish nationalists. This process was accelerated by the British who were trying to cut off that region from the oilfields, by communists who hoped to benefit from anarchy in the region, and by plunderers.[62] This attitude led to a great rebellion planned by the Azadi (Freedom) Society, founded in 1923 by former militia officers,[63] and the Naqshbandi Sheikh Sa'id of Palu, who was very influential among the Zaza tribes. The insurrection broke out in Diyarbakır and spread among all the Zaza and two Kormanji tribes, but divisions between the Kurds became apparent.[64] In the end the Kurdish rebels were pushed back into the mountains and Sheikh Sa'id was seized on 15 April 1925. He and his accomplices were sentenced to death by the Independence Tribunal in Diyarbakır on 29 June 1925.[65]

According to Zürcher, it was the Sheikh Sa'id rebellion that created the atmosphere and the mechanisms necessary to silence the opposition (through the *Takrir-i Sükun Kanunu* (Maintenance of Order Law)) and carry out the purges of 1926.[66] However, the Independence Tribunal in Diyarbakır sentenced the leaders of the Sheikh Sa'id rebellion to death. The same tribunal ordered the closing down of all Dervish convents in the southeastern region. The Independence Tribunal in Ankara called the attention of the government to this issue.[67]

Bediüzzaman Sa'id Nursi, who was sympathetic to, or even affiliated with, the Naqshbandiyya Order,[68] was allegedly involved in the incident, and was thus exiled to a little town (Barla, bound to Isparta) in western Anatolia. In exile he compiled his *tafsir* (Koran commentary) works, preached and became even more popular than before.[69] Some sources say that earlier, during his seclusion in Van, Kör Hüseyin Pasha, who furnished soldiers and arms/ammunition to the Sheikh Sa'id revolt, asked his help and gave him many gold coins. Sa'id Nursi did not want this money and told him to spend it on the poor in the region. He stated that he would not be associated with those who were making Turkish soldiers kill each other. He also received a letter from Sheikh Sa'id but replied to it with the words, 'Turks are a nation who carried Islam's flag to everywhere. They trained many saints and gave many martyrs for the cause of Islam. Swords cannot be drawn on the descendants of this nation.'[70] However, there were indications that he did not support the newly imposed reforms. For instance, he did not use the new alphabet and never wore a hat. He wrote and published his famous *Risale-i Nur* in the Arabic alphabet. As a result *Risale-i Nur* was continually persecuted until 1956. Only after that year did Tahsin Kola receive permission to publish these works in the Arabic alphabet.[71]

Sa'id Nursi tried to revive the Islamic faith in the community. He claimed not to be a Sufi or Sufi sheikh but wanted to be known as an *Imam* (leader) like Ghazali (d.1111) and Ahmed Sirhindi (d.1624), the great Naqshi revivalist.[72] It is generally known that although he was previously a great Sufi, after the reforms he changed his tactics and said that the time is not the time of Sufi orders, but of the faith.[73] Nevertheless many researchers believe that there were 'two Sa'ids' in Bediüzzaman Sa'id Nursi's lifetime: Sa'id before the republican regime and Sa'id after. Although the first Sa'id was very intimate with the Sufi orders, and counted them among the main institutions of Islam, along with *madrasa*s and schools, the second Sa'id distanced himself not only from the Sufi orders but from Sufism as well. He said, 'Our way is not the *Tarikat* (Sufi order), but the *Hakikat* (Reality, God)', meaning, 'I am not a Sufi.'[74]

Today his followers are known as *Nurcus*, and the most famous of them is Fetullahcıs (Fetullah Gülen and his group) who became associated with many modern, well-equipped schools in Turkey as well as other countries, beginning with Turkish states in Central Asia. Earlier they were accepted by some officials as the most modern Islamic group, but nowadays they too are under suspicion, beginning with their leader, who fled to the USA.[75]

Another instance was the case of two men, Mustafa Çavuş and Veli Dede, who tried to recruit a Bektashi battalion in April 1925 against the new government. They were tried by the Independence Tribunal of Ankara.[76] However, it was revealed during the trial that the former was a charlatan who tried to collect money by deceiving the Bektashis and Alevis around Antalya into believing that he was an inspector of Çelebi.[77]

The sources indicate that in the short-lived (founded in September 1930 and dissolved in November 1930) Free Republican Party (FRP),[78] there were some people who had previously attended the *tekkes*.[79] However, we do not possess any names.

The Menemen Incident. This incident was interpreted as, but never proven to be, the consequence of freedom granted through the establishment of the FRP in 1930.[80] The incident occurred on 23 December 1930. Giritli Derviş Mehmed (who claimed to be a *Mahdi*) and his accomplices revolted against the reforms. Kubilay, a teacher, who first reacted to this revolt, was murdered by the rebels. A court martial sentenced 28 rebels to capital punishment; all were hanged in Menemen.[81] It was claimed that this incident occurred as a result of the provocations of Mohammed Es'ad Erbili, the famous Naqshi sheikh.[82] (Laz Ibrahim, one of the suspected, had relations with his son, Mehmed Ali, an expert on snuff.[83]) He was an old man who decided not to go out of his home at Erenköy, Istanbul, after the *tekke*s were closed. He and his son Mehmed Efendi were captured, as they were thought to be involved in this incident. Sentenced initially to death, Es'ad Efendi's penalty, because of his age, was commuted to a life sentence. He died a year later. His body was not delivered to his family and he was buried somewhere in Menemen.[84]

'Abd al-Hakim Arvasi, Sheikh of Naqshi Kaşgari *Dargah*, was also under suspicion during this incident. He was confined in Izmir, but after a while was set free. Necip Fazıl Kısakürek (d.1983) and Hüseyin Hilmi Işık (d.2001) were among his most famous disciples.[85]

Mustafa Kara says that just as the Bektashis were the scapegoats in the 1830s, the Naqshis were treated the same in the 1930s. He continues: 'In the later years, *tekke*s, [those] who attend *tekke*s and Sufi orders were always the assumed culprits, labelled as "guilty" openly or in an allusive way.'[86] It was always stressed that it was the Naqshis, the most reactionary Sufi order who led all the revolts since the 31 March incident.[87] According to Mustafa Kemal: 'This order is a snake. It should be wiped out.'[88] It should be stressed here that although it is true that the Naqshis, in particular its Mujaddidiya branch, were conservative and very actively involved in socio-political matters, there were also very non-conservative Sufis among them from Kalandariyya and Malamatiyya.[89] For instance the last Malami representative, Muhammad Nuru'l-'Arabi (d. 1305/1878), was a Naqshi.[90] Also the Arusiyya, a mixed form of Naqshbandiyya and Kadiriyya,[91] was spread among progressive military men.[92]

Sufi circles do not accept that Derviş Mehmed and his accomplices were Sufis. Some Sufis stress that they were 'ignorant and unstable' (*cahil ve muvazenesiz*) 'miserables' (*zavallılar*).[93] This opinion was also stressed by Burhanettin Onat in a TBMM session.[94] As Mango says, 'the strictly orthodox Nakşibendis were unlikely to approve messianic claims of a Dervish, who, according to witnesses, was addicted to drugs.[95] Besides, Derviş Mehmed and his accomplices were so psychologically unstable that they perceived themselves to be the *Ashab-ı Kehf*,[96] as they have a dog named "Kıtmir".'[97]

It is also claimed that the Menemen Incident was a result of Jewish provocations, and there were some people from minorities (Cretans, Greeks and a Jew) among the suspects.[98]

Tijanis. Tijaniyya was an order made up of Kadiriyya and Naqshbandiyya, spread out mostly in Morocco, Senegal, Egypt and Hejaz, and related to Abu al-Abbas Ahmad b. Muhammad al-Tijani (d.1230/1815). He was born in southern Algeria.[99] It was Kemal Pilavoğlu (d.1977), a graduate of the faculty of law, who brought the order to Turkey. He became affiliated with the order in 1930s, and in 1942 one of his disciples, Sadık Çakırtepe, actually made it into the order.[100] Its adherents were very conservative and violent. (The word 'Tijani' even became an expression for violent people or kids. Mothers used to say to their naughty children, 'Are you a Tijani?') They were known for their attacks on statues of Atatürk and for opposing Turkish *Adhan*. They caused about 51 incidents between 1949 and 1951.[101] In 1951 Kemal Pilavoğlu was sentenced to ten years in prison, five years of exile in Bozcaada, and five years of compulsory residence on Imroz island. He published many books on religion. He was even the one who wrote the greatest number of religious works between the years 1950 and 1960.[102]

(4) Those who escaped abroad to continue their religious/political activities

Rıza Tevfik (Bölükbaşı, 1869–1949). A Bektashi. After the National Struggle, he escaped to Jordan. He was also among the 150 Undesirables.[103]

Zeynelabidin Efendi (1869–1940). A prominent Naqshi sheikh and Khoja, senator, MP for Konya. He was initially a member of the *Ahali Fırkası* (People's Party) that later merged with the *Hürriyet ve Itilaf Fırkası* (HIF, Freedom and Coalition Party). He was exiled to Gemlik during the reign of the *Ittihad ve Terakki Cemiyeti* (Union and Progress), but returned after the Mudros Armistice. According to Mewlanzade Rifat, it was he who revived the HIF in 1918, together with Mustafa Sabri Efendi.[104] He was an influential *khoja* sheikh in Konya, and, as an anti-nationalist, was the favourite of the sultan and the Entente powers.[105] Following the victory of the nationalists, he fled to Egypt. He was the 26th of the 150 Undesirables. [106] He died in Medina.[107] An eyewitness who knew Konya very well, Ali Osman Koçkuzu (1936–), says: 'His descendants are under suspicion. Hence, they always show extra attention to wear modern costumes and avoid any political activities, fearing persecution by the authorities.'[108]

Support and legitimization

(1) Those who accepted or pretended to accept the reforms

These mostly assumed official positions and pursued their Sufi activities in secret. The majority of Sufis followed this example.

Mehmed Şemseddin (Ulusoy) Efendi (1879–1936) was Sheikh of Mısri *dargah* (a Khalwati *dargah*) in Bursa and worked as *imam* after 1925.[109] 'As with any human being, Mehmed Şemseddin Bey's ideas and opinions had changed along with the circumstances and knowledge.'[110] For instance, after 1925 he stated that the caliphate did not help towards the liberation of the nation, and it was Ghazi and the Ankara government that did its best to this end.[111] He stated that the way of Sufis is a way between God and man, and hence there is no need to enter financial institutions (he means Sufi orders, *tekkes*).[112] As to the *dhikr*, man does not need *tekke* for it; according to the Koran's verses, which state 'remember God wherever you are', man can perform *dhikr* everywhere.[113]

'Abd al-Baki Baykara (1883–1935) was Sheikh of Mevlevi Yenikapı *dargah* since 1908. After 1925 he taught Persian at theology and arts faculties, and after the university (*Darulfünun*) reform taught at Bakırköy Armenian

Lyceum. His poem *oldum* (I became) illustrates very well the changes a Sufi underwent at that time:

> Cutting my white feathers, I changed into a pretty young girl,
> While previously, I was an old man.
> I became an elder Magi, while previously I was a Mevlevi Sheikh,
> I became neither a pure Muslim, nor completely infidel.
> On my tongue, the light of my faith, on my head a pitch-dark hat,
> So I became visible in the dark, like a false dawn.
> I left *Sema* (whirling), but did not learn how to dance.
> That is, I became a Muslim, worse than a Selanik Sabataist.
> Morning coat, cylinder hat became headdress of the Mullah
> I got myself ridiculed in front of the whole people.
> I could obtain neither any grace from my forefathers,
> Nor became beloved to the Republican regime.
> Thinking over the meaning of 'patience is the key to joys',
> Like the slow Patriarch of the time, I became non-conferred a favour.
> If I would be examined in ignorance and foolishness,
> *Madrasa* teachers would leave me behind.
> While previously I was dancing with the melody of *Ney*
> Now I became personified, distressed by the evil of dance.[114]

Sheikh Rahmi Baba (Sezgin, d.1935 or 1936).[115] It is very interesting that he, with a group of other Sufis, decided not to oppose Mustafa Kemal because of a dream he had. In the 1930s he invited some sheikhs and Sufis to a small Anatolian town to 'place/say a curse' on Mustafa Kemal. But the night before the gathering, he had a dream. In it he saw the Prophet Muhammad in front of a map, dividing the world among some people. Turkey, which clearly appeared in green, was surrounded with black, wide, but low walls. Mustafa Kemal stood somewhere on Thrace with his back turned to the Prophet. When Turkey's turn comes, the Prophet says, 'Give this to him.' 'This' is Turkey; 'him' is 'Mustafa Kemal. After describing the dream to the invitees, he interpreted it as follows: 'Turkey was green. This is a good sign, as green is a favourable colour according to Islam. It is surrounded with black walls. Black is not a good colour; it means *Küfr* (blasphemy). Nevertheless, the wall is low. This is also a good sign. Thus, in spite of everything, the Prophet gave Turkey to him [Mustafa Kemal]. This is the Prophet's unwilling approval of his leadership for Turkey.' After this event, he gave up placing curses on Mustafa Kemal and stopped opposing him.[116]

Ahmet Remzi Akyürek (d.1944). A Mevlevi. In 1919 he was Sheikh of Üsküdar Mevlevihane. After the banning of the orders, he worked at Üsküdar

Selimağa Library, and after 1937 at Ankara *Eski Eserler* (Ancient Works) Library.[117] A retired military man, Sadeddin Evrin is one of his admirers. His poem *Ankaraname* is one of his most interesting. Some couplets from the poem are as follows:

> A city of puzzle cannot be solved, Ankara,
> From all aspects, a very distinctive city is Ankara.
> It is understood what progress is,
> Each day Ankara is taking a step. ...
>
> By changing the alphabet, made things easier for the nation,
> Ankara made all the villagers 'clerks'. ...
>
> It taught us many languages we did not know,
> It solved all the problems concerning language. ...
>
> One direction, one front, one party, one administration at once,
> What a power! Ankara united all tendencies.[118]

Süleyman Hilmi Tunahan (1889–1959). A famous Naqshi, whose followers are now known as *Süleymancıs*. He worked as a preacher for the republican regime, but was arrested several times. His main services were in teaching the Koran, mostly in secret.[119] His disciples follow in his footsteps, holding illegal Koran courses at homes.

Bozkırlı 'Abd Allah Efendi (Tanrıkulu, 1883–1942). A Naqshi. Unlike Zeynelabidin *Khoja* from the same lineage, he worked first as *Khoja*, and later as an employee at the General Directorate of *Awkaf.*[120]

'Abd al-'Aziz Bekkine (1865–1952). One of the last Naqshi sheikhs. He also worked as *imam* in Istanbul (at the Zeyrek, Ümmü Gülsüm mosque).[121] He had many renowned disciples, including Nurettin Topçu (d.1975), leader of *Anadoluculuk* (Anatolian movement).[122] Naqshi groups in today's Turkey have *silsilas* going back to him.

Hacı Hasan (Yavuz) Efendi. For some 40 years he worked as an *imam* for the republican regime and used the basement of his home as a *madrasa*, teaching Islamic sciences. He especially instructed his students to teach the Koran even if only to one person, to learn the Ottoman script and to enter a Sufi order,[123] that is clandestinely.

Süheyl Ünver (1898–1986). A prominent medical and art historian. Besides his published works, he left more than 1,000 notebooks, some of which have not yet been inventoried.[124] He wrote many books concerning medical history and Ottoman–Islamic culture. He was a man of Dervish character and very much interested in Sufism.[125] In fact he was a Mevlevi-Malami, a close disciple of the famous Mevlevi Ahmet Remzi Akyürek[126] and Malami 'Abd al-'Aziz Mecdi Tolun.[127] He is also said to have been a *murid* of Naqshi Küçük Hüseyin Efendi, and an Arusi.[128] In outward appearance he was a modern man, inwardly he was a classical Sufi. He wore a hat and tie. However, 'he definitely knew that it was not the republican regime's promises which can help Turkish people stand firm and go further'. He always kept himself interested in Ottoman–Islamic culture.[129]

If we rely on contemporary publications, some Sufis accepted or continued their former high-ranking official jobs, and some famous Turkish politicians who lived before and after 1925 were affiliated with certain Sufi orders. For example, Fevzi Çakmak (1856–1950),[130] Alparslan Türkeş (1917–97)[131] and Rauf Orbay (d.1964)[132] are said to be Arusi, a branch of Shadhiliyya.[133]

Allegations concerning Fevzi Çakmak seem quite plausible because he now lies buried next to the tomb of Sheikh Küçük Hüseyin Hüsni Efendi (1244–1348/1828–1930) at Eyüp, Kırk Merdivenler, the Hill of Melek Efendi in Istanbul[134] although his grandson, A. Fevzi Çakmak, denies that he was an Arusi.[135] He was among the visitors to a Naqshi-Khalidi sheikh, Hüseyin Hüsni Efendi, who was known as 'Küçük Hüseyin Efendi' or Hüseyin Efendi Ankaravi. Ömer Fevzi Mardin, one of his disciples, was the representative of Arusiyya in Turkey.[136]

As for Türkeş and Orbay, I rather doubt it. At least, after a series of instalments in *Yeni Şafak* about Türkeş's being Arusi,[137] his family and close friends reacted harshly, saying that he had contacts with many sheikhs as a politician but never became a *murid* of anyone.[138]

Accepting official jobs is definitely a socio-economic phenomenon. Like ordinary members of society, Sufis needed credibility and a job to secure a living. After the Dervish convents were closed, the last Meshayikh and *Baba*s continued to receive allowances until their death. Some of these Meshayikh were already appointed to certain religious positions such as *imam* and *muedhdhin*, bound to the Directorate of Religious Affairs. Ordinary members established their private works.[139] However, accepting an official job is also a kind of acceptance and approval of official authority. Hence, there were Sufis/Sufi groups who did not accept any sort of official jobs, such as Süleymancıs.

(2) Those who actually supported the reforms

Some Sufi leaders favoured the reforms and, therefore, could be used as a medium of legitimization for those reforms. Indeed some were ready to fulfil this role. Some accepted or integrated into the new reforms, or even led them.

Sheikh Muhammed Razi (1889–1978). A sheikh of the Sümbüliyye Order (a branch of Khalwatiyya),[140] he was among the *Muntekhab-ı Thani* (Second Electorate)[141] of the *Koca* Mustafa Pasha in Istanbul. In a document dated 5 June 1923 we see that he gave his word to vote for Mustafa Kemal's candidates. The document states: 'I promise to support the announced principles of Mustafa Kemal Pasha.' Upon receiving this, Mustafa Kemal sent him a thank-you telegram saying that he strongly believed that he (Razi Efendi) would vote for Kemal's candidates.[142] This document means that he worked for the second TBMM, a strongly reformist assembly, and articulates his support for the republican regime. There were two other sheikhs among this *Muntekhab-ı Thani* group.[143] Sheikh Razi Efendi worked as *imam* for a while after the banning of the orders and later on, worked as an employee affiliated with the Ministry of Finance. He attended the '41st Nation School' to learn the new alphabet.[144]

Safvet (Yetkin, d.1950). A Khalwati sheikh and MP for Urfa in the second TBMM, he was chosen to present the bill putting an end to the caliphate and exiling the Ottoman dynasty.[145]

Yahya Galib (Kargı, 1874–1942). A Khalwati sheikh and MP for Kırşehir in the first, second and third terms of the TBMM, MP for Ankara in the fourth, fifth, and sixth terms of the TBMM. Along with Samih Rıfat, a Bektashi and MP for Biga in the first TBMM, he was one of those who proposed the above-mentioned bill.[146]

The Mevlevi sheikh at the main *dargah* in Konya, **'Abd al-Halim Çelebi** (1874–1925), sent a letter of congratulations to Mustafa Kemal for abolishing the caliphate and deporting the caliph, a member of the sultan's family, whom he described as a *'ta'un, bela'* (a pest).[147] In the letter he apologized for his late reaction because of his recurrent illness, and wished Mustafa Kemal success in his further endeavours.[148]

Some other prominent Mevlevi Meshayikh in Kastamonu, the *post-nishins* of the Shemsi-zade *dargah*, Ziyaeddin; of the Hazret-i Piri *dargah*, Sheikh Mehmed Ata; of the Mevlevi *dargah*, Tahir Çelebi, also sent a message of congratulations to the TBMM for the abolition of the caliphate. They endorsed the legality of this action and emphasized that 'the caliphate, which was never perceived among the main principles of Islam – because in Islam there was no need for a mediator between God and his creatures – was serving as a tool for the personal desires and interests of the ignorant, tyrannical sultans who could try to divide the people, and desire to govern the nation arbitrarily and ally with the enemies of Turkey to get their positions back.' Further, they added that 'therefore, it was harmful to the country, and its abolition complied with the will of nation and the *Shari'a*'.[149]

Veled Çelebi (Izbudak, 1869–1953). A Mevlevi sheikh and MP for Kastamonu in the second, third and fourth terms of the Assembly. In the sixth term he was MP for Yozgat. He was among the first to wear a hat.[150] In one of his poems, ending each quatrain 'Don't touch my hat, o *Khoja*', he said:

> If twelve thousand Muslims
> Wear the same costume
> It becomes religiously legal,
> Don't touch my hat, o *Khoja*!
> O *Khoja*, let's talk plainly,
> Did our Prophet wear a *kavuk*?
> All costumes are approved by (our) religion,
> Don't touch my hat, o *Khoja*![151]

Şükri Efendi. Sheikh of a former Rufai *tekke*, was among the personalities who received a telegram from Mustafa Kemal for their close concern regarding the reforms.[152]

Elmalılı Hamdi Yazır (1878–1942). A member of the Sha'baniyya Sufi order.[153] During the National Struggle, he was tried and consequently sentenced to death *in absentia* by the Independence Tribunal of Ankara. He worked officially for the Istanbul government as minister of *Awkaf* during the first and second Damad ferit Pasha cabinet. He was a member of A'yan Group (Senate) and a *Mudarris* at Süleymaniye at the same time. But he was released, as he was a member of the ITC.[154] After his trial, he did not go out of his house except to the mosque for prayer.[155] At the same time he was so trusted by the newly founded government that he was put in charge of compiling a Koran translation and commentary. According to Bilmen, this was because he was an adequate scholar, not involved in any kind of political activities, although he was previously an MP.[156] At that time there were rumours that the new government would use the translation/commentary for some reform purposes (such as for prayer in Turkish).[157] So, at the first instance, he noted down in the preface of his eight-volume commentary (*Hak Dini Kur'an Dili*) that the translation/commentary could not be used in the Arabic Koran's place. But after an official report was presented to the authorities by a commission entrusted with this task, he deleted that note.[158]

Hacıbeyzade Ahmed Muhtar (Yeğtaş, 1871–1955). A Bektashi *Baba*, he was connected to the Fıtriyya school, which defends the unity of all religions in the world. He had some other ideas, such as the legality of praying without a turban. Unlike some other Bektashi *babas*, he wore a hat.[159]

Ken'an Rifa'i (Büyükaksoy, d.1950). A sheikh of his mother's *dargah*, named 'Ümm-i Ken'an' (Ken'an's Mother). He did not voice any kind of dissent when the Sufi orders closed down. Once he met with Sheikh Baki Efendi, sheikh of Topkapı Mevlevikhane. Sheikh Baki Efendi complained to him about the closing down of the orders saying, 'We became like a pipe (short and tight), while previously we were playing together by Mevlana's *Nay*.' Ken'an Rifa'i replied, 'Why are we like a pipe? We are now, what we were earlier. Earlier we were in visible *tekkes*, now in an inner, heart *tekke*. Allah wished so, and made so. Everything from Him is fine. There is no reason to be a pipe.' He was of the opinion that Sufi orders had completed their roles, and now they had nothing to give the community. He did not give his students any kind of practical information regarding the Sufi orders. He was so obedient to the newly imposed laws that he did not allow the making of *sema* even in a small group consisting of three people including himself, and said, 'If the law said it is forbidden, it is forbidden.' In any case, he did not see any difference between Sufi *sema* and modern dance. He said, 'Only the goal is different.'[160] He was a liberal-minded person.[161] For instance, he was interviewed by the press concerning his ideas on the closing down of the *tekke*s. He stated that he approved of this, and added that only a few out of some 300 *tekke*s in Istanbul were in the service of knowledge, and in fact they had played their part in history.[162]

He worked as a teacher at the *Fener Rum Lisesi* (Lyceum) after the banning of the orders. His most famous disciples are women with a very modern orientation (such as Semiha Ayverdi (d.1993), Nezihe Araz (1922–) and Safiye Erol (d.1964)).[163] His understanding of Sufism can be described as 'intellectual Sufism'.[164]

Conclusion

The cases referred to in this article are the most conspicuous examples from the era. As to resolving the questions of 'Did the Sufis really change?', 'Were they sincere?', 'Did they pretend to have changed because they were afraid of the Independence Tribunals?', we do not know for sure. Nevertheless we can assume that some of them changed because they were afraid of the Independence Tribunals. Tahir al-Mevlevi is a distinctive example. When he heard the call to the court, he wore a hat, thinking that it was the reason for his call.[165] Maybe a Sufi saying can help us understand the majority Sufi stance: 'Sufi is son of the time; He does what must be done,'[166] or, as Sa'id Nursi says, 'Everything you say should be true, but you do not have the right to say everything is true. Everything you say must be right, but it is not right to say everything is right.'[167]

As to the motives that led Turkish Sufis to oppose the reforms, besides being 'religious', they were political: they opposed the abolition of the caliphate, as in the case of Şerafeddin Dağıstani, Mehmed Akif, Sa'id Nursi, Sheikh Sa'id, Veli Dede, Sufis in the Liberal Party, Derviş Mehmed, Tijanis, Rıza Tevfik and Zeynelabidin Efendi.

There were social motives: after 1925 Sufis' credibility in society and their colourful life came to an end; 'someone' turned into 'anyone'. Salih Niyazi, Bektash and some other Bektashi *Babas* sought refuge in Albania. Selman Cemali Baba's and Sa'id Nursi's rejection of wearing a hat was a protest against a reform with some social aspects. And the cases that involved minorities, such as the Sheikh Sa'id revolt and the Derviş Mehmed incident, carry an ethno-social colour.

There were economic motives: Süleymancıs and 'Abd al-'Aziz Mecdi Tolun, who were not offered any official jobs, were part of the silent opposition.

There were mystical motives: Mehmed Akif and 'Abd al-'Aziz Mecdi Tolun both chose silent opposition in accordance with the Sufi rule *'Riza'*.

There were cultural motives: Mehmed Akif did not deliver his Koran translation/commentary to the government, Sa'id Nursi rejected the use of the new alphabet, Süleymancıs refused to become teachers so as to avoid teaching the new regime's principles, and Tijanis opposed the 'Turkish' *adhan*.

Thus there were political motives (10 out of 14 cases treated here), social (six out of 14 cases), economic (two out of 14 cases), mystical (two out of 14 cases) and cultural (four out of 14 cases).

The motives that led Turkish Sufis to accept or pretend to accept or support the new regime, besides being religious, were political: Mehmed

Şemseddin Efendi, Muhammed Razi Efendi, Fevzi Çakmak, M. Safvet Yetkin, Yahya G. Kargı, 'Abd al-Halim Çelebi, Veled Çelebi and three other Mevlevi sheikhs all gave their support to banning the caliphate, legitimized the new regime and, in turn, became legitimized in the eyes of the new regime.

There were social motives: 'Abd al-Baki Baykara, Süleyman H. Tunahan, Bozkırlı 'Abd Allah Efendi, 'Abd al-'Aziz Bekkine, Hacı Hasan Efendi, Sa'id Özok, M.B. Pars, M.A. Ayni, Nüzhet Ergun, Fevzi Çakmak, Ken'an Rifa'i and Veled Çelebi all adapted themselves to a new status (job) in the community. Veled Çelebi and Hacıbeyzade Ahmed Muhtar, who supported the hat reform, a reform with a social aspect, can also be included in this group.

There were economic motives: the people discussed above, except Hacıbeyzade Ahmed Muhtar, who accepted an official job, naturally benefited financially from these jobs.

There were mystical motives: Rahmi Baba followed the signs he saw in a dream, and Ken'an Rifa'i became silent according to a Sufi rule, 'his punishment as well as his grace is nice', that is, 'Ri'a'.

Finally there were cultural motives: Elmalılı Hamdi Yazır composed a translation of and commentary on the Koran for the government.

Thus there were political motives (12 out of 26 cases), social (15 out of 26 cases), economic (14 out of 26 cases), mystical (two out of 26 cases), and cultural (one out of 26 cases). It is worth noting that although the number of opposition cases treated here (14) is lower than that of support cases (26), the number of culturally motivated opposition cases is higher than that of culturally motivated support cases (four to one), while mystically motivated ones are even (two to two).

In instances of both opposition and support, there were Sufis from all kinds of orders. Thus we cannot identify any Sufi order that can be perceived as a centre of opposition or support. In any case, we can claim that Turkish Sufism was (and still is) classical Sufism rather than neo-Sufism, which 'displays a radical departure from the tolerant, quietist and pacifistic tendencies of a classical Sufism'.[168] Yet if we compare the stance of Sufis in Turkey from the 1920s onwards to that of Shi'as in Iran during the shah's regime, we can say that although there are many common points between Sufism in general and Shi'ism,[169] their stance towards reforms definitely differed. Excepting Sheikh Sa'id's understanding of Sufism, which was very much mixed with ethnical awareness, 'Turkish Sufism did not lead to an armed reaction against the newly established regime, as was the case in Iran with Shi'ism. The vast majority of Turkish Sufis simply limited their religious thoughts to their individual lives.

Today, nearly all Sufi orders continue performing their functions and ceremonies, hiding themselves behind many civil public organizations and Waqfs. The focus of their activities is in an urban setting. The Mevlevis and Bektashis perform ceremonies openly under the labels of 'tourism initiative', or 'Turkish Sufism'.[170] Sufis take their places in a variety of political parties, changing their tendencies from right to left. Many Sufis do not see any harm in supporting left- or right-wing parties. Their only need is a space for their Sufi activities. Thus in a sense the Sufis became part of the new regime. This was how the nightingale turned into a crow.

A Reaction to Authoritarian Modernization in Turkey: The Menemen Incident and the Creation and Contestation of a Myth, 1930–31 [1]

Umut Azak

Turkish textbooks for secondary schools, covering the history of modernization of the Turkish Republic in the 1920s and 1930s and teaching the principles of Kemalism (*Atatürkçülük*), or the ideas of Mustafa Kemal Atatürk (1881–1938), the founder of the republic, include a reaction to the modernizing reforms. The event, which is listed among the most important 'reactionary movements/uprisings' (*irticai hareket*; *gerici ayaklanma*) against the republican regime, is narrated under the subtitle of 'The Menemen Incident' as follows:

> Those who were against the republic wanted to overthrow it and to re-establish the old order. However, they dissolved at their every attempt as the great majority was determined to protect the republic. The Menemen Incident was one of these attempts. Derviş Mehmed, a person affiliated with the Naqshbandiyya order, and ignorant people who gathered around him, came to Menemen on 23 December 1930. They began an uprising for the sake of religion. They martyred Kubilay, a teacher and second-lieutenant who tried to stop the uprising, by cutting his head off. Soldiers were sent to the town as soon as the event was heard of. The uprising was appeased. Rebels were caught, tried in military court and punished. [2]

This uprising is not only a 'historical event' which is chronicled and recorded, but more importantly an event which is still commemorated [3] every year on 23 December by the state, the army and Kemalist civil society organizations. In such official commemorative statements and ceremonies, the above narration of the event has been repeated with minor changes. The event in this narrative form has functioned as a model illustrating the 'perpetual conflict between conservative Islamists and secular Kemalists' [4] as the beheaded officer, Kubilay, the heroic victim of the incident, has been an icon[5] of Kemalist secularism.

This chapter aims to explain why and how this reaction to the Kemalist regime has become a 'commemorated event', unlike others, and why Kubilay has become an icon of Kemalist secularism. What follows is a review of the literature on the event and a reassessment of the uprising by focusing on its social and political context, the motivations and actions of the rebels, the state's use of the event to mobilize citizens and to delegitimize the opposition, and, finally, the silent resistance to this mobilization.

The official history and its contenders

The Menemen Incident has been studied mostly by amateur historians and journalists, and referred to by several, mostly Kemalist, sources, with little sociological or political analysis.[6] These sources narrate the event from the state's perspective and bring into focus the 'martyrdom' of Kubilay. They all point at a Sufi order, the Naqshbandiyya,[7] as the organization behind the uprising, and emphasize the fact that the latter was effectively suppressed.

However, the official history of the event has been contested by those who have claimed alternative pasts or 'counter-memories'.[8] In other words, the official/Kemalist memory of the event has sustained its dominance only under 'the pressure of challenges and alternatives'.[9]

The official account of the event has been challenged mainly by Islamist writers, who claim that the event was in fact a 'fake rebellion', planned and staged by the Kemalist regime for eliminating the opposition and oppressing the Naqshbandiyya Order.[10] Although these attempts to rewrite the history of the event contested the official account, their ideological bias has often led them to overemphasize the 'victims' of the regime and relied on conspiracy theories instead of historical facts.

The most important alternative account of the Menemen Incident was published by Necip Fazıl Kısakürek (1905–83) in 1969. Later descriptions of the incident by Müftüoğlu, Ceylan, Bursalı and İslamoğlu were duplications of his narrative. These writers questioned the glorification of Kubilay as a heroic martyr, but they appropriated the same theme of victimhood, though with a different content. Instead of Kubilay, they portrayed the Naqshbandiyya Order in general, and specifically Sheikh Es'ad,[11] a Naqshbandi sheikh from Istanbul, as the 'real victim' of the event. Sheikh Es'ad, who was charged by the state with planning the rebellion and finally sentenced to death, died – or was poisoned according to these writers – in the hospital of the town.[12] Hence, he has been highlighted as the counter-hero as opposed to the Kemalist icon of Kubilay.

In the Kemalist accounts of the event, the rebels are depicted as 'Naqshbandis,' 'reactionaries' (*mürteciler*) or 'fanatics' (*yobazlar*) who abused religion for political ends and incited the people against the republic. This was exactly how they were described by the press during the days after the incident.[13] In other words, the Kemalist discourse equated Naqshbandis with 'fanatics' and depicted the latter as the symbol of 'corrupt/wrong' Islam. Islamist accounts, however, opposed this equation between the Naqshbandis and fanaticism. Interestingly, they did so without questioning the category of 'fanatic' *per se*. Like Kemalists, they described Derviş Mehmed, the leader of the rebels, as a 'stereotypical vulgar fanatic',[14] or as a 'pawn', a 'vagrant' (*serseri*) or a 'hashish addict' (*esrarkeş*) who did not know what he was doing.[15] These writers wanted to disassociate Naqshbandis and even 'Muslims' as a whole from the incident, by claiming that the rebels 'were no true Muslims' or that 'Muslims were not responsible for the incident', on the basis of the argument that 'no foresighted Muslim would have had anything to do with this madness'.[16] Ironically, Islamists were no different from the Kemalists in their attempt to draw the line between the right and wrong belief, or, put differently, between true Muslims and fanatics. In short, both Kemalist and Islamist accounts saw the rebels as ignorant pawns of a larger Naqshbandiyya or Kemalist set-up and neither of them paid attention to the motivations of the rebels.

The second challenge to the Kemalist account of the Menemen Incident came from Marxist writers. For instance, Yalçın Küçük, quoting the memoirs of the American ambassador who in 1931 reported the event to Washington as a 'golden opportunity for the regime to reassert its prestige', questioned the official history of the event and argued that Kubilay's martyrdom was used by the state to consolidate the Kemalist regime.[17]

Recently other scholars similarly have challenged the Kemalist account by pointing at the lack of substantial proof of a larger Naqshbandiyya involvement in the event. According to Tunçay, such an involvement was very 'unlikely', because the Naqshbandi sheikhs of higher ranks would not take their minor disciples, such as Derviş Mehmed, seriously.[18] Bozarslan also concluded that although some local disciples of this order had participated in the movement, this was a local event and not a rebellion organized by the larger Naqshbandiyya network.[19]

Hikmet Kıvılcımlı (1902–71), a communist intellectual leader, was the first person who analysed the event by focusing on the rebels. He looked at the uprising from the perspective of the peasants in the villages between Manisa and Menemen who helped Derviş Mehmed and his companions. He concluded that villagers' support for the rebels showed their total lack of allegiance to the Kemalist state.[20] Besides criticizing the political elite's inability to see the material conditions that led to the rebellion,[21] he argued that people had not just been deceived by the 'reactionary sheikhs' who claimed that 'religion was in danger', but in fact needed to be deceived[22] as the only way to express their protest against the 'oppression and robbery' of the 'Kemalist bourgeoisie'.[23]

Bozarslan recently drew attention to Kıvılcımlı's work and approached the event as a 'millenarian movement' which should be understood in its religious, economic and political context. He contended that the incident was not only a 'religious resistance' but also a 'social event' caused by difficult economic conditions and political discontent.[24] Among recent studies which focused on the rebels and the political and sociological dynamics behind the rebellion, we can also cite Brockett depicting the rebellion as an example of 'collective action' from below, or Mazıcı, who approached it as a 'religious reaction' with specific socio-economic dimensions.[25] These studies also challenged the Kemalist historiography, as they aimed to understand the event from the perspective of 'reactionaries' or rebels instead of the state.

The political context and the opposition in 1930

The Menemen Incident occurred in December 1930, seven years after the proclamation of the Turkish Republic, ruled by the party-government of the Republican People's Party (*Cumhuriyet Halk Fırkası*, RPP). Under the leadership of Mustafa Kemal (Atatürk), republican leaders devoted themselves to what they called *İnkılâb* (Revolution), aiming at a complete transformation of society, a shift from Eastern to Western civilization.

Secularism, or *lâiklik*, as it is used in Turkish after the French word *laïcité*, has been a central principle of the Kemalist reforms aiming to speed up the process of secularization. Kemalist secularism aimed not only to separate the religious and political spheres but also to control religion. Thus, while the National Assembly abolished the caliphate and the function of Sheikh al-Islam, the highest religious authority in the Ottoman Empire, on 3 March 1924, it preserved the institution of religious administration by replacing the Ministry of Religious Affairs and Pious Foundations with the Directorate of Religious Affairs (*Diyanet İşleri Re'isliği*).

Following the outbreak of the Kurdish Rebellion (Sheikh Sa'id Rebellion) of 1925, the single-party regime was consolidated with the proclamation of martial law in the eastern provinces and the adoption of the Law on the Maintenance of Order (*Takrir-i Sükûn Kanunu*) which remained in force from 1925 to 1929 and gave the government dictatorial powers.[26] During this period of silenced opposition, the state implemented radical secularizing reforms. A major step to keep religious activity under control was taken on 30 September 1925 with the outlawing of Sufi orders (*tarikat*) and Dervish lodges (*tekke*), including the Naqshbandiyya Order which had played an important role in the Kurdish Rebellion.

Among several reforms which secularized the political, legal, educational and cultural spheres, one of the most resisted was that of the dress code or the so-called 'Hat Revolution' of 28 October 1925.[27] This reform, outlawing the *fez*, the traditional headgear for men, and replacing it by the Western brimmed hat, reflected the Kemalist urge to break with the past and to change even the daily habits of people for the sake of Westernization.

In 1930 the public discontent with RPP rule, the lack of civil liberties and the party's widespread corruption at the local level could be expressed for a short period via legal channels. On 12 August the Free Republican Party (*Serbest Cumhuriyet Fırkası*) was founded with the encouragement of Mustafa Kemal, under the leadership of the former prime minister Fethi (Okyar).[28] In the new atmosphere of toleration, two Istanbul-based daily newspapers, Arif Oruç's *Yarın* (Tomorrow) and Zekeriya Sertel's *Son Posta* (The Last Mail) began to criticize the government of İsmet (İnönü) and supported the Free Republican Party (FRP) against the RPP.

Shortly after its foundation, the FRP won considerable support, especially in western Anatolia, where the export-oriented agricultural region of İzmir and its hinterland had been hit by the economic depression of 1929.[29] Peasants and merchants in this region, as well as the urban and educated groups who resented the RPP's authoritarian rule, expressed their discontent via the FRP.[30] The latter followed a strategy of criticizing the RPP's economic policies. However, in the absence of any other channel, it attracted all anti-regime groups, including those who opposed the government's secularist policies.[31] The grassroots movement against the government, especially in western Anatolia, alarmed the RPP leadership who blamed the new party for being used by 'reactionaries' and 'enemies of the regime'. After the municipal elections in October 1930, the RPP leaders increased their attacks against the opposition party. No longer supported by Mustafa Kemal, the FRP leaders dissolved their party on 16 November 1930.[32]

Despite the electoral fraud of the RPP bureaucracy, the FRP had won in the local elections the majority of votes in about 30 of the 502 localities.[33] Most of these localities were in the provinces of Aydın and İzmir, among which there was also Menemen, a small town situated 30 kilometres away from the city centre of İzmir. The fact that the reactionary uprising of Menemen occurred in a town where the opposition party won the people's support led the RPP leaders and later commentators to infer that there was a link between the FRP and the uprising.

Kemalist historiography treats the closure of the FRP and the Menemen Incident as two events having a causal relationship. Official history text-books of Turkish secondary schools categorize the Menemen Incident in a subsection of the part titled 'Attempts to initiate the multi-party system and reactions against the Revolution'.[34] The selected 'reactionary rebellions', the Sheikh Sa'id revolt of 1925 and the Menemen Incident of 1930, are covered in these textbooks in conjunction with the opposition parties, the Progressive Republican Party (*Terakkiperver Cumhuriyet Fırkası*, founded on 7 November 1924; closed on 3 June 1925) and the FRP. Accordingly, both rebellions are associated with the formation of opposition parties, with the implication that their leaders 'abused the free atmosphere' and 'Mustafa Kemal's search for democracy'.[35] This way, Kemalist historiography not only echoes the RPP leaders who felt threatened by the popular support to the FRP in the autumn of 1930, but also legitimizes the continuation of the single-party regime. In this discourse, democracy should be delayed in order to protect it from 'fanatics' or 'enemies of the regime' who use religion for political ends.[36]

However, there is no proof of a connection between the FRP and the participants of the Menemen uprising. We can only suggest, following Rustow and Weiker, that the rebels might have been inspired by the general expression of social and economic dissatisfaction and the consequent support of the masses to the opposition party in their region.[37]

The rebels and the incident

The following account of the rebels' actions is largely based on the speeches they made in court.[38] The protagonists of the Menemen uprising were seven young men who were from Manisa, a city situated 50 kilometres away from Menemen. The leader of the group was Mehmed, called either Giritli (from Crete) Mehmed, implying that he was an immigrant from Crete, or Derviş Mehmed (Dervish), referring to his affiliation to a Sufi order. Derviş Mehmed was said to be a disciple of a Naqshbandi sheikh and to have worked as an official in the Municipal Marriage Office and later as a village guard for seven years in Manisa, where he married a woman from the village of Paşa Köy.[39] Since Derviş Mehmed was killed during the skirmish at the end of the uprising, as were his two companions, Sütçü (Milkman) Mehmed and Şamdan Mehmed, there is no information on them in the court records. We have, however, some information on the other members of the group, namely Mehmed Emin (b.1902, literate, married, with one child), Nalıncı

Hasan (b.1910, illiterate, single), Küçük (Giritli) Hasan (b.1913, single) and Çoban (Shepherd) Ramazan (b.1909, married, illiterate), who were tried in the court martial.[40]

The group that led the Menemen uprising had been introduced to the Naqshbandiyya Order by Derviş Mehmed. The latter interpreted their dreams and continuously told them to perform the *dhikr*, i.e. cite the name of the God.[41] The group began to grow beards[42] and met for *dhikr* in the coffeehouse of a certain Çırak (Apprentice) Mustafa. After the coffeehouse was closed down by the government, which had learned of these illegal gatherings, they began to meet in the house of a certain Hüseyin. In these meetings, Derviş Mehmed indoctrinated them against the government and said that all state officials were infidels because they let their wives and daughters wear inappropriate clothes.[43]

During one of these meetings, which they held on 6 December, Derviş Mehmed said to the group that they would perform *dhikr* in a cave outside of town for 15 days, at the end of which he would be inspired, as had happened to the Prophet. He told them that he would go as far as China and then Europe to call people to religion and that he would reopen the Dervish lodges in Turkey.[44] At that stage, he did not mention Menemen.

Derviş Mehmed, Sütçü Mehmed and Şamdan Mehmed first of all left Manisa.[45] They met with the others in the nearby village of Paşa Köy where they stayed in the houses of Derviş Mehmed's mother-in-law (Rukiye) and brother-in-law (Ahmet). Here Derviş Mehmed, who had already armed himself in Manisa, obtained two more weapons and took into his company a dog, which he symbolically named Kıtmir, after the Koranic story of *Ashab-ı Kehf* (*Ashab al-Kahf*, those of the cave).[46] According to the story, Kıtmir is the name of the dog which accompanied the *Ashab-ı Kehf*, a group of seven youths, who would be the helpers of the *Mahdi*.[47]

However, the group continued as a group of six, because Ramazan escaped on the way to the nearby village, Bozalan, the village of Sütçü Mehmed. In Bozalan, they first stayed in the house of Mustafa, a relative of Sütçü Mehmed, and told village people that they came for hunting. After seven to ten days, they moved to a hut that the villagers had built for them in a wood outside the village. During their 15-day stay in Bozalan, they spent their days smoking hashish and performing *dhikr*. Here Derviş Mehmed declared himself as the *Mahdi* and said that his companions were the *Ashab-ı Kehf*.[48] According to Mehmed Emin and Nalıncı Hasan, some villagers believed him, while some did not but did not interfere.

According to Goloğlu, the village of Bozalan was populated with immigrants coming from the Balkans in 1924 and, although they were Muslim, they did not have any knowledge of Islam, and hence it was easy for Derviş Mehmed to proclaim himself as the *Mahdi* without any challenge.[49] It seems, however, more logical to speculate that if the villagers believed in the *Mahdi*, they did so because of their familiarity with a common Islamic vocabulary rather than because of their ignorance. A messianic expectation, i.e. the belief in the *Mahdi* who will come to redeem the world and fill it with justice, as the Prophet Muhammad once did, has been part and parcel of both Shi'ite and Sunni traditions in Islam.[50] Therefore, if some villagers recognized Derviş Mehmed as the *Mahdi*, it was probably because they believed in the need to restore Islam in order to bring an end to their current condition. As mentioned in the previous section, peasants' discontent caused by the worsened economic conditions was also reflected in the ballot box during the local elections.

In the village of Bozalan, Derviş Mehmed told the group that they would go to Menemen. According to the plan, they would stay one night in the house of Saffet Hoca, an official preacher in Menemen; from there they would send telegrams to Sheikh Es'ad in Istanbul and other sheikhs; and after invading Manisa, Ankara and other towns, they would take over the government, restore the caliphate, reopen the Dervish lodges and appoint sheikhs in every town.[51] It is not clear, however, whether the villagers knew of this plan or not, nor is there any proof that Sheikh Es'ad in Istanbul or Saffet Hoca in Menemen knew about the *Mahdi* and his *Ashab-ı Kehf.* The link between the group of Derviş Mehmed and sheikhs in the upper echelons of the order remains obscure. Similarly, the reason for the choice of Menemen as the place to initiate the rebellion is unknown. Neither the court speeches of the three companions of Derviş Mehmed nor the final indictment of the prosecutor includes any substantial detail which explains these points.

Nalıncı Hasan seems to be the only one in the group who had personally met Sheikh Es'ad in Istanbul during his visit to the sheikh's house in Erenköy. Hasan told the court that when he was there he heard Sheikh Laz İbrahim, the retired *imam* of the Military Hospital in Manisa, and other sheikhs speaking against the government, planning to bring the *fez* back, to reopen Dervish lodges and to restore the caliphate. Similarly, Mehmed Emin referred to many sheikhs from the Manisa region, especially to Sheikh Laz İbrahim, as 'enemies of the Republic', and to Sheikh Es'ad as the one to whom all other sheikhs were linked. Both Mehmed Emin and Nalıncı Hasan insisted that suspects who denied their links to the order were lying and that their aim was to overthrow the government. At one point Mehmed Emin even said that this 'poisonous' order had to be eliminated in order to secure the peace of the republic.[52]

In short, during the trials, Derviş Mehmed's companions tried to prove their obedience to the state and presented themselves as ignorant persons who had been deceived by Naqshbandi sheikhs.[53] Their speeches were very much in line with the prosecutor's indictment that accused Sheikh Es'ad, his eldest son, Mehmed Ali, and some other sheikhs from Manisa, like Laz İbrahim Hoca, of hatching the plot. One should not forget, however, that these speeches were made by suspects who were charged with high treason against the state and who would be subject to capital punishment if they were found guilty.

The group arrived in Menemen on the morning of 23 December. They first stopped at a mosque in the centre of the town. After Nalıncı Hasan took the green banner of the mosque, Derviş Mehmed announced to the people who were there for morning prayer that he was the *Mahdi* and would restore the religion. He showed them the dog, Kıtmir, as proof, and told them that an 'army of the caliphate' with 70,000 soldiers was on its way to the town. Later, Küçük Hasan and Mahdi Derviş Mehmed began to tour the town, calling on the locals to join their revolt against the 'irreligious' state. According to Nalıncı Hasan, a hundred people followed them while another hundred just watched. At one point, Derviş Mehmed talked to Saffet Hoca, the official *imam* of the town, but the latter did not join them.[54] The rebels came to the square in front of the government office (*Hükümet Konağı*) and began to perform *dhikr*, together with a crowd of around a hundred people.

While the group was reciting *dhikr* in the town square and waiting for more people to join them under the green banner, one gendarme, Ali Efendi, and later the commander of the gendarmerie, Fahri Bey, asked Derviş Mehmed to disperse the crowd. Mehmed repeated that he was the *Mahdi*,[55] and that he would declare the *Shari'a* and no one could stop him. Gendarmes attempted to disperse the crowd, but they were ineffective. According to a publication of the chief of the general staff, this was because their arms were not filled with real bullets.[56] Unable to stop the rebels, the commander left the square and asked for reinforcements from the military barracks, which was on a hill close to the town centre. People in the square began to applaud the *Mahdi*, who proved at least for a while that no bullet would kill him.

On the request of the commander, a reserve officer, Mustafa Fehmi Kubilay, was put in charge of ending the disturbance. Kubilay arrived in the town square with his squad of 10 soldiers.[57] He tried to intervene alone and unarmed, leaving his soldiers behind. He pulled Mehmed's collar and told him to surrender.[58] Mehmed refused and shot him in the leg. The wounded officer tried to walk away towards a mosque adjacent to the government office, but fell after a while. Derviş Mehmed found the officer in front of the mosque, cut his head off with a saw and displayed it on top of the green banner.[59] The crowd watched and even applauded the rebels who continued to perform *dhikr*.[60] The terror and the shock of the rebels' act of defiance had a paralysing effect on the squad and the commander of the gendarmerie who was waiting at the government office. It was only after the arrival of reinforcements that the uprising could be stopped. During the skirmish, Derviş Mehmed, Sütçü Mehmed and Şamdan Mehmed were shot dead, while Mehmed Emin was wounded. Nalıncı Hasan and Küçük Hasan managed to escape, although they were arrested in Manisa three days later. Two village guards, Hasan and Şevki, also died while fighting the rebels.

The aftermath

Although it was suppressed in a few hours, the rebellion in Menemen was transformed into a national issue and a tool of official propaganda by the political elite. Shaken by the violence of the rebels and the people's alleged collaboration with them, the state needed to restore its authority. It was the collaboration of the people that most disturbed the political leadership. On 28 December Mustafa Kemal's message to the chief of the general staff, Fevzi Çakmak, was published on the front page of the newspapers. The message condemned the townspeople who applauded the brutality of reactionaries as 'disgraceful' and continued as follows:

> The nation will certainly regard this attack against the young and heroic officer, in a region which had the bitter experience of occupation, as a conspiracy against the Republic itself, and will pursue the perpetrators accordingly.[61]

The prime minister, İsmet (İnönü), also expressed his disappointment, which was caused by the fact that this 'reactionary' movement had taken place not in the east, as the Kurdish Rebellion of 1925 and the protests against the 'Hat Revolution', but in western Anatolia, the most modern and developed region of the country which was recently freed from Greek occupation.[62]

A few days after the event (on 28 December 1930), the home secretary, Şükrü Kaya, and army inspector, Fahrettin (Altay) Paşa, departed for Menemen to investigate the event.[63] Special meetings were held by Mustafa Kemal in Istanbul and in the National Assembly in Ankara, where official measures to be taken were discussed. Mustafa Kemal was so furious that during a meeting he wanted to declare Menemen as a '*vilmodit*' (*ville maudite*) and even insisted on the forced relocation of the townspeople, a measure which had been applied against rebellious Kurdish populations in the east. This initial idea was not to be realized, owing to the opposition of other RPP leaders who were in the meeting.[64]

Instead martial law was announced in Menemen and the provinces of Manisa and Balıkesir on 31 December.[65] Army inspector Fahrettin Paşa was appointed as the commander of the martial district, and Mustafa Muğlalı Paşa as chief of the martial court.[66] Martial law introduced a restriction on travelling and communication and applied censorship in the press until 8 March 1931. Meanwhile the court martial, which was temporarily based in the town's school, worked from 15 January to 16 February 1931. During the investigations, around 2,200 persons were arrested[67] and approximately 600 of those were tried.[68]

Many people arrested in Menemen were accused of acts such as applauding or helping the rebels, or just watching and not preventing the beheading of the officer. Nevertheless hundreds of persons from Menemen and nearby villages were arrested not only because of their alleged collaboration with the rebels but also because of their participation in *tarikat* activities banned by the state. Moreover the investigations were not limited to the Menemen region. The Office of the Public Prosecutor (*Cumhuriyet Savcılığı*) in Ankara sent telegrams to all local attorneys demanding that they investigate religious orders or convents in their regions.[69] As a result, many people in the provinces of Kayseri, Adana, İzmit, Yozgat, Konya, İzmir and İstanbul were indicted for breaking the laws protecting the secularizing reforms and were sent to the court martial in Menemen after their first interrogations.[70] Most of these suspects were religious functionaries, sheikhs and Dervishes allegedly connected with the Naqshbandiyya Order.

At the end of the trials, 37 suspects were found guilty of breaking the 64th and 146th articles of the Penal Code, which prescribed capital punishment for those who attempted high treason against the state by being involved in movements aimed at changing the constitutional law. Besides, 41 suspects were found guilty of breaking the 163rd and 151st articles of the Penal Code, which sentenced those who were involved in Sufi orders and who did not inform the government about the rebels to imprisonment from one to 15 years.[71]

Among those who were sentenced to death were Sheikh Es'ad, Sheikh Es'ad's son, as well as several sheikhs, villagers and townspeople who had allegedly collaborated with the rebels, such as Josef Hayim, a Jewish resident of Menemen, who was accused of applauding the *Mahdi*.[72] Six of the original 37 sentences were commuted to 24 years' imprisonment on the grounds of the youth or old age of some of the men, for instance, Sheikh Es'ad, who, as an old man, had already fallen ill and later died in hospital.[73]

Nalıncı Hasan, Küçük Hasan and Çoban Ramazan also avoided capital punishment owing to their youth. Mehmed Emin, however, was hanged along with 27 others on 4 February 1931, on gallows set up in the streets of Menemen.[74]

(a) Campaign against the *tarikats*

The hanging of 28 persons reflected the state's will to reassert its power and its determination to protect the secularist regime, especially against the Naqshbandiyya Order. The political leadership saw the order's continuing presence, despite the formal proscription of it in 1925,[75] as a major threat to the state's authority and was convinced that the rebellion was planned by Naqshbandi sheikhs who used Derviş Mehmed as a pawn.[76] Hence the court martial in Menemen became a tool for ending Naqshbandi activity and eliminating its still vibrant social network.[77]

In the minds of the ruling elite, the Naqshbandiyya Order in particular was associated with 'backwardness' and an 'unrelenting drive against secularization'.[78] This was a result of the traumatic effects of earlier uprisings such as the Kurdish Rebellion and several protest movements against the Hat Revolution in 1925, which were all led or supported by Naqshbandi sheikhs. The speeches of Muğlalı Mustafa Paşa, the chief of the court martial, reflected the ruling elite's disdain for this order.

During the trials, Muğlalı Paşa scolded Sheikh Laz İbrahim because he 'did not know his history' and explained to him that 'the nation had always suffered from the damage and disorder caused by the Naqshbandi', which 'poisoned and used the poor and naïve nation under the guise of religion and *tarikat*'. Muğlalı Paşa also instructed him that the government was not against religion as long as nobody interfered between the individual and God. On the statements of some suspects who wanted to be cleared by arguing that they did not even perform daily prayers, he said that this kind of defence was not acceptable and tried to correct their understanding of secularism: 'Individual prayer is a holy duty; what is wrong is to do it together with those who poisoned the minds of naïve people!'[79] Through these speeches the court martial became a stage where Kemalist secularism, which aimed to control and delimit religion as a private affair, clashed with popular perception of secularism as 'irreligion'.

(b) 'The martyr of the revolution' and the mobilization of the nation

The state also used Kubilay's 'martyrdom' (*şehâdet*) to mobilize popular support for the regime. In other words, the political elite turned the defeat in Menemen into a 'strategic advantage',[80] by depicting Kubilay as a heroic victim, a source of inspiration for the struggle against the enemies of the republic. Hence, at the end of his message to the chief of the general staff, Mustafa Kemal portrayed Kubilay's martyrdom as a regeneration rather than a loss: 'Kubilay's pure blood will refresh and strengthen the vitality of the Republic.'[81]

The martyrdom of Kubilay was recounted to the people by the pro-government press, portraying the rebels as 'reactionaries' (mürteciler), 'seditious' (şerir), 'traitors' (hainler) and 'savages' (vahşiler), who even drank the blood of the 'martyred officer' (şehit subay).[82] The brutal actions of the rebels were emphasized to such an extent that it caused a mild trauma among the newspaper-reading public. The childhood memoirs of the poet Ceyhun Atuf Kansu illustrate this trauma and the consequent self-identification with Kubilay:

> More than the political aspect of this bloody event, its frightening nature had struck me. Mosque courtyards, bearded dervishes, blooded stone in the court-yard of the mosque, green banners, the head, all were in my dreams. I woke up with fear after such nightmares. ... At the tensest moment of the event, my soul was unified with Kubilay. I was united, identified with him.[83]

Kubilay, with whom many young citizens of the republic identified, was a teacher who had begun his military service as a reserve officer (second-lieutenant) in the town. He was born in Aydın in 1906, but his parents settled in İzmir after migrating from Crete and moving around between several cities.[84] His real name was Mustafa Fehmi, but while studying at the Teachers' School in İzmir, he had chosen the name of Kubilay, following the fashion of the time to adopt the names of important Turks in pre-Islamic history as nicknames.[85] According to his close circle of friends and his wife, he was a nationalist and idealist teacher committed to the Kemalist revolution and its reforms.[86]

Kubilay's death, which could have also been interpreted as the result of a courageous but naïve act (he was unarmed), was portrayed instead as 'martyr-dom,' or as an honourable, altruistic self-sacrifice for the sake of protecting the republic against its enemies. Besides Kubilay, two village guards, Hasan and Şevki, were also killed while fighting the rebels. However, it was not the killing of these village guards but that of Kubilay (a teacher and an officer) that became central to the narration of the rebellion.

Intellectual and political leaders in their public speeches and newspaper articles called the nation to follow the path of Kubilay and to fight the enemies of the republic. This use of the concept of 'martyr' showed how the Kemalist elite successfully adopted Islamic concepts in order to use them in the service of the new national community redefined as a secular nation.[87] Martyrdom here was not for the sake of the Islamic faith, as in its Koranic meaning, but for the sake of the struggle for modernity against the old, degenerate religion.

Ironically, Necip Fazıl (Kısakürek), the later pioneer of the writers who argued that Kubilay was a 'fake hero' fabricated by the government, was at the time of the incident among those who participated in the collective damnation of religious reaction. As a young and ambitious intellectual committed to the Kemalist revolution, he wrote an article which was published in the official newspaper, where he recapitulated the reason why Kubilay's martyrdom was so significant: 'None of the earlier reactionary events can be compared to the Menemen Incident, because the latter has shown the resentment and the hatred towards youth, the educators, the soldiers, i.e. the whole ideal, which is represented in the person of Kubilay.'[88]

Kubilay was commemorated as 'the symbol of the republic' in several ceremonies and demonstrations organized against religious reaction, by local RPP branches all over the country as well as by the local branches of the *Türk Ocakları* (Turkish Hearths), nationwide social and cultural organizations that were used to spread nationalism and secularism in the country. In short, the Menemen Incident became a propaganda tool of the Kemalist regime which institutionalized its commemoration and made its hero, Kubilay, part of the Kemalist 'iconography'.[89] Hundreds of poems, leaflets and issues of magazines were dedicated to the memory of Kubilay the Martyr, the epic hero of the revolution.[90] Commemoration ceremonies were held in Menemen, Manisa and İzmir in the following years on 23 December.[91] In 1934 a monument dedicated to the memory of the 'martyrs' of the incident (Kubilay and the two village guards) was erected, on the initiative of the newspaper *Cumhuriyet* (Republic), on top of a hill in the military base in Menemen.[92]

(c) Local resistance to mobilization and the opposition

While official commemoration ceremonies took place all over the country, there were also some sections of society that kept their distance from this national campaign. For instance, the Menemen population found itself in an awkward situation because their town had become notorious all over the country as the embodiment of religious reaction. On 2 January 1931 thousands of students, scouts and civil servants rushed to Menemen for a ceremony organized by the RPP.[93] The townspeople preferred to watch the ceremonies from their windows. Some young members of the İzmir branch of the RPP tried in vain to persuade them to join the ceremony.[94] The townspeople had chosen – as pointed out also by Bozarslan – to 'boycott' the ceremonies of commemoration instead of joining in the collective damnation of their own town.[95] The local press of İzmir said that the identification of

Menemen with religious reaction was 'an injustice towards the republicans of Menemen', and affirmed that 'the event was exaggerated and that the Turkish people's allegiance to the revolution was beyond doubt'.[96]

After the event, opposition journalists and political leaders had to assert themselves as true republicans and secularists. During parliamentary sessions and in the editorials of pro-government daily newspapers such as *Vakit* (Time), *Akşam* (Evening) and *Cumhuriyet*, former leaders of the FRP, as well as opposition newspapers like *Yarın* (Tomorrow), were held responsible for inciting the incident and were blamed for abusing the atmosphere of freedom.[97] For instance Yusuf Ziya, the editor of the weekly satirical magazine *Akbaba*, argued that the incident in Menemen was the consequence of the freedom of the press, and that 'the Revolution (*Inkılab*) was suffering from its own tolerance'.[98]

Against such slander, opposition newspapers such as *Yarın* (Tomorrow) and *Hür Adam* (Free Man) criticized the government's tendency to overstate 'the threat of reaction', its lack of trust in the opposition and its blindness to the people's real problems.[99] Mehmed Fuat in *Hür Adam*, for instance, defended 'the need to trust the people's capacity to appreciate the Republican reforms' and suggested 'looking at the socio-economic causes of the reaction'.[100] Furthermore, Arif Oruç, in *Yarın*, stated that 'the Republic should win the hearts of the people instead of appearing behind bayonets'.[101]

Some other non-conformist interpretations of the event were brought forward by intellectuals in exile. For instance, *La République Enchainé* (*Zincire Vurulmuş Cumhuriyet*), a newspaper published by anti-Kemalist political exile Mehmed Ali Bey in Paris, criticized the Turkish state for portraying the incident as a Naqshbandi conspiracy and claimed that the incident was exploited as a pretext for creating terror and eliminating the political opposition.[102] Likewise, Rıza Nur (1878–1942), a former member of parliament and an anti-Kemalist exile in Paris, wrote in his journal, which would be published in Turkey after 1964 and then immediately banned, that this 'revolt was probably encouraged by the government' in order to create 'terror' and to 'eliminate' those figures who were detrimental to their own interests. Rıza Nur claimed that Mustafa Kemal had wanted to punish the people who were against the government. He also interpreted the townspeople's non-participation in the funeral ceremony as proof of the people's opposition to the regime.[103]

Conclusion

The voice of dissident intellectuals of the 1930s remained unheard for a long time because, as they had predicted, after the Menemen Incident the authoritarian regime was further consolidated and no opposition party was tolerated in Turkey until the transition to a multi-party system in 1946. Only in the late 1960s did Islamist and Marxist scholars, who criticized the authoritarianism of the Kemalist regime, begin to question the official narration of the Menemen Incident by unearthing the 'counter-memories' of those dissidents. My contention is that a fuller picture of the event can be seen under the light of both these official and dissident memories.

As shown above, the Kemalist state manipulated the event and used the 'martyrdom' of Kubilay as a tool of national mobilization and reinstitution of its authority vis-à-vis the continuing prestige of *tarikat*s. Thus the Menemen Incident has since been highlighted by the official history and commemorated in order to remind citizens of the need to protect the secular republic against its enemies. The enemy here referred to is an internal enemy, that is 'fanatics' and the remains of the old order such as the Naqshbandis who resisted the secularizing reforms.

However, a look at this local uprising from below, shifting the focus from the state to the rebels' side, enables one to see other dimensions of the event which are absent in the official memory. Considering the post-World Crisis socio-economic conditions in the region and the closure of the opposition party one month before the incident, this local uprising can be interpreted as an expression of popular dissent against the state in the absence of legal channels. The group of Derviş Mehmed could appeal to the Messianic expectations for a restored justice of at least some people in the villages where they had kinship connections, as well as in Menemen where popular dissent was earlier reflected in the people's support for the opposition party. The dissent against the republican regime was reflected also in the resistance of the townspeople to the state's mobilization by boycotting the commemoration ceremonies, as well as in the critical interpretations of opposition intellectuals of the time. The latter criticized the Kemalist state's exaggeration of the threat of religious reaction in order to postpone dealing with the real economic problems of the people and to delegitimize the opposition under the rubric of 'reaction'.

To conclude, the Menemen Incident cannot be read as a struggle between the republic and its enemies, as the official history textbook suggests. The event and its aftermath should rather be seen as an episode where the authoritarian regime was challenged and resisted by the opposition, which was in turn slandered by the regime as enemies of the secular republic.

10

Authority and Agency: Revisiting Women's Activism during Reza Shah's Period[1]

Afsaneh Najmabadi

The emergence of a vocal feminist identification and activism among Iranian Muslim and Islamist women in the 1990s came as a surprise (often mixed with scepticism) for many observers. For historians of the late nineteenth and early twentieth centuries it should not have. In fact, if there was a surprise, it was the extent of similarities between these two moments. The similarities include philosophical pragmatism – challenging Islamist anti-feminism with any combination of women-centred arguments, Islamic and secular, local and global – and an engaged, though autonomous, relation between women activists and governmental structures and power elites. Between these two moments, women's rights activism became increasingly state-dominated – ideologically and structurally – whether in alliance with or in opposition to the state. In my larger book manuscript, *Genealogies of Iranian Feminism*, I hope to offer an alternative narrative for this period of Iranian women's activism. For the present I shall focus on one piece of this puzzle: the 1920s and 1930s societal practices and debates on the woman's veil and social participation.

Rethinking Iranian feminism and secularism

Iranian politics of modernity, since the mid-nineteenth century, has been marked by the emergence of a spectrum of nationalist and Islamist discourses. Within that spectrum, one notion of Iranian modernity took Europe as its model of progress and civilization (*taraqqi va tamaddun*) – the two central terms of that discourse – and increasingly combined that urge with recovery of pre-Islamic Iranianism. Other trends sought to combine their nationalism and the urge to catch up with Europe, not with a pre-Islamic recovery but with Islam, by projecting Shi'ism as Iranianization of Islam in its early centuries.[2] I am emphatically putting the latter in the spectrum of modernity for two reasons: first, in order to distinguish it from counter-modernist trends, such as that led in the Constitutional Revolution (1905–9) by Sheikh Fazl'allah Nuri; and, second, because later twentieth-century developments largely led to ejection/abandonment of what may be called an Islamist nationalist modernist trend from the complex hybridity of Iranian modernity – until its re-emergence in new configurations in the late 1980s. Until recently, it had become a commonly accepted notion that Iranian politics is and has been a battleground since the nineteenth century, between modernity and tradition, with Islam always in the latter camp.[3]

The beginnings of Iranian feminism were not marked by a boundary, setting Islam to its beyond. Women's rights activists made rhetorical use of any available position to invent a female-friendly discourse. In the early twentieth century, we come across three kinds of self-identification by women: they referred to themselves as *khvaharan-i vatani* – patriotic sisters, *khvaharan-i dini* – sisters-in-religion, and *khvaharan-i naw'i* - gender sisters. Within Iranian constitutionalist discourse women claimed citizenship by writing themselves within the domains of Iranianism and Islamism. By calling each other gender sisters, on the other hand, they signalled their recognition that as women they needed to address particular concerns that the other two categories would not address.[4]

Though there were debates among women on certain issues, these differences were not consolidated as incompatible and contradictory positions, one negating the other. Nor was Islam viewed as inherently anti-women. Anti-constitutionalist forces, led by Sheikh Fazl'allah Nuri, grounded their political opposition to the constitution and to the reforms advocated by modernists in their interpretations of Islamic precepts. For instance, they argued that the establishment of new schools for girls was an example of abrogation of the laws of God. The advocates of the new girls' schools, however, also drew from the same sources to argue for female education. One woman, in an article directly addressed to Sheikh Fazl'allah Nuri (a gesture that put herself on the same plain of discourse as a prominent religious leader), first quoted one of his tracts as saying that 'schools for educating females are against religion', and then proceeded to argue against him in very strong language, worth quoting at length:

> If by your statement you mean that womankind should not be educated at all and should be like tail-less and horn-less animals until they pass away, and that this is the word of God, then please write down where God and his appointed guardians have said these words. ... If you are then proved right, then tell us what the reasons are for such disfavour of God, the prophets and the guardians toward womankind – they are made as effigies of humans but prohibited from throwing off their beastly disposition and entering the realm of humanity. And despite having been treated so unfavourably, God has imposed upon them

unbearable duties of worship, refined manners, and obedience to their husbands and fathers. For what good reason has God favoured men over women, and, in return for bestowing on men the gift of acquiring knowledge, what other duties, like those imposed on women, has God imposed on men, other than obeying God? But if God's blessing is equal for everyone, what has God rewarded and blessed women with for fulfilling all the hard duties imposed upon them for what God has blessed men with?

You may say that I have no right to dispute God's affairs. I humbly say to you that I am talking about the God that you have devised – a God free of justice and an oppressor of women. The God that we know and worship is far too elevated and great to intend such differences between men and women and command with no wisdom.

Our revered Prophet, exalted and glorious, has said that acquiring knowledge is obligatory upon all Muslim men and women; there is a very big difference between our God who makes acquiring knowledge obligatory for women, and yours who has made education for women forbidden and against religion.[5]

In other words, Nuri's clerical voice was not allowed to hold a monopoly of Islamic authority and truth. Women challenged him and his God, in their own language and in the name of their God.

Though in an earlier period and in the writings of a number of modernists, the Iranian women's veil had become a critical marker of difference between Europe and Iran/Islam, the contention over the veil was not simply between modernists and counter-modernists.[6] Not all reform-minded Iranians advocated unveiling; some actively opposed it, although they fully supported women's education and social participation. Among the latter were important groups of women. Moreover, by the turn of the twentieth century, reforming women's activism became centred on other issues. The common issues of women's activism in this period were, first and foremost, that of women's education and then the reform of marriage and divorce laws (restricting or eliminating polygyny, restricting the easy unilateral right of a husband to divorce his wife at any time, for any or no reason). Indeed women's rights activists diverged on the issue of veiling, *hijab*. In the pages of the women's journal *Shukufah* (published from late 1912 to 1916), for instance, while some writers, such as Shahnaz Azad and Shams Kasma'i, were known for (and sometimes wrote about) favouring unveiling, others, including the owner and editor of the journal, Muzayyan al-Saltanah, argued strongly against it.[7]

It is important to clarify here that the debate about veiling in the early decades of the twentieth century was very different from what in post-1979 Iran has been a subject of state policy and socio-cultural struggle under the same vocabulary.[8] The unveiling (*kashf-i hijab*) that some men and women began to advocate in the earlier period consisted of removal of the face veil, and changing to a scarf and a loose long mantle instead of the full-length chador.[9] My point is to emphasize the historicity of the meaning of unveiling – something that is often lost in general discussions of the veil.[10] What has been officially and forcefully put in place since early 1980s in Iran as veiling is not what constituted veiling in the early decades of the twentieth century; if anything, it looks much closer to what at that time women were advocating as unveiling.[11] Moreover, advocating or opposing unveiling was not the straightforward matter of modernity versus anti-modernity that it later became. Within the ranks of women's rights activists themselves there was a divergence on this issue that had not translated itself into antagonistic positions of one camp marking the other as anti-modern, anti-reform or traditionalist.

If in this earlier period a diversity of women's rights discourses and practices existed among activists, how did the conflation of modernist with non-Islamic and Islamic with tradition come about?

A critical period for transformation of these diversities into opposing categories was the reign of Reza Shah Pahlavi (1925–41). One of the major issues with which Reza Shah's reign has been marked in Iranian historical memory is the unveiling of women, both for those who supported the measure and those who fought it.[12] In its simplest form, the common narrative is that as part of his modernization measures, Reza Shah in 1936 ordered women's unveiling. For opponents of unveiling, the project has been seen not only as anti-Islamic, but also as part of a larger imperialist cultural offensive, with Reza Shah as an obedient pawn. Supporters of unveiling range from those who defend his methods (the scale of state coercion was unavoidable once several years of persuasion had not produced the desired result of mass voluntary unveiling by women) to critics who hold the brutality of the campaign responsible for its failure and the later Islamist backlash of the 1940s and eventually the Islamic Revolution of 1979.[13]

There are several problems with this account. For one thing, it ignores an actual shift in Reza Shah's policy on this issue. As late as autumn 1932, the government opposed *bi'chadori*, that is, replacing the chador with any other full-length outfit.[14] In an article in *Shafaq-i surkh*, Afzal Vaziri took the government to task on this issue:

> The police, with extreme severity, prevent girls from going to school without a chador. The Board of General Education is extremely strict on this, such that if a girl of seven or eight goes to school without a chador, the headmistress, on the order of the director of the Board of General Education, will throw her out

of school. ... People should be left free to choose; don't command *bi'chadori*, nor stop women who discard their chador. ... The government should simply take on the duty of defending order and protect women from men's harassment. It should write down and display the duties of men towards women in public places and on buses, and the police should first of all behave accordingly and then enforce these regulations.[15]

When the Second Congress of Women of the East was held in Tehran (27 November–2 December 1932),[16] Sheikh al-Mulk Awrang, a confidant of Reza Shah, sent there by minister of court Teymurtash, spoke repeatedly and vociferously against unveiling as it was proposed by a number of women. Three years later, in February 1936, the same Mr Awrang argued for the benefits of women's unveiling.[17] Something had changed between December 1932 and February 1936.

Indeed, current accounts ignore the early opposition of government to *bi'chadori*, and date Reza Shah's attention to unveiling to his journey to Turkey in June 1934 – a year prior to any sign of policy change on unveiling in spring 1935.[18] One memoir says that Reza Shah had always wanted to unveil, but feared the social upheaval that would ensue. The Turkey trip made him resolve that he must do it at any price.[19] Yet many contemporary sources indicate a more complicated inner-governmental picture. 'Ayn al-Saltanah, for instance, wrote in November 1931 that Reza Shah was indeed against *bi'chadori*; it was his powerful minister of court, Teymurtash, who was set to spread European practices in Iran. He continued:

> He has succeeded in most of them, such as women going to cinemas and promenades, cafés, etc. etc., except for removing the chador. This is because His Highness is against women going out *bi'chador* [without the chador]. Had it not been for his opposition, some six years ago women had become *bi'chador*. Generally he [Teymurtash] has not succeeded, though to some extent his intentions have materialized, for example, *hijab* in Tehran and other cities means only the black chador, otherwise the face, hands, chest and neck are all open. Even the *pichah* is set to make the face lovelier in its shade.[20]

In the debates staged in the pages of *Shafaq-i surkh* in 1929 and 1930, the majority of pieces, largely authored by men, were against women's employment outside the home and associated with it *bi'chadori*. This journal was edited by 'Ali Dashti and was considered from its inception to be in support of Sardarsipah (and later Reza Shah). It is not very likely that if the government was already inclined to support *bi'chadori*, then the pages of *Shafaq-i surkh* would be dominated as late as 1930 by a contrary position. The least one can surmise is that there were actual disagreements on this issue within and outside government circles.

Moreover, such accounts ignore the fact that by the 1920s women's unveiling had become a social debate and actual struggle, engaged in not only by male politicians but also by women themselves.

Even though unveiling had not been on the agenda of reformers during the years of the Constitutional Revolution, a changing social context had begun to bring the issue to the fore.[21] Women began to be more visibly part of the social scene, through their participation in constitutionalist activities, forming associations and holding patriotic meetings, establishing schools and holding public graduation ceremonies for students, writing in the press and publishing women's journals. They also began to circulate more openly in the streets. Urban middle- and upper-class women began to slowly challenge and expand their very restrictive gender spaces – a space much more restricted than that of lower-middle and working-class women who had a claim to the streets and moving around the city.

Apart from such daily presence, women from non-elite classes participated in *ta'ziahs*, in mosques and bazaars on particular occasions, in city gardens and outdoor spaces on *sizdah'bidar* (13th day of the Persian new year), and in Imamzadah Zayd and similar places for *hanabandan* (henna application ceremonies, practised on 27th of Ramazan, connected with special vows) and similar occasions. Another regular public appearance of women was when the ruling monarch appeared in public to allow them to express their allegiance and good wishes, or alternatively to air their grievances and protests. 'Ayn al-Saltanah's memoir provides us with a vivid account of these outings. Anticipating a rainy day, he wrote on 1 April 1890: 'May God have pity on women; they have all prepared new clothes and new chadors, and have prepared a lot of makeup for the day of *sizdah*; all of it will go to waste and their beauty will turn into ugliness [*badgili*, a play on soil turning into mud in rain]. Insha'allah, it will not rain and men will enjoy the sight of made-up women with new clothes.' Reporting on the actual event, he later wrote that he and his brother on the return journey had gone to Lalah'zar Avenue: 'There were so many women in the Lalah'zar garden that there was not a single empty spot. ... Similarly Amiriyah and other gardens were full of men and women. Streets were full of carriages and men and women on horses and on foot. It was a great spectacle [*tamasha-yi khubi dasht*]. Few days offer such spectacles. We looked at great length [*tamasha-yi kamili nimudim*] and then returned home.'[22] He observed that the daily *rawzah'khvanis* of Muharram and Safar were attended by more women than men.[23] He noted that there was an increasing tendency for women to treat these occasions as feasts, dress up, observe their veil less fully and display themselves. They even used the occasion to flirt with men.

By 1909 he was reporting that women were appearing in some *ta'ziyah* with fashionable *pichah* (*zanha-yi mud-pichah'i*).

He disapproved of women's behaviour when they expressed their ire and anger at the shah in public: 'One day we accompanied the Shah on his visit to Sipah'salar Mosque. I don't know what to write of women. We mingled among women, it was a great sight. They uttered much nonsense. … Regularly, they made up lines [*mazmun miguyand*] for the Shah and those accompanying him. I wonder what will happen with the passage of time.'[24]

Such participation was a contested one. Groups of men or the city police would regulate women's presence, on occasion close the doors of mosques and other holy places to them, or prevent them from leaving the gated cities. 'Ayn al-Saltanah reported that in *sizdah'bidar* 1308 (1891) women were not allowed beyond city gates; consequently most of the people in Dulab and Dushan'tappah were men. Women spent the day in various city gardens.[25] For 27 Ramazan 1310, a group of clerics closed the doors to Imamzahd Zayd at dawn and would not give in to the demands of thousands of women to open them; women dispersed among several mosques.[26] These restrictions began to be applied to women's participation in Muharram processions where in June 1898 women were prohibited from participating in the evening events of the 9th of Muharram (*tasu'a*). But they made up for it with increased participation on the tenth. When in Ramazan 1342 women were excluded from an important *va'z* by the popular Mirza Abdullah in Sipah'salar Mosque, they filled the adjoining streets and turned Baharistan's outer area into their domain. The police were helpless, 'Ayn al-Saltanah reported: 'I saw a woman who was screaming, "unless women all die, you will never be rid of us, women are everywhere!"'[27]

'Ayn al-Saltanah also reported on the changing fashion of court women's clothes, hairstyle and makeup. He credited Amin Aqdas, one of Nasir al-Din Shah's favourite wives, with introducing these changes and setting new trends followed by the rest of the urban elite women;[28] there were also reports that the royal *andarun* (inner quarters of the house) was observing the rules of gender segregation less and less rigorously.[29] On his visit back in Tehran in 1912, after four years in Alamut, 'Ayn al-Saltanah wrote, 'women's [in-door] clothes have become Europeanized, only a head-scarf [charqad] remains, … this too will go out of fashion soon.'[30]

The appearance of women on strolls was an emerging sight. Particular locations in and around Tehran, for instance, developed a reputation for being popular places for evening promenades. Many of these places had previously been frequented by women on special occasions, such as *sizdah'bidar*; now women began to go there for daily promenades or to spend their Fridays outdoors. These included Amiriyah Street, Lalah'zar, Qulhak, Tajrish and Darband. Many of the royal and private gardens were also open to public promenade (at least in particular periods), including to women. Women's presence in these locations immediately stirred public debate, satire and scrutiny by men and other women. The city officials (Baladiyah/later *azhans* and *pasbans*) would set rules to prevent the mingling of men and women; for instance, they would limit the hours when women were allowed in these spaces (e.g. *Bagh-i Zahir al-Dawlah*, where women were forced to leave at sunset),[31] they instituted opposite sidewalks as men's and women's to keep them apart.[32] This led to sometimes comic and not so comic problems. An aristocrat who had constructed benches in front of his garden for himself and his friends found his bench unusable because that side of street was marked for women's walks.[33] On occasion, women were banned from some of these popular locations. Dr Istipanian protested that the ban on women frequenting Lalah'zar Avenue in the afternoon had created a situation where respectable ladies were treated disrespectfully by the police and many had stopped coming to his practice.[34] In Muharram 1341 (September 1922) women were forbidden to come to the bazaars to see the processions, though they were allowed around Shams al-'Imarah, where 'the police [*azhans*] were very careful that men would not enter the women's throngs and would stand apart'. 'Ayn al-Saltanah continued approvingly, 'This was a very good decree, because women no longer cover their faces [*ru nimi'giraftand*] and all attention would be drawn to them.'[35] Regulations were also put in place on women's use of street carriages (*durushkah*).[36]

New socializing practices affected previous domains. The Majlis sponsored three days of *rawzah* (religious recitation) in September 1922 (Muharram 1341) but 'Ayn al-Saltanah wrote that it was more like a national feast, 'with only one difference: women were allowed to enter, there were more women than men; the whole space of the garden and all the surrounding streets were full of beautiful fashionable women, with silk chadors and excellent dresses. They would enter, take a walk, drink teas and leave. The MPs [*vukala*] and the *fukulis* enjoyed themselves and did not want the *rawzah* to come to an end.'[37]

Men's memoirs from this period indicate the voyeuristic novelty of encountering women on the streets.[38] As women became more comfortable on their strolls, they began to modify their outdoor outfits: *chaqchurs* gave way to socks, first black and slowly other colours. Colourful shoes began to make their appearance. Chadors were made shorter, 'so that women's nice socks, and of course their white flesh from under the silk/chiffon [*tur*] socks, would show.'[39] *Rubandah* and *niqab* were replaced by *pichah*, all three were often pushed aside, sometimes flirtatiously.[40]

Sayyid 'Ali Shushtari, famous for his opposition to women's schools during the Constitutional Revolution period, was outraged: 'Women first replaced their chaqchurs with black socks, then the socks turned red, yellow, blue; chests are open, sleeves went up, even an old man like me is aroused when I see them. They have turned the whole city into Shahr-i naw [the prostitutes' quarter].'[41]

There was also another arena in which the issue of *hijab* was being challenged. Urban women's activities and socializing was bringing women of different religious communities into closer interaction. Non-Muslim and Muslim women worked together in pro-constitutional activities (such as fundraising for the Majlis and the National Bank, or for schools, as well as through forming some of the earliest women's associations). Though non-Muslim women abided by public veiling on streets, in their private interactions they either did not observe veiling or did so to a lesser extent. In particular Baha'i women, many embedded within Muslim kin networks, began to be encouraged to socialize with men and go without the face veil.[42] Fabulous stories about unveiled 'Babi' (Baha'i) women began to circulate at large.[43] Women who formed associations during the constitutional period were suspected of being under the influence of Babi/Baha'i women and interested in going unveiled.[44] A new interest in Qurrat al-'Ayn's poetry, set to rhythmic music, was noted by 'Ayn al-Saltanah.[45]

Interactions with European women and with women in Muslim communities within the Russian domain constituted another element in changes of everyday life practices. Kasma'i's years of residence in the Caucasus and perhaps even more importantly in Ashkabad with a strong Baha'i community could not have but affected her views.[46]

Then there was 'the Bolshevik threat'! It was widely rumoured that 'the Bolsheviks' in Gilan were encouraging women to unveil and join the reform efforts of Mirza Kuchak Khan. Though 'Ayn al-Saltanah was relieved to report that women did not welcome these efforts, he noted that, 'Certainly the situation will not remain this way. It will follow the pattern of Egypt and the Ottomans; *hijab* will not totally disappear, but will not remain solidly in place either.'[47]

Gilan was not the only place where political conflict translated into a contest over the women's veil. From the earliest days of Reza Khan's rise to power, the spectre of women's unveiling was raised by his opponents. In the emerging debate about dissolution of the monarchy and its possible replacement with a republic, supporters of the republic were accused of advocating anti-Islamic measures, including unlawful mingling of men and women and women's *bi'hijabi*.[48] A chain of association had been established between republicanism, atheism, Babism and the advocacy of *rubazi* (showing face).[49] Pro-Qajar women, engaged in anti-republican activities, were told by 'the people of the city [*mardum-i shahr*]' that they did not have to come out. 'We will act on behalf of your coveredness.'[50] The popular Mirza 'Abdullah, speaking to an enthusiastic audience of mostly women in Sipahsalar Mosque (Ramazan 1342/April 1924), argued that what was going on in the country was Babi and atheistic propaganda; they aimed to remove *hijab*, mix men and women. The audience joined in by cursing them all.[51]

By the early 1920s, in certain neighbourhoods, mostly in north Tehran, women had begun to go out on the street without *rubandah*. 'Ayn al-Saltanah noted, on 2 May 1925, 'Our women's *hijab* today is only the black chador; hands, face, chests are open. It is a rare woman who would not display them.'[52] Some women began to venture out without the chador, replacing it with loose long tunics. When Dawlatabadi returned from Europe in 1927, she famously refused to take up the chador, even at work in the Ministry of Education.

Rumours of women attempting to hold mixed meetings, without covering their faces or even attempting to go on the streets without chador and *pichah*, would spread.[53] Such rumours invariably included stories of public outcry and opposition, narrated as part of the contemporary political struggles around the change of dynastic rule. The story of women holding theatre sessions under the cover of wedding parties, which were intercepted by the police, multiplied.[54] Among the women who were said to be involved in such activities were the wives of 'Ali Dashti,[55] Malik al-Shu'ara' Bahar and Saba – affiliations clearly marked by the political line-ups of the early 1920s (all three men were marked as supporters of Sardarsipah). Rumours about women's social practices did a great deal of political work. Other women were said to hold mixed family parties welcoming only men who were willing to come with their wives without the face veil.[56]

The *hijab* debates of the 1920s

The *hijab* debates of the 1920s unfolded in many domains, including the women's press, the general press (published in Iran and abroad), in clerical responses to such debates, literary production of poetry and moral novels.[57]

One of the earliest public ventures of women into the *hijab* debates unfolded in the pages of *Namah-i banuvan*, edited by Shahnaz Azad. She was already a familiar name in reform circles. Daughter of Hasan Rushdiyah, married to Abu al-Qasim Azad Maraghah-'i, she had been writing in *Shukufah* and *Zaban-i zanan*. In July 1920 she began to publish her own journal, *Namah-i banuvan*.[58] In its first two issues she openly advocated unveiling by serializing 'Ishqi's poem, 'Kafan-i siah' [Black Shroud], and an account of the debates in the Syrian parliament about women's franchise[59] in which the issue of unveiling had been raised. Clearly under attack, in an editorial in the third issue[60] she emphasized that by *hijab* she had meant solely the veil of superstition, ignorance and traditionalism; she had never intended to mean the chador and *rubandah*, and for now her message to the supporters of women's franchise or unveiling in Iran was that until women were educated such freedoms were harmful. She also ended serializing 'Ishqi's poem. Using the euphemism, 'removing the veil of superstition', was, however, not as innocent as Azad's detraction argued. It was used similarly in *Jahan-i zanan*,[61] where its editor, Fakhr Afaq Parsa, also more explicitly wrote about 'women not yet having the right to choose their own clothing, ... remaining deprived of breathing fresh air and freedom'.[62] This was clearly a tactical retreat. Shahnaz Azad and her husband, Abu al-Qasim Azad, had formed an association of men and women in 1914 (*guruh-i banuvan va banu'iyan*). In 1921 they suggested that women and *mahram* men should meet regularly, once or twice a week, to discuss social and ethical issues, and that these societies should use *Namah-i banuvan* as their organ to coordinate their activities and learn about each other's news. In 1926 they formed a league of supporters of the association (*Jam'iyat-i hamdilan*), stating in the preamble to its statutes, 'All the social, literary, economic, familial and even political problems of Iran are because of women's veiling which prevents them from entering public domains [*ijtima'at*].' The initial group, in addition to the Azads, included Fakhr Afaq Parsa, Batul Raf'at'zadah, Ahmad Sharifi and 'Ismat al-Muluk Sharifi.[63]

Another women's journal published in Rasht, *Payk-i sa'adat-i nisvan*, was more circumspect. In its second issue[64] it apologized to its readers for the many typographical errors of the first issue, explaining that this had been caused by the state of affairs in which a veiled woman could not go to a place such as the print shop, because men would stir at her avidly (*ba chashm'ha-yi pur az hirs*), 'because she was covered [*masturah*] and everything covered is unknown [*majhul*] and human beings are eager to uncover the unknown'.[65] Later that year it published an ode celebrating unveiling of women in Uzbekistan.[66]

As Rostam-Kolayi has amply documented, in the pages of *'Alam-i nisvan* there was a lively debate on this issue.[67] Women wrote not only in the pages of women's journals, but took the discussion to other pubic forums such as *Shafaq-i surkh*.[68]

In all these debates the issue of unveiling was closely linked with women's employment. Opponents argued that women's best occupation was good mothering and managing a good house for their husbands. Men seemed to be threatened by the prospect of women taking away their much-cherished civil servant occupations. Supporters, especially women writers, argued that women were being wasted at home and the country's prosperity would be imperilled without their participation. In part, this debate was an indication of a new generation of women coming of age: graduates of the first modern schools, some with post-secondary education, who were not satisfied with being educated mothers and housewives of the modernist imagination. In the wake of the constitutional activist years, they had begun to make a claim to public participation through employment. As the editorial in *Payk-i sa'adat-i nisvan* indicated, they felt their employment was hindered by the observance of chador. They proposed to remain covered and modest differently. They expected their patriotic brothers to be cooperative and welcoming of their aspirations to be part of the building of a new Iran. The general opposition of modernist men was disappointing. Women were particularly bitter that the government was restricting *bi'chador* women from going to school and participating in other social functions. Women themselves took a variety of positions. The disagreements were not lined up with pro-education/pro-employment/anti-veil fellows on the one side and the opposite position on the other. A number of men and women argued that women's education and employment were consistent with observation of *hijab*. This position had its own genealogy in the writings of the late nineteenth century and the constitutionalist period. It was also the position advocated by Muzayyan al-Saltanah in *Shukufah*. The journal *Nawbahar*, edited by Malik al-Shu'ara', advocated a similar position in 1914. Yet the weight of subsequent developments and its effect on Pahlavi historiography have made all anti-unveilers into opponents of 'women's progress', and virtually eliminated this voice from Iranian history.[69] Moreover, some women activists and writers argued that the focus on *bi'chadori* and employment was wrong. In particular Masturah Afshar, president of the leading Tehran women's organization, *Jam'iyat-i nisvan-i vatankhvah* (Society of Patriotic Women, henceforth referred to as SPW), argued for the reform of marriage laws and practices as the precondition for any meaningful change in women's status and life. Both in the pages of SPW's journal and in the pages of *Shafaq-i surkh* and other journals, she wrote on this issue and campaigned for it by sending petitions to the Majlis.[70] Her subsequent support for the 1931 and 1938 laws, far from being a submission of compromising women to a strong state, was for her indicative of her success. That some women were turning to men of state, and perhaps most particularly the rising strong man Reza Khan, is evident as early as 1921. Fakhr Afaq Parsa, for instance, argued, 'To gain freedom and our usurped rights, Iranian women need a revolution, and that revolution will happen in the hands of men. ... Therefore, in order to reach our goals we need to cultivate supporters for ourselves, not with harshness and threats, but with peaceful reasoning! Now if you want to call this flattery and sweet talk, that's up to you!'[71] The relation to the centralizing state proved to be a difficult challenge for campaigning women.

Women of the East

The 1932 congress of Women of the East marked a very important shift in the evolution of the SPW (which hosted the congress) and a significant reconfiguration of some of these debates. Founded in 1922, the Society had been headed by Masturah Afshar after the death of one of its founders and its first president, Muhtaram Khanum Iskandari (d. July 1924). Shortly after the 1932 congress, the SPW ceased any activity. The current oppositional story combines an emphasis on Reza Shah's violence in implementing unveiling with his repressive policy of closing down all independent parties, journals, unions and organizations, including women's presses and associations. This account ignores the fact that more than coercion was at work: women themselves were divided on the issue of unveiling and on how to relate to the increasingly centralized and autocratic government of Reza Shah. The differences on the unveiling question were voiced at length from the floor of the congress of Women of the East. A number of Iranian women spoke in favour of unveiling as a necessary step towards women's progress. Others spoke for progress but in opposition to unveiling. The organizational issues are not very evident from the congress proceedings, but later memoirs of participants, and some details of congress presentations, are quite indicative of a rift. The site of the congress was shifted from a private girls' school, 'Iffatiyah, where the first session was held, to the private residence of the SPW's president, Masturah Afshar,[72] and finally to the hall of the Ministry of Education for its sixth and concluding session. This shift in site consolidated a critical move by the government that aimed to control women's activism. Though the congress was hosted by the SPW, the government played an increasingly interventionist role. In addition to Awrang, who attended the planning meetings in early November 1932, the wife of Brigadier General 'Abd al-Reza Afkhami, Associate Director of the Red Lion and Sun (Iranian equivalent of the Red Cross), her name not given in the records, and Khanum 'Iffat al-Muluk Khwajah'nuri, representing Princess Shams Pahlavi, went to Masturah Afshar's house to greet and welcome the planning group. Nour Hamadé from Lebanon, Hanifa Khouri from Egypt and Saʿida Murad from Syria arrived in Tehran in early November to organize the congress. The minister of the court, Teymurtash, visited the delegation and indicated the government's support for the congress and for 'women's emancipation'.[73] Awrang officially opened the congress on 27 November, and Mrs Afkhami, now representing Princess Shams Pahlavi, informed the congress that the princess had agreed to act as its honorary president.[74] She then proceeded to read a lecture in praise of Reza Shah and his efforts in rejuvenating the Iranian nation and his actions to improve women's education and welfare. She was followed by Masturah Afshar. According to Nur al-Hudá Manganah, one of the leading women's rights activists and a member of the board of directors of SPW, this lecture was not what had been planned by the society. She recalled bitterly:

> We had set up a number of commissions [within SPW to deal with organiza-
> tion of the congress], but Masturah Khanum would negotiate matters in the
> absence of commissions [behind the scenes]. I reminded her several times that
> she was carrying things out without consulting the commissions and without
> informing other women, and that all women, members of these commissions,
> are very upset at her behaviour. ... When the Congress was convened ... Mrs
> Masturah Afshar's report was not about the positive activities and achievements
> of the Society of Patriotic Women. Members began to murmur their discontent,
> 'This report had nothing to do with us; it was out of subject; why didn't she
> mention our activities and services; why didn't she honour the founders of our
> society such as Mrs Iskandari and yourself (that is, me)?' After this untruthful
> report of Mrs Masturah Afshar, the personal side of which overrode the general
> interests of the Society, all the hard-working members of the Society who were
> committed to general interests, including myself who had carried the heavy
> burden of the Society's work, lost heart and resigned. After that, there was
> no one to pursue the Society's goals with steadfastness and hard work and re-
> establish it on a firm and beneficial foundation. The Society fell apart.[75]

What was the content of the 'untruthful report of Mrs Masturah Afshar' that had caused such commotion and demoralization? What had she said in place of reporting 'the positive activities and achievements of SPW'? Afshar's lecture on the first day of the congress was filled with praise and appreciation, favourably comparing the situation of Iranian women under Reza Shah to other women of the East, on the one hand, and to the piti-ful state of Iranian women prior to the 'shining dawn' of the Pahlavi era, on the other. Throughout the congress, while many Iranian women used the occasion as a platform from which to address the Iranian government critically and raise their demands, largely speaking on issues of concern to women, others were more concerned with displaying the achievements of

Reza Shah's government, expressing their thanks to him. When there were disagreements among Iranian women (such as on unveiling, or on whether they should demand that the government send women abroad for higher education), Awrang would intervene to weigh the argument along the lines of government policy.[76]

If Awrang had failed to stop women from speaking for unveiling when it was not yet government policy, he had succeeded in bringing a wing of the movement under the government mantle. Is it possible that the change of government policy on the issue of unveiling was in part a bargain that these women had struck? The current dissident historiography of women's organizations not only credits (blames) Reza Shah with the unveiling campaign, but it often considers women such as Masturah Afshar, Hajir Tarbiat and Sadiqah Dawlatabadi as traitors to the cause of an independent women's movement and as stooges of Reza Shah.[77] *Kanun-i banuvan* – a women's organization established in May 1935 under the auspices of the Ministry of Education to lead the educational and propaganda campaigns for unveiling and other policies to do with women – is considered simply as a state organization that was formed on the dead bodies of all previous independent women's organizations. But a woman such as Dawlatabadi could hardly be thought of as a stooge of the government. She had been active since the late 1910s in opening schools and publishing journals. In 1923 she went to Europe to study and represented SPW at the 1926 congress of the International Alliance for Women's Suffrage in Paris, and upon her return to Iran in 1927 she worked for girls' schools in Tehran – many years before *Kanun-i banuvan* came on the scene. She continued to do much of the same after the 1941 abdication of Reza Shah until her death in 1961. A more persuasive account would see her as informing what became government policy on women's issues while being formed by those very possibilities and limiting conditions we codename 'government'.[78] Dawlatabadi can be seen as using the government as much as the government can be seen as using her.[79]

Hajir Tarbiat recalled her own surprised dismay that as late as 1932, when she was appointed to be the director of *Dar al-mu'allamat* (the post-secondary college for women), she was ordered to wear the chador even inside the college, since all girls had been required to do so. She took the initiative of negotiating with the girls' parents an acceptable black uniform that would replace the chador inside the college grounds. This initiative, she recalled, was gradually followed by other girls' schools.[80] More interestingly, her narrative continues to state that from early March 1935 she encouraged a group of women educators and colleagues to come to work without chador and allowed the girls to come to the college without chador as well. She takes credit for the formation of *Kanun-i banuvan*: 'In April/May 1935, I asked for permission from the Ministry of Education to form an association for women called *Kanun-i banuvan*. This request was granted.'[81] She was its first president, before she was replaced by the government by Dawlatabadi. That her initiatives were important in the state's eyes is indicated by a rarely noted detail from Reza Shah's much quoted speech of 17 Day 1314 (7 January 1936). He opened his brief speech with these words: 'As Khanum Tarbiat has noted, women in this country could not develop their innate capabilities because they were kept outside society.'[82] In other words, the most powerful man in the country sought affirmation of what has been recorded as his bold move to liberate Iranian women by relying on a woman's words.

Yet the (self-) erasure of these women's agencies was almost immediate. Already on 18 January 1936, in his talk at *Kanun-i banuvan*, Hasan Vusuq would speak of 'an angel of mercy, a courageous child of the country with a strong mentality, a vision, and a capable iron hand who arose to save the miserable women [*badbakht'ha*]'.[83] Tarbiat herself confirmed Vusuq's narrative by emphasizing that it was Reza Shah who had just removed all obstacles on the path of women's development.[84] I am not seeking to reverse the story and project what these women had achieved up to that moment as determinative of governmental action. We need a much more nuanced view of the relationship between women's activities and the government. Not only were Iranian women divided in the 1930s on how to relate to the increasingly autocratic government of Reza Shah on the issue of unveiling. Unlike on the issues of women's education and reform of the laws of marriage and divorce, there was a deep division among Iranian women themselves, going back at least to the constitutional period, as the pages of *Shukufah* attest, as women's writings and actions in the 1920s show and as the arguments presented in the 1932 congress confirm.

I stress this division among women because after the official ban on the chador was imposed, not only did state violence enter into the picture but, more critically, an unbridgeable chasm opened up among women. Girls were withdrawn from schools and kept at home. Women teachers who did not want to unveil resigned from their jobs or were dismissed, which opened up room for the immediate promotion of other women.[85] Girls' schools that had been the venues of women's public togetherness, with women acting not only as students and teachers but also as citizens, actively shaping 'gender and patriotic sisterhood', now became sites of a division. As later recalled by women who accepted (or embraced) unveiling, schools suddenly 'became empty'. Becoming empty evidently cannot be taken literally, since these very women who narrate the emptiness of these spaces were there to observe and report that emptiness. They had become empty only of women who would not (or could not, if forbidden by fathers, brothers or husbands) unveil. Yet it is the women who did unveil who recall the space as empty; the emptiness they experienced was their site of gender and national sisterhood being emptied of those 'sisters-in-religion' who did not return to school. In the previous site, all women who wanted modern education, who wanted to refashion themselves as educated mothers and spouses, to escape marriage, or to become professional, all who were advocating reforms of marriage and divorce laws seen to be in conformity with the reforming spirit of Islam, had crafted a space of solidarity and common activity. All these reforms were considered Islamicly acceptable. Not so with unveiling. The unveiling campaign as enforced by the government now expelled some from this common site. As with other measures taken by Reza Shah's government, increasing modernization became conflated with that modernity in which becoming modern was disaffiliated from Islam and made to coincide with pre-Islamic Iranianism.[86] It is highly indicative of the stakes played out on women's dress code that official government memoranda of the 1930s repeatedly referred to the new dress code as *libas-i tajaddud-i nisvan*, clothes of modernity of women.[87] Those who had sought to combine their quest for modernity with a reconfiguration of Islam were unmistakably marked as traditional and anti-modern – an identification that has only in the recent decade been re-shaped. This process changed the meanings of modernity, Iranianism and Islam. Iranian modernity took increasingly a non-Islamic (though not necessarily anti-Islamic) meaning. Iranian secularism and nationalism were critically re-shaped through the expulsion of a different kind of modernity, one that had attempted to produce a different hybrid made of grafting Iranian nationalism with Shi'ism.

Current accounts of the period, by focusing on the issue of violence or on the issue of struggles between the state and clerical establishment over social authority and power, occlude modernity's expulsion of part of its own spectrum to produce its secularism. In another place, I have argued:

> The rift between traditionalist and modernist women ... resulted largely from particular sets of state policies initiated by Reza Shah, and the reaction of the clerical establishment to those policies. ... Twice, once in the 1930s and once again in the 1950s and 1960s, the Pahlavi state closed off all possibilities for independent women's initiatives and took over 'the woman question' as a domain of state policy. In response, in each period, the clerical faction opposed to any changes in women's social conditions constructed women's liberation as un-Islamic, as illegitimate, and as corruption perpetuated by the state. Thus ...

[the] 'modernizing state' and the Shi'ite clergy constructed each others' domains
of authority and produced Islam and feminism as mutually exclusive.[88]

What my own earlier assessment is missing is that women activists and organizations themselves were critically involved in the production of these reconfigurations. In fact, feminism became a most privileged category marking
Iranian secularism. Perhaps more than any other socio-political and cultural
issue of contention, women's rights issues – as the expressions 'clothes of
modernity', 'clothes of civilization', best narrate it – became markers of secularism of modernity. Feminism became a screen category (a veil) occluding
a historical process by which one kind of modernity was fashioned through
the expulsion of Islam on to the beyond of modernity, where backwardness and religion became conflated by secularism as its abject other.[89] It is
this historical legacy that I suggest lies at the heart of current fears about
contamination of secularism and feminism with religion.

One consequence of this process has been that women's issues, as
symbolized by the unveiling controversy, proved to be an issue on which
it became impossible to build a consensus. Not only did those opposed to
giving up independent women's activities to state tutelage (such as Nur al-
Hudá Manganah) withdraw and become demoralized, but those who did
not want to unveil stayed at or were driven home. This is a chasm that
only recent developments have begun to challenge and change. There is a
re-emergence of conversation and cooperation between secular and Islamist
women activists today. Islamist women activists in today's Iran are products of the previous era, not only sociologically, as many have observed, but
also in the sense that the terms of 'the woman question' they have received
bear the markings of decades of socio-cultural transformations. They take
issues as self-evidently Islamic as their mothers' generation took them as un-
Islamic.

The emergence of a vocal feminist position from within the ranks of the
Islamist movement over the past decades in Iran constitutes an important
break from the past, positioning all Islam to the beyond of the modern.
By opening up the domain of Islamic interpretation to non-believers and
non-Muslims, by insisting on the equality of women and men in all areas,
by disconnecting the presumed natural or God-given differences between
women and men from the cultural and social constructions of gender, these
currents have opened up a space for dialogue and alliance between Islamist
women activists and secular feminists, reversing a 60-year-old rift in which
each treated the other as antagonist.

Conclusion

The purpose of my historicization of secularism, nationalism and feminism is not to evoke some golden age narrative in which women were united and then became divided, hoping that one could re-enact some new moment of unity. But if Islam, secularism, nationalism and feminism are historically defined and in a changing relationship, there is no reason not to imagine reconfigurations of these terms.[90]

If the Islamist movement and the revolution and the government established in 1979 have provided the threat to projects of Iranian secularism and feminism, they turn out to have produced at once some of the possibilities of a reconfiguration of these modernist projects. Thinking of Islam as the antithesis of modernity and secularism forecloses the possibilities of recognition of these emergences, of working for these reconfigurations; it blocks off the formation of alliances;[91] it continues to reproduce Islam as exclusive of secularism, democracy and feminism, as pollutants of these projects; it continues the work of constituting each as the edge at which meaning would collapse for the other.

The points I have raised so far through a discussion of feminism and Islamism pertain to a reconsideration of Iranian nationalism and Islamism as well. Like many other modern nationalisms, the dominant concept of Iranian nationalism has demanded assimilation of differences of religion, language, ethnicity, gender and sexuality into a unitary notion of Iranian-ness. Citizenship seemed to require erasure of difference. But Iranian-ness achieved through such erasures could speak confidently of its inclusivity only if Muslim-ness, Persian-ness, masculinity and heterosexuality could be taken for granted. Iranians who could not take such privileges for granted had to assimilate into the manly woman, Persianized Turks, Islamicized non-Muslims, and accept heteronormativity as natural – in other words keep silent, if not be silenced – on their language, gender and sexuality, religious and ethnic differences.

If, however, we begin to re-imagine an Iranian identity that would entertain a different relationship between citizenship and difference, then the possibility that one can speak as Iranian and as Muslim, by explicitly marking Islam and Iran as separate domains, can make it more possible also to speak as Iranian and Jewish, as Iranian and Armenian – though it still remains tragically dangerous to try to speak as Iranian and Baha'i. To open up an explicit claim to Iranian-ness as Muslim and feminist could thus open up other speaking-as positions. Far from being threatening to secularism, feminism or Iranianism, it could promise a different sense of Iranian-ness that allows new reconfigurations of these terms.

11

Polygamy Before and After the Introduction of the Swiss Civil Code in Turkey

Nicole A.N.M. van Os

In February 1926 the rulers of the young Turkish Republic introduced a new Civil Code. Ever since, this has been celebrated by Kemalist feminists as a major step forward in the emancipation of Turkish women and, of course, in modernization. Every year in February Turkish newspapers carry articles celebrating the anniversary of the introduction of the code and testifying to its importance for the modernization of the republic. Others, however, have been more critical and questioned the effectiveness of these laws and therefore the success of modernization.

This chapter contributes to this discussion. In the first place, I want to put the introduction of the code into its historical context, looking at the various family-related laws/codes of the late Ottoman Empire and the Turkish Republic, concentrating on those parts that deal with contracting a marriage. Laws and regulations can indeed be a useful tool of authoritarian modernization but only, however, if they can be enforced. The question whether the authorities were successful in enforcing the laws will be the subject of the second part of my study. I will concentrate on one aspect of the family code in this second part: polygamy, and more specifically polygyny, or marriage of a man to more than one woman. I will try to compare the situation before and after the introduction of the Swiss Civil Code: how often did (or does) polygyny occur and under what circumstances? How should we interpret the developments in this respect in the context of modernization and its (lack of) success?

Modernization in the late Ottoman Empire and the early Republic of Turkey: secularization of law and education

Although the two terms should be separated conceptually, 'modernization' and 'secularization' are often used interchangeably. This approach to modernization has been criticized heavily for being Eurocentric over the past few decades, and the existence of alternative forms of modernization has been discussed extensively.[1] However, secularization is undeniably part and parcel of Western-inspired modernization. Thus, also in the late Ottoman Empire and the early Turkish Republic, the dominant – and victorious – form of modernization was closely intertwined with secularization.

One of the books which for a long time put an important stamp on the historiography of the late Ottoman Empire and the early Turkish Republic is *The Development of Secularism in Turkey* by Niyazi Berkes.[2] In Turkish this book is called *Türkiye'de Çağdaşlaşma*. The choice of title, meaning 'Modernization in Turkey' in Turkish, reveals two things. In the first place, the development of secularism is put on an equal footing with moderniza-tion. This probably happened with the knowledge of the author, who was still alive when the book, which originally appeared in English, was trans-lated into Turkish. In the second place, the literal meaning of the word *çağdaşlaşma* ('modernization') is 'to become of the same era'. Implicitly this meant becoming of the same era as Western Europe (and the US). From this we can conclude that according to Niyazi Berkes and quite a few other scholars, Turkish modernization was inevitably connected with seculariza-tion according to European examples.

This was not only the analysis of scholars in hindsight, but also the point of view of the 'victorious' part of the ruling and intellectual elites in the late Ottoman Empire. During the nineteenth century some of the bureaucrats within the Ottoman ruling class felt that their increasing relative weak-ness vis-à-vis the European powers was due to the lack of knowledge of modern science. They developed highly positivist views and thought the panacea to cure the 'sick man of Europe' lay in the adaptation of secu-lar and scientific forms of education. Parallel with the traditional religion-based educational system under the control of local religious authorities, a new secular-based and state-controlled educational system firmly based in European Enlightenment traditions was developed.

Not only was the educational system reformed along more secularist lines, but also the Ottoman law system was gradually secularized. On the initiative of reform-minded bureaucrats and under the pressure of European states that wanted to improve the position of their citizens in the Ottoman Empire and of the minority groups under their protection, the influence of *fikh* and *Shari'a* on the Ottoman law system was diminished. Along with the secularization of the law system, the judiciary system was also secular-ized.

From its earliest years the Ottoman state had known a kind of dual law system with *Shari'a* and *fikh*-based laws existing next to a more secular law system of *kanun*s, generally based on existing traditions and sanctioned by the Padishah, both the spiritual leader of the Muslim world community and the worldly leader of the Ottoman Empire, through a decree and/or the highest religious authority, the Sheikh al-Islam, through a *fatwa*. *Kanun*s dealt mainly with questions of taxation, land tenure and criminal law, fields in which the *Shari'a* lacked clarity.

In the nineteenth century the law system was further, or rather more formally, secularized: existing laws were reformed, new laws were issued and, importantly, secular courts, initially in the form of councils, were installed parallel with the existing religious courts. A commercial code based on parts of the French commercial code was introduced in 1850. This first example of translating and adapting a European code to the local Ottoman situation was followed by others.[3]

After the inglorious end of the Ottoman Empire the process of secularization gained momentum. Under Mustafa Kemal (Atatürk) the secularization of education and law that had started in the nineteenth century was finalized. While the changes during the last century of Ottoman rule led to a dual system in law and education, with institutions controlled by religious authorities existing next to state-controlled secular institutions, Kemal was decisive in removing the last remnants of control by religious authorities over education and law.

In March 1924 the power of the religious authorities was dealt a severe blow. Three laws were, after due discussions in the parliament, accepted, which ended the caliphate, put the religious foundations under the control of a Directory falling under the Prime Ministry and put an end to the dual educational system.[4] With the *Tevhid-i Tedrisat Kanunu* (Unity of Education Law) the opening of religious schools was not prohibited, but the new laws demanded that compulsory primary education until the age of 12 was to be taken at a secular state school. Henceforth all schools fell under the supervision of the Ministry of Education, and religious authorities were denied all control over education.[5]

Mustafa Kemal Atatürk also replaced the last remnants of the *Shari'a*. By the 1920s the *Shari'a* and the courts dealing with cases related to it were only concerned with matters of marriage, divorce and succession. While these courts were now placed under the jurisdiction of the Ministry of Justice, family law, as in most societies that underwent a process of secularization of their law system, remained the last part of the system to be secularized in Turkey.

The secularization of civil codes and family law

Although the process of secularization of law systems in countries over the world shows a great variety in the times it started and the length of the process, what is common in most countries, if not all, is that the last element of law to become secularized is family law. The first country to secularize its family law was France. In the wake of the French Revolution, the French Civil Code was introduced in 1804. Other countries followed suit.

With the introduction of secular civil codes, family law, the authority to legitimize the conjugal bond between a man and a woman, was transferred to the state, while before it belonged to the church or religious authorities. In general, this legitimizing authority is the third element needed to create a conjugal unit or family, besides a man and a woman.[6] Not always are the two authorities completely separated. In some states of the USA, for example, the religious functionary can at the same time represent the secular authority.

Although in secular states official civil marriage is sufficient to create a legal conjugal bond, many religious people do not feel a marriage to be complete unless sanctioned by a higher power represented by a religious authority. Therefore the official marriage ceremony is still often followed by a wedding service before a religious authority. Interestingly enough this can lead to a still-existing dual system of religious courts, such as that of the Roman Catholic Church next to the secular courts, as is the case in the Netherlands. The Roman Catholic court still deals with matters of family law such as marriage and divorce and can prevent someone who has been officially divorced before a secular court from getting married in church for a second time, because it does not recognize the 'religious divorce'. Only after the Roman Catholic Church acknowledges the divorce (which only happens in very exceptional cases) is a second marriage in church possible.

Especially in newly formed secular or secularizing states with a variety of religious communities living within their borders, family laws are often seen as the last stronghold through which religious authorities can officially exert control over the personal lives of their community members and through which the continuation of a cultural identity can be guaranteed.

In the dominantly Muslim countries of the Arab world, secularization of the *Shari'a*-based family law was not an issue. For Muslims, the *Shari'a* forms the law of God. Based on the Koran, the Sunna and the Hadith, it regulates without any formal codification all legal aspects of a Muslim society. However, in the twentieth century, the rulers of these countries also felt that the *Shari'a* and its application were no longer meeting the demands of their society. The divine source of the *Shari'a* was open to multiple interpretations, which caused a lack of transparency not only for the laymen, but also for the judiciaries. Through codification this lack of transparency was to be lifted and a set of general legal provisions was to facilitate the work of the judges. Thus family law in these countries was codified, but certainly not secularized. The *Shari'a* remained the framework on which the codification was based. In most Arab countries, this codification was modelled on a book published in Egypt in 1875 by Muhammed Qadri Pasha on family law[7] and the 1917 Law of Family Rights of the Late Ottoman Empire.[8] The book by Muhammed Qadri Pasha was a codification based on the Hanafi school, but was never enacted as a law.[9]

The late Ottoman Empire and the early Republic of Turkey

With the reforms of the *Tanzimat* era and the ongoing secularization and codification of the Ottoman law system, the need was also felt to develop a civil law. This led to a fierce discussion between those in favour of adopting the secular French Civil Code, represented by Ali Pasha, the *Tanzimat* reformer, and those in favour of basing this civil law on Islamic principles, headed by Ahmet Cevdet Pasha, the historian. While the former wanted to create equality for all citizens of the Ottoman Empire through a French-based civil code and mixed courts, the latter was convinced that such a Christian-based law would not be acceptable to the Muslim population. Ahmet Cevdet Pasha, therefore, opted for a codification in which the Muslim legal rules relating to civil law would be collected and systematized. A commission was put to work to discuss the issue and the result was that Cevdet Pasha was asked to form a committee to write a work based on Muslim principles. This four-man committee, *Mecelle Cemiyeti*, set to work and between 1867 and 1876 developed what became known as the *Mecelle-i Ahkam-i Adliye*, or, in short, *Mecelle*, the first civil code of the Ottoman Empire based on Hanafi principles.[10]

Although the *Mecelle* was a very extensive work, it was not a complete civil code. Among others, the part on family law was absent. Family law remained uncodified, and *fikh* and collections of *fatwa* continued to form its source of reference. Aydın gives two main reasons for the fact that the committee did not include family law in its work. One reason was lack of time. Before it had finished its work, the *Mecelle* Committee was dissolved in 1876 by Abdulhamid II, who did not allow for any independent bodies. Another reason was the development of the *nizamiye* (secular) courts that were in need of a codification of the laws, which were indeed included in the *Mecelle*. On the other hand, he argued, family law remained under the jurisdiction of the religious courts of the respective communities and therefore there was no need for a uniform codified family law.[11] The religious authorities of the various communities in the Ottoman Empire were probably not really interested in such a codification either. Nor were the conservative forces in the committee that had been formed by Ahmet Cevdet Pasha, who, as we have seen, was not in favour of a European-based civil code.

The first codifications of family law were in the form of imperial decrees issued during the First World War. Under one of these decrees a woman gained the right to file for divorce if she had not heard from her husband for four years and his absence caused her to live in poverty. Another decree issued in March 1917 gave women the right to divorce their husband if he had a serious or contagious illness such as psychiatric problems, venereal diseases or leprosy.[12] They had to apply to the religious judge (*kadı*), who would grant them a divorce. Both decrees were confirmed by a *fatwa* from the Sheikh al-Islam, although neither accorded with the teaching of the Hanafi school, but with that of the Hanbali and Maliki schools respectively.[13] The idea of using the principles of other schools was a novelty that proved to be very useful in the first real codification of Ottoman family law. Using these principles, especially where they were more flexible than the Hanafi school, enabled the committee codifying family law to meet the demands for change and at the same time not to jeopardize their relations with the more conservative religious circles.

These two decrees were followed by a more comprehensive codification of Ottoman family law in the *Hukuk-u Aile Kararnamesi* (Decree on Family Law). This was issued in October 1917 and only contained regulations relating to marriage and divorce. It was repealed before it could become law by the Sheikh al-Islam who was acting Grand Vizir under the occupying forces after the end of the First World War on 19 June 1919. The reason was the violent opposition against the law from Muslim conservative forces and leaders of non-Muslim communities.[14]

The decree had been prepared by one of the three commissions installed to review the *Mecelle* and the trade law and to codify Ottoman family law. The commissions were explicitly ordered not to base themselves only on the Hanafi school, but to also include views from the other schools. They also studied the relevant laws of Switzerland, Germany and France and, where necessary, other countries. The decree on family law that was issued was valid for all Ottomans, Muslim and non-Muslim. However, it was stressed that the commission had tried to form a system, which was applicable to all communities, but that, if the need was felt, separate laws and rules could be issued for the non-Muslim communities. In practice the decree ended up having a partially separate text to suit the wishes of the empire's

Muslim, Jewish and Christian communities. Still, according to Article 56, all communities, Muslim and non-Muslim, henceforth had to apply to the Muslim (*Shari'a*) courts in cases relating to family law. This decision led to fierce protests from the leaders of the non-Muslim communities, among them the Vatican, and Article 156 which stated this was repealed.[15]

With the cancellation of the decree, the old situation was restored and the courts of the separate communities were again allowed to deal with the family law cases of their own people. Meanwhile the commissions continued to work, trying to formulate a new law. After the abolition of the sultanate in 1922 and the promulgation of the republic in 1923 a new Civil Code Commission was formed. This was to follow, in the first place, the principles of *fikh* and use the principles of the modern state only in the second instance. It drafted a new law that, with its 142 articles, looked very much like the old *Hukuk-u Aile Kararnamesi*.[16] This did not meet the aspirations for modernization and secularization of Mustafa Kemal and his men, however, and by 1925 the minister of law, Mahmud Es'ad (Bozkurt), declared that a new commission would be installed to investigate, translate and annotate the Swiss Civil Code. Based on the Swiss Civil Code, the Civil Code of the Republic of Turkey was drafted. It was accepted on 17 February 1926 and promulgated on 4 October 1926.[17]

Despite referring to the Civil Code of the Republic of Turkey as a translation with minor changes, a closer scrutiny of the text reveals that quite substantial changes were made. These changes were not just random, but clearly designed to satisfy the more conservative, religious forces in the religious and political arena and to

> facilitate the merging of a Swiss inspired Code into the pre-existing situation which had become the Republic of Turkey. ... The discrepancies, ... are at least partially the result of an inheritance by the Turkish Code of certain legal sensibilities which were expressed both in earlier Ottoman documents – such as ... the 1917 Family code – and in earlier Ottoman/Islamic legal tradition.[18]

Law and marriage[19]

Although the *Shari'a* covers all aspects of life, at its heart is family law, the rules regulating the relations between the partners within a conjugal unit and their relatives and dependants. According to Muslim law, marriage is a legal agreement between two parties, a man and a woman, or, if they are minors, between their guardians or their families. As such marriage is a purely civil act and has no religious implications at all. It is concluded at the moment one of the parties accepts the offer of the other party in the presence of two male witnesses. According to the Hanafi school an adult woman can contract her own marriage. However, if she asks for too low a dowry, her guardian can force her to dissolve the marriage bond. He has the same right if, in his eyes, there is no 'equality' between the parties according to the law. Not only can a woman contract her own marriage, she also has to give her consent explicitly if she is an adult woman. If she is a virgin this consent does not have to be verbally stated, but may be concluded based upon her behaviour. If she is not a virgin, she has to state her consent explicitly. If she is dumb she may do this through signs, and if she cannot be present, because she is at a distance, she can do it in writing.[20]

Although the fact that women can contract their own marriage seems to give them some freedom, this freedom is very limited. Except for the Hanbali school, none of the other Sunni schools allow for extra stipulations in the marriage contract. Nor does the Hanafi school. So a stipulation stating that the woman has the right to divorce her husband, if he takes a second wife, is void, it does not make the marriage contract as such invalid.[21]

Marriages according to Hanafi law do not need an authority to legitimize the bond nor do they need to be registered. In fact the contract does not even have to be made in writing. The presence of two male witnesses or two female and one male witness is sufficient to make it legally binding.[22]

Invalid or irregular marriages

According to Islamic law marriages that have not been concluded according to the rules of the *Shari'a* and do not fulfil the preconditions needed are either invalid (*batil*) or irregular (*fasid*). If a marriage is concluded *knowingly* while impediments exist and these impediments cannot be removed by the parties themselves, the marriage is invalid. If a marriage is concluded while the parties were not aware of the impediments existing and/or the impediments can be lifted by the parties, the marriage is irregular. The parties then have the option either to regularize the marriage or to separate.

So what is important is whether or not the parties are acting in good faith and whether or not the irregularity is curable to determine whether the contract is void or valid and whether the parties have to abide by the regulations resulting from a marriage contract. This matter is very complicated and the various schools differ in opinion on minor details that are beyond the scope of this chapter. Therefore I will give only an outline here of the impediments to marriage.[23]

The first category of impediments to marriage is the existence of blood ties, ties of affinity or foster ties of a certain degree that prohibit the conclusion of a marriage. One cannot marry his or her mother or father, his or her grandmother or grandfather, his or her daughter or son, his or her granddaughter or grandson, nor his or her aunts, uncles, nieces and nephews. However, marriage between cousins, i.e. one's aunt's or uncle's children, is permitted and in some communities even preferred to prevent family property from being dispersed. One cannot marry the husband or wife of one's ascendants or descendants nor the ascendants or descendants of one's spouse. So a man cannot marry his father's or his son's widow, just as he cannot marry his father-in-law's or stepson's widow. Furthermore, the Koran prohibits explicitly a marriage to one's wet nurse or her daughters. The various schools have extended this rule and virtually prohibit marriage to the relatives of the wet nurse, as if they are related by blood ties or ties of affinity.

A second factor that can hinder marriage is *idda*, the waiting period for women after a divorce from or death of her husband. If a woman is still in her period of *idda* she cannot be married. This waiting period is designed to prove that she is not bearing his child. The period is three months after a divorce and four months and ten days after a death. In both cases the *idda* also ends after birth if the woman happens to be pregnant at the moment the marriage is terminated.

Thirdly, one cannot marry if one already has the maximum-allowed one husband or four wives for a woman and a man respectively. Furthermore if a woman has not married another man after having been repudiated by her husband three times, she cannot marry her first husband again unless she first marries and divorces someone else.

Finally, marriage is prohibited if one of the partners is physically or mentally unfit. Age is not an impediment to marriage. According to the Hanafi school minors can be married off by their guardians without their consent. Both males and females have, however, the right to reject the marriage when they reach puberty, but only if the marriage guardian was not their father or paternal grandfather. For females this is more relevant, because the man can use his regular right of repudiation, while for a woman the possibilities to file for divorce are limited in Hanafi law. To terminate the marriage, she will have to indicate this immediately upon reaching majority in front of two witnesses and ask the judge to dissolve the marriage. The marriage will be terminated only after he has issued a decree to that effect.[24]

Polygamy

According to Islamic law a woman can have one husband, while a man can have a maximum of four wives. The source for this rule is the *Sura al-Nisa* (Chapter of Women) in the Koran:

> But if ye fear that ye cannot do justice between orphans, then marry what seems good to you of women, by twos, or threes, or fours; and if ye fear that ye cannot be equitable, then only one, or what your right hands possess. That keeps you nearer to not being partial.[25]

The central word in this quotation is 'equitable'. Polygamy as such has no legal implications; no permission or other form of formality is needed, but Islamic courts deal with cases in which equality between the spouses is supposedly not maintained. According to *Shari'a* law the wives of a man have a right to separate households. If a wife does not get her own household she can refuse her husband cohabitation without any legal repercussions. Although most schools state that all the wives should be treated equally the Hanafi school leaves space for differential standing of wives. According to this school, the standing of a wife should be the average standing of the husband and the wife before her marriage.

The principle of equality requires a husband to spend an equal amount of time – in practice this often is interpreted as 'nights' – with all his wives. This right to companionship does not automatically imply that he also has to divide his sexual attentions equally between his wives. However, if he does not spend time with the wife whose turn it is, he has to pay compensation to her. Only if the new wife is a virgin may he spend seven nights in a row with her without having to make it up to his other wives.

Although marriages in societies where the *Shari'a* was applied were formally regulated, for marriages to be socially and sometimes even legally accepted other elements were often essential. Besides the existing formal law, encoded or not, there exist other socially accepted (local) rules, regulations and traditions and customs, which can be regarded as a form of law, a system of directives organizing, legitimizing and sanctioning the actions and interactions of the members of a society.

Understanding these multiple layers of law and their interaction may help us to understand the continued existence of polygamy in modern Turkish society, despite the profound changes in its formal legal system.

Marriage in the Ottoman Empire

In the Ottoman Empire the doctrine of the Hanafi school prevailed and Ottoman family law was based on the interpretations of that school. However, we will see that marriages in the Ottoman Empire were much more regulated than the Hanafi school required. Most likely, these extra requirements were based on old Turkish habits, which as such had been codified.[26] Moreover, besides the discrepancies caused by the requirements of the Ottoman authorities beyond those of the Islamic law *per se*, there were local mores and habits which also regulated the ways a marriage was contracted.

Although Hanafi law merely states that marriage should take place in the presence of two witnesses, it seems that the Ottoman authorities felt that some religious official representing at the same time the state authorities had to be present. Although this was only put into legal terms during the *Tanzimat* era, this seems to have been the practice long before.

We know that at least in Istanbul, according to local practices, an *imam* (religious functionary) was present at most marriages. His presence, however, never bestowed any religious authorization on the marriage.[27] Some of these *imams* took notes on the contracts that were concluded in their presence, but these notes had no official status. In 1883 the Ottoman state introduced marriage registration. This demanded a legal registration of the marriage, which had to take place within six months after the marriage itself took place. Since registration was not sanctioned legally or religiously, it remained low, even though penalties were supposed to be given to those not fulfilling the requirements. Only after 1905, when fines were more effectively given and other legal sanctions were introduced, did the registration, at least in Istanbul, increase slightly.[28]

According to Islamic law, officials like religious judges (*kadıs*) did not have to be involved in the process of concluding a marriage contract. In the religious court records (*sicil-i şeriyye*), one can find, however, several decisions on the validity of individual marriage acts. The local religious judge also had to provide an *izinname*, a certificate stating that there were no religious obstacles to marriage, which couples who wanted to get married needed to obtain.[29]

The *izinname* was a specifically Ottoman 'invention'. This document issued by the *kadı* stated that there were no impediments to marriage. Obtaining such permission for marriage from the religious authorities became mandatory for both Muslims and non-Muslims in the Ottoman lands with a regulation issued on 2 September 1881.[30] Although obtaining such an *izinname* was mandatory for administrative purposes, not obtaining it did not make the marriage invalid. Only with the issuing of a temporary law (*Kanun-u muvakkat*) in 1913 could an *imam* performing a marriage ritual without an *izinname* be punished with three months to two years of imprisonment. A few months later, when the *Hukuk-u Aile Kararnamesi* was issued, this was changed to one to six months of imprisonment for the male partner in the marriage, one week to one month for the witnesses present and two to 12 months behind bars for the authority concluding the marriage without the required *izinname*.[31]

The religious authority contracting the marriage was also obliged to send a certificate to the State Registry of Persons within 15 days. To check whether this was really done, the persons giving the *izinname* had to send a list once a month of the names of the persons to get married and their full addresses. Religious functionaries neglecting to perform this duty had to pay a fine of half a Turkish lira.[32]

Another quirk of the Ottoman marriage regulations was the habit of putting certain stipulations in the marriage contract. According to Hanafi law a marriage does not need a detailed marriage contract. Despite the fact that detailed stipulations in a marriage contract do not carry any validity according to Hanafi law, we know that Ottoman women in the late nineteenth and early twentieth century included such clauses in their marriage contracts. Thus Fatma Aliye, in the second conversation of a book in which she describes three (fictional) conversations between European women visiting a harem and their hosts, refers to such a practice.[33] Also the author Halide Edib Adıvar divorced her husband when he married a second wife. She could do this because she had stipulated it in her marriage contract, following the Hanbali rather than the Hanafi school of law.[34] The possibility of making such stipulations was codified with the *Hukuk-u Aile Kararnamesi* of 1917.

Hukuk-u Aile Kararnamesi (Decree on Family Law) of 1917

The *Hukuk-u Aile Kararnamesi* was the first codification of family law in the Ottoman Empire. It was based on the existing practices of the Muslim community in the empire and as such based on Islamic law but included extra articles for the non-Muslim communities. It consisted of two books of six and three chapters respectively, of which the first was dedicated to marriage and the second to divorce. These books were followed by a kind of epilogue of 'various articles'. Furthermore it contained a series of articles in which their legal implications were further explained.[35] The decree is quite limited in its text. It laid out the headlines, and some details in the supplements, but still left a lot to be worked out by the persons involved. Details such as the exact procedures to be followed or the implications when one failed to follow the rules laid out in the decree were lacking.

With the decree, the authorities went beyond the regulations of the Hanafi school. It included articles based on the teachings of the other schools of thought or on Ottoman practices, but it also incorporated articles that were new. The introduction of an age limit was one such element. Men had to be 18 and women 17 to be able to get married. Only under certain conditions could they marry earlier. However, under no circumstances could boys under 12 and girls under nine get married (Articles 4–7). In accordance with Hanafi law (except for the clear age limit), a girl of 17 years or older wanting to get married had to apply to a judge who had to announce her wish to her legal guardian. If her legal guardian did not object or his objection was not deemed valid, she was allowed to get married (Article 8). Marriages of mentally weak persons were not permitted (*caiz değildir*), if there was no need to get married. If there was such a need, they could marry only with the permission of a judge (Article 9).

The decree listed those persons for whom marriage was forbidden (Articles 13–19). In this it followed the Hanafi school. In Article 14 the decree explicitly allowed for polygyny. Men were allowed to marry up to four wives.[36] An article based on the Maliki school, however, gave women the right to prevent their husbands from marrying a second wife. According to Article 38 a woman could stipulate in the marriage contract that in case her husband married another woman, she or the other woman would be regarded as divorced.[37] Thus an already existing practice was codified.

With the decree some of the specifically Ottoman practices were also codified. The intention to marry had to be officially announced beforehand (Article 33). In a further regulation the procedure to follow was explained. The prospective bride and groom had to get a paper from the Board of Elders with information on their family backgrounds and on whether or not there were any impediments to marriage. After due research by the court, the couple would be told whether or not there were indeed any impediments to their marriage. They could object to the decision. If they were then allowed to get married, the information on the paper would be compared to the official existing registers and, if found in order, the marriage would be announced at least ten days before the date of the ceremony. One copy of the announcement would be displayed at the courthouse, another at a crowded place in town. It was also possible to make the announcement through a newspaper. If someone raised objections, he or she would be heard by the court.[38]

The presence of a judge or state-appointed official was required. This official had to be present at the moment the parties expressed their consent to the marriage and he had to take down and register the marriage contract or deed. Although such a presence was deemed necessary, the absence of such an official did not make the marriage invalid (Article 37).

The decree remained valid until June 1919, after which the old situation, without any codification of family law, was restored. This situation continued until 1926, when the new Civil Code was issued.

The Civil Code of 1926

With the introduction of the Civil Code on 17 February 1926, polygamy was no longer allowed. Marriages concluded while one of the partners was married were automatically null and void. Persons contracting a polygamous marriage knowingly were subject to the Criminal Code, Article 237/5. A man's multiple marriages (up to four) concluded before 4 October 1926 remained valid. New marriages, however, could no longer be polygamous.[39]

A woman could only get married 300 days after a former marriage was ended (either through divorce or death). Furthermore the party that caused a marriage to be ended with a divorce could be prohibited from re-marrying for a period of between one and two years, this to be at the discretion of the judge declaring the divorce (Articles 96 and 142).[40] People having syphilis, gonorrhoea, leprosy or mental illness were not allowed to get married.[41]

The distinction between a religious marriage (*imam nikahı* or *dini nikah*) and an official or civil marriage (*resmi* or *medeni nikah*) was clearly made for the first time. For a marriage to be officially recognized the persons involved had to follow certain procedures. The marriage had to be announced 15 days before the actual marriage took place (Article 97). An official had to be present at the marriage. Unlike the *Hukuk-u Aile Kararnamesi*, a marriage where such an official was not present was invalid. At the marriage itself the spouses had to declare their decision to get married clearly and without any hesitation in front of two witnesses, as was the case under Islamic law as well. This way a civil marriage was actually also valid according to the *Shari'a*.

Religious marriages were no longer of any relevance to the state and carried no legal weight. The children born out of such marriage bonds were regarded as being born out of wedlock, could not be registered and were devoid of any legal rights. The problems caused by the high number of such illegal children prompted the Turkish government several times to issue laws legalizing them.[42] For the fruits of polygamous marriages, however, this was not possible. Polygamy now being illegal, men wanting to marry more than one wife could no longer be married by state officials and often sought the help of an *imam nikahı*.

Polygyny in the Ottoman Empire

Contrary to common belief in Europe, polygyny was rather rare in the Ottoman Empire, as Lady Montague had already remarked at the beginning of the eighteenth century. In seventeenth-century Istanbul approximately 7.5 per cent of the men appearing in the court records had more than one wife.

Most of them had two. In Bursa in the sixteenth through to the nineteenth century the percentage did not exceed five. Registers of inheritances from the main towns of Anatolia over a broader period of time show that of the men in these records approximately 10 per cent were polygamous. However, the fact that they were mentioned in these records might mean that they were relatively well off. Given that polygyny occurred somewhat more frequently among the wealthier, the general average of polygamous men was probably less than 10 per cent. The vast majority of these had two wives only.[43] Duben and Behar found that in 1885 only 2.51 per cent of the married males in the Istanbul districts they studied were married polygynously. In 1907 this percentage had declined to 2.19. Again, almost all polygynous men had only two wives. Of the 108 cases of polygyny there were only nine cases where the man had three wives, and none had the maximum of four wives permitted by Islamic law. Of course, one must keep in mind that these were wives with an official status based on a marriage ceremony as prescribed by Islamic law. It may well be that some men had more sexual partners within their households in the form of concubines and slave-servants. The children of such relationships would be free and have the same social and legal status as the children of his wife, if they were acknowledged to be his.[44] Often the father would manumit and marry his concubine after she had borne him a child. Davis states that in most instances of polygyny this was the case. In such a situation the first wife of the master would remain the *büyük hanım* (grand lady) and keep her status as mistress of the house.[45]

Most cases of polygyny occurred among religious scholars and high-ranking government officials.[46] Respectively 30 and 10 per cent of them had more than one wife. Accordingly the number of cases of polygyny was higher in the areas where government officials lived, for example, in the areas surrounding the imperial palace on the lower shores of the Bosphorus. Duben and Behar suggest that the fact that polygyny occurred more frequently among government officials was not only because of their relatively high wealth. In most cases the male head of the household seems to have married a second time only because his first wife had not borne him any (male) children or because, after the early death of a son, she was too old to give him a new heir.

Ottoman literature reflects the findings described by Duben and Behar relating to polygyny. The study of Esen shows that in novels polygyny is also rarely mentioned and only occurs among men of religious learning or high rank. In these novels polygyny as such seems to have been accepted as part of daily practice for some. Esen mentions only one case in which the first wife of a man who wants to take a second wife considers committing suicide and eventually runs away. It is worthwhile mentioning that this book was written by a female author, Fatma Aliye, in the early 1880s.[47]

Fatma Aliye gave voice to the rejection of polygyny in public through her writings. In the second conversation of her above-mentioned book, a British woman is introduced who indeed is convinced that polygyny is current among middle-class Ottoman families. She is eager to know whether or not there would be rivalry and jealousy between the different wives of one man. She is immediately corrected. The host tells her that polygyny is very rare indeed even though it is permitted according to religious law. The explanation she gives is that it is very difficult to comply with the rules of Islam that demand from a polygynous man that he treats all his wives equally. It is, she tells her visitor, already difficult to maintain one wife. The reason for not abolishing polygyny completely is, according to the narrator-host, to prevent women who are barren or ill from being divorced and left to their own devices by their husbands.[48] The cases in which men take second wives while having a pretty and healthy first wife is explained with a reference to the nature of men. Although the Ottoman Muslim woman agrees that such a practice is undesirable, the visitor is told that the law grants women the right to ask for a divorce. After thus having defended the system of marriage in the Ottoman Empire, she takes the offensive and points out that the situation of women in Europe is much worse. She argues that if a man in Europe is engaged in more than one sexual relationship it means that the illegitimate partner and her children do not have any rights at all.[49] It seems that even though Fatma Aliye rejects polygyny in principle, she allows for it in certain cases, as does Şemseddin Sami,[50] but only with the consent of the first wife. In 1896 Fatma Aliye would take up the issue of polygyny again in a vehement polemic against the religious scholar Mahmud Es'ad Efendi, who argued that men were by nature polygamous and that this natural law was only confirmed by the religious law.[51]

Polygyny in the Republic of Turkey

Figures on the numbers of polygynous marriages in the Republic of Turkey are scarce. This is logical, since these marriages, being illegal, were never registered officially. Still some figures are available.

According to the census of 1960, 5,960,104 men and 5,981,430 women aged above 15 were married.[52] The difference between these two figures gives us an idea of the number of polygamous marriages. If we presume that most of these polygamous men limited themselves to two wives, there must have been about 42,652 (21,326 x 2) women involved in a polygynous marriage. That is approximately 0.71 per cent of all married women above the age of 15 and 0.36 per cent of all men.[53] One could perhaps argue that these polygamous marriages in 1960 formed the debris of the era predating the introduction of the Civil Code of 1926.

These percentages, based on the data of the 1960 census, seem lower than other estimates, however. Paul Stirling in his study *Turkish Village* published around 1968, for example, estimated that 2 per cent of all marriages in Turkey were polygamous.

Andras Riedlmayer mentions that he 'can cite anecdotal accounts from the 1970s of people [he] met in small-town Western Anatolia who had more than one wife'. In most cases, he added, the children born to the second wife were registered in the name of the first wife, with the result that, according to the official records, a woman would have given birth to two children within a period of less than nine months.[54] Clearly the reason behind this was to save the children from being illegal and, according to Turkish law, virtually non-existent, with the result that they were denied a school education.[55]

A study by Serim Timur from Hacettepe University showed that in the late 1960s and early 1970s the percentage of polygamous marriages in the west of Turkey was less than 0.5 per cent, approximately 2 per cent in central Anatolia, the Black Sea and the Mediterranean areas, and 5 per cent in eastern Anatolia. Most of the polygamous families were living in villages. In the three big cities of Izmir, Ankara and Istanbul there were virtually no polygamous marriages.[56]

A study by the Institute of Demographic Studies at the same university concluded in 1988 that 1.6 per cent of all marriages in Turkey were polygamous, with different percentages for the regions varying from 0.6 per cent in the west of Turkey to 2.9 per cent in the east.[57] Another research study found that the rate of polygamy in the area around Diyarbekir was about 4.4 per cent.[58] Elmacı gives a rate for the whole of Turkey of around 2 per cent.

It is difficult to draw far-reaching conclusions based on the scarce and diverse figures mentioned here. One thing that can definitely be concluded, however, is that polygamy did not end with the introduction of the Civil Code of 1926. Kumbetoğlu even states that the number of incidents of polygyny had been increasing throughout the 1990s.[59] At the turn of the millennium the percentage of women aged between 15 and 49 involved in a polygamous marriage in the eastern province of Şırnak was as high as 10.7 per cent.[60]

Although there are scarcely any figures to prove an increase in polygamous marriages, it is definitely possible to say that polygyny has become increasingly more *salonfähig* in the last decade. Characters in locally made television series are polygamous, women talk openly about their polygamous households in the discussion programmes for women on television, newspapers report on polygyny and its (often sad) consequences[61] and members of parliament and ministers of the cabinet do not hesitate to demand separate state housing for their multiple households.

Legitimacy of polygyny

The above numbers give an indication of the frequency with which polygyny occurs. However, more important is whether and under what circumstances it is legitimized by society. Legitimacy of polygynous marriages in the eyes of the community is closely related to the reasons for polygyny. Also relevant for the degree of legitimacy is whether or not certain ceremonies have been completed.

The reasons for polygynous marriages seem to be similar to those in Ottoman times. Romantic love is one reason, although this seems to be less acceptable to the public.[62] Often the polygamous marriage is only entered into after a period of secrecy. The second wife first becomes the mistress of a married man and only after the relationship has become more stable or widely known does the woman achieve the more public status of second wife.

Often more utilitarian reasons are behind a second marriage. There might be a need for one or more extra pairs of hands in the fields.[63] This seems to be occurring less and also seems to be less accepted by the public. More accepted is the case in which the first wife fails to provide her husband with a male heir, or she is too old to 'give' him a replacement for a son who died before his father.[64]

A research study made in the early 1960s in two villages around Diyarbekir in the eastern region where polygamy is relatively frequent shows that polygyny was more accepted in one village than in another. While of the 69 interviewed (38 women, 31 men) in one village only two men thought polygyny would be acceptable if the man's economic situation was convenient, the inhabitants of another village had a different opinion. Of the 43 interviewed there (20 women, 23 men) eight women and 18 men thought it acceptable in such a situation. Approval increased considerably when asked whether polygyny would be acceptable if a man did not have a son. In the first village 36 women and 21 men answered this question affirmatively. In the second village, however, 18 out of 29 women and all 23 men considered this acceptable. Asked more specifically whether they would give their daughter to a wedded man, they confirmed their points of view. The number of people interviewed is too limited to draw far-reaching conclusions. Moreover, although the author indicated that the two villages are at 'a different level of social cultural change', she did not give more details.[65] Still the data confirm that polygyny was more acceptable in cases where a man did not have a son. A more recent article in the newspaper *Hürriyet* confirms that this is still the case. In the article a medical specialist indicates that the number of requests for *in vitro* fertilization is higher in the east of Turkey than in the rest of the country. The reason for this is that women are afraid that their families-in-law will start looking for a *kuma*, a second wife, if she does not give birth (to a son).[66]

For legitimacy in the eyes of society a sort of ceremony is generally required. For polygamous marriages, by definition, this cannot be an official or legal ceremony. A *resmi nikah* in such a case is impossible. Couples, therefore, often seek recourse in an *imam nikahı*.[67] Although it is, according to Article 237 of the Penal Code, forbidden to perform a religious marriage ceremony while no official marriage has taken place, the figures show that this happens quite regularly, not only in polygamous marriages, but also in single marriages.[68] Certainly, if the religious marriage is celebrated with a *düğün*,[69] such a liaison is sufficiently legitimate in the eyes of society. The five-minute ceremony in the presence of a state official is often seen as bestowing even less legitimacy in the eyes of society than a religious marriage combined with a *düğün*.

Conclusion

Despite the introduction of the Civil Code in February 1926, polygamy has not been eradicated from Turkish society. Although the figures are very scanty and a full picture cannot be obtained, it is safe to state that, especially in certain areas of the country, polygamy continues to exist up to the present day. A change of the formal law is not enough to change the locally accepted mores and habits. What Starr called the different 'layers of law' are not congruent. Despite the modernization of the Turkish family law through the introduction of the Civil Code of 1926, society's alternative normative orderings, such as local customs which were based on the adherence to religious law, remained more traditional. Polygamy and religious marriage remained legitimate in the eyes of large parts of society and continued to exist. Yılmaz refers to this situation as 'post-modern Turkish socio-legal reality' or 'Turkish post-modern legality'.[70] This 'reality', however, was never 'modern' in the first place. What was modern, was the discourse. Polygamy was virtually non-existent in republican discourse. Television, schoolbooks and newspapers hardly referred to its existence. Where it was mentioned, it was to accentuate especially the lack of modernity of those involved, for example, the head of a Kurdish tribe with his four wives and more than 30 children. In recent years this has changed. Polygamy has become part and parcel of everyday conversations and no longer carries the negative connotation of backwardness. Ministers openly demanding state housing for their multiple families nowadays is what I would call Turkish post-modernity.

Notes

Introduction

1. Eric Hobsbawm, *On History* (London: Weidenfeld & Nicolson, 1997), p 73.
2. Albert Hourani, *A History of the Arab Peoples* (Cambridge, Massachusetts: Harvard University Press, 2002).
3. Halil Inalcik and Donald Quataert (eds), *An Economic and Social History of the Ottoman Empire 1300–1914* (Cambridge: Cambridge University Press, 1994).
4. Abdulhussein Zarinkoub, *Du Qarn Sokut* (Two Centuries of Silence) (Tehran: Amir Kabir, 1951).
5. Hobsbawm, *On History*, p 201.
6. Ervand Abrahamian, 'Crowd in Iranian Politics, 1905–53', *Past and Present* 41 (December 1968), pp 184–210.
7. Huri Islamoğlu-Inan, *State and Peasant in the Ottoman Empire: Agrarian Power Relations and Regional Economic Development in Ottoman Anatolia during the Sixteenth Century* (Leiden: Brill, 1994).

Chapter 1. Time, Labour-Discipline and Modernization in Turkey and Iran

1. In developing this article I benefited from the advice of Mohamad Tavakoli-Targhi, Donald Quataert, Houchang Chehabi and Hans Timmermans. I would like to express my gratitude to them all.
2. One of the first public clocks to strike the hour was in Milan in about 1335. This clock had only one hand, the hour hand. Later, with the weight-driven clocks, which were introduced before 1400 and regulated by a verge escapement, a mechanism known as the verge and foliot or balance beam with a crown wheel was introduced resulting in a mechanical relaxation oscillator.
3. *The Turkish Letters of Ogier Ghiselin de Busbecq*, trans E.S. Forster (Oxford: Clarendon Press, 1927), p 55.
4. *Ibid.*, p 214.
5. John Evelyn, *The Diary*, ed E.S. de Beer (London, 1955), vol. 4, p 358. See also O. Kurz, *European Clocks and Watches in the Near East* (Leiden: Brill, 1975), p 63.
6. Hafez Isfahani, *Sih risalah dar san'at* (Tehran: Bunyad-i Farhang-i Iran, 1971), pp 11–19.
7. Adnan Adivar, *Osmanli Türklerinde Ilim* (Istanbul: Maarif Matbassu, 1943), pp 88–90.
8. *Encyclopedia of Islam*, CD-ROM edition, v. 1.0 (Leiden: Brill, 1999).
9. Manuchehr Qodsi, 'Saat va Lughz-i Saat', *Ayandah* 10, no. 1 (1984), p 15.

10. Michele Membré, 'Relazione di Persia' (1542). *Ms. Inedito dell' Archivio di Stato di Venezia*, Studie e materiali sulla conscenze dell'Oriente in Italia 1, ed G.R. Cardona (Naples: 1969), pp 37–8, cited in Willem Floor, 'Clock', *Encyclopaedia Iranica* (California: Mazda Press, 1992), vol. 5, pp 713–18.

11. Floor, 'Clock', *Encyclopaedia Iranica*, vol. 5, p 715.

12. *Ibid.*, p 716.

13. *Ibid.*

14. Hakki Acun, *Anadolu Saat Kuleleri* (Ankara: Kütür Bakanliği, 1994), p 6.

15. Ja'far Shahri, *Tarikh-i ijtema'i Tehran dar qarn-i sinzdahom, zandegi, kasb va kar* (Tehran: Resa, 1999), vol. 3, p 235.

16. Floor, 'Clock', *Encyclopaedia Iranica*, vol. 5, p 716.

17. Kurz, *European Clocks and Watches in the Near East*, pp 83–4.

18. Bernard Lewis, *What Went Wrong? Western Impact and Middle Eastern Response* (New York and London: Oxford University Press, 2002), pp 129–30.

19. *Ibid.*

20. Carlo M. Cipolla, *Clocks and Culture 1300–1700* (London: Collins, 1967), p 88.

21. Bernard Lewis, *The Emergence of Modern Turkey* (London: Oxford University Press, 1962), p 271.

22. Ja'far Shahri, *Tarikh-i ijtema'i Tehran*, p 247.

23. For a detailed study of the introduction of the summer-time regulation in Iran see Siamak Movahedi, 'Cultural Preconceptions of Time: Can We Use Optional Time to Meddle in God's Time?', *Comparative Studies in Society and History* 27, no. 3 (1985).

24. In 1971, when the shah celebrated 2,500 years of the inauguration of the Kingdom of Iran, the Iranian government decided to make the year 1971 AD correspond to the year 2500 in the Iranian calendar. However, in 1976, when the shah adopted the new kingdom calendar as the the country's official calendar, he opted for a different inter-calendar correspondence and selected 1941 (the year of his accession to the throne) as the year corresponding with 2500.

25. Movahedi, 'Cultural Preconceptions of Time', p 385.

26. *Ibid.*, p 386.

27. *Ibid.*

28. *Ibid.*

29. Karl Marx, *Das Kapital* (Frankfurt am Main: Ullstein, 1975), I:4.

30. Donald Quataert, 'Ottoman Workers and the State, 1826–1914', in Zachary Lockman (ed), *Workers and Working Classes in the Middle East: Struggles, Histories, Historiographies* (New York: University of New York Press, 1994), p 22.

31. Charles James Wills, *Persia As It Is. Being Sketches of Modern Persian Life and Character* (Persian trans *Tarikh-i ijtema'i Iran dar 'ahd-i Qajariyah*) (Tehran: Zarin, 1984), p 306.

32. *Encyclopedia of Islam*, CD-ROM edition, v. 1.0.

33. Yıldırım Koç, *Türkiye Işçi Sinifi ve Sendikacilik Tarihi. Olaylar-değerlendirmeler* (Ankara: no publisher, no date), pp 7–9.

34. Lewis, *The Emergence of Modern Turkey*, p 84.

35. Qahriman Mirza Salur and Iraj Afshar (eds), *Khatirat-i 'Ayn al-Saltanah* (Tehran: Asatir, 1995), vol. I, p 263.

36. Lütfü Erişçi, *Türkiye'de İşçi Sınıfının Tarihi* (Ankara: no publisher, 1997), p 8.
37. Erol Kahveci, Nadir Sugur and Theo Nichols, *Work and Occupation in Modern Turkey* (London and New York: Mansell, 1996), p 84.
38. Roy A. Church, *The History of the British Coal Industry* (Oxford: Clarendon Press, 1986), pp 254–5.
39. Quataert, 'Ottoman Workers and the State', pp 34–5.
40. *Ibid.*, p 32.
41. For a not very asymptotic eyewitness account of the strike, see *Ikdam*, 15 and 16 September 1908.
42. Hüseyin Avni Şanda, *1908 İşçi hareketleri, Yarı Mütemleke Oluş Tarihi* (Istanbul: no publisher, 1932), pp 32–40.
43. Yıldırım Koç, *Türkiye İşçi Sınıfı ve Sendikacılık Tarihi*, pp 83–7.
44. *Ibid.*, pp 108–11.
45. Willem Floor, *Labour Unions, Law and Conditions in Iran, 1900–1941* (Durham: Centre for Middle Eastern and Islamic Studies; Persian trans, Tehran, 1371), p 82.
46. FO 248/1072, 62, 7 April 1913; 68–70, 14 April 1913.
47. Floor, *Labour Unions*, p 84.
48. *Ibid.*, p 88.
49. *Ibid.*, p 92.
50. Ardeshir Avanesian, *Safahati chand az junbish-i karigari va kumunisti da duwran-i avval saltanat-i Reza Shah (1922–1933)* (Tudeh Publication House, 1979), pp 75–83.
51. Floor, *Labour Unions*, p 54.
52. Vizarat-i Sana'at va Ma'adin, *Nizamnamah-i karkhanijat va mo'asisat-i san'ati* (Tehran: Vizarat-i Sana'at va Ma'adin, 1936).
53. Vizarat-i Kar, *Qanun-i kar* (Tehran: Vezarat-e Kar, 1946).
54. Movahedi, 'Cultural Preconceptions of Time', p 395.

Chapter 2. Workers and the State during the Late Ottoman Empire

1. An earlier version of this paper is entitled 'Labor and State in the Ottoman Empire during the Nineteenth Century', in Walid Arbid, Salgur Kançal et al (eds), *Mediterranee, Moyen-Orient: Deux Siècles de Relations Internationals, Recherches en Homage à Jacques Thobie* (Paris: Harmattan, 2003), pp 145–57.
2. See, for example, Joel Beinin and Zachary Lockman, *Workers on the Nile* (Princeton: Princeton University Press, 1987); Zachary Lockman (ed), *Workers and Working Classes in the Middle East* (Albany: State University of New York Press, 1994); Donald Quataert and Erik-Jan Zürcher, *Workers and the Working Class in the Ottoman Empire and the Republic of Turkey, 1839–1950* (London: I.B.Tauris, 1995); Ellis Goldberg (ed), *The Social History of Labor in the Middle East* (Boulder: Westview, 1996).
3. Joel Beinin, *Workers and Peasants in the Modern Middle East* (Cambridge: Cambridge University Press, 2001); John Chalcraft, *The Striking Cabbies of Cairo and Other Stories: Crafts and Guilds in Egypt, 1863–1914* (Albany: State University of New York Press, 2004). See also Peter Carl Mentzel, 'Nationalism and the Labor Movement in the Ottoman Empire, 1872–1914' (unpublished PhD thesis, University of Washington, 1994).

4.   See, for example, the record of mixed agricultural, industrial and peddling activities documented in the *Temettuat Defterleri* found in the Prime Ministry Archives in Istanbul.

5.   Uri Kupferschmidt, 'The Social History of the Sewing Machine in the Middle East', *Die Welt des Islam* 44 (2001), pp 1–19.

6.   Here I am particularly indebted to the studies of Ellis Goldberg.

7.   The best account of the 1908 strikes is Yavuz Selim Karakışla, 'The 1908 Strike Wave in the Ottoman Empire', *Turkish Studies Association Bulletin*, September 1992, pp 153–77. See also Donald Quataert, *Social Disintegration and Popular Resistance in the Ottoman Empire, 1881–1908* (New York: New York University Press, 1983).

8.   Donald Quataert, 'Ottoman Workers and the State, 1826–1914', in Lockman (ed), *Workers and Working Classes in the Middle East*, pp 21–40.

9.   Karakışla, 'The 1908 Strike Wave'; Quataert, *Social Disintegration*; and Quataert in Lockman (ed), *Workers and Working Classes*.

10.   Quataert, *Social Disintegration*; Oya Sencer, *Türkiye' de işçi sınıfı* (Istanbul: Habora Kitabevi Yayınları, 1969), p 160.

11.   Donald Quataert, 'Janissaries, Artisans and the Question of Ottoman Decline' (working paper, International Congress of Historical Sciences, Madrid, 1990). I am very grateful to Cemal Kafadar for giving me his unpublished works on this subject.

12.   Mehmed Esʿad, *Üss-ü Zafer* (Istanbul, AH 1293); Ismail Hakkı Uzunçarşılı, *Osmanli Devleti Teşkilatından Kapıkulu Ocakları* (Ankara: Türk Tarih Kurumu, 1943), vol. 1, pp 524–5.

13.   Ghazzi as cited in Herbert Bodman, *Political Factions in Aleppo, 1760–1826* (Chapel Hill: University of North Carolina Press, 1963), pp 64–5; Howard Reed, 'The Destruction of the Janissaries in June 1826' (unpublished PhD thesis, Princeton University, 1951), p 258, reports that in 1826 the town guilds in Edirne 'were all closely associated' with the Janissaries.

14.   Ghazzi as cited in Bodman, *Political Factions in Aleppo*, pp 64–5.

15.   I am giving these events a different interpretation than the sources that reported them, e.g. Uzunçarşılı, *Osmanli Devleti Teşkilatından Kapıkulu Ocakları*, p 501.

16.   Perhaps this alliance between the various groups of Ottoman workers soured, for reasons presently unclear. The behaviour of the urban skilled workers in 1826 needs further investigation. See Kafadar's unpublished works.

17.   Quataert, 'Janissaries, Artisans and the Question of Ottoman Decline' (working paper, Madrid, 1990).

18.   *Ibid*.

19.   Quataert, *Social Disintegration*, pp 95–145; Quataert, 'Labor Policies and Politics in the Ottoman Empire: Porters and the Sublime Porte, 1826–1896', in Heath W. Lowry and Donald Quataert (eds), *Humanist and Scholar: Essays in Honor of Andreas Tietze* (Istanbul: ISIS Press, 1993), pp 59–69.

20.   Quataert, 'Labor Policies and Politics in the Ottoman Empire'.

21.   *Ibid*.

22.   *Ibid*.; Quataert, *Social Disintegration*, pp 96–103.

23.   Quataert, *Social Disintegration*, pp 94–145; Quataert, 'Labor Policies and Politics in the Ottoman Empire'.

24. Elsewhere, long ago, I noted the economic crisis and rising food prices preceding the July revolution and the objective of most strikers to obtain higher wages in compensation. Donald Quataert, 'The Economic Climate of the "Young Turk Revolution" in 1908', *Journal of Modern History* (1979), pp D1147ff. See also Carter Findley, 'Economic Bases of Revolution and Repression in the Late Ottoman Empire', *Comparative Studies in Society and History* 28 (1986), pp 81–106.

25. Şehmus Güzel, 'Faire la Grève en Turquie', in A. Gökalp (ed), *La Turquie en Transition* (Paris: Maisonneuve et Larose, 1986), p 219; Karakışla, 'The 1908 Strike Wave in the Ottoman Empire'.

26. Karakışla, 'The 1908 Strike Wave in the Ottoman Empire'; Quataert, *Social Disintegration*.

27. For example, Sherry Vatter, 'Militant Textile Weavers in Damascus: Waged Artisans and the Ottoman Labor Movement, 1850–1914', in Quataert and Zürcher (eds), *Workers and the Working Class in the Ottoman Empire and the Republic of Turkey*, pp 35–57.

Chapter 3. Disgruntled Guests: Iranian Subalterns on the Margins of the Tsarist Empire

1. This article was first published in the *International Review of Social History*, no. 48 (2003), pp 401–26. It is reproduced with permission of Cambridge University Press. For their comments and suggestions regarding this article I would like to thank Teressa Walczak, Hans Timmermans, Ulla Langkau-Alex and Marcel van der Linden.

2. My use of the word 'subaltern' is based on the description given by Antonio Gramsci in his *The Modern Prince* and *The Prison Notebooks*. According to Gramsci, the subaltern classes are those subordinated by hegemony and excluded from any meaningful role in a regime of power. Although Gramsci himself had workers in mind, the term was later used to describe other groups who are excluded and do not have a position from which to speak. See Antonio Gramsci, *Prison Notebooks* (New York: Columbia University Press, 1991), and *The Modern Prince and Other Writings* (London: Lawrence and Wishart, 1957).

3. For a detailed study of the Babi movement see Abbas Amanat, *Resurrection and Renewal: The Making of the Babi Movement in Iran, 1844–1850* (Ithaca: Cornell University Press, 1989).

4. Charles Issawi (ed), *The Economic History of Iran 1800–1914* (Chicago: University of Chicago Press, 1971), p 20.

5. Homa Katouzian, *The Political Economy of Modern Iran* (London: Macmillan, 1981), p 27.

6. Abbas Amanat, *Pivot of the Universe, Nasir al-Din Shah Qajar and the Iranian Monarchy 1831–1896* (London: I.B.Tauris, 1997), pp 204–11.

7. French consulate report, Tabriz to Paris, 7 August 1895, quoted in Homa Nategh, *Karnamah va zamanah Mirza Reza Kermani* (Bonn: Hafez, 1984), p 117.

8. *Ibid.*, p 120.

9. Said Nafisi, *Tarikh-i ijtima'i va siyasi-i Iran dar durih-i mu'asir* (Tehran: Bunyad, 1961), vol. 2, p 143.

10. Homa Nategh, *Iran dar rahyabi-i farhangi* (London: Payam, 1988), p 161.
11. *Ibid.*
12. For a detailed account see Amanat, *Pivot of the Universe*, p 382.
13. *Ibid.*, pp 212–13.
14. Moojan Momen (ed), *The Babi and Bahai Religion 1844–1944: Some Contemporary Western Accounts* (Oxford: G. Ronald, 1981), p 145.
15. N.K. Belova, 'Ob Otchodnichestve iz Severozapadnego Irana v Kontse XIX–Nachale XX Veka', *Voprosy istorii*, no. 10 (1959), p 112.
16. *Ibid.*
17. *Ibid.*
18. Malcolm E. Fakus, *The Industrialisation of Russia, 1700–1914* (London: Macmillan, 1972), pp 44–6, 64–6.
19. *Encyclopedia of Islam*, CD-ROM edition, v. 1.0 (Leiden: Brill, 1999).
20. Republic of Georgia State Central Archive (hereafter RGSCA), record 13, dossier 1, file 267, 18.
21. A.M. Nikolskii, *Letnie Poezdki Naturalista: v Turkestane, na Ledovitom Okeane v Severnoy Persii, na Sakhaline* (Leningrad: Gos. Iz-do, 1924), p 129.
22. A.Z. Arabadzian and N.A. Kuznetsova (eds), *Iran. Sbornik Statey* (Moscow, 1973).
23. Republic of Azerbaijan State Central Archive (hereafter RASCA), record 44, dossier 1, file 45, 3.
24. *Ibid.*
25. *Ibid.*
26. *Ibid.*
27. RGSCA, record 13, dossier 1, file 267, 16.
28. RGSCA, record 11, dossier 4, file 3104, 38–9.
29. V. Miller, *Dvizhenie Persidskikh Rabochikh v Zakavkaz'e. Sbornik Konsul'skikh Doneseniy Ministerstva Inostrannikh Del* (St Petersburg, 1903), vol. 3, p 205.
30. Issawi, *The Economic History of Iran 1800–1914*, p 52.
31. Miller, *Dvizhenie Persidskikh Rabochikh v Zakavkaz'e.*
32. L.S. Sobosinskej, *Persiya* (St Petersburg, 1913), pp 288–9.
33. RASCA, record 45, dossier 1, file 149, 68–9.
34. *Mulla Nasriddin*, no. 6 (1906).
35. G.N. Illinskii, 'Agrarnie Otnosheniya v Irane v Kontse XIX – Nachale XX Veka', v *Uchenie Zapiski In-ta Vostokovedniya Akademii Nauk SSSR*, no. 8 (1953), p 120.
36. L.F. Tigranov, *Iz Istorii Obshchestvenno-economicheskikh Otnoshenii Persii* (St Petersburg, 1905), pp 159–60.
37. *Kaspii* (April 1897).
38. I.V. Strigunov, *Iz Istorii Formirovaniya Bakinskogo Proletariata 70-90-e gody XIX v.* (Baku: Izd-vo Akademii Nauk Azerbaidzhanskoj SSR, 1960), p 134.
39. RGSCA, record 13, dossier 23, file 745, 1.
40. Belova, 'Ob Otchodnichestve iz Severozapadnego Irana', p 117.
41. RGSCA, record 13, dossier 1, file 267, 14.
42. I.M. Rasanova et al (eds), *Azerbaidzhan v Gody Pervoy Russkoy Revoliutsii, Sbornik Statey* (Baku, 1966), p 95.
43. *Baku*, no. 42 (1907).

44. *Bakinskoe ekho*, no. 16 (1907).

45. Strigunov, *Iz IstoriiFformirovaniya Bakinskogo Proletariata*, p 134.

46. *Novii Vostok*, no. 20 (1920).

47. Beeby Thompson, *The Oil Fields of Russia and the Russian Petroleum Industry* (London, 1908), p 126.

48. RGSCA, record 13, dossier 1, file 267, 16.

49. Hassan Hakimian, 'Wage Labour and Migration: Persian Workers in Southern Russia, 1880–1914', *International Journal of Middle East Studies*, no. 17 (1985), p 446.

50. Republic of Azerbaijan Archive of the History of Political Parties and Social Movements (hereafter RAAHPPSM), record 153, dossier 1, file 78, 2–3.

51. *Ibid.*, record 509, dossier 1, file 68, 1, 8; Strigunov, *Iz Istorii Formirovaniya Bakinskogo proletariata*, p 139.

52. *Ibid.*, p 138.

53. RGSCA, record 13, dossier 1, file 267, 14.

54. Belova, 'Ob Otchodinichestve iz Severozapadnego Irana', p 115.

55. Michael Honey, 'Racism and the Labor Market in the American South: Memphis, Tennessee in the Segregation Era', in Marcel van der Linden and Jan Lucassen (eds), *Racism and the Labour Market* (Bern and New York: P. Lang, 1995), p 225.

56. Strigunov, *Iz Istorii Formirovaniya Bakinskogo Proletariata*, pp 88–9.

57. Muhammad Amin Rasulzadah, *Guzarish-ha'i az Inqilab-i Mashrutah*, trans Rahim Reisnia (Tehran: Shirazah, 1998), p 78.

58. RGSCA, record 13, dossier 1, file 267, 16.

59. *Ibid.*

60. RAAHPPSM, record 153, dossier 1, file 78, 3

61. Beeby Thompson, *The Oil Fields of Russia*, p 376.

62. RAAHPPSM, record 153, dossier 1, file 78, 3.

63. Archive of the Ministry of Foreign Affairs, Tehran (hereafter AMFA), B. 12, D. 32, 1910, B. 13, D. 51, 1912.

64. AMFA, B. 13, D. 34, 1912.

65. Hakimian, 'Wage Labour and Migration', p 450.

66. S.M. Aliev, 'K Voprosu o Sviaziakh Bakinskogo i Tiflisskogo Komiteta RSDRP s Iranskimi Revoliutsionerami v 1903–1911', in *Slavnie Stranitsy Bor'by i Pobed. Mat-y Nauchnoi Sessii, Posviashchnnoy 60-letiyu II S'ezda RSDRP i Vseobshchikh Zabastovok v Baku i na Yuge Rosii Letom 1903 g.* (Baku, 1965), p 192.

67. Ahmad Kasravi, *Tarikh-i mashrutah-i Iran* (Tehran: Amir Kabir, 1978), p 151.

68. *Revolutionary Movements in Armenia 1905–1907: Collection of Documents* (Yerevan, 1955), p 185. See also *Nor Khosk* 6 (1906).

69. AMFA, B. 7, D. 5, 23 April 1905.

70. *Ibid.* See also S. Shaumian, 'Failed Strike', *Nor Khosk* 6 (1906). At the Fifth Congress of the RSDRP (1907) Shaumian presented a detailed report on the Alaverdi strike. See S. Shaumian, *Collected Works* (Moscow, 1957), vol. 1, p 236. In articles published in *Kavkozkii Rabochii Listok*, no. 3 (1905), Jalil Muhammad Qulizadah also presented a detailed account of the strike and the fate of those Iranian miners deported to Iran.

71. RAAHPPSM, record 13, dossier 27, file 533, and record 15, dossier 1, file 78.

72. *Ibid.*
73. S.M. Aliyev, *People of Asia and Africa* (Moscow, 1965).
74. Salmullah Javid, *Iran Sosyal Dimoktar (Adalat) Firqasi Haqinda Khataralarim* [mimeo] (Tehran, 1980), p 11.
75. *Ibid.*
76. Muhammad Sa'id Maraghah'i, *Khatirat-i siyasi* (Tehran: Nashr-i Namak, 1994), p 59.
77. Cosroe Chaqueri, *The Soviet Socialist Republic of Iran, 1920–1921: Birth of a Trauma* (Pittsburgh: University of Pittsburgh Press, 1995), p 154.
78. *Ibid.*, p 48.
79. FO 371/4358, 1918.
80. *Açiq Söz*, 17 January 1918.
81. Muhammad Khan Tarbiyat was founder of the Democrat Party's Baku committee. He was also director of the Iranian Ittihad school in Baku. The committee's other members included Mirza Mahmud Khan Parvarish, Mitza 'Abdullah 'Abdulahzadah, Sheikh Baqir Shirazi, Azhdar 'Alizadah, Hussein Khayyat, Hussein Mahmudzadah, Mir Hussein Mutazavi, Mirza 'Aliquli (from Ashgabat; he later became the editor of *Azarbayjan, joz'-i la-yanfak-i Iran*), Mir Jafar Javadzadah Pishavari, Haji Mo'alim Ja'farzadah Kalkhali, Mirza Aqa Valizadah, Sayfullah Ibrahimzadah and 'Ali Akbar Osku'i (founder of the Iranian guild and a member of its executive committee). Parvarash had to leave Baku in 1916 on account of his political activities. He left illegally for Iran. After the Russian Revolution of February 1917, the Democrat Party began to operate legally. See Javid, *Iran Sosyal Dimoktar ('Adalat) Firqasi haqinda khataralarim*, pp 9–10.
82. On the origins of reconstructing Iran's pre-Islamic history in the nationalist discourse, see Mohamad Tavakoli-Targhi, 'Contested Memories: Narrative Structure and Allegorical Meaning of Iran's Pre-Islamic History', *Iranian Studies*, nos. 1–2 (1996), pp 149–75.
83. *Azarbayjan, Juz'-i la-yanfak-i Iran*, no. 2 and 3 (1918).
84. Javid, *Iran Sosyal Dimoktar ('Adalat) Firqasi haqinda khataralarim*, pp 14–15.
85. On the process of self-identification see Thomas Hylland Eriksen, *Ethnicity and Nationalism: Anthropological Perspectives* (London: Pluto Press, 1993), pp 9–10.
86. I. Gershoni, 'Imagining and Re-imagining the Past: The Use of History by Egyptian Nationalist Writers, 1919–1952', *History and Memory*, no. 2 (1992), p 7.
87. T. Nipperdey, 'In Search of Identity: Romantic Nationalism: Its Intellectual, Political and Social Background', in J.C. Eade (ed), *Romantic Nationalism in Europe* (Canberra: Australian National University, 1983), p 11.

Chapter 4. The Modernization of the Empire and the Community 'Privileges'

1. On the role of community institutions and symbolic practices in the integration of diverse social groups into community life, see Charis Exertzoglou, 'Μετά μεγάλης παρατάξεως', συμβολικές πρακτικές και κοινοτική συγκρότηση στις αστικές ορθόδοξες κοινότητες της ύστερης οθωμανικής περιόδου' ('With Pomp and Circumstance': Symbolical Practices and Communal Construction in Urban Orthodox Communities of the Late Ottoman Period), *Τα Ιστορικά*, 31 December 1999, pp 349–80.

2. On the efforts of the Ottoman state to legitimize its existence towards both its own subjects and the outside world, see Selim Deringil, *Well-Protected Domains: Ideology and the Legitimisation of Power in the Ottoman Empire, 1876–1909* (London and New York: I.B.Tauris, 1998).

3. The most sophisticated analysis of the impact of the *Tanzimat* on the internal structure of the ethno-religious communities has been provided by Athanasia Anagnostopoulou, *Μικρά Ασία, 19ος αι. –1919, Οι ελληνορθόδοξες κοινότητες. Από το μιλλέτ των Ρωμιών στο ελληνικό έθνος* (Asia Minor 19th Century–1919, The Greek-Orthodox Communities from *Millet-i Rum* to the Greek Nation) (Athens: Ελληνικά Γράμματα 1998). For an abridged version of her conclusions in Turkish see Athanasia Anagnostopoulou, 'Tanzimat ve Rum milletinin kurumsal çerçevesi', pp 1–35, in Pinelopi Stathis (dir.), *19. Yüzyıl İstanbul'unda Gayrimüslimler*, çeviri Foti ve Stefo Benlisoy, Tarih Vakfı Yurt Yayınları, 2inci baskı (İstanbul, 2003).

4. Dimitris Stamatopoulos has argued that the purpose of this process was not the separation of the church from the state but rather the eventual state control over church affairs. The first step of this process was the involvement of lay individual members of the Ottoman administration. See Dimitris Stamatopoulos, *Η Εκκλησία ως Πολιτεία, Αναπαραστάσεις του Ορθόδοξου Μιλλέτ και το Μοντέλο της Συνταγματικής Μοναρχίας (δεύτερο μισό 19ου αι.)* (Church as a Polity: Representations of the Orthodox Millet and the Model of Constitutional Monarchy (second half of 19th c.)) (Mnimon, 23, Athens, 2001), pp 183–220.

5. This reorganization of community administration coincided with the development of national historiographies in the Balkans but also the increasing need of the Patriarchate itself to legitimize its authority and its power against the challenge of emerging nationalisms. On the historiographical canons developed by the Patriarchate, see Minas & Christos Chamoudopoulos, *Ιστορία της Οθωμανικής Αυτοκρατορίας* (History of the Ottoman Empire) (Smyrna, 1874). Constantinos Paparrigopoulos, *Ιστορία του Ελληνικού Έθνους* (History of the Hellenic Nation) (Athens, 1874) relied on the assumption that the 'privileged status' of the Patriarchate after the *Tanzimat* had been established already with the Ottoman conquest of Constantinople. Legends rather than actual documents were used to support this argument. According to them, Mehmed II, within his policy of harmoniously incorporating the conquered population in the new state structure, had assigned to Gennadios Scholarios, a clergyman famous for his anti-Catholic sentiments, the task of taking over the administration of the Patriarchate, with authority reaching far beyond the religious. He was actually given the authority to rule over his flock. However, as contemporary research has pointed out, neither did his flock exceed the population of Constantinople nor did the assigned 'privileges' refer to the institution, but rather to the person itself, thus generating the need which was to be respected ever after for any new Patriarch to acquire similar authority from the Ottoman sultan. See 'Το Πατριαρχείο και η έννομη οθωμανική τάξη' (The Patriarchate and the Ottoman Legal Order) in Paraskevas Konortas, *Οθωμανικές Θεωρήσεις για το Οικουμενικό Πατριαρχείο* (Ottoman Perceptions of the Ecumenical Patriarchate) (Athens:Alexandreia, 1998), pp 295–361. Konortas's seminal account is based on the *berats* and *fermans* provided by the Ottoman administration to the Patriarchs and Metropolitans throughout the Ottoman

period. On the genealogy of the *millet* system and the privileges, see Benjamin Braude, 'Foundation Myths of the Millet System', in B. Braude and B. Lewis (eds), *Christians and Jews in the Ottoman Empire: The Functioning of a Plural Society* (New York, London: Holmes & Meier Publishers, 1982), vol. 1, pp 69–88.

6.   Anagnostopoulou, 'Tanzimat', pp 31–2.

7.   Ayşe Ozil, *Education in the Greek Orthodox Community of Pera in 19th c. Istanbul* (unpublished MA thesis, Bogaziçi University, 2001), p 42. Ozil's study is one of the first attempts in Turkish historiography to deal with the problem from the point of view of the non-Muslim communities. On state education policies, see Selçuk Akşin Somel, *The Modernization of Public Education in the Ottoman Empire, 1839–1908: Islamization, Autocracy, and Discipline* (Leiden and Boston: Brill, 2001), and Benjamin C. Fortna, *Imperial Classroom: Islam, the State, and Education in the Late Ottoman Empire* (Oxford and New York: Oxford University Press, 2002).

8.   This distinction between 'spiritual affairs' (πνευματικές υποθέσεις) and 'material affairs' (υλικές υποθέσεις) would also be the point of contention among the clergy and the lay element of the Patriarchate during the debates of the National Council between 1858 and 1862 for a new community regulation, when finally education as a 'material affair' was taken over by the lay Mixed National Council.

9.   Having said that, we should point out that the *Tanzimat* sanctioned and officially recognized the pre-existing practices. Paraskevas Konortas reached the conclusion that the state attributed a great importance to the activities of the clergy and wished to control it politically. This 'legal status' that the clergy enjoyed, however, was not a result of the 'understanding' and incorporation into the administration of a structured organism, which in any case was alien to the Islamic law. It was due to the fact that the Patriarch and the Metropolitans were considered 'instruments for the application of their decisions', whereas at the same time were liable to the political control of the state. On their part, the Patriarchs, through their access to state administration, achieved an authority even larger than the one they had before the fall of Constantinople, and developed into administrative, political and economic figures in Ottoman society in general while being involved in international politics, as well. See Konortas, *Οθωμανικές Θεωρήσεις*, p 36.

10.   Ozil, *Education in the Greek Orthodox Community of Pera*, p 46.

11.   Ioachim III was among the most fervent supporters of the *Tanzimat* and also one of the last champions of the ecumenical character of the Greek Orthodox Patriarchate. His first patriarchy (1878–84), apart from its conflict with the Sublime Porte, coincided with the first cabinet of the Hellenic prime minister Charilaos Trikoupis and was also marked by a conflict with him. Trikoupis, who initiated the first significant modernization projects in Greece, was a liberal anglophile who could not tolerate the pro-Russian sentiments of the Patriarch, in a period when Russia was openly supporting the aspirations of the newly born Bulgarian principality. On the other hand, the Patriarch, who was advocating an 'Orthodox Commonwealth', severely opposed the efforts of the Hellenic state to take over control of the education and the appointment of Metropolitans among the Greek Orthodox of the empire. See Evangelos Kofos, 'Patriarch Ioachim III

(1878–1884) and the Irredentist Policy of the Greek State', *Journal of Modern Greek Studies* IV, no. 2 (1986), pp 107–20.

12. *Ekklisiastiki Alithia*, 6 December 1883, quoted in Charis Exertzoglou, 'To Προνομιακό Ζήτημα' (The Privileges Question), Τα Ιστορικά, p 67.

13. *Ekklisiastiki Alithia*, 30 December 1883, quoted in Exertzoglou, 'The Privileges Question', p 67.

14. Exertzoglou, 'The Privileges Question', p 67.

15. Enver Ziya Karal and İsmail Hakkı Uzunçarşılı, *Tanzimatan Cumhuriyete Türkiye Ansiklopedisi* (Cilt I, Ankara: Türk Tarih Kurumu Basımevi, 1988), p 317.

16. Bülent Atalay, *Fener Rum Ortodoks Patrikhanesi 'nin Siyasi Faaliyetleri (1908–1923)* (Istanbul: TATAV yayınları, 2000), p 71.

17. *Nea Efimeris*, 8 January 1891, quoted in Exertzoglou, 'The Privileges Question', p 69.

18. Exertzoglou, 'The Privileges Question', pp 74–6.

19. See Anagnostopoulou, *Μικρά Ασία*, Chapter 3, 'Η επανάσταση των Νεοτούρκων, το νέο οθωμανικό πλαίσιο εξουσίας' (The Young Turk Revolution, the New 'Ottoman' Frame of Authority, 1908–1914) especially pp 453–8. Anagnostopoulou refers to the seminal work of David Kushner, *The Rise of Turkish Nationalism* (Frank Cass, 1977), pp 97–9. It is interesting that Kushner distinguishes this 'political nationalism' from the 'cultural nationalism' advocated by Ottomanists and Islamists of the previous period. However, he sees the development of this 'political nationalism' towards the end of the period, that is after the First World War, and also admits that, for economic and social issues, the appeals were articulated in Ottoman terms (against foreigners) or in Muslim ones (against non-Muslims). I would suggest, however, that this different vocabulary in economic and social issues is also instrumental in the second constitutional period. Moreover, 'political nationalism' appears with the Young Turk movement and not at the end of the period, again in the forms of 'Ottoman' or 'Muslim nationalism'.

20. We should not fail to mention that there is a very rich debate on whether and to what extent the nationalist ideology advocated by the Young Turks instrumentalized religion. Hanioğlu, for instance, sees religion as a necessary tool which the Young Turks unwillingly utilized in order to manipulate the masses. See Sükrü M. Hanioğlu, *The Young Turks in Opposition* (New York: Oxford University Press, 1995). On the other hand, Kansu stresses the secular character of Young Turk nationalist ideology, and claims that they did not manage to impose their view, because of the inertia of the system. See Aykut Kansu, *The Revolution of 1908 in Turkey* (Leiden: Brill, 1997). Both authors, however, follow a rather mechanistic approach, which disconnects political action from political discourse, and thus downplays the importance of the latter in decision making. Erik-Jan Zürcher has suggested that allowing more space for the religious element in Turkish nationalism might prove more useful and he describes the ideology of the period as 'Muslim nationalism'. See Erik-Jan Zürcher, 'Young Turks, Ottoman Muslims and Turkish Nationalist Identity Politics 1908–1938', in Kemal H. Karpat (ed), *Ottoman Past and Today's Turkey* (Leiden and Boston: Brill, 2000), pp 150–79.

21. For an interesting account of the interrelation between culture and nationalism see Charis Exertzoglou, 'The Cultural Uses of Consumption: Negotiating Class,

Gender and Nation in the Ottoman Urban Centers during the 19th Century', *Journal of Middle Eastern Studies*, no. 35 (2003), pp 77–101.

22.   Anagnostopoulou, Μικρά Ασία, pp 457–8. Anagnostopoulou's analysis stems from the very significant methodological precondition that 'neither Turkish nationalism constitutes from the beginning the main element of the Young Turk policies, nor Hellenic nationalism that of the policies of the Greek-Orthodox deputies'.

23.   Athanassios Souliotis-Nicolaidis, Οργάνωσις Κωνσταντινουπόλεως (Society of Constantinople), ed Catherina Boura and Thanos Veremis (Athens, 1984), p 72.

24.   Anagnostopoulou, Μικρά Ασία, p 459. Anagnostopoulou also suggests that since the concept of the *millet* was abolished, from 1908 onwards we cannot talk any more of *Milleti-i Rum*. However, I argue, the abolition of an institution does not automatically bring about the elimination of its 'imagined' perceptions.

25.   In other words, his fate would be parallel to that of the sultan. When Ioachim III visited Mehmed Resat V to protest against the new law on schools, churches and cemeteries voted in parliament on 12 June 1910, the latter confessed his inability to intervene. Since the law was constitutional, any interference on his part would be against the constitution. See Anagnostopoulou, Μικρά Ασία, p 462.

26.   Anagnostopoulou, Μικρά Ασία, p 464.

27.   *Ibid.*, p 464.

28.   Helleno-Ottomanism was a widespread ideology among the traditional elite groups of Istanbul, a product largely of the *Tanzimat*. It also found support in the Hellenic state in the 1860s and 1870s among intellectuals and politicians such as Epaminondas Diligeorgis, who advocated peaceful relations with the Ottoman Empire. This policy sought to provide the Greek Orthodox elites with the necessary conditions for prosperity, thus paving the way for their participation in the administration of the Ottoman state.

29.   Anagnostopoulou, Μικρά Ασία, p 475.

30.   This is how the newspaper *Amalthia* (no. 9156, 17 November 1910), the most well-known Greek newspaper in the Ottoman Empire, published in Izmir by Sokratis Solomonidis, a fervent supporter of the Patriarch, describes the place of Hellenism in the Empire: 'The Hellenic race claims ... that it lived and lives in this Empire on its own. It did not lose its existence in the dark years of slavery, nor the cover of Christianity intermingled it with other Christian races. ... The Hellenic race constitutes part of the valuable material through which the beautiful structure of the constitution, not of Turkey but of the Ottoman Empire, will be built, or according to the view of more liberal ones of the Eastern Empire.'

31.   The most detailed and thorough account of the issue is provided by Veremis and Boura (eds), Οργάνωσις Κωνσταντινουπόλεως, pp 9–23.

32.   Caterina Boura, 'The Greek Millet in Turkish Politics: Greeks in the Ottoman Parliament (1908–1918)', in Dimitris Gonticas and Charles Issawi (eds), *Ottoman Greeks in the Age of Nationalism* (Princeton: Princeton University Press, 1999), pp 193–206.

33.   On the policy of the Hellenic state, see Th. Veremis, 'The Hellenic Kingdom and the Ottoman Greeks: The Experiment of the Society of Constantinople', in Gondicas and Issawi (eds), *Ottoman Greeks in the Age of Nationalism*, pp 181–91. Veremis and Boura suggest that the policy of the Hellenic state towards the

Young Turks is marked by inconsistency and obscurity. It seems, however, that in the course of events, and at least until the Balkan War, the Hellenic authorities managed to have a channel of communication both with the liberal opposition (through the Political Association) and the Unionist circles (through Carolidis).

34. The 'Hellenic Programme' (Ελληνικὸν Πρόγραμμα) was submitted to the Ministry of Foreign Affairs. The whole text can be found in Veremis and Boura, *Οργάνωσις Κωνσταντινουπόλεως*, pp 273–4.

35. Anagnostopoulou, *Μικρά Ασία*, p 477. On the conceptual ambiguities in the public discourse during that period see Vangelis Kechriotis, 'Greek-Orthodox, Ottoman-Greeks or Just Greeks? Theories of Coexistence in the Aftermath of the Young Turks Revolution', *Études Balkaniques* 1 (2005), pp 51–72.

36. Similar concerns were expressed by the Armenian middle-class political and intellectual elite figures in the capital, such as the parliamentary deputy Krikor Zohrab. See Rober Koptaş, *Armenian Political Thinking in the Second Constitutional Period: The Case of Krikor Zohrab*. On Anatolia, see Ohannes Kılıçdağı, *The Bourgeois Transformation and Ottomanism among Anatolian Armenians after the 1908 Revolution*. (Both of these are unpublished MA theses presented at the ATA, Bogaziçi University.) In both cases, the authors argue that these individuals were loyal to the Ottomanist ideal, while also supporting the cultural autonomy of their community.

37. 'Τω υπουργείω της Παιδείας' (To the Ministry of Education), *Ekklisiastiki Alithia*, 9 January 1910, p 3.

38. 'Ζήτημα Εκπαιδευτικό' (The Issue of Education), *Ekklisiastiki Alithia*, 5 February 1911, p 35.

39. Atalay, *Rum Patrikhanesi*, p 40.

40. Şûra-yı Ümmet, 1 Teşrinisani 1324/24 Kasım 1908 quoted in *ibid.*, p 41.

41. Atalay, *Rum Patrikhanesi*, p 36.

42. This is supported by the fact that the Patriarchate was accusing the government of trying to unify the Greek Orthodox with the Otttomans (Osmanlı). However, it is well known that the Greek Orthodox elites were using the term 'Ottoman' in order to describe the Muslim Turks. As we have already seen, the ultimate fear of the Patriarchate was the 'Turkification' of the Greeks.

43. Atalay, *Rum Patrikhanesi*, p 48.

44. 'Τα περί στρατολογίας των χριστιανών πατριαρχικά τακρίρια' (The Patriarchal Memoranda Regarding the Mobilization of Christians), *Ekklisiastiki Alithia*, 22 April 1910, p 50.

45. *Ekklisiastiki Alithia*, 29 April 1910, p 61.

46. 'Η άρσις του σχίσματος' (The Removal of the Schism), *Ekklisiastiki Alithia*, 12 August 1909, p 254.

47. Pavlos Carolidis, *Λόγοι και Υπομνήματα* (Speeches and Memoranda) (Athens, 1913), p 337

48. Atalay, *Rum Patrikhanesi*, p 72, who also quotes *Tanin*, 21 Mayis 1325/13 Haziran 1909.

49. *Meclisi Mebusan Zabıt Ceridesi*, içtima senesi: 1, devre: 1, 16 Mayis 1325–11 Haziran 1325 (16 May–11 June 1909), 26 May 1909, p 206.

50. In order to avoid confusion, we translate the term *kavmi* as 'ethnic' and *millî* as 'national'. In fact, the term first used for 'nationalism' was *kavmiyet*. Thus this

distinction is schematic, but since it forms part of the contemporary argument, we abide by this.

51. *MMZC*, içtima senesi: 1, devre: 1, 26 May 1909, p 206.

52. G. Pappamerkourios, *I Ekklisia kai i syntagmatikai eleftheriai* (The Church and the Constitutional Rights) (Constantinople, 1911), pp 5–6.

53. *Ibid.*, p 206.

54. Cosmidis's reference has a particular symbolic significance. The Great School of the Nation, or the Patriarchal School (widely known as *kırmızı okul* because of the colour of the new building which was designed by Constantinos Dimadis and was completed in 1881 under the auspices of Patriarch Ioachim III) had been founded by Gennadios Scholarios in 1454 in order to provide educated individuals who would staff the patriarchal administration. Thus it is closely connected with the foundation myths of the *millet* and the concession of the 'privileges'. Cosmidis's residence, built in a neo-classical style, was within five minutes' walk of the school. The impressive mansion was one of the few in the Fener area which have survived in a good shape and are used to this very day. Despite Cosmidis's fears, the school has also survived and in 2004 celebrated the 550th anniversary of its foundation.

55. *MMZC*, 26 May 1909, p 207.

56. According to the history professor and Izmir deputy Pavlos Carolidis, Choneos was one of the best-educated Greek Orthodox deputies, with knowledge of both political and legal matters. He had always been well connected to the Unionist circles of Salonica, when he had worked underground and was working as a translator at the Hellenic consulate. He retained these relations so efficiently that he even managed to wage a party war against the Unionists without losing the superb personal contacts he had with their leaders and used them for his own benefit. See Pavlos Carolidis, *Speeches*, p 212.

57. *MMZC*, içtima senesi: 1, devre: 1, 26 May 1909, p 207

58. *Ibid.*

59. *Ibid.*

60. *Ibid.*

61. Atalay, *Rum Patrikhanesi*, p 51. We have already demonstrated the inability of the Patriarchate to impose its control over the new political representatives of the community. Thus it would be wiser to see the firm refusal of the Greek Orthodox deputies to compromise as one of the instances of the severe conflict between Greek and Bulgarian nationalism in Macedonia.

62. *Ibid.*, p 52.

63. *MMZC* VI, 19 August 1909, p 68.

64. *Ibid.*, p 53.

65. *Ibid.*, p 60.

66. *Amalthia*, 28 June 1910. Relevant information is provided in Aydın Vilayeti'nden Dahiliye Nezareti'ne tahrirat, 27 Haziran 1326/10 Temmuz 1910, BOA, DH. SYS, nr. 29-1/1-1, lef 5/2, quoted in Atalay, *Rum Patrikhanesi*, p 60.

67. Atalay, *Rum Patrikhanesi*, p 61.

Chapter 5. Reform from Above, Resistance from Below

1. For a recent example of this approach, see Cyrus Ghani, *Iran and the Rise of Reza Shah: From Qajar Collapse to Pahlavi Power* (London and New York, 1998).

2. For an attempt to widen the discussion of the period beyond the regime and the political elite, see the articles collected in Stephanie Cronin (ed), *Iran under Riza Shah* (London, 2002).

3. The reform drive may actually be said to have begun in 1925 but was interrupted and delayed by the multiple crises afflicting both the new regime and especially the army during 1926. See Stephanie Cronin, *The Army and the Creation of the Pahlavi State in Iran, 1910–1926* (London and New York, 1997).

4. 'Conscription and Popular Resistance in Iran (1925–1941)', in Erik-Jan Zürcher (ed), *Arming the State: Military Conscription in the Middle East and Central Asia 1775–1925* (London: I.B.Tauris, 1999), pp 145–67.

5. Lambton, *Landlord and Peasant in Persia* (Oxford, 1953), p 189.

6. A.C. Millspaugh, *The American Task in Persia* (New York and London, 1925), p 190.

7. For elections in the early Pahlavi period, see *Asnadi az Intikhabat-i Majlis-i Shuravi-yi Milli dar Durah-i Pahlavi-yi Avval* (Idarah-i Kull-i Arshiv, Asnad va Muzih-i Daftar-i Ra'is-i' Jumhur, Tehran, 1378).

8. Ervand Abrahamian, *Iran between Two Revolutions* (Princeton, 1982), pp 151–2.

9. Houchang E. Chehabi, 'Staging the Emperor's New Clothes: Dress Codes and Nation-Building under Reza Shah', *Iranian Studies*, 26, nos. 3–4 (1993), pp 209–33. The Uniform Dress Law as passed by the Majlis actually came into effect from 21 March 1929.

10. Cronin, *The Army and the Creation of the Pahlavi State*, p 126.

11. A translation of the bill as originally presented to the Majlis in April 1923 may be found in Loraine to Curzon, 28 April 1923, FO371/9021/E5823/71/34.

12. Intelligence Summary no. 1, 8 January 1927, FO371/12285/E512/34/34; Intelligence Summary no. 2, 22 January 1927, FO371/12285/E883/34/34.

13. Consul Chick, Shiraz, to Clive, 22 October 1927, FO371/12293/E4979/520/34.

14. Husayn Makki, *Tarikh-i Bist Salah-i Iran*, 8 vols (Tehran, 1323), vol. 4, pp 415–39.

15. Annual Report, 1927, Clive to Chamberlain, 21 May 1928, FO371/13069/E2897/2897/34.

16. See, for example, document no. 2, 'A'laniyyah-i Hakim-i Isfahan (Nizam al-Din Hikmat) Khitab bih Ahali-yi Isfahan dar khusus-i Luzum-i Taba'iyyat az Qanun-i Nizam Vazifah va Tahhdid-i Mukhalifin bih Sarkub va Mujazat', Ali Riza Isma'ili, *Ganjinah-i Asnad*, 1375, pp 15–16; Intelligence Summary no. 21, 15 October 1927, FO371/12286/E4742/34/34.

17. Chick, Shiraz, to Clive, 22 October 1927, FO371/12293/E4979/520/34.

18. Clive to Chamberlain, 19 November 1927, FO371/12293/E5207/520/34.

19. Clive to Chamberlain, 5 November 1927, FO371/12293/E4979/520/34.

20. Chick, Shiraz, to Clive, 8 November 1927, FO371/12293/E5208/520/34.

21. Translations in Chick, Shiraz, to Clive, 1 December 1927, FO371/13056/E40/40/34.

22. Clive to Chamberlain, 29 December 1927, FO371/13056/E375/40/34.
23. Isfahani's death immediately gave rise to rumours that he had been poisoned on the orders of the Tehran authorities. Since he was aged and unwell, he may well have died of natural causes, although the shah's regime was certainly developing a habit of secretly murdering its opponents.
24. Mandatory female unveiling was, however, postponed, probably owing to concern at the fate of King Amanullah in Afghanistan, overthrown after advocating similar reforms.
25. Gilliat-Smith, Tabriz, to Parr, 19 October 1928, FO371/13056/E5211/40/34.
26. Even the quietist Ayatullah Shaykh Abd al-Karim Ha'iri, in Qum, was moved to telegraph Riza Shah expressing concern that the clothing reform was contrary to the Law of Islam. Shahrough Akhavi, *Religion and Politics in Contemporary Iran: Clergy–State Relations in the Pahlavi Period* (New York, 1980), p 44.
27. Gilliat-Smith, Tabriz, to Parr, 19 October 1928, FO371/13056/E5211/40/34.
28. *Ibid.*
29. Extract from Tabriz Consulate Diary, no. 11, November 1928, Clive to Chamberlain, 12 December 1928, FO371/13781/E95/95/34.
30. *Ibid.*
31. Annual Report, 1929, Clive to Henderson, 30 April 1930, FO371/14545/E2445/522/34; Gilliat-Smith, Tabriz, to Clive, 28 January 1929, FO371/13781/E1658/95/34; Clive to Chamberlain, 12 March 1929, FO371/E1658/95/34.
32. Kavih Bayat, *Shurish-i 'Asha'ir-i Fars* (Tehran, 1365).
33. For a full account of the 1929 tribal rebellions see Stephanie Cronin, *Tribal Politics in Iran: Rural Conflict and the New State, 1921–1941* (RoutledgeCurzon, 2006).
34. See Cronin, *Tribal Politics in Iran*; Kaveh Bayat, 'Riza Shah and the Tribes: An Overview', in Cronin (ed), *The Making of Modern Iran*.
35. For a full examination of this point, see Cronin, *Tribal Politics in Iran*.
36. For a fuller discussion of this point see Cronin, 'Resisting the New State: Peasants and Pastoralists in Iran, 1921–1941', *Journal of Peasant Studies* 32, no. 1 (January 2005), pp 1–47.
37. For a discussion of peasant protests and rebellions in Iran see Janet Afary, *The Iranian Constitutional Revolution, 1906–1911: Grassroots Democracy, Social Democracy, and the Origins of Feminism* (New York, 1996), pp 145–76. For the concept of 'social banditry' see Eric Hobsbawm, *Bandits* (London, 2000).
38. Chick to Nicolson, 12 July 1926, FO371/11502/E4812/4323/34.
39. Bayat, *Shurish-i 'Asha'ir-i Fars*, pp 125–6.
40. Clive to Henderson, 27 July 1929, FO371/13782/E3918/95/34.
41. Clive to Henderson, 10 August 1929, FO371/13782/E4086/95/34.
42. See Cronin, 'Riza Shah and the Disintegration of Bakhtiyari Power in Iran'.
43. See, for example, Clive to Henderson, 12 July 1929, FO371/13781/E3668/95/34; Extract from the Tehran newspaper *Iran* of 5 July 1929, FO371/13781/E3668/95/34; Taimourtache to Clive, le 13 juillet 1929, FO371/13781/E3659/95/34; Clive to Henderson, 29 June 1929, FO371/13781/E3557/95/34.
44. Clive to Henderson, 29 June 1929, FO371/13782/E3554/96/34.
45. Summary of Events and Conditions in Fars during the Year Ended March 31, 1930, Davis, Shiraz, to Clive, 24 April 1930, FO371/14551/E3025/3025/34;

Annual Report, 1929, Clive to Henderson, 30 April 1930, FO371/14545/ E2445/522/34.

46. Hoare to Simon, 16 December 1933, FO371/17889/E41/40/34.

47. See Hamid Riza Dalvand, *Majarayi-yi Qatl-i Sardar As'ad Bakhtiyari* (Tehran, 1379).

48. Knatchbull-Hugessen to Simon, 1 December 1934, FO371/17889/E7530/40/34. See also Rawshanak Bakhtiyar, 'Zindigi va Marg-i Khan Baba Khan As'ad', *Kitab-i Anzan, Vizhah-i Farhang, Hunar, Tarikh va Tamaddun-i Bakhtiyari*, vol. 1, pp 76–98.

49. Nikki Keddie, 'The Origins of the Religious-Radical Alliance in Iran', in Nikki R. Keddie, *Iran: Religion, Politics and Society* (London, 1980), pp 53–65.

Chapter 6. The Ottoman Legacy of the Kemalist Republic

1. Erik-Jan Zürcher, 'Young Turks, Ottoman Muslims and Turkish Nationalists: Identity Politics 1908–1938', in Kemal H. Karpat (ed), *Ottoman Past and Today's Turkey* (Leiden: Brill, 2000), p 170.

2. *Ibid.*, p 169.

3. Erik-Jan Zürcher, 'The Ottoman Empire and the Armistice of Mudros', in Hugh Cecil and Peter H. Liddle (eds), *At the Eleventh Hour: Reflections, Hopes and Anxieties at the Closing of the Great War, 1918* (London: Leo Cooper, 1998), pp 266–75. This was still true as late as 1923, as Nimet Unan (ed), *Atatürk'ün söylev ve demeçleri II (19-6-1938)* (Ankara: TTK, 1959), p 60, shows.

4. Erik-Jan Zürcher, 'The Borders of the Republic Reconsidered, Bilanço 1923/1998', *International Conference on History of the Turkish Republic: A Reassessment, vol. 1: Politics – Culture – International Relations* (Ankara: TUBA, 1999), pp 53–9.

5. Erik-Jan Zürcher, 'Between Death and Desertion. The Experience of the Ottoman Soldier in World War I', *Turcica* 28, pp 235–58.

6. These data have been taken from Justin McCarthy, *Muslims and Minorities: The Population of Ottoman Anatolia and the End of the Empire* (New York: New York University Press, 1983), and in particular from chapter 7, 'The End of Ottoman Anatolia'. Although McCarthy has often been criticized for his interpretation of the Armenian massacres, I am not aware of a better analysis of population statistics than his.

7. Cf. Richard Hartmann, *Im neuen Anatolien* (Leipzig: Hinrichs, 1928), p 86; Lilo Linke, *Allah Dethroned. A Journey through Modern Turkey* (London: Constable, 1937), p 278; Erik-Jan Zürcher, 'Two Young Ottomanists Discover Kemalist Turkey: The Travel Diaries of Robert Anhegger and Andreas Tietze', *Journal of Turkish Studies* 26/11 (2002), pp 359–69.

8. The population movements are described in Engin Berber, *Sancılı Yıllar: İzmir 1918–1922 Mütareke ve Yunan işgali döneminde İzmir sancağı* (Ankara: Ayraç, 1997), pp 57–70, 317–30 (for the Sanjak of Izmir only) and by Erkan Şenşekerci, *Türk devriminde Celal Bayar (1918–1960)*, pp 35–8. The latter work is based in part on the memoirs of Bayar, who together with the military commanders Pertev (Demirhan) and Cafer Tayyar (Eğilmez) was in charge of the deportations.

9. McCarthy, *Muslims and Minorities*, chapter 7.

10. Kemal Atatürk, *Nutuk* (Istanbul: Millî Eğitim Basımevi, 1967), vol. 2, p 684.

11. For a comprehensive discussion of the problem, see Rıdvan Akın, TBMM, *devleti (1920–1923). Birinci meclis döneminde devlet erkleri ve idare* (Istanbul: İletişim, 2001), pp 197–217.

12. Tarik Zafer Tunaya describes the legal aspects of the transition to a new state in his 'Türkiye Büyük Millet Meclisisi hükümetinin kuruluşu ve hukukî karakteri', *İstanbul Hukuk Fakültesi Mecmuası* 23 (1957), pp 227–47.

13. Nimet Unan (ed), *Atatürk'ün söylev ve demeçleri II (19-6-1938)* (Ankara: TTK, 1959), pp 70, 92.

14. Erik-Jan Zürcher, 'How Europeans Adopted Anatolia and Invented Turkey', *European Review* 13/3 (2005), pp 379–94.

15. Erik-Jan Zürcher, *The Unionist Factor: The Role of the Committee of Union and Progress in the Turkish National Movement (1905–1926)* (Leiden: Brill, 1984).

16. Nur Bilge Criss, *Istanbul under Allied Occupation, 1918–1923* (Leiden: Brill, 1999), pp 9ff.

17. Bülent Tanör, *Türkiye'de yerel kongre iktidarları (1918–1920)* (Istanbul: AFA, 1992), pp 52ff.

18. Erik-Jan Zürcher, *Political Opposition in the Early Turkish Republic: The Progressive Republican Party (1924–1925)* (Leiden: Brill, 1991); Mete Tunçay, *T.C.'nde tek parti yönetimi'nin kurulması (1923–1931)* (Istanbul: Cem, 1989).

19. Gotthard Jaeschke, *Türk inkılâbı tarihi kronolojisi*, trans Niyazi Recep Aksu (Istanbul: İstanbul Üniversitesi, 1941), vol. 2, p 73.

20. Erik-Jan Zürcher, 'Two Young Ottomanists Discover Kemalist Turkey', pp 359–69.

21. İlhami Soysal, *Yüzellilikler* (Istanbul: Gür, 1985).

22. Mete Tunçay, *T.C.'nde tek parti yönetimi'nin kurulması (1923–1931)*, p 178.

23. Tevfik Çavdar, 'Halkevleri', in Murat Belge (ed), *Cumhuriyet dönemi Türkiye ansiklopedisi* (Istanbul: İletişim, 1984), p 878.

24. Cf. Paul Dumont, 'The Origins of Kemalist Ideology', in Jacob M. Landau (ed), *Atatürk and the Modernization of Turkey* (Boulder: Westview, 1984), pp 25–44.

25. Şükrü Hanioğlu, *The Young Turks in Opposition* (Oxford: Oxford University Press, 1995), pp 7–18.

26. Robert A. Nye, *The Origins of Crowd Psychology: Gustave Le Bon and the Crisis of Mass Democracy in the Third Republic* (London: Sage, 1975). Le Bon was extremely popular and influential not only among the Young Turks but also among contemporary intellectuals in the Balkans and the Arab world.

27. Erik-Jan Zürcher, 'Ottoman Sources of Kemalist Thought', in Elisabeth Özdalga (ed), *Late Ottoman Society. The Intellectual Legacy* (London: Routledge/Curzon, 2005), pp 14–27.

28. Kazim Karabekir, *İttihat ve Terakki cemiyeti 1896–1909* (Istanbul: private publication, 1982), p 176 (the text dates from 1947).

29. Among the most important studies are: Şerif Mardin, *Jön Türklerin siyasi fikirleri 1898–1908* (Ankara: İş Bankası, 1964); Şükrü Hanioğlu, *The Young Turks in Opposition*; Uriel Heyd, *Foundations of Turkish Nationalism: The Life and Teachings of Ziya Gökalp* (London: Luzac, 1950); Taha Parla, *The Social and Political Thought of Ziya Gökalp 1871–1924* (Leiden: Brill, 1985); A. Holly Shissler, *Turkish Identity between Two Empires: Ahmet Ağaoğlu 1869–1919* (unpublished PhD thesis, Chicago, 2000); François Georgeon, *Türk milliyetçiliğinin kökenleri*.

Yusuf Akçura (1876–1935) (Ankara, 1986); Şükrü Hanioğlu, *Bir siyasal düşünür olarak doctor Abdullah Cevdet ve dönemi* (Ankara: Üçdal, 1981); Füsun Üstel, *Türk Ocakları*; Masami Arai, *Turkish Nationalism in the Young Turk Era* (Leiden: Brill, 1992); Esther Debus, *Sebilürreşad: eine vergleichende Untersuchung zur islamischen Opposition der vor- und nachkemalistischen Ära* (Frankfurt: Peter Lang, 1991).

30. Erik-Jan Zürcher, 'The Vocabulary of Muslim Nationalism', *International Journal of the Sociology of Language* 137 (1999), pp 81–92.

31. Şükrü Hanioğlu, 'Garbcılar: Their Attitudes toward Religion and Their Impact on the Official Ideology of the Turkish Republic', *Studia Islamica* 86/2 (1997), pp 134–58.

32. Uriel Heyd, *Foundations of Turkish Nationalism*, pp 63ff.

33. Zafer Toprak, *Türkiye' de milli iktisat 1908–1918* (Istanbul: Yurt, 1982, and later editions).

34. François Georgeon, *Türk milliyetçiliğinin kökenleri. Yusuf Akçura (1876–1935)* (Ankara, 1986), p 109.

35. For detailed discussions of Turkish populism, see Zafer Toprak, 'İkinci meşrutiyette solidarist düşünce: halkçılık', *Toplum ve bilim* 1 (1977), pp 92–123; and İlhan Tekeli and Gencay Şaylan, 'Türkiye' de halkçılık ideolojisinin evrimi', *Toplum ve bilim* 6–7 (1978), pp 44–110.

36. Tarik Zafer Tunaya, *Türkiye'de siyasal partiler. Cilt 3: İttihat ve Terakki* (Istanbul: Hürriyet, 1989), p 214.

Chapter 7. With or Without Workers in Reza Shah's Iran

1. For example, see Abulfazl Lissani, *Tala-i siah ya bala-i Iran* (Tehran, 1329); Mustafa Fateh, *Panjah Sal Naft* (Tehran, 1334); Fuad Rohani, *Tarikh-i Melli shodan-i San'at-i Naft-i Iran* (Tehran, 1352).

2. For an early attempt to portray the Abadan events as a purely 'workers' affair' see 'Vaz'iat-i kargaran-i naft-i jonoub dar Iran', *Sitarah-i surkh* 2, nos. 9–10, in Hamid Ahmadi (comp), *Documents and Historical Studies: Socialist and Communist Organizations in Iran*, vol. 2, pp 461–7. See also W.M. Floor, *Labour Unions, Law and Conditions in Iran, 1900–1941* (Durham: Centre for Middle Eastern and Islamic Studies; Persian trans, Tehran, 1371), pp 61–74.

3. Ronald W. Ferrier, 'The Development of the Iranian Oil Industry', in H. Amirsadeghi (ed), *Twentieth Century Iran* (London: William Heineman, 1977), pp 93–8.

4. *Ibid.*; Floor, *Labour Unions*, p 62.

5. 'Labour Welfare', 17 June 1929, British Petroleum Archive (BPA), 59011. I am grateful to Dr Majid Tafreshi who provided me with copies of the relevant files of the BPA on this subject.

6. Ronald W. Ferrier, *The History of the British Petroleum Company* (Cambridge and London, 1982), vol. 1, p 432; Elwell-Sutton, *Persian Oil: A Study in Power Politics* (London, Lawrence & Wishart, 1955), p 68.

7. Sir John Cadman to Brigadier General Sir Gilbert Clayton, British High Commissioner in Baghdad, 24 May 1929; Copies of Telegrams Regarding Recent Dispatches in Persia, 2 May–July 1929, 1–2, BPA 59010.

8. From Tehran to Abadan, 5 May 1929, no. 97, Copies of Telegrams, 1, BPA 59010.

9.   From Abadan to London, 6 May 1929, no. 92, Copies of Telegrams, 2.

10. 'A Report by the Head of Khoramshahr's Post and Telegraph Office on the Abadan Disturbances', no. 1026, 16 Urdibihisht 1308 (6 May 1929), in *Naft dar durah-i Reza Shah*, Sazman-i Chap va Intisharat-i Vizarat-i Farhang va Irshad-i Islami (Tehran, 1378), pp 99–100.

11. E.H. Elkington (Abadan), to H.E. Medlicott (London), 22 June 1929, BPA 59010.

12. 'Persia, Annual Report, 1928', in R.M. Burrell (ed), *Iran Political Diaries, 1881–1965, 8: 1927–1930* (Archive Editions, 1997), p 455. For a set of British reports and documents on this affair see also Cosroe Chaqueri (ed), *The Condition of the Working Class in Iran* (Florence, 1978), pp 214–22.

13. Hugh Seton-Watson, *The Pattern of the Communist Revolution* (London: Methuen and Co., 1960), pp 104–10.

14. Sepehr Zabih, *The Communist Movement in Iran* (University of California Press, 1966; Persian trans, Tehran, 1378), pp 108–21.

15. For further information see Yusif Iftikhari, *Khatirat-i duran-i sipari shudah, 1299–1329*, be kooshesh-e Kaveh Bayat va Majid Tafreshi (Tehran: Firdowssi, 1370), pp 29–36, 115–34.

16. *Ibid.*

17. Iftikhari, *Khatirat-i duran-i sipari shudah*, p 126.

18. *Ibid.*

19. E.H. Elkington, 'An Appreciation of the Political Situation in Kkuzestan with Special Reference to the Present Unrest at Abadan', 17 June 1929, 4, BPA 59010.

20. *Shafaq-i surkh*, 12 Azar 1307 (3 December 1929). For the British embassy's interpretation of these comments and developments see 'Persia, Annual Report, 1928', in *Iran Political Diaries*, vol. 7, p 273.

21. Elkington, 'An Appreciation of the Political Situation in Kkuzestan'.

22. *Ettela'at*, 29 Aban 1307 (20 November 1928).

23. See *Naft dar dorih-i Reza Shah*, pp 15–17, 32–4, 42.

24. *Ibid.*, pp 35–8.

25. For an early example of *Toufan*'s anti-APOC comments see an article by Fakhr al-din Shadman under the title of 'B.P.', 28 Shahrivar 1306 (20 September 1927).

26. *Shafaq-i surkh*, 8 Mihr 1307 (6 September 1928).

27. *Ibid.*

28. *Ibid.*

29. For further information on Muvaqqar, see Zahra Shaji'i, *Namayan-digan-i majlis-i shura-i melli dar bist-u yik durah-i ganunguzari* (Tehran: Mu'assasih-i Mutali'at va Tahghighat-i Ijtima'i, 1344), p 371. For his family background, see Mahammad Hussein Roknzadah Adamiyat, *Danishmandan va sukhansarayan-i Fars* (Tehran: Ketabforoushi Khayam, 1340), vol. 5, p 562.

30. For further information on Badi' see Mirza Mihdi Khan Mumtahen-i-Duwlah Shaqaqi, *Rijal-i vizarat-i kharijah*, ed Iraj Afshar (Tehran: Asatir, 1365), pp 154–5. On his literary reputation, see Saeed Nafissi, *Bi ravayat-i Saeed Nafissi* (Tehran: Nashr-i Markaz, 1381), p 384.

31. Jacks to E.H. Elkington, 7 June 1929, BPA 59010. For the generally favourable attitude of the local authorities towards the Iranian workers and their organiza-

tional endeavours, see also Iftikhari, *Khaterat-i duran-i sipari shudah*, pp 33–44, 115–43.

32.   E.H. Elkington, 'An Appreciation of the Political Situation in Kkuzestan'.

33.   Notice, enclosed with a letter from Abadan, 15 June 1929, BPA 59010.

34.   Sir John Cadman to Brigadier General Sir Gilbert Clayton; see also 'Annual Report, 1928', in *Iran Political Diaries*, p 455.

35.   'Interview with His Highness Teymurtash on 29 May 1929', 2, BPA 59010.

36.   E.H. Elkington to Medlicott, 2 June 1929, 4, BPA 59010.

37.   *Shafaq-i surkh*, 30 Mordad 1308 (21 August 1929).

38.   *Ibid.*

39.   *Ibid.*

40.   M.H. Badi' to the Ministry of Foreign Affairs, 24-2-1308 (14 May 1929), in *Naft dar durah-i Reza Shah*, pp 108–11.

41.   *Ibid.*

42.   *Habl al-matin* 37, 14 Khordad 1308 (4 June 1929), p 27.

43.   For this new approach see the debates initiated in Iran upon the publication of APOC's annual report for the year 1931, *Ittila'at*, 28 Tir 1311 (19 July 1932).

Chapter 8. Sufi Reactions Against the Reforms After Turkey's National Struggle

1.   The author wishes to thank her copy-editor Robert N. Stacy, Cambridge Centre for Adult Education, MA, USA.

2.   Alexander Knysh, 'Sufism as an Explanatory Paradigm: The Issue of the Motivations of Sufi Resistance Movements in Western and Russian Scholarship', *Die Welt Des Islams* 42, 2 (2002), pp 140–73. As examples of these kinds of work, Knysh refers to Ziadeh, *Sanusiyah: A Study of a Revivalist Movement in Islam* (Leiden: E.J. Brill, 1958); J. Abun Nasr, *The Tijaniyya: A Sufi Order in the Modern World* (London, New York and Toronto: Oxford University Press, 1965); N.R. Keddie (ed), *Scholars, Saints, and Sufis: Muslim Religious Institutions since 1500* (Berkeley: University of California Press, 1972); N. Levtzion and J. Voll (eds), *Eighteenth-Century Renewal and Reform in Islam* (Syracuse, NY: Syracuse University Press, 1987); R. Schulze, *Islamischer Internationalismus im 20. Jahrhundert* (Leiden: Brill, 1990), pp 19–26. For further references see R. O'Fahey and B. Radtke, 'Neo-Sufism Reconsidered', *Der Islam* 70, no. 1 (1990), pp 53–87. See also B. Radtke, 'Erleuchtung und Aufklärung: Islamische Mystik und europäische Rationalismus', *Die Welt des Islams* 34 (1994), pp 48–66, and K. Vikør, *Sufi and Scholar on the Desert Edge: Muhammad b. 'Ali al-Sanusi and His Brotherhood* (London: Hurst and Company, 1995), pp 2–4, 6–13.

3.   See further in this chapter.

4.   For reforms and reactions against them, see Mahmud Gologlu, *Devrimler ve Tepkileri (1924–1930)* (hereafter *Devrimler ve Tepkileri*) (Ankara: Başnur Matbaası, 1972); Osman Ergin, *Türkiye Maarif Tarihi* (hereafter *Maarif*), 5 vols (Istanbul: Eser, 1977).

5.   See Gologlu, *Devrimler ve Tepkileri*, pp 236–7.

6.   The imposition of the hat, and later of the European calendar, script, etc. For details see G. Jäschke, *Yeni Türkiye'de İslamlık*, trans H. Örs (Ankara: Bilgi, 1972), pp 28–33.

7.   Şerif Mardin, *Din ve İdeoloji* (Istanbul: İletişim, 2002), p 101.

8.   Şerif Mardin, *Türk Modernleşmesi* (Istanbul: İletişim, 2002), p 18.

9.   Bernard Lewis, *The Emergence of Modern Turkey*, 2nd ed (Oxford and New York: Oxford Paperbacks, 1968), p 410. See also Andrew Mango, *Atatürk*, 2nd ed (London: John Murray Publishers, 2000), pp 433–4.

10.   Gologlu, *Devrimler ve Tepkileri*, p 214.

11.   For details see Mardin, *Türk Modernleşmesi*, pp 246ff.

12.   Mustafa Kara, 'Bir Şeyh Efendinin Meşrutiyet ve Cumhuriyete Bakışı' (hereafter 'Bir Şeyh – Cumhuriyet'), *Tasavvuf. İlmi ve Akademik Araştırma Dergisi*, no. 6 (2001), p 32.

13.   Mustafa Kara, *Metinlerle Günümüz Tasavvuf Hareketleri* (hereafter *Günümüz Tasavvuf*) (Istanbul: Dergah, 2002), p 17.

14.   *Ibid.*, p 155.

15.   Ergin says *Milli Mecmua* interviewed some famous writers of the time about the reforms (Ergin, *Maarif*, vol. 5, pp 1961–2). Some Sufis like Ken'an Rifa'i (Büyükaksoy, d.1950) were also interviewed by the press (see, for instance, Semiha Ayverdi et al, *Ken'an Rifai ve Yirminci Asrın Işığında Müslümanlık* (hereafter *Ken'an Rifai*) (Istanbul: Hülbe, 1983), p 98. But no public surveys were taken then.

16.   Cf. Mardin, *Din ve İdeoloji*, p 100.

17.   Turkish educator, writer and calligrapher. For his biography, see M.F. Bayraktar, 'Baltacıoğlu, Ismayıl Hakkı', in *İslam Ansiklopedisi (TDV)*, no. 5 (1992), pp 36–8.

18.   Ergin, *Maarif*, vol. 5, pp 1961–2.

19.   İsmail Kara, *Şeyhefendinin Rüyasındaki Türkiye* (hereafter *Şeyh Efendi*) (Istanbul: Dergah, 2002), p 45.

20.   *Ibid.*, pp 52, 53.

21.   See Kara, *Günümüz Tasavvuf*, pp 17, 155; Kara, 'Bir Şeyh – Cumhuriyet', p 34; Osman Ergin, *Balıkesirli Abdulaziz Mecdi Tolun. Hayatı ve Şahsiyeti* (hereafter *Tolun*) (Istanbul: Kenan, 1942), p 258; Ayverdi et al, *Ken'an Rifai*, p 99; F.A. Tansel, *Mehmed Akif Ersoy. Hayatı ve Eserleri* (Istanbul: İrfan, 1973), p 123. (He does not say this directly. He says: 'My disposition towards Sufism is increasing as much as it can. Man should do his best to achieve his goal. But if he does not reach the goal, he should not cry out. I feel that I am going through this point out of my will.') See also Mardin, *Din ve İdeoloji*, p 100; Kara, *Şeyh Efendi*, p 18. The Sufi is someone who absolutely consents to what God does. This outlook is called *rıza* in Sufism. To be a good Sufi, man has to say to everything '*Eyvallah*: By Allah, it is good'. Those who cannot accept this must say goodbye to the *tekke*. This case is rephrased in the idiom '*Al külahını Eyvallahı içinde*: take your (dervish) cap, its *eyvallah* is in it'. Furthermore some Sufis who attain God-granted knowledge (*Ilm-i Ledun* and *Irfan*), which includes knowledge of meta-physical as well as worldly things, cannot even pray for change of these things, as they hold this also to be against God's will; they are all governed by this *Ilm-i Ledun* and *Irfan*. Mawlana describes them in his *Mathnawi* as '*Qawm-i diger mi şinasam za Awliya, ki dihanşan basta başad az du'a*': 'I know another group of saints whose tongues are prevented from praying.' Another group of Sufis act in accordance with the exoteric rules of the Koran; that is they pray at least. For details see Şeyh Galib, *Şerh-i Cezire-i Mesnevi*, eds T. Karabey et al (Erzurum:

Atatürk üniversitesi Fen edebiyat Fakültesi, 1996), pp 72–3.

22. Kara, *Günümüz Tasavvuf*, p 156; Kara, *Şeyh Efendi*, pp 66–7.

23. See Kara, *Şeyh Efendi*, pp 80–2.

24. The law on the Maintenance of Order was passed on 4 March 1925. It empowered the government for two years to ban by administrative measures any organization or publication that it considered caused disturbances prejudicial to law and order. Two Independence Tribunals (one for the eastern provinces and one for the rest of the country) were reinstated to promote this desired order: (2nd Term) TBMM, *Zabıt Ceridesi* (Ankara: TBMM Basımevi, 1976), 15, p 166; Erik-Jan Zürcher, *Turkey: A Modern History* (London and New York: I.B.Tauris, 1997), p 179; Mango, *Atatürk*, p 424.

25. Kara, 'Bir Şeyh – Cumhuriyet', p 34.

26. Cf. Kara, *Günümüz Tasavvuf*, p 46.

27. See Abdülbaki Gölpınarlı, *Melamilik ve Melamiler* (Istanbul: Gri, 1992), p 300.

28. Abdülbaki Gölpınarlı, *Türkiye'de Mezhepler ve Tarikatlar*, 2nd ed (Istanbul: İnkılap, 1997), p 257; and *Melamilik ve Melamiler*, pp 22–6.

29. Gölpınarlı, *Türkiye'de Mezhepler ve Tarikatlar*, p 257; Gölpınarlı, *Melamilik ve Melamiler*, pp 299–300.

30. Gölpınarlı, *Melamilik ve Melamiler*, VII (Murat Bardakçı's foreword).

31. See Gölpınarlı, *Türkiye'de Mezhepler ve Tarikatlar*, p 263.

32. See Gölpınarlı, *Melamilik ve Melamiler*, pp 315, 320, 323–4.

33. Kara, *Şeyh Efendi*, p 73.

34. Şerafeddin Zeynelabidin Dağıstani. We have little information about his life. He was descended from Sheikh Shamil (d.1871), the leader of Dağıstan resistance to the Russian conquest of the Caucasus from 1834 to 1859. He and his family lived on a small mountain (near the village of Reşadiye, bound to Orhangazi, Bursa) during the National Struggle. He expended great efforts in mediating between the sultan and the nationalists and in mobilizing public opinion. Unfortunately his services are unknown to contemporary researchers. For sources see Hülya Küçük, *The Role of the Bektashis in Turkey's National Struggle* (hereafter *Bektashis*) (Leiden and Boston: Brill, 2001), pp 280–1.

35. See *Hakimiyet-i Milliye*, 19 October 1341 (1925), p 1.

36. According to Naqshi sources, it is not true that he went, or rather escaped, to Jordan and stayed there until 1936. See Arif Ekim, 'Şeyh Şerafettin Efendi', in Nuri Taner (ed), *Yalova Araştırmaları* (Yalova: Ortipa, 2005), pp 77–95.

37. For Bediüzzaman Sa'id Nursi, see further in this chapter.

38. Hamid Algar et al, *Bediüzzaman ve Tasavvuf* (Istanbul: Gelenek, 2002), pp 25–6. Habibis, who does not mention his imprisonment, says that he returned to Turkey and died shortly afterwards in Guneykoy in Istanbul. Tayfun Atay, *Batı'da Bir Nakşi Cemaati. Şeyh Nazım Kıbrısi Örneği* (Istanbul: İletişim, 1996), p 73, quoted in D. Habibis, *A Comparative Study of the Workings of a Branch of the Naqshbandi Sufi Order in Lebanon and the UK* (London: London University Press, 1985), p 73.

39. For a detailed account of his services in support of the nationalists, see Küçük, *Bektashis*, pp 150–92.

40. Here it should be remembered that Albania was under Italian occupation from 1939 onwards. On the other hand, it is also said that he was killed by

the communists because of his collaboration with the Italians. Yusuf İzzettin Ulusoy (uncle of Veliyyettin Ulusoy, the current sheikh of the main *tekke* in Hacıbektaş) claims that Salih Niyazi Baba had received a large sum of money from the government and collected from the people for the construction of a *tekke*. After he had taken this money to his *dargah*, he was killed and the money stolen. For the sources, see Küçük, *Bektashis*, pp 295–6.

41.   A disciple of Nafi'Baba, sheikh of the Shehidlik *tekke* in Rumelihisarı, Istanbul, from the branch of the 'Celibate Babagan'. In 1331/1913 he was the sheikh of the Bektashi Kazimiye *tekke* (in Iraq). According to Turgut Koca, he came to Denizli during the National Struggle and served in the national forces. According to Koca, Cemal (Bardakçı) and Birge (the author of *The Bektashi Order of Dervishes*) were initiated into the Bektashi Order by Selman Cemali Baba. For sources, see Küçük, *Bektashis*, p 298.

42.   For neo-Salafiyya's attitude towards Sufism, see Suleyman Uludağ, *İslam Düşüncesinin Yapısı* (Istanbul: Dergah, 1985), pp 70–2.

43.   See 'Ersoy, Mehmed Akif', in *Yeni Türk Ansiklopedisi* (Istanbul, 1985), vol. 3, pp 831–4. See also M. İz, *Yılların İzi* (Istanbul: İrfan, 1975), pp 124, 148.

44.   For details, see Tansel, *Mehmed Akif Ersoy*, pp 124–9.

45.   *Ibid.*, p 123.

46.   İsmail Kara, *Türkiye'de İslamcılık Düşüncesi* (hereafter *İslamcılık*), 3 vols (Istanbul: Kitabevi, 1997), vol. 1, p 402; Tansel, *Mehmed Akif Ersoy*, p 129.

47.   Tansel, *Mehmed Akif Ersoy*, p 129.

48.   See A. Abdülkadiroğlu and N. Abdülkadiroğlu, *Mehmed Akif'in Kur'an Tefsiri, Mev'ıza ve Hutbeleri* (Ankara: Diyanet İşleri Başkanlığı, 1992), pp 5–6.

49.   For details see Ergin, *Maarif*, vol. 5, pp 1934–5. See also Kara, *İslamcılık*, vol. 1, p 402. For a list of first Turkish Koran translations, see Ergin, *Maarif*, vol. 5, pp 1928ff.

50.   Kara, *Şeyh Efendi*, p 23. This visit is not mentioned in the TBMM minutes of meetings. Cf. Gölpınarlı, *Türkiye'de Mezhepler ve Tarikatler*, pp 224–5.

51.   Gölpınarlı, *Türkiye'de Mezhepler ve Tarikatler*, pp 222–3.

52.   For details on his life and teaching, see Ergin, *Tolun*; Nihat Azamat, 'Abdulaziz Mecdi Efendi', in *İslam Ansiklopedisi (TDV)* (Istanbul, 1988), vol. 1, pp 191–2

53.   Ergin, *Tolun*, pp 16, 216–17.

54.   *Ibid.*, pp 54, 56, 230–6.

55.   *Ibid.*, pp 257–8.

56.   *Ibid.*, p 94.

57.   *Ibid.*, pp 257–8.

58.   *Ibid.*, pp 230–6.

59.   See Martin van Bruinessen, *Agha, Shaikh and State: The Social and Political Structures of Kurdistan* (hereafter *Agha, Shaikh and State*) (London and New Jersey: Zed Books, 1992), p 281; Zürcher, *Turkey*, p 178.

60.   Van Bruinessen, *Agha, Shaikh and State*, p 265

61.   Robert Olson, 'The Shaikh Sa'id Rebellion in Turkey in 1925: Estimates of Troops Employed', *Turcica* 5, no. 25 (1992), p 263. See also Olson, 'The International Sequels of the Shaikh Sa'id Rebellion', in M. Gaborieau, A. Popovic and T. Zarcone (eds), *Naqshibandis, Cheminements et situation actuelle d'un ordre mystique musulman (Historical developments and present situation of a*

Muslim mystical order). Actes de la table ronde Sèvres (Istanbul and Paris: ISIS, 1990), pp 379–406.

62. Goloğlu, *Devrimler ve Tepkileri*, p 127.
63. According to some Kurdish people, it was founded in 1921 by Halit Beg Cibran, former commander of the garrison at Erzurum. It was Halit Beg Cibran who mobilized for rebellion at the first congress of the Azadi. In 1924 he was arrested and imprisoned in Bitlis, and later killed in prison: Robert Olson, *The Emergence of Kurdish Nationalism and the Sheikh Sa'id Rebellion, 1880–1925* (Austin: University of Texas, 1989), pp 41, 42, 92.
64. For ethnic differentiation among the Kurds, see P. White, 'Ethnic Differentiation among the Kurds. Kurmanci, Kızılbaş and Zaza', *Journal of Arabic, Islamic and Middle Eastern Studies* 2, no. 2 (1995), pp 67–90.
65. For a complete account, see W.F. Tucker and R.W. Olson, 'The Shaikh Sa'id Rebellion in Turkey in 1925: A Study in the Consolidation of a Developed Uninstitutionalized Nationalism and the Rise of Incipient (Kurdish) Nationalism', *Die Welt des Islams* XVIII, nos. 3–4 (1978), pp 195–211; Bruinessen, *Agha, Shaikh and State*, pp 265–305. For the reports on the rebellion in the newspapers of the time, see *Tanin*, 1 and 3 March 1341 (1925); *Hakimiyet-i Milliye*, 16 April 1341 (1925) and 8 May 1341 (1925); *Açıksöz*, 21 June 1341 (1925) and 25 June 1341 (1925).
66. Mustafa Kemal had opponents among former leaders of the UPP (Union and Progress Party) and the PRP (Progressive Republican Party). He was aware of the capabilities of his opponents and their underground organization (going back to the days before the revolution of 1908), and he still felt insecure. During his inspection tour of the south and the west of the country a plot to assassinate him was uncovered when he was about to arrive in Izmir on 15 June. The small band of plotters led by Ziya Hurşid (a former representative in the TBMM and secretary of the Defense of Rights Group) was arrested and tried by the Ankara Independence Tribunal which arrived there on 18 June 1926. See Erik-Jan Zürcher, *The Unionist Factor: The Role of the Committee of Union and Progress in the Turkish National Movement* (Leiden: Brill, 1984), pp 144–67, and Goloğlu, *Devrimler ve Tepkileri*, p 132.
67. *Hakimiyet-i Milliye*, 4 September 1341 (1925), no. 1518, p 1.
68. See Algar et al, *Bediüzzaman ve Tasavvuf.*
69. Şerif Mardin, *Türkiye'de Din Ve Siyaset* (Istanbul: İletişim, 1995), pp 170ff.
70. Vehbi Vakkasoğlu, *Maneviyat Dünyamızda İz Bırakanlar* (hereafter *İz Bırakanlar*) (Istanbul: Cihan, 1994), pp 85–6.
71. Şerif Mardin, *Bediuzzaman Said Nursi Olayı* (Istanbul: İletişim, 2002), p 163. See also Kara, *Şeyh Efendi*, pp 25–6.
72. Mardin, *Bediuzzaman Said Nursi Olayı*, p 303; Vakkasoglu, *İz Bırakanlar*, p 90.
73. For his life and struggle, see Mardin, *Bediuzzaman Said Nursi Olayı*; Mardin, *Din ve Siyaset*, pp 170–89; Vakkasoglu, *İz Bırakanlar*, pp 62–115: Kara, *Şeyh Efendi*, pp 23–9: Kara, *Günümüz Tasavvuf*, pp 296–305.
74. See Bediüzzaman Said Nursi, *Lemalar*, in *Risale-i Nur Külliyatı* (Istanbul: Yeni Asya, 1996), pp 669–70. See also Kara, *Günümüz Tasavvuf*, pp 297–300.
75. For details see Ruşen Çakır, *Ayet ve Slogan. Türkiye'de İslami Oluşumlar* (Istanbul:

Metis, 1991), pp 77–122; *The Muslim World* LXXXIX, nos 3–4 (special issue: 'Said Nursi and the Turkish Experience'), ed M.H. Yavuz; Bayram Balcı, *Fethullah Gülen's Schools in Central Asia* (Grenoble: Institute d'Etudes Politiques, 2002).

76. Başbakanlık Cumhuriyet Arşivi, *Karar* (Decision) no. 1735; *Hakimiyet-i Milliye*, 15 April 1341 (1925), 1 and 12 May 1341 (1925), p 1; *Tanin*, 15 April 1341 (1925), p 1.

77. Mustafa Çavuş was sentenced to two years' imprisonment for fraud, and Veli Dede was acquitted as he had been cheated by Mustafa Çavuş who said that he was entrusted by Çelebi with the task of collecting money (Çelebi had the right to send people to collect money according to the order's regulations). See 'Bektaşi Ordusu', *Yakın Tarihimiz* II, no. 18 (28 June 1962), pp 133–4.

78. Although this was an opposition founded initially by Mustafa Kemal with the twin aims of channeling the social discontent and of shaking up the lethargic Republican People's Party, in the elections it managed to win 30 of the 520 councils. Even though this was a small minority of the seats, the governing party was alarmed. Fethi Okyar, an old friend and the leader of the party, accused the governing party of large-scale irregularities and electoral fraud. This in turn led to fierce attacks on his party, in which he and his party were accused of high treason. After talks with Mustafa Kemal, Fethi Okyar felt that he had no choice but to close down the party. For the rest of his life, he remained bitter about Mustafa Kemal's desertion at this juncture. For details see Gologlu, *Devrimler ve Tepkileri*, pp 273–301; Zürcher, *Turkey*, pp 186–7.

79. See Gologlu, *Devrimler ve Tepkileri*, p 297.

80. Kemal H. Karpat, *Turkey's Politics: The Transition to a Multiparty System* (New Jersey: Princeton University, 1959), pp 137–69, 278.

81. U. Kocatürk, *Atatürk ve Türkiye Cumhuriyeti Tarihi Kronolojisi 1918–1938* (Ankara: Türk Tarih Kurumu, 1983), pp 513, 515, 517.

82. Gologlu, *Devrimler ve Tepkileri*, pp 304, 308. For Erbili's life, see H.K. Yılmaz, 'Es'ad Erbili', in *İslam Ansiklopedisi (TDV)*, vol. 11, pp 348–9; Kara, *Günümüz Tasavvuf*, pp 185–9; Ömer Çelik, 'Muhammed Es'ad Erbili (1847–1931) 'nin Kur'an-ı Kerim Ayetlerini Yorumlama Yaklaşımı' (hereafter 'Muhammed Es'ad Erbili'), *Tasavvuf. İlmi ve Akademik Araştırma Dergisi*, no. 6 (2001), pp 177–210.

83. Gologlu, *Devrimler ve Tepkileri*, p 308.

84. Çelik, 'Muhammed Es'ad Erbili', p 179.

85. Kara, *Günümüz Tasavvuf*, p 165; Vakkasoğlu, *İz Bırakanlar*, pp 23–36.

86. Kara, *Günümüz Tasavvuf*, p 186.

87. The counter-revolution against the constitution, which broke out on 31 March 1325/13 April 1909, and was suppressed by the *Hareket Ordusu* (Action Army). See A.H. Ongunsu, 'Abdulhamid', in *İslam Ansiklopedisi (MEB)* (Istanbul, 1993), vol. 1, p 79.

88. See Gologlu, *Devrimler ve Tepkileri*, pp 306–7; Gölpınarlı, *Türkiye'de Mezhepler ve Tarikatler*, pp 219–20.

89. See Gölpınarlı, *Türkiye'de Mezhepler ve Tarikatler*, pp 220, 263.

90. *Ibid.*, p 263; and *Melamilik ve Melamiler*, pp 291–92. For some notes on Malamis, see further in this chapter.

91. Abdullah Muradoğlu, *Öldüren Sır. Garih: Sıradışı bir Musevi'nin Portresi* (hereafter *Öldüren Sır*) (Istanbul: Bakış, 2001), pp 113–14.

92. *Ibid.*, pp 121–30. For Arusis, see further in this chapter.

93. Necip F. Kısakürek, *Son Devrin Din Mazlumları* (Istanbul, 1976), p 116. Kısakürek thought the opposite way before he became a disciple of Arvasi. See Kara, *Günümüz Tasavvuf,* p 188.

94. Kara, *Günümüz Tasavvuf,* p 186. For the literature on the Menemen Incident, see *ibid.*, pp 186–7.

95. Mango, *Atatürk,* p 476.

96. It is the name of a Koran Surah which tells the story of six or seven young Christian men who slept in a cave for years to escape from a tyrannical ruler. Their dog, Kıtmir, also slept with them.

97. Gologlu, *Devrimler ve Tepkileri,* p 308.

98. *Ibid.* For further details on the Menemen Incident see Umut Azak's chapter in the present volume.

99. For details on Tijaniyya see J. Abun Nasr, *The Tijaniyya: A Sufi Order in the Modern World* (London, New York and Toronto: Oxford University Press, 1965); J.S. Trimingham, *The Sufi Orders in Islam* (Oxford: Clarendon, 1971), pp 107–10; Gölpınarlı, *Türkiye'de Mezhepler ve Tarikatler,* pp 221–2; Kara, *Günümüz Tasavvuf,* pp 242–6.

100. Kara, *Günümüz Tasavvuf,* p 242.

101. Gölpınarlı, *Türkiye'de Mezhepler ve Tarikatler,* p 222. For an article about them in a contemporary newspaper see 'Alçak bir yobazın Hacıbayram Camiinde marifeti', *Zafer,* 30 June 1951, p 1.

102. For a list of his works see Kara, *Günümüz Tasavvuf,* p 242.

103. For brief information on his life, see Küçük, *Bektashis,* pp 293–4.

104. For details see Mewlanzade Rifat, *Türkiya Inkılabının İç Yüzü* (Haleb, 1929), part 2, pp 66–7.

105. For sources see Kamil Erdeha, *Milli Mücadele'de Vilayetler ve Valiler* (İstanbul: Remzi, 1975), p 281.

106. See '150'likler Albümü', *Tarih ve Toplum* XII (Ekim, 1989), no. 70 (Special Affix).

107. For details see M. Ali Uz, *Baha Veled'den Günümüze Konya Alimleri ve Velileri* (Konya: Alagöz, 1993), pp 153–4; Caner Arabacı, *Osmanlı Dönemi Konya Medreseleri 1900–1924* (Konya: Konya Ticaret Odası, 1998), pp 515–25.

108. Koçkuzu was professor at the Theology Faculty, Selçuk University, Konya, from our talks on 30 January 2003.

109. For his life and teaching see Mustafa Kara, 'Bursalı Bir Tarihçi. Mehmed Şemseddin (Ulusoy) Efendi', *U.Ü. İlahiyat Fakültesi Dergisi* III, 3 (1991), pp 131–7; Kara, 'Bir Şeyh – Cumhuriyet'.

110. Kara, 'Bir Şeyh – Cumhuriyet', pp 32–3.

111. *Ibid.*, pp 28, 30.

112. *Ibid.*, pp 26–8.

113. *Ibid.*, p 29.

114. Kara, *Günümüz Tasavvuf,* p 171, quoted in A. Baykara's unpublished *Enfas-ı Baki [Divan]* (Ali Emiri Manzum, no. 533/1).

115. Worked at the Meshikhat during the reign of Abülhamid II. See Kara, *Şeyh*

Efendi, p 15.

116. *Ibid.*, pp 15–16 (narrated from Ahmed Başoğlu (d.2001), an eyewitness and *murid* of a *murid* of Sheikh Rahmi Baba).

117. For details of his life and works see A.C. Haksever, *Son Dönem Osmanlı Mevlevilerinden Ahmet Remzi Akyürek* (hereafter, *Ahmet Remzi Akyürek*) (Ankara: Kültür Bakanlığı, 2002); Hasibe Mazıoğlu, 'Akyürek, Ahmet Remzi', in *İslam Ansiklopedisi (TDV)*, vol. 2 (1989), pp 304–5.

118. See his *Mecmu'a-ı Eş'ar*; Mevlana Museum Archive, no. 963 (contains all the poems he wrote after the banning of the Sufi orders). See also Kara, *Günümüz Tasavvuf*, p 166.

119. Vakkasoğlu, *İz Bırakanlar*, pp 52–9, 61.

120. For details see Arabacı, *Osmanlı Dönemi Konya Medreseleri. 1900–1924*, pp 533–4.

121. Kara, *Günümüz Tasavvuf*, p 262.

122. Kara, *Şeyh Efendi*, pp 191–7; Kara, *Günümüz Tasavvuf*, pp 262, 334–52.

123. Kara, *Şeyh Efendi*, pp 66–7.

124. For his biography see A.G. Sayar, *Süheyl Ünver. Hayatı, Şahsiyeti, Eserleri* (hereafter *Süheyl Ünver*) (Istanbul: Eren, 1994).

125. Kara, *Şeyh Efendi*, pp 44–7.

126. See Haksever, *Ahmet Remzi Akyürek*, pp 85–6.

127. See Sayar, *Süheyl Ünver*, pp 118–34. For his Sufi inclinations and thoughts, see pp 299ff., 481ff., 493–504.

128. Muradoğlu, *Öldüren Sır*, pp 104–5, 109.

129. Kara, *Şeyh Efendi*, pp 44–7.

130. For details see Muradoğlu, *Öldüren Sır*, pp 104, 109, 114–15, 118, 121.

131. *Ibid.*, pp 118–20, 132.

132. *Ibid.*, pp 114–15, 121.

133. Louis Massignon, 'Tarikat', in *İslam Ansiklopedisi (MEB)* (Istanbul, 1993), 12/1, p 15; See also Muradoğlu, *Öldüren Sır*, pp 121–30, which states that it was a branch of Kadiriyya in North Africa related to Sheikh 'Abd al-Salam al-Asmar (881–981/1460–1560).

134. Cemaleddin S. Revnakoğlu, 'Tarikat Mensublarında Zarafet, Nüktedanlık ve Hazırcevaplık', *Tarih Konuşuyor* VII, no. 39 (April 1967), p 3127.

135. Muradoğlu, *Öldüren Sır*, pp 109–10.

136. *Ibid.*, pp 115, 125–6, 129.

137. Abdullah Muradoğlu, 'Türkeş'in Gizli Dünyası', *Yeni Şafak*, 14–18 August 2003, p 5.

138. *Yeni Şafak*, 20 August 2003, p 5, and 27 August 2003, p 12.

139. For sources see Küçük, *Bektashis*, p 234.

140. For details on Sümbüliyya, see Nazif Velikahyaoğlu (Öztürk), *Sümbüliyye Tarikatı ve Kocamustafapaşa Külliyesi* (hereafter *Sümbüliyye Tarikatı*) (Istanbul: Çağrı, 2000), pp 75–123.

141. Those who were elected by people to elect the MPs representing their region.

142. See Velikahyaoğlu, *Sümbüliyye Tarikatı*, pp 235–7.

143. *Ibid.*, p 41.

144. *Ibid.*, p 237.

145. For details on the debates, see (2nd Term) TBMM, *Zabıt Ceridesi*, 7, pp 17, 21,

27–69. On Sheikh Safvet Yetkin, see M. Birol Ülker and Ö. Faruk Bahadır, 'Şeyh Mustafa Safvet (Yetkin) ve Tasavvuf Dergisi', *Müteferrika*, no. 24 (Winter 2003–2), pp 145–57.

146. See (2nd Term) TBMM, *Zabıt Ceridesi*, 7, p 28.

147. It should be remembered here that formerly he had good relations with the last sultan, Wahid al-Din, and the caliph, Abdülmajid Efendi. He was the one who first informed the latter that he had been elected as caliph. See Jäschke, *Yeni Türkiye'de İslamlık*, p 35.

148. Mevlana Museum Archive, Envelope, no. 108.

149. (2nd Term) TBMM, *Zabıt Ceridesi*, 7, pp 136–7, the meeting on 6.3.1340 (1924).

150. Nevin Korucuoğlu, *Veled Çelebi İzbudak* (Ankara: Kültür Bakanlığı, 1994), p 45.

151. Kara, *Günümüz Tasavvuf*, p 105.

152. His telegram dated 8 September 1925. See *Atatürk'ün Tamim, Telgraf ve Beyannameleri, (1917–1938)* (Ankara, 1964), vol. 4, p 526 (from *Hakimiyet -i Milliye*, 9 September 1925).

153. See Y.Ş. Yavuz, 'Elmalılı Muhammed Hamdi', in *İslam Ansiklopedisi (TDV)*, vol. 11 (1995), p 59. Sha'baniyya is a branch of the Khalwatiyya Order. For details on the order, see Reşat Öngören, *Osmanlılarda Tasavvuf* (Istanbul: İz, 2000), pp 79–89.

154. Yavuz, 'Elmalılı Muhammed Hamdi', pp 57–8.

155. Kara, *İslamcılık*, vol. 1, p 520.

156. Ö.N. Bilmen, *Büyük Tefsir Tarihi. Tabakatu'l-Müfessirin* (Istanbul: Bilmen, 1974), vol. 2, p 786.

157. Ergin says (*Maarif*, vol. 5, p 1965): 'Such a thing never happened in Mustafa Kemal's lifetime. Why he did not carry out this reform is not known.'

158. Ergin, *Maarif*, vol. 5, pp 1934–7.

159. For an account on Hacıbeyzade Ahmed Muhtar, see Hülya Küçük, *Kurtuluş Savaşı'nda Bektaşiler* (Istanbul: Kitap, 2003), pp 229–30; Gabriele Karayel, 'Der religiöse Aspekt im Leben Ahmed Muhtars (1871–1955)', *Deutsche Morganländische Gesselschaft e.v., XXVIII.* Deutscher Orientalistentag. Orientalistik Zwischen Philologie und Sozial Wissenschaft, Bamberg, 26–30 März 2001.

160. Ayverdi et al, *Ken'an Rifai*, pp 17–100.

161. *Ibid.*, p 141.

162. *Ibid.*, p 98.

163. Kara, *Günümüz Tasavvuf*, pp 163, 382–9.

164. Mardin, *Türkiye'de Din ve Siyaset*, p 34. For details on him see Ayverdi et al., *Ken'an Rifai*.

165. Tahir'ul-Mevlevi, *Matbuat Alemindeki Hayatım ve İstiklal Mahkemeleri* (Istanbul: Nehir, 1991), p 216. During his questioning it turned out that he was called because of his connection with the *Te'ali İslam* Society. For details see *ibid.*, pp 203ff.

166. Abd al-Karim al-Qushayri, *al-Risalatu'l-Qushayriyya*, eds M. Zerrik and A.A. Baltaji (Beirut: Daru'l-Khayr, 1413/1993), p 55. The famous Ibn 'Arabi interprets this as follows: 'Sons of time (*'abidu'l-wakt*), i.e., those whose spiritual levels

are high, always see Allah's continuously changing manifestations as they are, and worship Him as the time orders them. He is always flexible and obedient. Doing so, they are not worshipping these changing forms, but One God only, who possesses all these forms. (Things and happenings, etc are all different manifestations of Allah.)' See Toshihiko İzitsu, *İbn Arabi'nin Fusus'undaki Anahtar-Kavramlar*, trans A.Y. Özemre (Istanbul: Kaknüs, 1998), pp 133–4.

167. Bediüzzaman Sa'id Nursi, *Mektubat. Yirmi ikinci Mektup*, in *Risale-i Nur Külliyatı* (Istanbul, 1996), vol. 1, p 471.

168. For an account of neo-Sufism and classical Sufism, see R. O'Fahey and B. Radtke, 'Neo-Sufism Reconsidered', *Der Islam* 70, no. 1 (1990), pp 53–87; Knysh, 'Sufism as an Explanatory Paradigm', pp 141ff.

169. For details and sources see Hülya Küçük, 'Bektaşilik ve Aleviliğin Sufi ve esoterik Boyutu: Karşılaştırmalı Kavram Analizi', *İslamiyat* VI, no. 3 (July–September 2003), pp 151–63 (162–3).

170. For some details on Sufi orders today see Küçük, *Bektashis*, pp 242–50.

Chapter 9. A Reaction to Authoritarian Modernization in Turkey

1. I would like to thank Prof. Erik-Jan Zürcher, Erdoğan Azak, Annemarie Stremmelaar, Özgür M. Ulus, Pınar Yelsalı-Parmaksız, Seda Altuğ, Yüksel Taşkın, Didem Danış, Harriet Fitski and Arzu Meral as well as librarians of ISAM in Istanbul and TBMM Library in Ankara.

2. Güler Şenünver et al, *Türkiye Cumhuriyeti İnkılâp Tarihi ve Atatürkçülük* (Istanbul: M.E.B, 2005), p 126. The translation is mine.

3. For the separation between historical and commemorated events, see Barry Schwartz, 'The Social Context of Commemoration: A Study in Collective Memory', *Social Forces* 61, no. 2 (1982), p 377.

4. Gavin D. Brockett, 'Collective Action and the Turkish Revolution: Towards a Framework for the Social History of the Atatürk Era, 1923–38', *Middle Eastern Studies* 34, no. 4 (1999), p 48.

5. 'Icon' is used here in the wider sense of the term, i.e. an 'enduring symbol'. *American Heritage Dictionary* (TLC Properties Inc, 1997).

6. The most referred to and comprehensive source on the event is Kemal Üstün, *Devrim Şehidi Öğretmen Kubilay: 60.yıl (1930–1990)*, 4th ed (Istanbul: Çağdaş, 1990). See also Mustafa Baydar, *Kubilay*, Türk Kahramanları Serisi: 20 (Istanbul: Üstünel, 1954); Celal Kırhan, *Öğretmen Kubilay ve Uydurma Mehdi* (Istanbul: Sıralar Matbaası, 1963); Cemaleddin A. Saraçoğlu, 'Menemen İrticaının İçyüzü', *Cumhuriyet*, 23–29 December 1958; Cemalettin A. Saraçoğlu, 'Menemen İrticaı Adı Altındaki Cinayetin Esrar Dolu İç Yüzü I-III', *Tarih Konuşuyor* 5, no. 28 (1966), pp 2290–4, no. 29, pp 2429–33, no. 30, pp 2513–16; Abdullah Neyzar Karahan, *Şehit Edilişinin 50. Yılında Kubilay* (Ankara: Spor Toto, 1981); Hikmet Çetinkaya, *Kubilay Olayı ve Tarikat Kampları*, 3rd ed (Istanbul: Çağdaş, 1995). For the works of Kemalist scholars see Tarık Zafer Tunaya, *İslamcılık Cereyanı* (Istanbul: Baha Matbaası, 1962), p 186; Bernard Lewis, *The Emergence of Modern Turkey* (London: Oxford University Press, 1967), p 411; Çetin Özek, *100 Soruda Türkiye'de Gerici Akımlar* (Istanbul: Gerçek, 1968), pp 158–9; Mahmud Gologlu, *Devrimler ve Tepkileri (1924–1930)* (Ankara: Başnur Matbaası, 1972), pp 303–9; Muzaffer Sencer, *Dinin Türk Toplumuna Etkileri* (Istanbul: Garanti

Matbaası, 1968), pp 137–8; Neşet Çağatay, *Türkiye'de Gerici Eylemler: 1923'ten Bu Yana* (Ankara, 1972), pp 33–4; Suna Kili, *Türk Devrim Tarihi* (Istanbul: Tekin, 1982), pp 177–8.

7. The Naqshbandiyya Order (*Nakşibendi tarikatı*), which took its name from Sheikh Baha ud-Din Naqshband of Bukhara (d.1390), was introduced into the Ottoman Empire in the fifteenth century. The order is characterized by 'its concern for the integrity of the *Shari'a*' and 'for the replacement of *adat* – customary law – by ordinances of the *Shari'a* in several places'. See Hamid Algar, 'A Brief History of the Naqshbandi Order', in Marc Gaborieau et al (eds), *Naqshbandis: Historical Developments and Present Situation of a Muslim Mystical Order* (Istanbul: ISIS, 1990), pp 14–15.

8. Jeffrey K. Olick and Joyce Robbins, 'Social Memory Studies: From "Collective Memory" to the Historical Sociology of Mnemonic Practices', *Annual Review of Sociology* 24 (1998), pp 105–40, here p 126.

9. Natalie Zemon Davis and Randolph Starn, 'Introduction', *Representations*, special issue: 'Memory and Counter Memory', 26 (Spring 1989), p 2.

10. Necip Fazıl Kısakürek, *Son Devrin Din Mazlumları*, 18th ed (Istanbul: Büyük Doğu, 1997); Mustafa Müftüoğlu, *Yalan Söyleyen Tarih Utansın*, 8th ed (Istanbul: Çile, 1988), pp 287–302 (*Yakın Tarihimizde Bir Olay: Menemen Vak'ası* (Istanbul: Risale, 1991)); Hasan Hüseyin Ceylan, 'Ulemaya Yapılan Zulümler. Rejim Tarafından Zehirlenerek Şehid Edilen Nakşi Şeyhi', *Cumhuriyet Dönemi Din-Devlet İlişkileri*, III, 9th ed (Ankara: Rehber, 1991), pp 159–85; Mustafa İslamoğlu, *Devrimlere Tepkiler ve Menemen Provakasyonu*, 7th ed (Istanbul: Denge, 1998); Necati Bursalı, *Yakın Tarihin Din Mazlumları* (Istanbul: Beyda, 1996), pp 138–62. The incident could even be described as a 'Zionist conspiracy' by an ultra-nationalist anti-Semitist writer, on the basis that one of the suspects, Josef Hayim, was a Jewish resident of Menemen. See Cevat Rifat Atilhan, *Menemen Hadisesinin İç Yüzü*, 3rd ed (İzmir: Aykurt Neşriyatı, 1972).

11. Sheikh (Muhammed) Es'ad (b. Erbil, 1848), a Kadiri sheikh and the *postnişin* at the Kelami Naqshbandi lodge in Kocamustafapaşa, Istanbul, after 1888. See Algar, 'A Brief History of the Naqshbandi Order', pp 34–5. Exiled to Erbil by Sultan Abdulhamid until 1909, appointed in 1914 by Sultan Reşad as the *Şeyhü'l-Meşayih*, the head of all Sufi orders in the country. See İslamoğlu, *Devrimlere Tepkiler*, p 109. After the outlawing of lodges in 1925, he continued to receive guests in his house in the Istanbul suburb of Erenköy. See Saraçoğlu, 'Menemen İrticaı', p 2294.

12. Islamist writers claim that the incident was planned earlier in 1930 by some prominent members of the political elite who, during their visit to Bursa, were struck by the traffic of people paying their respects to Sheikh Es'ad, staying in a hotel opposite to their own. See Kısakürek, *Son Devrin Din Mazlumları*, pp 137–8; İslamoğlu, *Devrimlere Tepkiler*, pp 85–6, 115–16; Müftüoğlu, *Yalan Söyleyen Tarih Utansın*, pp 292–4.

13. For instance, *Cumhuriyet*, 25 December 1930.

14. Kısakürek, *Son Devrin Din Mazlumları*, p 130.

15. İslamoğlu, *Devrimlere Tepkiler*, p 71.

16. Müftüoğlu, *Yalan Söyleyen Tarih Utansın*, p 302.

17. Yalçın Küçük, *Türkiye Üzerine Tezler 1908–1978*, 4th ed (Istanbul: Tekin, 1985),

vol. 1, pp 236–40.

18. Mete Tunçay, *Türkiye Cumhuriyeti'nde Tek-Parti Yönetimi'nin Kurulması (1923–1931)*, 3rd ed (Istanbul: Tarih Vakfı Yurt, 1999), p 304.

19. Hamit Bozarslan, 'Messianism et Mouvement Social: l'Evenement de Menemen en Turquie (Décembre 1930)', *C.E.M.O.T.I.* 11 (January 1991), pp 73–89, here p 79. Brockett too contends that the event was not a 'Naqshbandi plot', because if it were, it would be set somewhere more remote and receive much larger popular support. 'Collective Action', p 56.

20. Hikmet Kıvılcımlı, *Müttefik: Köylü* (Stockholm: Arşiv, 1980), pp 226–7.

21. *Ibid.*, p 218.

22. *Ibid.*, pp 233–4.

23. *Ibid.*, p 205.

24. Bozarslan, 'Messianism et Mouvement Social', p 83.

25. *Ibid*; Brockett, 'Collective Action'; Nurşen Mazıcı, 'Menemen Olayı'nın Sosyo-Kütürel ve Sosyo-Ekonomik Analizi', *Toplum ve Bilim* 90 (Fall 2001), pp 131–46.

26. Erik-Jan Zürcher, *Turkey: A Modern History* (London: I.B.Tauris, 1997), pp 178–80.

27. Protests against the 'Hat Revolution' of 1925 took place in Kayseri (22 November), Erzurum (24 November), Rize (25 November) and Maraş (26 November) and resulted in several death sentences. See Sencer, *Dinin Türk Toplumuna*, p 134; Özek, *100 Soruda*, p 155; Tunaya, *İslamcılık Cereyanı*, pp 176–8. Among other secularizing reforms were: the adoption of the Swiss Civil Code and the Italian Penal Code in 1926; the replacement of the Arabic alphabet by the Latin one in 1928; and finally the removal of the second article of the 1924 constitution, which made Islam the official religion of the state, in 1928.

28. For the history of this short-lived opposition party see Ahmet Ağaoğlu, *Serbest Fırka Hatıraları*, 3rd ed (İstanbul: İletişim, 1994); Osman Okyar, Mehmed Seyitdanlıoğlu, *Fethi Okyar'ın Anıları, Atatürk, Okyar ve Çok Partili Türkiye* (Ankara: Türkiye İş Bankası Kültür Yayınları, 1997); Walter F. Weiker, *Political Tutelage and Democracy in Turkey: The Free Party and Its Aftermath* (Leiden: Brill, 1973); Çetin Yetkin, *Atatürk'ün Başarısız Demokrasi Devrimi, Serbest Cumhuriyet Fırkası* (Istanbul: Toplumsal Dönüşüm, 1997); Cem Emrence, 'Politics of Discontent in the Midst of the Great Depression: The Free Republican Party of Turkey (1930)', *New Perspectives on Turkey* 23 (Fall 2000), pp 31–52.

29. Bozarslan, 'Messianism et Mouvement Social', p 77. The export-oriented agricultural sector was severely hit in this period by the reduction in the prices of crops such as grapes, olives etc by up to 50 per cent. Producers' conditions were worsened also by new taxes imposed on this sector. See Şevket Pamuk and Roger Owen, *A History of Middle East Economies in the Twentieth Century* (London: I.B.Tauris, 1998), p 16; Çağlar Keyder, *State and Class in Turkey: A Study in Capitalist Development* (London: Verso, 1987), pp 95–6, 101; İlhan Tekeli and Selim İlkin, *1929 Buhranında Türkiye'nin İktisadi Politika Arayışları* (Ankara: ODTÜ, 1977), pp 86–7. Besides, state monopolies in the sectors such as tobacco, alcohol and sugar had worsened the economic condition of the commercial bourgeoisie. See Muzaffer Sencer, *Türkiye'de Siyasal Partilerin Sosyal Temelleri* (Istanbul: Geçiş, 1971), p 142.

30. Emrence, 'Politics of Discontent'. See also Cem Emrence, 'Buhranlı Yıllar: Ödemiş'te Serbest Cumhuriyet Fırkası', *Toplumsal Tarih* 72 (1999), pp 28–32.

31. Sencer, *Partilerin Sosyal Temelleri*, p 142.

32. Emrence, 'Politics of Discontent'; Ağaoğlu, *Serbest Fırka Hatıraları*, pp 109–15; Okyar, *Fethi Okyar'ın Anıları*. For the anti-government demonstrations held in İzmir on the occasion of the FRP leaders' visit to the city, see Weiker, *Political Tutelage*, pp 88–91, 135.

33. Weiker, *Political Tutelage*, p 115. In 42 localities, according to Emrence, 'Politics of Discontent'.

34. Kamil Su and Kazım N. Duru, *Ortaokullar için Tarih, III* (Istanbul, 1943–49); Hamza Eroğlu, *Türk İnkılap Tarihi* (Istanbul: MEB, 1982), pp 292–6; Kemal Kara, *Türkiye Cumhuriyeti İnkılap Tarihi ve Atatürkçülük 2* (Istanbul: Önde Yayıncılık, 1994); Şenünver et al, *İnkılâp Tarihi ve Atatürkçülük*.

35. Büşra Ersanlı Behar, *İktidar ve Tarih: Türkiye'de 'Resmi Tarih' Tezinin Oluşumu (1929–1937)* (Istanbul: Afa, 1996), pp 229–30.

36. Some writers could even argue that the FRP had to be closed '*because* it incited the Menemen Incident' (emphasis is mine), ignoring the fact that the FRP was closed one month before the incident. See Kili, *Türk Devrim Tarihi*, p 169; İrfan Orga, *Phoenix Ascendant: The Rise of the New Turkey* (London: Robert Hale, 1958), p 177.

37. Weiker, *Political Tutelage*, p 138; Dankwart A. Rustow, 'Politics and Islam in Turkey, 1920–55', in Richard N. Frye (ed), *Islam and the West* (The Hague: Mouton, 1957), p 88.

38. The records of the court martial, which tried the suspects of the incident between 15 January and 16 February 1931, were published in the written proceedings of the National Assembly in 1931: 'Menemen hadisesini ika ve teşkilâtı esasiye kanununu cebren tağyire teşebbüs edenlerden 37 şahsın ölüm cezasına çarptırılması hakkında 3/564 numaralı Başvekâlet tezkeresi ve Adliye Encümeni mazbatası', 31 January 1931, TBMM, *Zabıt Ceridesi* 25 (3), no. 4.

39. 'Menemen hadisesini ika', pp 16, 47, 51.

40. For information on the age and marital status of other suspects, see 'Menemen hadisesini ika', p 5.

41. TBMM, *Zabıt Ceridesi* 25 (3), no. 4, pp 8–9.

42. *Ibid.*, p 11.

43. *Ibid.*, p 9.

44. *Ibid.*, p 74.

45. *Ibid.*, p 9.

46. The Surat al-Kahf in the Koran tells the story of *Ashab al-Kahf*, the seven (or three or five) youths, who in the Christian tradition are usually called the 'Seven Sleepers of Ephesus', a group that fled into a cave in order to remain true to their belief in one God and slept miraculously for 309 years, which appeared to them as a single day. See R. Paret, 'Ashab al-Kahf', *Encyclopedia of Islam*, CD edition, v. 1.0 (Leiden: Brill, 2003). See also *Türkiye Diyanet Vakfı İslam Ansiklopedisi*, vol. III (Istanbul, 1991), p 466.

47. The *Mahdi* (or *Mehdi*) is the name given in Islamic belief to the messianic figure that, as 'the restorer of religion and justice', 'will rule before the end of the world'. W. Madelung, 'Al-Mahdi', *Encyclopedia of Islam*, CD edition, v. 1.0 (Leiden:

Brill, 2003).

48.   'Menemen hadisesini ika', p 14.

49.   Gologlu, *Devrimler ve Tepkileri*, pp 303–4.

50.   Zeki Sarıtoprak, 'The Mahdi Tradition in Islam: A Social-Cognitive Approach', *Islamic Studies* 41, 4 (2002), pp 651–74.

51.   'Menemen hadisesini ika', p 10.

52.   *Ibid.*, pp 10, 12, 18, 31–2.

53.   According to the reporter of *Cumhuriyet*, just after their arrest they had accused the prosecutor of infidelity and claimed that their leader Mehmed was the *Mahdi* and would be resurrected. *Cumhuriyet*, 26 December 1930, quoted in Kıvılcımlı, *Müttefik*, p 230.

54.   During his trial in the court martial, Saffet Efendi said that he was a faithful official of the Directorate of Religious Affairs and did not have any relationship with the rebels, 'Menemen hadisesini ika', pp 21–2. He was then acquitted by the court. Üstün saw this as the proof of the innocence of Menemen's inhabitants. See Üstün, *Devrim Şehidi*, p 13.

55.   'Menemen hadisesini ika', p 15.

56.   Genelkurmay Harb Tarihi Başkanlığı, *Türkiye Cumhuriyeti'nde Ayaklanmalar 1924–1938* (Ankara: Genelkurmay, 1972), p 363.

57.   Kan Demir, *Şehit Kubilay* (Kanaat Kütüphanesi, 1931), p 33.

58.   According to a witness, Mehmed Yetimoğlu, who ran a barber shop during the event, 'nothing would have happened if Kubilay had not held the rebels by their collar'. Yetimoğlu had told the court that he had not seen the rebels, although he had in fact seen them, as those who said they had were hanged. 'İşte Menemen Olayının İçyüzü' (interview by Sadullah Amasyalı, Şirin Kabakçı, Mehmed Deniz), *Zaman*, 23–29 December 1988.

59.   According to the report of *Cumhuriyet* (25 December 1930) and the accounts by Özek and Üstün, Mahdi Mehmed also drank the blood of Kubilay. Özek, *100 Soruda*, p 159; Üstün, *Devrim Şehidi*, p 24.

60.   'Menemen hadisesini ika', p 15.

61.   'Gazi Hz.'nin mektubu', *Cumhuriyet*, 28 December 1930.

62.   TBMM, *Zabıt Ceridesi* 24 (3), no. 4, 1 (Ocak, 1931), p 3.

63.   *Yarın*, 30 December 1930, pp 1, 3.

64.   Kazım Özalp's memoirs were published in the newspaper *Milliyet* in 1969: 'Özalp, Atatürk'ü Anlatıyor: Kubilay Şehit Ediliyor', *Milliyet*, 22 November 1969. For Fahrettin Altay's notes of this meeting, see his memoirs: *Görüp Geçirdiklerim, 10 Yıl Savaş ve Sonrası* (Istanbul: İnsel, 1970), pp 433–40.

65.   Doğan Akyaz, 'Menemen Olayı Üzerine İlân Edilen Sıkıyönetim', in *5. Askeri Tarih Semineri Bildirileri (I)* (Ankara: Genelkurmay Basımevi, 1996), pp 341–55, here p 345.

66.   General Mustafa Muğlalı was also tried by a court martial in 1950, accused of having illegally executed 32 people in Van-Özalp in 1943. Condemned to 20 years of imprisonment, he died in hospital in December 1951. Mete Tunçay, *Tek-Parti Yönetimi*, p 304; Suat Akgül and Kenan Esengin, *Orgeneral Mustafa Muğlalı ve Van-Özalp Olaylarının İçyüzü* (Ankara: Berikam, 2001), p 32; H. Neşe Özgen, *Toplumsal Hafızanın Hatırlama ve Unutma Biçimleri: Van-Özalp ve 33 Kurşun Hadisesi* (Istanbul: TÜSTAV, 2003), pp 61–3.

67. Özek, *100 Soruda*, p 159.
68. Akyaz, 'Sıkıyönetim', p 353.
69. *Ibid.*, p 344.
70. *Ibid.*, p 350. For instance, some Mevlevi sheikhs were arrested in Konya (*Yarın*, 8 January 1931); an old woman was caught by the police while she was lighting a candle on the tomb of Laleli Baba in the quarter of Laleli in Istanbul (*Son Posta*, 6 January 1931); and in Çanakkale a group around a Kadiri sheikh was accused of forming a secret society to depose the government (*Son Posta*, 16 February 1931, quoted in Kıvılcımlı, *Müttefik*, p 206).
71. 'Menemen hadisesini ika', pp 1–4.
72. *Ibid.*, pp 23, 26. His sister, Raşel Biton, in vain wrote a letter to the head of the court martial protesting his innocence and that he was a member of the Jewish community obedient to the fatherland (*ibid.*, p 84). When Muğlalı Mustafa Paşa was later interviewed about his decision to hang a Jew, his answer was, 'I would not hesitate to burn down all Anatolia in the case of even the smallest anti-revolutionary incident', quoted in Barlas, 'Menemen'deki İrtica Olayı', *Cumhuriyet*, 25 December 1966. See also Akgül and Esengin, *Orgeneral Mustafa Muğlalı*, p 33.
73. 'Menemen hadisesini ika', p 2.
74. Saraçoğlu, 'Menemen İrticaı'.
75. According to a report in the newspaper *Son Posta*, at that time there were 52 lodges of the Naqshbandiyya Order in Istanbul alone (*Son Posta*, 2 January 1931).
76. Yunus Nadi, 'Mürettep bir irtica karşısındayız', *Cumhuriyet*, 28 December 1930.
77. Altay, *Görüp Geçirdiklerim*, pp 435–7.
78. Şerif Mardin, 'The Naqshibendi Order of Turkey', in Martin E. Marty and R. Scott Appleby (eds), *Fundamentalisms and the State: Remaking Polities, Economies, and Militance* (Chicago: University of Chicago Press, 1993), pp 204–32, here p 206.
79. *Ibid.*, pp 62, 63, 70.
80. Jeffrey A. Sluka, 'From Graves to Nations: Political Martyrdom and Irish Nationalism', in Joyce Pettigrew (ed), *Martyrdom and Political Resistance: Essays from Asia and Europe* (Amsterdam: VU University Press, 1996), pp 35–60, here p 39.
81. 'Gazi Hz.'nin mektubu', *Cumhuriyet*, 28 December 1930.
82. *Cumhuriyet*, 25 December 1930.
83. Ceyhun Atuf Kansu, *Cumhuriyet Bayrağı Altında, Yaşam-Öykümde Devrim* (Istanbul: Varlık, 1973), pp 78–9.
84. Üstün, *Devrim Şehidi*, p 9.
85. *Ibid.* According to Kan Demir, Kubilay had once told his friends about his dream of changing everybody's name to a pure Turkish name. See Kan Demir, *Şehit Kubilay*, p 50.
86. Kemal Üstün, *Devrim Şehidi Öğretmen Kubilay*. In the words of Kubilay's wife, Fatma Vedide, who was interviewed by the journalist Çetinkaya in 1983, he was not religious and was committed to the Kemalist regime. In her words again, both she and Kubilay had 'adopted the reforms of Atatürk, the great saviour' and they were proud of being the first couple in Aydın to have a civil marriage under

the Civil Code adopted in 1926. Çetinkaya, *Kubilay Olayı*, pp 11–12.

87. Cf. the use of the term 'Gazi' (Ar. *ghāzī*) to refer to Mustafa Kemal. See Şerif Mardin, *Religion and Social Change in Modern Turkey: The Case of Bediüzzaman Said Nursi* (Albany: State University of New York Press, 1989), pp 3–4.

88. *Hakimiyet-i Milliye*, 5 January 1931, quoted in Mustafa Kara, *Metinlerle Günümüz Tasavvuf Hareketleri* (Istanbul: Dergah, 2002), pp 187–8. Necip Fazıl (Kısakürek, 1905–83) 'converted' to Islam under the spiritual influence of a Naqshbandi sheikh, Ziyaeddin Arvasi, who was also among those who were arrested after the Menemen Incident. See his autobiography, *O ve Ben* (Istanbul: B.D., 1974).

89. Ertan Aydın, *The Peculiarities of Turkish Revolutionary Ideology in the 1930s: The* Ülkü *Version of Kemalism, 1933–1936* (unpublished PhD thesis, Bilkent University, Ankara, 2003), p 82. Aydın shows in detail that the regime aimed to create a 'revolutionary religion' and 'to convert people from their traditional religious ties to the new revolutionary faith'. *Ibid.*, p 263.

90. For early examples of the mythicization of Kubilay see Kan Demir, *Şehit Kubilay*; Enver Benhan, *İnkılap Ötkünçleri* (Istanbul: Devlet Matbaası, 1934), pp 95–100.

91. *Cumhuriyet*, 26 December 1931, 23–24 December 1932.

92. *Cumhuriyet*, 26–27 December 1934. On the supporting stone of the monument, the following statement was engraved: 'They believed, fought and died; we are the guardians of the trust they left behind.'

93. Kan Demir, *Şehit Kubilay*, pp 43–5; Üstün, *Devrim Şehidi*, p 27; Aslan Tufan Yazman, 'Devrimlere Karşı bir Direniş. Menemen Olayının Yankıları', *Sigorta Dünyası* 14, no. 159 (1973), p 13.

94. 'Menemen'de Bazılarının Çekingen Duruşları Nazarı Dikkati Celbetti', *Son Posta*, 4 January 1931.

95. The townspeople continued to boycott these ceremonies, and during the multi-party period the RPP never won the majority of the votes in the elections until 1983 when it took a new name and image. See Bozarslan, 'Messianism et Mouvement Social', p 84. For other expressions of the townspeople's resentment, see Emin Abalı, *Kubilay'ın Mezarında ve Yanmıyan Şehrin Hikayesi* (İzmir: Meşher Basımevi, 1937); 'Menemen bir irtica yuvası değildir', *Yeni Istanbul*, 9 January 1960; Mümtaz Arıkan, 'Menemenli 58 Yıldır Kubilay Burukluğu Yaşıyor', *Cumhuriyet*, 23 December 1988.

96. Bahriye Acar, 'İzmir Basınında Menemen Olayı', *Çağdaş Türkiye Tarihi Araştırmaları Dergisi* 3, no. 8 (1998), pp 137–46, here pp 140–2. See also Serap Tabak, 'Menemen Olayının İzmir Basını'nda Yankıları', *Tarih İncelemeleri Dergisi*, no. 10 (1995), pp 313–28.

97. For the discussion between Ahmet Ağaoğlu and Ali Saip Bey, the deputy of Urfa, during the session in the National Assembly, see TBMM, *Zabıt Ceridesi* 24(3), no. 4, 1 (Ocak, 1931), p 9.

98. Yusuf Ziya, 'İrtica', *Akbaba*, 29 December 1930.

99. *Hür Adam*, 'Menemen'daki İrtica', 27 December 1930; *Yarın*, 'Biraz da Bizi Dinleyin', 28 December 1930; 'Cumhuriyetin Hainleri Kimlerdir?', 29 December 1930.

100. Mehmed Fuat, 'Değişmek Meselesi', *Hür Adam*, 31 December 1930.

101. 'Derinleri Görelim', *Yarın*, 31 December 1930.
102. Mehmed Ali, 'La Révolution/La Terreur'; Nedjati Rifaat, 'L'Assassinat', *La République Enchaînée*, 15 February 1931, quoted in Mete Tunçay, 'Zincire Vurulmuş Hürriyet', *Tarih ve Toplum* 91 (July 1991), pp 6, 19.
103. Rıza Nur, *Hayat ve Hatıratım, Rıza Nur Atatürk Kavgası* (Istanbul: İşaret, 1992), pp 479–82.

Chapter 10. Authority and Agency: Revisiting Women's Activism during Reza Shah's Period

1. My deepest gratitude goes to friends, colleagues and librarians whose help in accessing the archival material used in this paper has been invaluable: Azar Ashraf, Homa Hoodfar, Ghulamriza Salami and Matthew Smith. I have benefited enormously from conversations with Camron Amin and Parvin Paidar on many of the issues explored here.
2. The literature on the politics of Iranian modernity is enormous. I have found the following particularly insightful and helpful: Fariba Adelkhah, *Being Modern in Iran*, trans Jonathan Derrick (London: Hurst & Co., 1999); Mehrzad Boroujerdi, *Iranian Intellectuals and the West: The Tormented Triumph of Nativism* (Syracuse: Syracuse University Press, 1996); Roy Mottahedeh, *The Mantle of the Prophet* (New York: Simon and Schuster, 1985); and the many writings of Mohamad Tavakoli-Targhi, especially *Emergence of Two Revolutionary Discourses in Modern Iran* (PhD thesis, University of Chicago, 1988) and *Refashioning Iran: Orientalism, Occidentalism and Historiography* (New York: Palgrave, 2001).
3. Haideh Moghissi, feminist Iranian sociologist and activist, for instance, argues: 'What is happening in Iran today, in my view, is not indicative of legitimacy of political Islam as a native solution for cultural, social, and political problems arising from modernization policies and the experience of modernity in Iran; it constitutes the continuation of the battle between tradition and modernity that in political developments of Iran from the constitutional era to the present has existed with many ups and downs in Iran's social life.' Haideh Moghissi, 'Zanan, tajaddud, va Islam-i siasi' (Women, Modernity, and Political Islam), Proceedings of the Ninth Annual Conference of The Iranian Women's Studies Foundation, Washington DC, 26–28 June 1998, pp 98–114, quote from pp 101–2.
4. Inclusion of non-Muslim women within the categories of patriotic sisters and gender sisters, though possible, was precarious. It was possible largely as assimilation rather than as recognition of difference. Armenian, Jewish, Zoroastrian, Azali and Baha'i women – all active within the early women's associations – could speak only as Iranians, whereas Muslim, and more specifically Shi'ite Muslim, women would retain the privilege of speaking as Iranian and as Muslim.
5. The letter continues at some length. For the full text, originally published in *Habl al-matin* (Tehran edition) 1, 105 (1 September 1907), pp 4–6, see Mihrangiz Mallah and Afsaneh Najmabadi (eds), *Bibi Khanum Astarabadi and Khanum Afzal Vaziri: Pioneering Mother and Daughter for Women's Education and Rights in Iran* (New York: Nigarish va Nigarish-i Zan, 1996), pp 65–70. For similar arguments, see letters by Bibi Khanum Astarabadi in the same volume. This rhetoric is common in writings of women in the constitutionalist press of the period.

6.   As Muhammad Tavakoli-Targhi has extensively documented and persuasively argued, in the nineteenth century European and Iranian/Islamic women (perceived as radically different) emerged as 'terrain[s] of political and cultural contestations'. 'Imagining Western Women: Occidentalism and Euro-eroticism', *Radical America* 24, 3 (1990), pp 73–87, here p 74. These contestations, he has further suggested, 'resulted in the valorization of the veil (*hijab*) as a visible marker of the self and the other. For Iranian modernists, viewing European women as educated and cultured, the veil became a symbol of backwardness. Its removal, in their view, was essential to the advancement of Iran and its dissociation from Arab-Islamic culture. For the counter-modernists who wanted to uphold the Islamic social and gender roles, the European woman became a scapegoat and a symbol of corruption, immorality, Westernization, and feminization of power' (*Refashioning Iran*, p 54).

7.   See, for instance, the following issues: *Shukufah* 1, no. 14 (31 August 1913), p 3; 1, no. 15 (21 September 1913), pp 3–4; 2, no. 5 (22) (1 February 1914), pp 1–2; 2, no. 6 (23) (16 February 1914), p 4; and 2, no. 7 (24) (2 March 1914), p 3.

8.   In early twentieth-century Iran, an urban woman's outdoor attire, *hijab*, consisted of a chador (a full-length loose-enveloping robe), a *rubandah* (face veil, made of see-through material), and for more strict circumstances a *chaqchur* (a leg garment that would protect whatever one was wearing from a stranger's eyes, in case the wind should blow away the chador; more in use in the nineteenth century; by the early-twentieth century the *chaqchur* had become far less frequent). For further information and sources, see Hamid Algar, 'Çador in Islamic Persia', in *Encyclopaedia Iranica*, ed Ehsan Yarshater, vol. IV, pp 610–11 (London: Routledge and Kegan Paul, 1990).

9.   For a fuller history of male advocacy of unveiling as a measure of progress and improvement of women's life in Iran in the nineteenth century, see Camron Amin, *The Attentions of the Great Father: Reza Shah, 'The Woman Question', and the Iranian Press, 1890–1946* (PhD thesis, University of Chicago, 1996). See also Farzaneh Milani, *Veils and Words: The Emerging Voices of Iranian Women Writers* (Syracuse: Syracuse University Press, 1992); Tavakoli-Targhi, 'Imagining Western Women' and 'Zani bud, zani nabud', *Nimeye Digar*, no. 14 (Spring 1991), pp 77–110. For a photographic sample of what women advocated as unveiling in this period, see the photograph of Afzal Vaziri, 18, in Mallah and Najmabadi, *Bibi Khanum Astarabadi and Khanum Afzal Vaziri*; or the photograph of Sadiqah Dawlatabadi, in Mahdokht Sanati and Afsaneh Najmabadi (eds), *Namah'ha, nivishtah'ha, va yadha* (Letters, Writings, and Remembrances) (New York: Nigarish va Nigarish-i Zan, 1999), vol. 3, p 611. Afzal Vaziri made her proposal in print first in the pages of *Shafaq-i surkh* 9, 1565 (18 August 1930), p 3, as part of the debates of that year which I will shortly discuss.

10.   For a discussion of this point see my paper presented at the American Association of Religion, 23 November 1999, a shorter version of which was published in *Social Text*, no. 64 (2000), pp 29–45.

11.   Jasamin Rostam-Kolayi makes a similar observation in her richly informative essay, 'Expanding Agendas for the "New" Iranian Woman: Family Law, Work, and Unveiling', in Stephanie Cronin (ed), *The Making of Modern Iran: State and Society under Riza Shah, 1921–1941* (London: Routledge, 2003), pp 157–180.

12.   The other marker of his reign in Iranian national memory is the construction of
      countrywide railways. But whereas this is considered an achievement, women's
      unveiling is a disputed legacy, considered an achievement by some, and a disgrace,
      if not a catastrophe, by others.

13.   In addition to several memoirs, three documentary collections of government
      decrees, memoranda and reports related to the unveiling campaign have been
      published that make a more thorough historical reassessment possible. For a full
      documentation of sources, see Amin, *The Attentions of the Great Father*. As Amin
      has noted (p 270), these documents attest to the government's concern that local
      authorities should not act recklessly. In memorandum after memorandum, it is
      repeated that 'utmost caution' must be exercised in implementing the campaign,
      that educational and demonstrative meetings must be held, that women should
      be persuaded through officials (that is the officials' wives and other female rela-
      tives) setting an example for the larger population. Yet the pressure to produce
      quick results, the continuous reprimands and dismissals of officials in whose
      locality a favourable outcome could not be demonstrated, produced a violent
      dynamic: where local authorities could not achieve the implementation of central
      government orders through persuasion, they resorted to daily violence, ranging
      from dismissing women who refused to unveil from their jobs, to pressuring local
      bath-attendants to report on women who went to public baths veiled (sometimes
      through roof-hopping), to instructing shopkeepers to refuse business and services
      to veiled customers, to tearing women's veils in public. See Amin, *The Attentions
      of the Great Father*, for a fuller discussion. The similarities between these measures
      and those undertaken by the Islamic Republic in the 1980s to achieve imposi-
      tion of veiling are truly astounding. For a recent restatement of the impossibility
      of achieving women's rights without Reza Shah's forceful measures, see Shireen
      Mahdavi, 'Reza Shah Pahlavi and Women: A Re-Evaluation', in Cronin (ed), *The
      Making of Modern Iran*, pp 181–92.

14.   In the 1920s and early 1930s, increasing numbers of urban middle-class women
      had discarded the face veil. What had remained controversial was replacing the
      chador with other full-length outfits, as advocated by women such as Afzal Vaziri
      and Sadiqah Dawlatabadi.

15.   Afzal Vaziri, 'Mardha khayli zirangi mi'kunand' (Men Try to be Clever), *Shafaq-
      i surkh* 9, 1565 (18 August 1930), p 3, in Mallah and Najmabadi (eds), *Bibi
      Khanum Astarabadi and Khanum Afzal Vaziri*, pp 94–5.

16.   For a partial French translation of the proceedings and lectures, see *Revue des
      études Islamiques* VII, no. 1 (1933), pp 45–141.

17.   *Ittila'at* 2721 (25 February 1936), p 5.

18.   For a thoughtful analysis of the significance of the Turkey trip, see Afshin
      Marashi, 'Performing the Nation: The Shah's Official State Visit to Kemalist
      Turkey, June to July 1934', in Cronin (ed), *The Making of Modern Iran*, pp 99–
      119. While I agree with Marashi's emphasis on the importance of this journey in
      a 'cultural and representational sense', in the context of 'the emerging narrative
      of modern culture in the region' (p 102), I think the weight repeatedly put on
      this journey as a causal event that produced dress reform and in particular the
      women's unveiling campaign has worked to displace the effect of the previous
      two decades of social change and cultural activism within Iran itself. It is also

important to note that years before Reza Shah's trip to Turkey, changes in Turkey were followed closely by Iranians. The change of men's outer wear was read as a regression into absolutism (*qahqara bih istibdad*). See Qahriman Mirza Salur ('Ayn al-Saltanah), *Ruznamah-i khatirat-i 'Ayn al-Saltanah*, eds Mas'ud Salur and Iraj Afshar, 10 vols (Tehran: Asatir, 1995–2001), vol. IX, 6897/3 April 1924; see also vol. IX, 7361/15 October 1925; vol. IX, 7485/2 May 1926. Abrogation of Islamic marriage laws was noted with alarm (vol. IX, 7223/29 January 1925). The government would disavow any similar intentions; at least for the time being (vol. IX, 7368/12 November 1925). The coverage of developments in Turkey was also a persistent feature of *Ittila'at*, *Shafaq-i surkh* and the women's press.

19. See Yahya Dawlatabadi, *Hayat-i Yahya* (Tehran: Ibn Sina, 1952), vol. 4, pp 430–6. For other accounts, see Murtiza Ja'fari, Sughra Isma'ilzadah and Ma'sumah Farshchi (eds), *Vaqi'ah-'i kashf-i hijab* (Tehran: Sazman-i Madarik Farhangi-i Inqilab-i Islami, 1993), second introductory essay by Ghulamhusayn Zargarinizhad, p 21; 'Ali Asghar Hikmat, *Si khatirah az 'asr-i farkhudah-'i Pahlavi* (Tehran: Pars, 1976), pp 87–102; Mahdiquli Hidayat, *Khatirat va khatarat* (Tehran: Zavvar, 1965), pp 405–8; Muhsin Sadr, *Khatirat-i Sadr al-Ashraf* (Tehran: Vahid, 1985), pp 302–7. Based on anecdotal accounts of later memoirs, such as those referred to here, Chehabi echoes the same judgement that unveiling had been on Reza Shah's agenda even when he had been a prime minister (1923–25). See H.E. Chehabi, 'The Banning of the Veil and its Consequences', in Cronin (ed), *The Making of Modern Iran*, pp 193–210. Contemporaneous accounts do not support this proposition.

20. 'Ayn al-Saltanah (1872–1945), a nephew of Nasir al-Din Shah and a Qajar statesman who harshly criticized all Qajar politicians who supported Reza Shah, is unlikely to have written these lines to lend his approval of Reza Shah. He did oppose *bi'chadori*, so he was thankful in this instance to the shah. The *pichah* was the stiff face cover made from horsehair that could be lifted up, showing the face and allowing more flexibility. Women in the 1910s and 1920s were often accused of using their semi-lifted *pichah*s to flirt with men in public. For a cartoon depiction of such scenes, see *Nahid* 3, no. 50 (Autumn 1924), p 4. (This number (and also numbers 47–9) are undated. Number 46 is dated 18 November 1924 and number 51 is dated 6 December 1924.)

21. There were very few, and oblique, references to the issue of *hijab* in the constitutionalist press. One such reference was in the graduation speech of Badr al-Duja Imam al-Hukama, a student of the American School for Girls in Tehran, printed in *Iran-i naw* 3, no. 80 (29 June 1911), and 3, no. 81 (1 July 1911), pp 2–3, in which she expressed regret that women, because they were veiled (*bih vasitah-i mahjub budan*), had been deprived of participation in sports in recent centuries and were consequently mostly weak and unfit. Even women who practised unveiling in private and within their own religious community, such as Ta'irah, did not advocate it in their public writings.

22. For other *sizdah'bidar tamashas*, see 'Ayn al-Saltanah, *Ruznamah-i khatirat*, vol. I, p 917. For his description of *hanabandan* on 27 Ramazan 1307 (17 May 1890), see vol. I, p 273; for his account of women's presence in Sipah'salar mosque for shopping (and their less frequenting of the bazaar), see vol. I, pp 274, 577, 707–8, 905.

23. For Safar 1308 (September/October 1890), see vol. I, pp 299–300; for subsequent years and other occasions, see vol. I, pp 385, 599, 908.

24. See also vol. I, pp 711–12, 850, 906. Many of these one-liners have been preserved in nineteenth- and early-twentieth-century sources. Unlike his father, Muzaffar al-Din Shah did not know how to deal with protesting urban female crowds and had ordered the complaining women arrested and imprisoned. His prime minister had to intervene to prevent a big explosion by releasing the women and apologizing for the arrests (vol. II, p 1333). In the early 1920s women would turn to Sardarsipah on similar occasions to complain about daily hardships. See the description of the Majlis's three-day *rawzah* at the end of Safar in September 1925, vol. IX, pp 7337–8.

25. See also 'Ayn al-Saltanah, *Ruznamah-i khatirat*, vol. I, p 721; vol. II, p 1135.

26. See also *ibid.*, vol. I, p 716.

27. *Ibid.*, vol. IX, p 6988.

28. *Ibid.*, vol. I, pp 908–9; vol. II, p 1070. On the changing fashion of men's clothes and hairstyles, see vol. II, p 1873; vol. III, p 1931; vol. VIII, pp 6486–7.

29. *Ibid.*, vol. I, pp 751–2 (8 June 1895); vol. I, p 794 (17 July 1895); vol. I, p 889 (3 February 1896), where 'Ayn al-Saltanah expressed concern that the practice was bound to spread: 'soon the situation in Iran will become chaotic, all women will begin to do so. Already some have begun.'

30. *Ibid.*, vol. V, p 3822; vol. VI, p 4849.

31. *Ibid.*, vol. IX, p 7126.

32. *Ibid.*, vol. VIII, p 6495.

33. *Ibid.*, vol. IX, p 7087; vol. IX, p 7154.

34. Dr Istipanian, 'Maktub-i sargushudah', *Iran-i naw* 3, no. 35 (6 May 1911), p 4.

35. See 'Ayn al-Saltanah, *Ruznamah-i khatirat*, vol. VIII, p 6501.

36. *Ibid.*, vol. IX, pp 7269; 7328.

37. *Ibid.*, vol. VIII, p 6507.

38. Mu'ayyir al-Mamalik, *Vaqayi' al-zaman*, pp 30–1, 38–9, 50, 56, 58, 70, 105, 192; 'Ayn al-Saltanah, *Ruznamah-i khatirat*, vol. VIII: 6484-87/5 July 1922, vol. VIII: 6642/July 1923; vol. IX: 6832/March 1924; vol. IX: 7158/12 July 1924. Concern about impropriety of men's gazing and flirting practices was expressed at length in the women's press. See, for example, *Danish*, no. 2 (29 September 1910), p 2; *Shukufah* 2, no. 8 (17 March 1914), pp 3–4; 2, no. 19 (27 September 1914), pp 3–4; 2, no. 20 (21 October 1914), p 4; 2, no. 21 (9 November 1914), p 4; 3, no. 2 (16 December 1914), pp 2–3; 3, no. 8 (29 March 1915), pp 2–3; 4, no. 7 (11 March 1916), pp 1–2; and 4, no. 10 (13 May 1916), pp 1–2. For a discussion of articles in *Danish* and *Shukufah* in the context of a 'moralizing discourse' of the Iranian turn-of-the-century press, see Camron Amin, *The Making of the Modern Iranian Woman: Gender, State Policy, and Popular Culture, 1865–1946* (Gainesville: University Press of Florida, 2002), pp 57–9.

39. See 'Ayn al-Saltanah, *Ruznamah-i khatirat*, vol. VIII, p 6487; vol. IX, p 6832.

40. See *Nahid* 3, 50 (Autumn 1924), p 4; 'Ayn al-Saltanah, *Ruznamah-i khatirat*, vol. V, p 3811; vol. VI, pp 4795–6.

41. See 'Ayn al-Saltanah, *Ruznamah-i khatirat*, vol. VIII, p 6529. Until the early 1920s, Shahr-i naw was a rural hamlet of gardens, popular for outdoor pass-time activities. As part of the transformation of Tehran into a more disciplined and

proper capital city, in the early 1920s, women prostitutes, at the time located in many districts of Tehran, were collected and relocated in Shahr-i naw, facilitating imposition of a series of regulations, financial and medical included. See Ja'far Shahri, *Tihran-i qadim*, 5 vols (Tehran: Mu'in, 1991–96), vol. 3, pp 394–420.

42. See Milani, *Veils and Words*, and Juan Cole, *Modernity and the Millennium: The Genesis of the Baha'i Faith in the Nineteenth-Century Middle East* (New York: Columbia University Press, 1998).

43. See, for instance, 'Ayn al-Saltanah, *Ruznamah-i khatirat*, vol. I, pp 739–40 (19 May 1895).

44. See, for instance, *ibid.*, vol. III, p 2009 (28 March 1908).

45. *Ibid.*, vol. VIII, p 5912.

46. Abbas Amanat has pointed out to me such intellectual traces in Kasma'i's poetry.

47. See 'Ayn al-Saltanah, *Ruznamah-i khatirat*, vol. VII, p 5693; vol. VII, p 5718. On the Gilan movement, see Cosroe Chaquèri, *The Soviet Socialist Republic of Iran, 1920–1921: Birth of the Trauma* (Pittsburgh: University of Pittsburgh Press, 1995).

48. 'Ayn al-Saltanah, *Ruznamah-i khatirat*, vol. VIII, pp 6520–21; 6527/26.

49. While anti-Qajar campaigners circulated a picture of Ahmad Shah posing with a European woman to prove his unfitness to remain the shah of Iran, anti-Sardarsipah campaigners circulated a picture of Reza Khan holding a Baha'i template. Each transgression proved the un-Islamicness of the opponent. 'Ayn al-Saltanah, *Ruznamah-i khatirat*, vol. IX, p 7066.

50. See *ibid.*, vol. IX, pp 6836–9, quote from p 6841.

51. *Ibid.*, vol. IX, p 7011.

52. *Ibid.*, vol. IX, p 7269; similarly vol. X, p 7701; See also vol. IX, p 7449 (21 March 1926), where 'Ayn al-Saltanah on his visit to Shiraz noted that while women there wore *rubandah* and *chaqchur*, very few wore the *pichah*: 'In our eyes who have not seen the *rubandah* in a long while, the scene is worth looking at; it reminds us of old times.'

53. *Ibid.*, vol. IX, p 7266.

54. Nur al-Hudá Manganah, *Divan* (Tehran: Ibn Sina, 1957), pp 10–12; Badr al-Muluk Bamdad, *Zan-i Irani az inqilab-i mashrutiyat ta inqilab-i sifid*, 2 vols (Tehran: Ibn Sina, 1968 and 1969), vol. 1, pp 56–7; 'Ayn al-Saltanah, *Ruznamah-i khatirat*, vol. IX, p 7015 (14 April 1924); *Nahid*, 45 (15 November 1924), pp 6–7; Pari Shaykh al-Islami, *Zanan-i ruznamah'nigar va andishmand-i Iran* (Tehran: Chapkhanah-i Mazgirafik, 1972), pp 155–7.

55. Who in fact had never married! As Iraj Afshar has noted in 'Ayn al-Saltanah, *Ruznamah-i khatirat*, vol. IX, p 7015.

56. *Ibid.*, vol. IX, p 7262 (12 April 1925); vol. X, p 7702 (November 1931).

57. In this article I am largely concerned with the women's press. In the larger project, these other arenas are analysed. A selection of clerical writings, including many of the writings of the 1920s, has been recently published. See Rasul Ja'farian (ed), *Rasa'il-i hijabiyah* (Qum: Intisharat-i Dalil-i Ma, 2001). For an analysis of two such texts, see Mohamad Tavakoli-Targhi, 'Zani bud, zani nabud: bazkhvani-i vujub-i niqab va Mafasid-i sufur', *Nimeye Digar*, no. 14 (Spring 1991), pp 77–110.

58. For an adversarial conversation between 'Ayn al-Saltanah and Abu al-Qasim Azad about this journal, see *Ruznamah-i khatirat*, vol. IX, p 7080 (2 June 1924). 'Ayn al-Saltanah spoke in the most derogatory terms about Shahnaz Azad and was scandalized that a journal like hers should be allowed to be published.

59. *Namah-i banuvan*, no. 2 (16 August 1920), pp 1–4.

60. *Namah-i banuvan*, no. 3 (4 September 1920), pp 1–2.

61. *Jahan-i zanan*, no. 1 (5 September 1921), pp 9–13.

62. *Jahan-i zanan*, no. 1 (5 September 1921), p 25.

63. See also *Ittila'at*, no. 227 (29 May 1927), p 1.

64. 'Murdah bad 'adat', *Payk-i sa'adat-i nisvan*, no. 2 (December 1927/January 1928), pp 1–5.

65. *Payk-i sa'adat-i nisvan*, no. 2, p 2.

66. 'Bih dukhtaran-i Iran', *Payk-i sa'adat-i nisvan*, no. 6 (August/September 1928), p 167.

67. Rostam-Kolayi, 'Expanding Agendas for the "New" Iranian Woman'. Rostam-Kolayi's narrative is one of the few accounts of this period that is women-centred (as distinct from state-centred), but it remains tied to the idea that women's use of the state was out of necessity; there was no other choice. It is not clear why women should not have tried to use the state. This seems to be a trace of subsequent political developments and its impact on historiography of the earlier period.

68. For 'Ayn al-Saltanah's evaluation of the press debates on the *hijab* in this period, see *Ruznamah-i khatirat*, vol. X, p 7704. See also his discussion of club meetings and private parties as forums for practising unveiling and mixed socializing (vol. X, pp 7701–5). *Shafaq-i surkh* had series of debates in 1929 and 1930. I review these debates in Chapter 4 of *Genealogies*.

69. '[T]he idea that women can wear a veil and still be active and have access to a common public sphere with men, i.e. veiling without *purdah*, does not seem to have occurred to many people in the Iran of the 1920s and 1930s.' And again: 'The idea that women's participation in social activities could be broadened while allowing them freedom of choice in matters of dress did not occur to the modernizers, but nor, to be fair, did it occur to the ulema.' Chehabi, 'The Banning of the Veil and its Consequences', pp 193, 203.

70. For a review of critical debates in *'Alam-i nisvan* of marriage practices and laws, see Rostam-Kolayi, 'Expanding Agendas for the "New" Iranian Woman'.

71. *Jahan-i zanan*, no. 1 (5 September 1921), pp 25–6.

72. Sessions 2–5.

73. H. Shajarah, 'Nihzat-i nisvan-i sharq' (Eastern Women's Movement), *Iran*, 3944 (4 November 1932), p 1.

74. The actual presiding committee consisted of Nour Hamadé, president, Masturah Afshar, vice president, Mrs Jamil and Sadiqah Dawlatabadi as secretaries. *Iran* 3963 (27 November 1932), p 1.

75. Nur al-Hudá Manganah, *Divan* (Tehran: Ibn Sina, 1957), pp 15–16.

76. At one point several women objected to his interjections, saying that he had no right to speak at this congress; the congress had specified that only women could speak. At this point Awrang said that he was there on behalf of the SPW, and Masturah Afshar confirmed his statement. Note that at this stage not only could

his presence and right to speak be challenged by Iranian women, but he seemed to need to invoke the SPW's authority, either because of the presence of international delegations or because the government's relation to women's organizations was not (yet?) of as secure and brutal a character as is generally assumed.

77. Hajir Tarbiat and Sadiqah Dawlatabadi served as the first and second presidents of *Kanun-i banuvan*.

78. Rostam-Kolayi reaches a similar conclusion in her discussion of *'Alam-i Nisvan*: *'Alam-e Nesvan*'s agenda for the 'progress of women' overlapped with Reza Shah's project of the 'Women's Awakening'. See 'Expanding Agendas for the "New" Iranian Woman', p 159. I am grateful for Sima Shakhsari's critical comments that helped me articulate this point.

79. A similar process could be documented for many women activists of the 1950s through to the 1970s. See Mana Kia, *Negotiating Women's Rights: Activism and Modernization in Pahlavi Iran* (MA thesis, New York University, 2001).

80. 'Sih Khatirah qabl az 17 Day 1314', *Tehran-i musavvar*, no. 10 (January/February 1957), pp 12–13, 35.

81. *Ibid.*, p 13. Dawlatabadi's recollection of the formation of *Kanun-i banuvan* narrates it as an idea suggested by 'Ali Asghar Hikmat, Minister of Education at the time, after Reza Shah's return from Turkey. She also recalls that on his suggestion she set out to design a school uniform for girls that was adopted and ordered for all schools. That it was a state order, she argues, was important to take the responsibility off the shoulders of teachers and school administrators when some parents protested. See 'Sih Khatirah qabl az 17 Day 1314', p 12. There are clearly competing narratives here that need further historical research.

82. 'Abd al-Reza Sadiqi'pur (ed), *Yadgar-i guzashtah: majmu'ah-'i Sukhanraniha-yi a'lahazrat-i faqid Reza Shah-i kabir* (Tehran: Javidan, 1968), p 137, my emphasis.

83. *Khitabah'ha-yi Kanun-i banuvan dar sal-i 1314* (Tehran: Matba'ah-i Majlis, n.d.), pp 91–2.

84. *Ibid.*, pp 110–11.

85. As my mother recalled her own instant promotion! Homa Hoodfar in her essay, 'The Veil in Their Minds and on Our Heads: Veiling Practices and Muslim Women', in Lisa Lowe and David Lloyd (eds), *The Politics of Culture in the Shadow of Capital* (Duke University Press, 1997), pp 248–79, insightfully details how the imposition of the veil, contrary to dominant perceptions, did not translate into universal increased opportunity for women's education and work. For substantial layers of urban women, unwilling to venture out unveiled, the government measures resulted in restriction of their education, economic activities and venues for socialization, making them more dependent on men of the household.

86. The official unveiling campaign literature emphasized over and over again that not only was doing away with the face veil and chador not un-Islamic, but the kind of clothes advocated had been what Iranian women wore from time immemorial. See, for instance, *Khushunat va farhang* (Violence and Culture), published by Department of Research Publication and Education, Iran National Archives Organization (Tehran, 1992), p 3.

87. Alternatively *libas-i tamaddun*, clothes of civilization, was used. See Ja'fari et al (eds), *Vaqi'ah-i kashf-i hijab*, pp 105, 148.

88. Afsaneh Najmabadi, '"Years of Hardship, Years of Growth": Feminisms in an Islamic Republic', in Yvonne Haddad and John Espositopp (eds), *Islam, Gender, and Social Change* (Oxford: Oxford University Press, 1998), pp 59–84, quote from p 76.

89. In fact, it was a screen that covered from sight the state's refusal to secularize the law. The Iranian Civil Code, drafted in the 1930s, on issues of marriage, divorce, child custody, inheritance, among other things, was largely the contemporary Islamic code reworded without reference to Islamic texts, and re-directed to be under control of state institutions instead of local religious leaders. Secular feminism's more radical position has been that the state did not secularize thoroughly enough. But it has remained oblivious to its own implication as a screen and border setter for modernity's construction of secularism.

90. It also brings to our attention the challenge of not reversing the bifurcation in the other direction, as it is already being attempted, namely, by considering Islamist feminism as the authentic voice of women's rights activism and secular feminism as some foreign importation. For one such attempt, see Anouar Majid, 'The Politics of Feminism in Islam', *Signs: Journal of Women in Culture and Society* 23, no. 2 (Winter 1998), pp 321–61.

91. As I had begun thinking about this project, I was coincidentally reading Janet Jakobsen's *Working Alliances and the Politics of Difference: Diversity and Feminist Ethics* (Bloomington: Indiana University Press, 1998), which deeply affected my thinking and writing.

Chapter 11. Polygamy Before and After the Introduction of the Swiss Civil Code in Turkey

1. See, for example, Nilüfer Göle, 'Snapshots of Islamic Modernity', *Daedalus* 129, no. 1 (Winter 2000), pp 91–117.

2. Niyazi Berkes, *The Development of Secularism in Turkey*, facsimile edition (London: Hurst & Co., 1998).

3. June Starr, *Law as a Metaphor: From Islamic Courts to the Palace of Justice* (Albany: State University of New York Press, 1992), pp 21–33.

4. Reşat Genç (ed and trans), *Türkiye'yi lâikleştiren yasalar: 3 Mart 1924 tarihli meclis müzakereleri ve kararları* (Ankara: Atatürk Kültür, Dil ve Tarih Yüksek Kurumu, Atatürk Araştırma Merkezi, 1998).

5. Berkes, *The Development of Secularism*, p 466.

6. Or, nowadays, also between two men or two women.

7. Also translated into English and French: Mohammed Kadri Pasha (Muhammed Qadri), *Code of Mohammedan Personal Law According to the Hanafite School*, trans Wasey Sterry and N. Abcarius, printed for the Sudan government (London: Spottiswood, 1914); Mohammed Kadri Pacha, *Droit Musulman: statut réel d'après le rite hanafite / Mise en articles d'après le système des codes égyptiens*, Traduit de l'arabe par Abdulaziz Kahil Bey (Le Caire: Imprimerie Nationale, 1893); Muhammad Qadri, *Kitab Al-Ahkam ash-shar'iya fi 'l-ahwal ash-shahsiya 'ala madab al-imam Abi Hanifa an-Nu'man*, Tab'a 4. (Misr: Matba'a Hindiya, 1318).

8. See below.

9. Dawoud Alami and Doreen Hinchcliffe, *Islamic Marriage and Divorce Laws of*

the Arab World (London: CIMEL, SOAS; London: Kluwer Law International, 1996), pp 35–7, 51.

10. Gülnihal Bozkurt, *Batı Hukunun Türkiye'de Benimsenmesi: Osmanlı Devleti'nden Türkiye Cumhuriyeti'ne Resepsiyon Süreci (1839–1939)* (Ankara: Türk Tarih Kurumu, 1996), pp 159–63; Starr, *Law as a Metaphor*, pp 33–6.

11. M. Akif Aydın, 'The Codification of the Islamic–Ottoman Family Law and the Decree of "Hukuk-ı Aile"', in Halil İnalcık et al (eds), *The Great Ottoman– Turkish Civilisation* (Ankara: Yeni Türkiye, 2000), pp 705–13.

12. *Nikah-i Medeni ve Talak Hakkında Hukuk-u Aile Kararnamesi* (Istanbul: İbrahim Hilmi, 1336), pp 2–9.

13. Starr, *Law as a Metaphor*, p 39.

14. Aydın 'The Codification', pp 711–12.

15. Bozkurt, *Batı Hukunun Türkiye'de Benimsenmesi*, pp 166–73; Gülnihal Bozkurt, 'Review of the Ottoman Legal System', *Ankara Üniversitesi Osmanlı Tarihi Araştırma ve Uygulama Merkezi Dergisi*, no. 3 (Ocak 1992), pp 115–28; Aydın, 'The Codification', p 711.

16. Bozkurt, *Batı Hukunun Türkiye'de Benimsenmesi*, pp 184–7.

17. *Ibid.*, pp 187–96.

18. Ruth A. Miller, 'The Ottoman and Islamic Substratum of Turkey's Swiss Civil Code', *Journal of Islamic Studies* 11, no. 3 (2000), pp 335–61, quotation p 337.

19. Although there are four main schools of interpretation within Sunni Islam, I will take the opinions of the Hanafi school as the main point of reference, since this school was the one adopted in the Ottoman Empire. Where other schools were followed, I will indicate this.

20. El Alami and Hinchcliffe, *Islamic Marriage and Divorce Laws of the Arab World*, pp 5–6; Cem Behar and Alan Duben, *Istanbul Households: Marriage, Family and Fertility 1880–1940* (Cambridge: Cambridge University Press, 1991), pp 107–8; Halil Cin, *İslâm ve Osmanlı Hukukunda Evlenme* (Ankara: Ankara Üniversitesi, 1974), pp 135–6.

21. El Alami and Hinchcliffe, *Islamic Marriage and Divorce Laws of the Arab World*, pp 8–10.

22. Cin, *İslâm ve Osmanlı Hukukunda Evlenme*, pp 136–43.

23. For details see Şamil Dağcı, 'İslam Aile Hukukunda Evlenme Engelleri (Sürekli Evlenme Engelleri)', *Ankara Üniversitesi İlâhiyat Fakültesi Dergisi*, no. 39 (1999), pp 173–237; Şamil Dağcı, 'İslâm Aile Hukukunda Evlenme Engelleri (Geçici Evlenme Engelleri)', *Ankara Üniversitesi İlâhiyat Fakültesi Dergisi*, no. 41 (2000), pp 137–94. See also Feyzi Necmeddin Feyzioğlu, 'Cumhuriyetin 50. Yıldönümünde "Medeni Nikâh"', in *İstanbul Üniversitesi Hukuk Fakültesi'nin 50. Yıl Armağanı: Cumhuriyet Döneminde Hukuk* (Istanbul: İstanbul Üniversitesi Hukuk Fakültesi, 1973), pp 233–90, 238–58.

24. El Alami and Hinchcliffe, *Islamic Marriage and Divorce Laws of the Arab World*, pp 6–7; Halil Cin, *Eski Hukukumuzda Boşanma* (Ankara: Ankara Üniversitesi Hukuk Fakültesi, 1976), pp 91–2.

25. *Chapters from the Koran*, translated and annotated by E.H. Palmer, vol. XLV, part 5 (New York: The Harvard Classics; New York: P.F. Collier & Son, 1909– 1914; Bartleby.com, 2001: http://www.bartleby.com/45/5/205.html).

26. Cin, *İslâm ve Osmanlı Hukukunda Evlenme*, p 284.

27. Fanny Davis, *The Ottoman Lady: A Social History from 1718 to 1918* (New York: Greenwood Press, 1986), p 66; Behar and Duben, *Istanbul Households*, pp 107–8.
28. *Ibid.*, pp 108–9.
29. *Ibid.*, p 110. See also Davis, *The Ottoman Lady*, p 66.
30. An example of such an *izinname* from a rather late date (April 1920) gives us an idea of the possible contents: it states that the woman involved has reached puberty, has no mental illnesses and is not engaged to be married to a soldier-in-arms. It states that both parties have agreed to the marriage and that the parents have given their permission and that there are no impediments to the marriage. Furthermore it gives information on the bride-price to be paid before and after the marriage. The *izinname* was signed by an official, the representatives of the bride and groom, and by two witnesses for each party. İsmail Ünver, 'Bakire İzinnamesi', *Ankara Üniversitesi Osmanlı Tarihi Araştırma ve Uyguluma Merkezi Dergisi*, no. 5 (1994), pp 529–34.
31. *Kanun-i Cezanın 200'üncü Maddesininin 19 Rebiülahir 1332 Tarihli Zeyl-i Sanisini Muaddil Kararname* in *Aile Hukûkû Kararnâmesi*, ed Orhan Çeker (Konya: Mehir, n.d.), pp 107–9.
32. Cin, *Islâm ve Osmanlı Hukukunda Evlenme*, pp 287–9.
33. Alihé Hanoum, *Les Musulmanes Contemporaines: Trois Conférences, Traduites de la Langue Turque par Nazimé-Roukie* (Paris: Alphonse Lemerre, 1894), pp 45–67.
34. Said Öztürk, 'Osmanlı'da çok eşlilik'. http://www.osmanli.org.tr//web/maka-leler/044.asp.
35. *Nikah-i Medeni ve Talak Hakkında Hukuk-u Aile Kararnamesi* (Istanbul: İbrahim Hilmi, 1336).
36. Although the article states it differently. It says that a man is not allowed to marry if he already has four wives.
37. Cin, *Islâm ve Osmanlı Hukukunda Evlenme*, pp 300–2.
38. *Ibid.*, pp 299–300.
39. *Ibid.*, p 319; Feyzioğlu, 'Cumhuriyetin 50. Yıldönümünde "Medeni Nikâh"', p 247n.
40. Cin, *Islâm ve Osmanlı Hukukunda Evlenme*, p 336.
41. This impediment was not mentioned in the Civil Code but was part of the Law for Public Health (*Umumî Hıfzıssıha Kanunu*), no. 1593, Articles 122 and 123. Cin, *Islâm ve Osmanlı Hukukunda Evlenme*, p 322.
42. *Ibid.*, pp 315–16.
43. Said Öztürk, 'Osmanlı'da çok eşlilik'.
44. Colin Imber, 'Women, Marriage and Property: *Mahr* in the Behcetü'l-Fetava of Yenişehirli Abdullah', in Madeleine C. Zilfi (ed), *Women in the Ottoman Empire: Middle Eastern Women in the Early Modern Era* (Leiden: Brill, 1997), pp 81–104.
45. Davis, *The Ottoman Lady*, pp 88–9.
46. Behar and Duben, *Istanbul Households*, pp 156–7. See also Grace Ellison, *Turkey To-Day* (London: Hutchinson & Co. Ltd, n.d.), p 131. That it was more prominent among the higher classes is confirmed by Davis who quotes several sources. However, it seems that some of her sources exaggerate the incidence of such

polygamous households if we take into account the figures given by Duben and Behar. Davis, *The Ottoman Lady*, pp 87–8.

47. Nükhet Esen, *Türk Romanında Aile Kurumu, 1870–1970* (Istanbul: Boğaziçi Üniversitesi Yayınları, 1997), pp 208–10, 221–2. For a summary of the novel *Muhadderat* (Virtuous Ladies) by Fatma Aliye, see *ibid.*, pp 39–52.

48. Another argument put forward by Şemseddin Sami was that although men and women were born in equal numbers, men were more likely to die early because of the dangerous tasks they had to perform. The change of ratio between the sexes would have led to the introduction of polygamy. Özer Ozankaya, 'Reflections of Şemseddin Sami on Women in the Period before the Advent of Secularism', in Türköz Erder (ed), *Family in Turkish Society: Sociological and Legal Studies* (Ankara: Turkish Social Science Association, 1985), pp 127–45.

49. Alihé Hanoum, *Les Musulmanes Contemporaines*, pp 45–67.

50. Şemseddin Sâmi, *Kadınlar* (Istanbul: Mihran Matbaası, 1311 (1296)), trans İsmail Doğan (Ankara: Gündoğan Yayınları, 1996 (1983)), pp 56–67; Ozankaya, 'Reflections of Şemseddin Sami', pp 141–2.

51. Berkes, *The Development of Secularism in Turkey*, pp 285–8. See also Said Öztürk, 'Osmanlı'da çok eşlilik', for a more extensive description of the discussions on polygamy in the last years of the Ottoman Empire.

52. Sabine Dirks, *La Famille Musulmane Turque* (Paris and La Haye: Mouton, 1969), p 84.

53. Dirks reaches different conclusions based on the numbers of marriages. Simply deducting the number of married women from the number of married men she reaches a number of 21,326 women living in a polygamous marriage. However, that number should, of course, at least be doubled. On what calculation she bases her conclusion that 1.8 per cent of the total number of marriages are polygamous is unclear to me. Dirks, *La Famille Musulmane Turque*, pp 84–5.

54. Andras Riedlmayer through personal correspondence (19 August 2003).

55. See also Altan Eserpek, 'Türk köyünde poligam evliliğe ilişkin formel – enformel norm çatışması', in Beylü Dikedigil and Ahmet Çiğdem (eds), *Aile Yazıları 4: Evlilik Kurumu ve İlişkileri* (Ankara: T.C. Başbakanlık Aile Araştırma Kurumu, 1991), pp 401–12 (reprint from *Ankara Üniversitesi Dil Tarih Coğrafya Fakültesi Felsefe Araştırmaları Enstitüsü Dergisi*, no. 11 (1979), pp 153–63).

56. Serim Timur, *Türkiye'de Aile Yapısı* (Ankara: Hacettepe Üniversitesi Yayınları, 1972), p 89.

57. Nilüfer Narlı, 'Türk Toplumunda İmam Nikâhı Olgusu', in Necla Arat (ed), *Kadınların Gündemi* (Istanbul: Say Yayınları, 1997), pp 79–88.

58. Rezan Şahinkaya, *Diyarbakir İli Merkez Köylerinde Aile Strüktürü* (Ankara: Ankara Üniversitesi, 1983), p 50.

59. Nuran Elmacı, 'Polygamy: Çok-eşli Evlilikler', in Necla Arat (ed), *Türkiye'de Kadın Olmak* (İstanbul: Say, 1994); Belkıs Kumbetoğlu, 'Aile, Evlilik, Nikah: Farklılaşan Kavramlar', *Toplum ve Bilim*, no. 73 (1997), pp 111–28.

60. Tülay Yavan, Şırnak ilinde yaşayan 15–49 yaş grubu evli kadınların demografik özellikleri ve üreme sağlığı sorunlarının saptanması'. http://www.gata.edu.tr/hyo/tgezler/Tulay_Yavan_Tez.asp.

61. See, for example, '3'üncü eş 4'üncüyü kıskanınca kan aktı', *Hürriyet*, 10 October 1998.

62. See also Eserpek, 'Türk köyünde poligam evliliğe', pp 401–12.

63. *Ibid.*; Cin, *İslâm ve Osmanlı Hukukunda Evlenme*, p 317n.

64. Eserpek, 'Türk köyünde poligam evliliğe', pp 401–12.

65. Fatma Başaran, 'Birden fazla kadınla evlenmeye karşı vaziyet alışlar', in Dikedigil and Çiğdem (eds), *Aile Yazıları 4*, pp 183–91 (reprint from *Araştırma* 4 (1966), pp 155–163).

66. http://www.hurriyetim.com.tr/haber/0,,sid-5@tarih-2003-07-26-m@nvid-294864,00.asp.

67. See, for example, 'Kumayı benzinle yakmak istedi', *Hürriyetim*, 17 June 1998.

68. Both local and central authorities still regularly organize large marriage events where several couples that have been married for years through an *imam nikâhı* are officially wed.

69. The festivities around the celebration of a marriage (or a circumcision) are called *düğün*. The festivities for a *düğün* may last anything from a few hours to several days according to the local habits and the financial means of the families involved.

70. İhsan Yılmaz, 'Non-Recognition of Post-modern Turkish Socio-legal Reality and the Predicament of Women', *British Journal of Middle Eastern Studies* 30, no. 1 (2003), pp 25–41.

Index